Working Memory, Thought, and Action

OXFORD PSYCHOLOGY SERIES

Editors

Mark D'Esposito   Daniel Schacter

Jon Driver   Anne Treisman

Trevor Robbins   Lawrence Weiskrantz

Working Memory, Thought, and Action

ALAN BADDELEY
Department of Psychology
University of York
UK

OXFORD
UNIVERSITY PRESS

OXFORD

UNIVERSITY PRESS

Great Clarendon Street, Oxford OX2 6DP

Oxford University Press is a department of the University of Oxford.
It furthers the University's objective of excellence in research, scholarship,
and education by publishing worldwide in

Oxford New York

Auckland   Cape Town Dar es Salaam   Hong Kong   Karachi
Kuala Lumpur Madrid Melbourne Mexico City   Nairobi
New Delhi Shanghai Taipei Toronto
With offices in
Argentina Austria Brazil Chile Czech Republic France Greece
Guatemala Hungary Italy Japan South Korea Poland Portugal
Singapore Switzerland Thailand Turkey Ukraine Vietnam

Oxford is a registered trade mark of Oxford University Press
in the UK and in certain other countries

Published in the United States
by Oxford University Press Inc., New York

ISBN 978-0-19-852801-2

Printed and bound in Great Britain by CPI Antony Rowe,
Chippenham and Eastbourne

To
Hilary

Contents

Preface

This is a book that I said I would never write. It is a sequel to *Working Memory*, a book I completed some 20 years ago which was basically an account of an extended programme of research that began in the 1960s when the study of short-term memory (STM) was in its hey day and continued during its loss of popularity in the 1970s as the broader and more functionally-based concept of working memory proposed by Graham Hitch and myself (Baddeley and Hitch, 1974). By the publication of *Working Memory* in 1986, interest had substantially begun to increase, with some 51 papers published with 'working memory' in their title, a process that has continued to a point at which there are now around 800 papers a year with working memory in their title and some 3700 papers in their title, key words or abstract. Not all of these, of course, will be of direct relevance to the multicomponent model, but when, from time to time, it was suggested that I should update the 1986 book, realizing the huge literature that was accumulating, I declared that I never would.

And yet, I kept noting that colleagues would make statements about our model, usually by suggesting that their data were incompatible with it, despite the fact that the model had subsequently evolved, in a way that made the specific criticism no longer appropriate. There was clearly a need for an updated account of the model, but I still baulked at the sheer amount of material to be covered by a through review. I then hit on the apparently more tractable plan of writing an extended essay, setting aside a summer for this purpose. As autumn arrived, I found I was only half way through the first section on the phonological loop. So much for tractability. Somewhat later, the opportunity for a second attempt came along when I was invited to spend the academic year 2001-2002 at the Center for Advanced Study in Behavioral Sciences at Stanford. I decided to try again.

The Center seemed a particularly appropriate place for such an enterprise, given that the term 'working memory' appears to have been invented there by Miller, Galanter and Pribram (1960) in producing their classic contribution to cognitive science, *Plans and the Structure of Behavior*. Furthermore I discovered that I was assigned the room previously occupied there by Richard Atkinson, whose model together with Shiffrin (Atkinson and Shiffrin, 1968) is probably where Graham Hitch and I acquired the term 'working memory', although our own model differed in important ways from theirs. The omens seemed good.

Each year, the Center hosts some 40 fellows with backgrounds ranging from history and political science through anthropology and sociology to psychology and neuroscience. The availability of this breadth of expertise encouraged me, perhaps foolishly, to undertake the even more ambitious task of locating the concept of working memory within a broader intellectual context. There is always a temptation when introducing the concept of working memory to make rather grand claims for its importance as the basis of complex cognition and rational thought. And yet, from our very first experiments, much of the progress in refining the model has come from finding out what it *does not* do. With a full year ahead, and my prior commitments cleared away, I decided I would think more deeply about the broader implications of the multicomponent working memory model, and investigate a range of areas that might throw interesting light on how the model should be developed. I began my task in late summer, hoping to have completed it by Christmas. Some five years later I am finally completing the book that has turned into rather more than an extended essay. So what went wrong?

Having previously begun with the phonological loop, and finding myself drowning in detail, I decided I would start with the central executive component, on the misguided grounds that this was the topic we knew least about; indeed in the 1986 book, it had only emerged as the final chapter. There has however, been a huge amount of research in recent years concerned with executive processing, much of it related to the study of the frontal lobes. Furthermore, the central executive is the component of working memory that most naturally links to a range of other fields. For example, discussions with two social psychologist colleagues at the center, John Bargh and Roy Baumeister, suggested that their research could be linked very neatly to the account of action control given by Norman and Shallice (1986) that formed the basis of my own account of the central executive. I began also to see potential links with some of the classic philosophical issues such as the nature of consciousness and freewill. At the same time I discovered exciting and important evidence from cognitive neuroscience that appeared to bear directly on the multicomponent working memory model. The result is both a longer, broader and more ambitious book than I ever anticipated.

I would like to have produced a book that was a seamless whole, with detailed experimentation building up to general theory which in turn leads to speculation as to the broader role of the theory. Sadly, this did not work. The gap was just too large between, for example, the detailed analysis of the phonological loop, and speculations on the broader implications of the concept of working memory for consciousness and the control of action. Consequently, the book divides into two halves, the first concerned with developments within the multicomponent model, and the second with its potential role in social and emotional behaviour, consciousness and the control of action.

The first section takes on the task which, perhaps wisely, I declared that I would never attempt, namely that of surveying the last 20 years of research on working memory. Its strength lies in the fact that I have been actively involved in most of the areas discussed. However, I make no claim to having covered the enormous literature that has occurred over this period in a thorough, balanced and scholarly manner, although I have tried to do so. Inevitably, I have tended to view the literature from the perspective of the mulitcomponent WM model, and to make more use of my own research than would be ideal. I can certainly not claim to have read all the literature, even in areas closest to my own research. Furthermore, I am sure that, in line with the self-performed-task literature (Englekamp, 1998), I remember what I have done rather better than what I have read. So if you are working in this area yourself, then I am sure you will know studies, perhaps performed by yourself, that could and should have been included. Please accept my apologies.

The second part of the book is very different in both its strengths and weaknesses. It attempts to place the concept of working memory in a broader context, looking for links with the study of social behaviour, emotion, conscious awareness and the control of action, which in turn raises some of the classic philosophical issues of consciousness and freewill. I found these potential links fascinating, and hope that my enthusiasm might encourage further work on these interface areas. I cannot however claim expertise in the topics covered, and have relied more on review papers than I would have liked. In a few cases I have found such reviews particularly helpful, and have tried to make this clear in the text. So what has emerged?

I wanted to produce a book that would be accessible and useful to a wide range of potential readers. I therefore begin with an introductory chapter providing an overview of the model as it stood when I completed my 1986 book. I then move on to discussing the phonological loop, which is probably the simplest and best understood component of working memory. This immediately presented a problem however. It is an area that has seen a great deal of detailed analysis, leading to complex controversies and sophisticated computational modelling. It is I think, essential to cover this as it reflects most clearly the potential for development of what began as a simple verbally described model. However, a reader from outside the field encountering this in the first chapter could very reasonably decide that 'this is not for me!' So, rather than start by bombarding the reader with computational models and third order interactions, I begin with the question of what function the phonological loop might serve, with a view to convincing the reader that this is an area of some importance, whether or not they proceed to the more specialised Chapter 3. It is perhaps worth stressing at this point, that I have tried to write the chapters in such a way that they do not depend upon the book being read sequentially from start to end, although where, as is often the case, the topic is covered by two chapters, it is sensible to read them in that order.

From the phonological loop, I move on to the visuospatial sketchpad, with one chapter focusing on the short-term storage of visual and spatial information, and a second concerned with imagery and the manipulation of visuospatial information. Chapter 6 is concerned with a rather different method of storage that was classically linked to the concept of STM, namely the recency effect which is interpreted as a combination between passive priming and an active retrieval mechanism.

The next three chapters are concerned with the central executive and episodic buffer components of working memory. They do not attempt to review the vast and growing literature on executive control but focus on my own attempt to fractionate and elaborate the initial concept of a central executive, leaving the broader implications of executive and attentional control to later chapters, with the analysis of executive processing featuring prominently in the next two chapters on individual differences in working memory. The first part of book concludes with a discussion of the application of neuroimaging techniques to the study of working memory.

As mentioned earlier, the second part of the book attempts to place working memory in a broader perspective. A chapter concerned with potential links with social psychology is followed by two concerned with working memory and emotion. The first of these focuses on the effects of fear and anxiety, an area in which clear links between working memory and the disruption of cognition by emotion are already being actively explored, and extended to other clinically important issues such as craving and addiction. The link between working memory and depression, explored in Chapter 15 is less clear. I found this the most challenging chapter to write, but potentially the most productive, in that it led to a more detailed specification of the links between emotion and working memory, together with a new theoretical framework that has the potential to provide a conceptual link between psychological and neurobiological approaches to depression.

Continuing in a speculative mode, Chapter 16 is concerned with empirically-based explanations of the phenomenon of conscious awareness, stressing the potential link between working memory and theories of consciousness based on the global workspace hypothesis. The role of conscious awareness, and by implication, working memory in the control of action forms the focus of the next chapter. The book ends with an attempt to place working memory in a broad evolutionary context and to explore its implications for tackling the classical philosophical questions of consciousness and free will. If you think this is rather a heady way for an experimental psychologist to end a book, I can only agree with you; I blame it on my year in California.

Acknowledgements

This book was largely written during a year spent in Stanford California at the Center for Advanced Studies in the Behavioural Sciences, generously supported by a fellowship from the John D. and Catherine T. MacArthur Foundation. I am also grateful to the British Medical Research Council who have supported the programme of research on working memory which forms the basis of the book since its inception over 30 years ago, latterly through grant G9423916. I am also grateful for financial support to the Universities of Bristol and York.

It will be clear I hope, that the book has gained from interaction and collaboration with a range of colleagues that is too numerous to list. Over the years however, I have gained particularly from discussions with Sergio Della Sala, Susan Gathercole, Graham Hitch, Chris Jarrold and Robert Logie. During my time at the Center in Stanford, I benefited greatly from discussions with my fellow Fellows, and in particular with Robert Bjork, and with John Bargh and Roy Baumeister, whose influence on the chapter relating working memory to social psychology will be obvious. The two chapters on working memory and emotion also profited greatly from advice and discussion from a range of colleagues, notably including Rainer Banser, Joseph LeDoux, Karin Mogg and Mark Williams.

I am grateful to Nelson Cowan, who read the whole book in draft form, providing timely and constructive advice, and to Bernard Baars, Donna Bayliss Gary Green, Graham Hitch, Satoru Saito and Tim Shallice, all of whom read and commented on one or more chapters. The book gained substantially from their suggestions.

I always produce my first writing drafts by dictation, largely while walking through the countryside. While this is a pleasant way of writing, it does require someone with greater transcription skills than I process. I would therefore like to acknowledge the major part played by Megan Stokes-Holt, who came to my rescue at the Center, when a combination of ambient noise and my English accent proved too much for the available automatic speech recognition package. Back in Bristol I was fortunate that Dee Roberts was happy to split her time between completing a PhD and applying her combined secretarial and psychological skills to advance progress on the book. I am particularly grateful to Lindsey Bowes for applying her considerable secretarial and IT skills, not only to the last stages of writing, but also to the tricky process of tracking down the elusive references that inevitably seem to slow down the final stages of producing a book.

Finally, this book is dedicated to my wife Hilary with thanks for her sustained support and encouragement, and her stoicism in the face of sympathy from neighbours for having an idle husband who paces the countryside talking to himself when he should be mowing the lawn or painting the fence. Her support is greatly valued.

Chapter 1

Introduction and overview

Working memory is assumed to be a temporary storage system under attentional control that underpins our capacity for complex thought. Consider the task of instructing a friend how to get from the railway station to your house: you probably need to form some kind of visuospatial representation of the district, work out the best route, and turn this into verbal instructions your friend is likely to understand. They will have to perform a similar task, although in the reverse order, then taking notes or relying on long-term memory. Or consider the simple exercise of multiplying 27 by 9. Having multiplied the 7 by 9, you need temporarily to store the 3, and 'carry' the 6, holding it while you multiply 2 by 9, then adding the 6, retrieving the 3 and coming up with the answer 243. Once complete, you can no doubt remember the result, at least briefly, but probably not the results of the individual stages.

The study of working memory is concerned with the way in which such temporary manipulation and storage is carried out. Its study was based initially on the concept of a simple unitary temporary memory store, short-term memory (STM). Over the years, however, it has become increasingly clear that considerably more than simple storage is required for a system that effectively forms the crucial interface between perception and memory, and between attention and action.

There are many approaches to working memory, most of which have common features, although this basic agreement may be obscured by the fact that different theorists often emphasize different phenomena and use a range of methods of theory development. My own approach has been largely empirically driven, relying principally on the methods of cognitive memory research, and influenced strongly by neuropsychology. As such, it has tended to stay close to the data, neglecting the broader implications of the model that was evolving. The chapters that follow attempt to do two things; to give an updated account of the more empirically based model, and then to place the concept of working memory in its broader theoretical context. Inevitably this requires a good deal of speculation, extending as it does to such classic issues as the nature of consciousness and the will. I will begin with a brief historical overview.

1.1 **Some history**

William James (1890) proposed a distinction between a temporary *primary memory*, which he described as 'the trailing edge of consciousness', and the more durable *secondary memory*. By the middle of the twentieth century, however, the dominant view within experimental psychology was of a single memory system in which learning reflected the formation of associations, and forgetting was due to interference between competing associations (McGeoch and Irion 1952). In 1949, Donald Hebb revived the two-component view, speculating that there may be two types of memory, short-term memory (STM) which depended upon temporary electrical activity in the brain, and long-term memory (LTM) which was represented by more durable neuro-chemical changes. This view was supported by Brown (1958) in the UK, and Peterson and Peterson (1959) in the US. In each case, they observed a rapid loss over a matter of seconds of even small amounts of information if rehearsal was prevented. Since the rehearsal prevention task did not involve material that was similar to the items being recalled, they ruled out classic similarity-based interference theory, proposing instead the existence of a memory trace that faded rapidly over time.

1.1.1 **How many kinds of memory?**

This led in the 1960s to a vigorous controversy. Keppel and Underwood (1962) showed that forgetting in the Peterson task was minimal on the first trial of the experiment, building up rapidly over the next few trials, suggesting that forgetting could readily be interpreted in terms of proactive interference from earlier items in the experiment. Melton (1962) demonstrated that digit span, the classic STM task involving immediate serial recall of a string of digits, also had a long-term component, concluding that there was no need to assume a separate STM system. In response to this, Waugh and Norman (1965) pointed out the need to distinguish between experimental paradigms and the hypothetical cognitive system, or systems that were assumed to con-tribute to performance on such tasks. Following William James (1890), they use the term *primary memory* for the hypothetical short-term system, and *secondary memory* for the long-term system, using STM and LTM to refer to the respec-tive experimental paradigms, accepting that performance on STM tasks was always likely in practice to have a component based on LTM.

Further evidence for at least two memory systems came from a detailed study of neuropsychological patients. Classic amnesic patients who typically had bilateral damage to the temporal lobes and hippocampi (Milner 1966) show a devastatingly poor capacity for performance on LTM tasks, but perform well on classic STM tasks such as digit span (Baddeley and Warrington 1970).

At the same time, Shallice and Warrington (1970) described patients who showed the opposite pattern, with normal LTM, coupled with a digit span of only one or two items, and very poor Peterson performance. This so-called double dissociation between performance on LTM and STM tasks strongly suggested the need to assume separate processes.

Further evidence for a dichotomy came from two-component tasks such as free recall in which subjects attempt to recall a list of words in any order: the most recent items tend to be well recalled if recall is immediate, the recency effect. The recency effect is lost, however, if a brief filled delay is introduced between presentation and test, while earlier items assumed to reflect the long-term component are unaffected by this brief delay (Glanzer 1972; Glanzer and Cunitz 1966). The recency effect is preserved in amnesic patients but impaired in patients with defective STM performance, while recall of earlier items, assumed to depend on LTM, shows the opposite pattern, being greatly impaired in amnesic patients but preserved in patients with defective STM (Baddeley and Warrington 1970; Shallice and Warrington 1970).

1.1.2 **The modal model**

By the late 1960s, the weight of opinion was tending to favour a distinction between two or more kinds of memory, a state of affairs that was reflected in a number of models of memory, of which the most influential was that of Atkinson and Shiffrin (1968), which became known as the modal model. This model assumed three separate types of memory (see Fig. 1.1). The briefest of

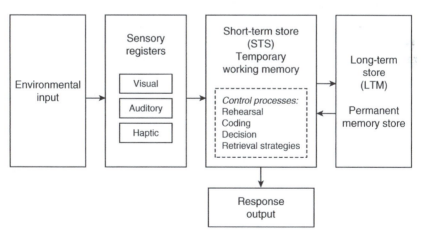

Fig. 1.1 The information-processing model of memory proposed by Atkinson and Shiffrin (1968). Information flows from the environment through a series of sensory registers into a short-term store, which plays a crucial role in controlling the flow of information into and out of the long-term store.

these was a series of sensory memory systems that are perhaps best regarded as components of perceptual processing. These included visual sensory memory (Sperling 1960) sometimes termed iconic memory, and its equivalent sensory acoustic storage system (Crowder and Morton 1969), termed echoic memory by Neisser (1967). Other sensory systems, however, were also thought to include some form of temporary storage (Atkinson and Shiffrin 1968). Information was assumed to flow from a parallel array of sensory memory systems to a single short-term store. This acted as a working memory of limited informational capacity, the *short-term store* (STS). The STS could both hold information and manipulate it, and was assumed to be responsible both for encoding information into LTM and subsequently retrieving it. The limited capacity STS system thus interacted with the much larger capacity *long-term store* (LTS). Hence long-term learning depended on both LTS and STS.

1.1.3 **Problems with the modal model**

Initially, it seemed as if the modal model provided a good account of the available data. It did however, run into at least two problems. The first of these concerned its learning assumptions, which proposed that merely holding information in the STS was sufficient for it to be transferred to LTS; the longer the information was held, the higher the probability of transfer, and the better the learning. However, attempts to test this directly were unsuccessful (e.g. Craik and Watkins 1973; Tzeng 1973; Bjork and Whitten 1974). Much more important than simple time was the nature of the operations performed on the material being learned, with items that were processed purely in terms of their physical appearance being poorly retained and items that were verbalized being somewhat better recalled, but not as well as items that were richly encoded in terms of their meaning, interpreted by Craik and Lockhart (1972) in terms of their highly influential Levels of Processing hypothesis. This proposed that degree of long-term learning depended on the depth and richness of encoding and not on the length of time the material was held in the STS, as Atkinson and Shiffrin had assumed.

A second problem was inherent in the neuropsychological evidence. If the STS provides a crucial stage in the process of long-term learning, then patients with a deficit in the STS system should also show impaired LTM performance, which they did not (Shallice and Warrington 1970). Furthermore, if the system serves as a general purpose working memory, then such patients should be handicapped on many different cognitive tasks. This was clearly not the case. One STM patient was performing effectively as a secretary, while another ran a shop and a family and a third was a successful taxi driver. Their problems appeared to be limited in nature, showing no evidence of a general cognitive dysfunction such as one might expect of a patient with a grossly impaired working memory.

1.2 **Multicomponent working memory**

This was the situation when Graham Hitch and I began research using a grant that was targeted at understanding the relationship between long- and short-term memory, at a point when the study of STM was rapidly losing its popularity in favour of research into new and exciting areas of LTM such as levels of processing (Craik and Lockhart 1972), and the nature of semantic memory (Collins and Quillian 1969; Collins and Loftus 1972).

We chose to tackle the simple question of what function was served by STM, if it was not a working memory? We did not have access to STM patients, but instead decided to use dual task methodology in order to selectively disrupt STM in normal subjects. Despite their differences, all existing models of STM appeared to agree that it was necessary for the immediate serial recall of digits, and all agreed that the limited span for digits resulted from the limited capacity of the STS. We therefore required our subjects to continuously repeat random sequences of digits, while performing a second task which was assumed to depend upon the operation of a limited capacity working memory system. Simply requiring one item to be repeated would prevent overt vocal rehearsal, but impose only a minimal storage load. Increasing the number of digits to three or six or more should take up a successively greater proportion of available STS capacity. This successive increase in concurrent digits should be reflected in the progressively impaired performance of any task that was heavily dependent on working memory.

We chose to study verbal reasoning, comprehension and long-term learning in this way, in each case performing the task while reciting strings of digits. Our reasoning task involved the verification of sentences that varied in their syntactic complexity. Each sentence purported to describe the order of two letters, A and B and was followed by a letter pair, for example, *A follows B – BA*, to which the subject should respond 'true'. The difficulty of the task was manipulated by also using negatives and passives, for example *B is not preceded by A – AB*, which should evoke the response 'false'. Subjects performed this visually presented task while overtly rehearsing sequences of random numbers ranging in length from zero to eight digits. The results are shown in Fig. 1.2, which gives both the mean time to respond and mean percentage of errors at each level of digit load. There is a clear increase in response time with increasing digit load, although it is important to note that even the heaviest load increases response time by only 50 per cent. Perhaps more surprising is the error rate, which is quite unaffected by a concurrent load that reaches and in

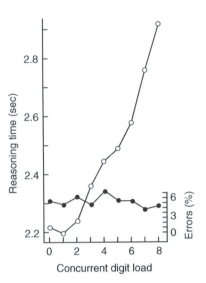

Fig. 1.2 The influence of a concurrent memory task on verbal reasoning. The longer the concurrent digit sequence, the slower the response. However the decrement was far from massive, and there was no effect on accuracy. Data In: *Working Memory* from Baddeley (1986). Reproduced with permission from Oxford University Press.

some subjects' cases exceeds, digit span. Broadly similar results were obtained when we studied the effect of concurrent digit load on tasks involving either learning or prose comprehension. The system that underpins the retention of digits therefore *does* resemble a working memory system in that decreasing its capacity impairs cognitive functioning, but the degree of impairment is far less than would be predicted by the modal model. We decided to abandon the assumption of a unitary STS, and replace it with a multimodal system, which we termed *working memory*.

We chose the term working memory in order to emphasize the functional role of the proposed system, rather than simply its storage capacity. The term was already current though not common in cognitive psychology. It appears to have been coined by Miller, Galanter and Pribram (1960), although they say little about its characteristics. The term was also used by Atkinson and Shiffrin to describe the functional role of their short-term store. Both of these usages are broadly equivalent to our own, however two other usages that are different should be mentioned. The term working memory is also applied to a component of production system models in artificial intelligence (Newell and Simon 1972), referring to a system of unlimited capacity that holds the if-then production rules that underpin such models. It has also been used in yet another way within the animal learning literature (Olton 1979) to refer to performance on tasks such as the radial arm maze in which animals are required to remember the outcome of a series of related trials performed on the same day.

However, for better or worse, the term working memory has increasingly come to be used in the sense that we adopted, to refer to a limited capacity temporary storage system that underpins complex human thought. Such a system is often, though not always, assumed to comprise multiple components (Miyake and Shah 1999a; Smith and Jonides 1996, 1997). The term STM continues to be used to describe tasks in which the immediate recall of small amounts of information is required with the term working memory being used to refer to a broader system typically involving attentional control and allowing the *manipulation* of information held in short-term storage. The term STM is still used to describe a range of tasks such as digit span or the short-term Peterson forgetting paradigm. As previously noted, such tasks are likely to have both long-term and short-term components. However, many studies that focus explicitly on short-term *storage* (see Chapters 2-4) may continue to use the term STM to refer both to tasks and to the theoretically assumed underlying processes, relying on the context to make clear whether they are referring to a task or a system (e.g. Gathercole 1996; Vallar and Papagno 2002).

1.3 The multicomponent model

In order to explain our pattern of data, we suggested that the unitary short-term store proposed by Atkinson and Shiffrin should be replaced by a three-component working memory (Baddeley and Hitch 1974). This comprised an attentional control system – the *central executive* – together with two subsidiary storage systems, the *phonological loop* and the *visuospatial sketchpad* (see Fig. 1.3). All three systems were limited in capacity, although the nature of their limitations differed. The phonological loop was assumed to be capable of holding speech-based and possibly purely acoustic information in a temporary store. The storage was assumed to be dependent on a memory trace that would fade within seconds unless refreshed by rehearsal. Rehearsal was assumed to depend on either overt or covert vocalization.

The visuospatial sketchpad performed a similar function for both visual and spatial information. Rehearsal was assumed to occur, possibly though not necessarily involving eye movements (Baddeley 1986, p. 116-121; Postle *et al.* 2006). In the initial model, the central executive was assumed to comprise a limited pool of general processing capacity. We left its precise nature unspecified, concentrating instead on the subsystems, which seemed to offer a more tractable challenge. In the longer term of course, a working memory model that gives no account of executive control becomes effectively a simple storage model, albeit a two-component STS. Over the years the attempt to fill the gap left by the unspecified executive has been a major concern, and is reflected repeatedly in later chapters. Each of the three components is described in more detail below.

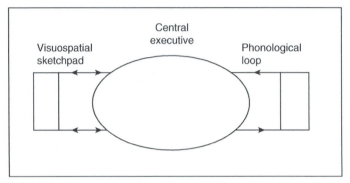

Fig. 1.3 The three-component working memory model proposed by Baddeley and Hitch (1974). Reproduced with permission from Oxford University Press.

1.3.1 **The phonological loop**

The loop was assumed to comprise a phonological store and an articulatory rehearsal mechanism: evidence of the nature of the store came principally from the phonological similarity effect. Conrad (1964) observed that when subjects attempted to recall sequences of *visually* presented consonants, that they tended to make 'acoustic' errors, for example mis-recalling *B* as *V* or *F* as *M*. Conrad and Hull (1964) demonstrated that sequences of phonologically similar letters such as *B D T G C P* were recalled less accurately than dissimilar sequences such as *F K Y W R Q*. They proposed that STM depended upon an acoustic memory trace, with visually presented items being converted into an acoustic code by subvocalization. Conrad used the term 'acoustic' similarity, since it was defined in terms of listening errors in noise. I myself prefer the term 'phonological' to refer to the underlying storage systems. The term is intended to leave open the precise nature of the code, earlier attempts to specify this having proved inconclusive (Hintzman 1967; Wickelgren 1969). I myself extended this finding to words, finding that a sequence such as *man cat cap map can* was recalled correctly only about 10 per cent of the time, in contrast to a dissimilar sequence such as *pit day cow pen sup*, which was correct on approximately 80 per cent of occasions. Similarity of meaning (e.g. *huge big long wide tall*) reduced recall by a significant but very small amount (Baddeley 1966a).

A very different pattern of results emerged when the same sets of words were used in a study of long-term memory, presenting a sequence of ten items for several trials. Under these circumstances similarity of meaning disrupted performance, while phonological similarity had little effect (Baddeley 1966b). These results were consistent with the use of a phonologically based store for immediate recall of small amounts of information, in contrast to long-term learning which, in line with the subsequent levels of processing hypothesis (Craik and Lockhart 1972) appeared to rely principally on semantic coding.

The process of rehearsal was assumed to be reflected in the word length effect. Immediate memory for sequences of words declined as the words became longer, with a sequence of five short words such as *wit, sum, pad, beg, top* being correctly recalled on 90 per cent of trials, compared to around 50 per cent for a polysyllabic sequence such as *university, refrigerator, hippopotamus, tuberculosis, auditorium* (Baddeley *et al.* 1975). This result was consistent with the assumption of a fading trace, coupled with a rehearsal process that operates in real time. Memory span is thus assumed to be set by two factors – the rate at which the trace fades, and the speed at which items can be rehearsed. Shorter words can be rehearsed more rapidly leading to a greater span, and subjects who rehearse rapidly tend to have longer spans (Baddeley *et al.* 1975). The process of rehearsal can, however, be blocked by requiring the subject repeatedly to utter an irrelevant sound such as the word 'the'. Although this involves only a minimal memory load, it prevents rehearsal and impairs performance (Murray 1968).

One further assumption was made, namely that items presented auditorily gained automatic access to the phonological store, while those presented visually had to be subvocalized to gain access. This latter point is reflected in an interaction between acoustic similarity, modality of presentation and suppression of articulation. The finding in question contrasts the phonological similarity effect – which is assumed to reside within the store – and the word length effect – which is assumed to reflect the process of transfer and rehearsal. When material is presented visually, articulatory suppression through the repetition of a single word removes both the phonological similarity effect and the word length effect. This is because the visually presented items cannot readily be translated into an appropriate phonological code. However, when presented auditorily a phonological similarity effect is again found (Murray 1968; Levy 1971), but there is still no effect of word length. This is because auditory items gain automatic access to the store. The word length effect still does not occur because it depends directly on subvocal rehearsal which is prevented by articulatory suppression (Baddeley *et al.* 1975; Baddeley *et al.* 1984a).

The storage-rehearsal distinction was subsequently supported by neuropsychological evidence from patients with lesions that disrupted either storage or rehearsal (Vallar and Papagno 2002), and by neuroimaging evidence which located the storage component in the temporo-parietal region of the left hemisphere, while rehearsal was more frontally located in Broca's area (Paulesu *et al.* 1993; Jonides 1998).

As we shall see in Chapter 3, the concept of a phonological loop has not gone unchallenged. However, as Chapter 2 illustrates, despite (or perhaps because of) the fact that this remains an area of theoretical controversy, it has proved very fruitful in stimulating research on language acquisition and processing. It is important to bear in mind however, that the loop is only one relatively small component of the complex of systems and processes that constitute working memory.

1.3.2 The visuospatial sketchpad

This system performs the same function for visual and spatial information as is served by the phonological loop for verbal and acoustic stimuli. My own involvement with studying this system stemmed from a personal experience. While on sabbatical in California, I became very interested in American football. On one occasion, when driving on the freeway from Los Angeles to San Diego, I listened to the Stanford-UCLA game on the radio, forming a clear image of the field and the relevant teams. I then noticed that I was drifting from one lane to another, switched to music and survived.

On returning to Britain, I attempted to simulate my experience experimentally. We did not have access to a driving simulator, so instead used a pursuit rotor. This involved a spot of light following a circular path, which the subject was required to track with a stylus. Difficulty level could be set by varying the speed of rotation. Tracking was combined with a range of memory tasks, some involving rote verbal rehearsal while others encouraged the use of imagery. One such task, for example, used the classic location mnemonic, first teaching the subjects a route through the campus involving a number of specific locations. They were then instructed to form an image of each of the sequence of objects, one at each location, and to retrieve them by mentally performing the walk. When the task was performed alone this reliably enhanced recall performance as compared to rote rehearsal. Concurrent tracking, however, removed this advantage while having no effect on rote memory. As we shall see in Chapters 3 and 4, subsequent studies have investigated the relationship between visual STM and visual imagery, showing that it is possible to separate *visual* aspects of the system, concerned with patterns or objects, from a *spatial* component concerned with location. This distinction has been supported by studies on brain-damaged patients and by studies of normal brain function using neuroimaging techniques (Jonides *et al.* 1993; Smith and Jonides 1997; Della Sala and Logie 2002). Unlike the loop, the sketchpad relies principally on the right hemisphere of the brain.

1.3.3 **The central executive**

Our initial studies were concerned almost exclusively with the two subsystems, principally on the grounds that they seemed to offer more tractable problems. However in writing a book that attempted to summarize the progress made on the model (Baddeley 1986), I came to final chapter before fully realizing that I had said nothing about the executive. I set out to remedy this, basing my speculations on a model of attentional control proposed by Norman and Shallice (1986) which was unusual in being concerned with the attentional control of action, rather than with the role of attention in perception, of which there were a range of well-developed models. It is significant to note that the Norman and Shallice model, which I think continues to be extremely fruitful theoretically, was initially only available as a technical report and subsequently as a book chapter, apparently because of the difficulty in persuading a journal to accept it (Shallice, personal communication). Our journal reviewing system does not appear to favour innovation!

Norman and Shallice were both interested in the attentional control of action, but from somewhat different viewpoints. Norman was interested in slips of action, and wanted a framework that would provide a potential explanation as to why and when they might occur. Such lapses are usually trivial, such as absentmindedly driving to the office rather than the shopping centre on a Saturday morning. They can occasionally be devastating, however, for example in air accidents based on pilot error. Shallice on the other hand was interested in the control of behaviour by the frontal lobes, and wanted to explain the paradoxical behaviour of certain patients with bilateral frontal lobe damage. Such patients are found to perseverate, repeatedly performing the same action and showing considerable difficulty escaping that pattern. On other occasions they show what is apparently the opposite behaviour and their attention is captured by any passing stimulus.

In order to provide a framework for explaining both everyday lapses and frontal lobe performance, Norman and Shallice proposed that behaviour is controlled at two levels. One of these is relatively automatic, based on habits and schemas whereby predicable events give rise to appropriate behaviour. Driving along a familiar route would be a good example of this. The other component, which they term the *Supervisory Attentional System* (SAS), is a mechanism for overriding such habits. It is used when the existing habit patterns are no longer adequate, for example finding a traffic jam and needing to take appropriate action to circumvent it. The lapses of everyday attention such as setting off to drive to the market on a Saturday morning and finding oneself driving to work instead, represent the inappropriate dominance of such habit patterns over control by the SAS, and typically occur when one's attention is diverted from the task in hand – planning a future holiday, for example, rather than thinking about the current shopping trip. Patients with frontal lobe damage are assumed to have defective operation of the SAS, with the result that attention may be captured by a single persistent stimulus or by a succession of irrelevant stimuli in the absence of central attentional control: their habit system is preserved while the frontally located SAS is not.

I proposed to accept the Norman and Shallice model as a basis for conceptualizing the central executive (Baddeley 1986). As subsequent chapters will indicate, I continue to find the model extremely useful.

1.3.4 The episodic buffer

One problem in having an executive that comprises general processing capacity is that it is potentially able to explain any result. This excessive flexibility means that it is not empirically productive in generating experiments that tell us more about how the system works. In an attempt to remedy this problem, I proposed to explore the possibility that the executive had a purely attentional role, and was itself incapable of storage (Baddeley 1993; Baddeley and Logie 1999). This led to a series of studies that attempted to fractionate the executive into an alliance of separate attentional control processes, each performing a different function. As Chapter 7 shows, this proved to be a major task, although one that was not without success.

However, it became increasingly clear that some form of additional storage was necessary if the model was to give an adequate account of some of the more complex functions of working memory, such as the capacity for remembering large chunks of prose. Furthermore, research on individual differences in working memory performance was yielding some very exciting results. The measure used in these studies was working memory span. This required subjects to combine memory with processing, for example verifying a sequence of sentences and then recalling the last word of each (Daneman and Carpenter 1980). Span was measured by the maximum number of such sentences which the subject could successfully process and recall. Working memory span predicts a wide range of complex cognitive activity from comprehension to computer programming (Daneman and Merikle 1996; Engle *et al.* 1999a).

At one level the success of this complex span measure was very gratifying in that it illustrates the breadth and usefulness of the general concept of working memory. On the other hand, however, it was far from easy to see how performance on such complex span tasks could be explained within the existing framework, where memory storage was limited to the loop and the sketchpad, each of which could hold information only briefly, and which had no specified means of interaction. This prompted the addition of a fourth component, the *episodic buffer* (Baddeley 2000). This system was assumed to form an interface between the three working memory subsystems and long-term memory. It served as a binding mechanism that allowed perceptual information, information from the subsystems and from long-term memory to be integrated into a limited number of episodes. It was a buffer in the sense that it provided an interface between a number of different codes – visual, verbal, perceptual – and from LTM, semantic and episodic. Finally, it was assumed to be accessible through conscious awareness. It differs from episodic LTM in being temporary in nature, but provides an interface that allows access to LTM both for learning and retrieval. It is assumed to act as a workspace for which conscious awareness plays a crucial role (see Chapter 13). As such it provides a conceptual bridge between the Baddeley and Hitch model and a range of other approaches to working memory (Miyake and Shah 1999a). The episodic buffer is discussed in more detail in Chapters 8 and 9.

1.4 **Conclusions**

The multicomponent working memory model assumes a four- component system, comprising (1) an attentional controller, the central executive, and three temporary storage systems, namely (2) the visuospatial sketchpad, (3) the phonological loop, and (4) a more general integrated storage system the episodic buffer. The chapters that follow aim both to give a more detailed account of the model, and to place it in a broader context. Research in this area has developed enormously since the model was proposed more than 30 years ago, with the result that the account given will inevitably be selective, and determined by my own personal views on the topic. I have however attempted to acknowledge alternative approaches, providing references that would allow such approaches to be further explored, and explaining why I hold my current views, which are, of course, continually evolving as we learn more about working memory.

As the book progresses, I attempt to place the more detailed empirically based multicomponent model in a wider theoretical context. In attempting to say where, when and why working memory is important, I am led to discuss at least briefly those situations in which it plays little part. As a result, the final chapters are considerably broader in scope and more speculative in tone than I anticipated when I set out on what was planned originally as an extended essay on the current state of the multicomponent model.

Chapter 2

Why do we need a phonological loop?

Despite the fact that the phonological loop is limited in capacity to a few items and is only used in certain circumstances, it has generated a huge amount of research over the last 30 years. It also appears to be the component of working memory that is most strongly associated with the Baddeley and Hitch model, with the result that data that do not fit into the phonological loop component are often quite wrongly cited as evidence against the multicomponent model. One example of this will discussed in detail later.

The amount of work that it has generated, and the fact that it remains both controversial and empirically productive after 30 years, presents a dilemma. Devoting a single chapter to the loop would inevitably mean skimming over controversies that are still active, and neglecting alternative hypotheses. On the other hand, a thorough treatment would be likely to involve a degree of detail that is out of balance with the rest of the book. Indeed, some might regard the system as one of minor importance, rather colourfully described by Jim Reason (personal communication) as little more than 'a pimple on the face of cognitive psychology'. If this is the case, then it would be hard to justify further extensive coverage. I will therefore begin by discussing the question of what function might be served by the phonological loop. This will be followed by a chapter that attempts to summarize the controversies and gives a brief account of ways in which the loop model had been elaborated and extended.

2.1 The evolutionary relevance of the loop

In the days when digit span was assumed to be a good measure of STM, one could readily justify its study as reflecting the capacity of a general working memory (Atkinson and Shiffrin 1968). However, as noted earlier, patients whose span was a single digit appeared to have few problems in their everyday life, which clearly seemed inconsistent with a general working memory impairment. If digit span, and by implication the phonological loop does not reflect a general working memory system, what biological function might it serve?

2.1.1 **Language comprehension**

The possibility of working with PV, a patient with a very pure deficit in short-term phonological memory, offered an opportunity to tackle this question (Vallar and Baddeley 1984). My colleague, Giuseppe Vallar and I began by exploring the possibility that the loop might play an important role in language comprehension (Vallar and Baddeley 1987). We found that PV had no difficulty in processing simple sentences, but she did show a deficit in the capacity to verify certain complex sentences. These were constructed so as to require her to hold the initial part of the sentence until the end of the sentence, before the verification decision could be made. Hence, she could successfully reject short sentences such as *Sailors are lived on by ships*, and accept the converse (*Ships are lived on by sailors*), but was virtually at chance with a longer version, such as *Ships are believed, and with some considerable justification, to often be lived on by sailors*. This problem in processing and understanding long sentences is characteristic of STM-deficit patients (Vallar and Shallice 1990). It is, however, hard to argue convincingly that the capacity to interpret such convoluted sentences is likely to have bestowed a sufficiently major biological advantage as to justify the evolution of an apparently specialized system such as the phonological loop.

2.2 **Language acquisition**

Our second hypothesis was that the loop might conceivably play an important role in language *learning*, making it a crucial component for a child, but much less so for adults who have already acquired their native language. Some support for this view came from the observation that dyslexic children who often have delayed language development frequently show impaired digit span (Miles 1993). We decided to test this hypothesis by asking PV to learn items of the vocabulary of a foreign language, Russian (Baddeley *et al.* 1988). If the phonological loop plays an important role in language acquisition, she should perform poorly on this phonological long-term learning task.

2.2.1 **Evidence from patients**

Our test simply involved eight Italian words and eight Russian equivalents, for example, when the familiar Italian word *rosa* (rose) was presented, PV had to learn to respond with the Russian word *svieti*. In order to control for a general verbal learning deficit, we also required her to learn to link eight pairs of words in her native Italian, for example, to associate *cavallo* (horse) and *tavola* (table). We also tested a group of control subjects who were matched for age and educational level. PV proved quite normal in her capacity to learn to associate pairs of Italian words, a task that is known to rely principally on semantic coding, but over ten successive trials she completely failed to master even one item of Russian vocabulary, whereas by this time the control subjects had learned all eight. She did indeed have a problem in new phonological learning.

A later study based on a highly intelligent US graduate student extended this finding to a developmental STM subject, identified because he had very poor phonological STM. Like PV he showed normal acquisition of word pairs together with very poor learning of a foreign language vocabulary (Baddeley 1993). We subsequently discovered that he had previously experienced enormous difficulty in second language learning.

Vallar and Papagno (1993) describe a subject with Down syndrome who shows the converse. Despite her reduced level of general intelligence, she was fluent in three languages. She proved to have excellent phonological STM, rather than the impairment in STM that is typical of Down syndrome (Bellugi *et al.* 1994; Jarrold *et al.* 1999). In a similar vein, a study of polyglots who were fluent in several languages showed that they had longer digit spans than monoglot control subjects who were otherwise similar in age and educational background (Papagno and Vallar 1995).

2.2.2 Second language learning

The evidence so far described relies on data from rare cases in which the phonological loop is either specifically impaired, or is preserved despite more general cognitive deficits. A second approach to the issue studied the impact on new vocabulary learning of disrupting phonological processing in normal subjects. Papagno *et al.* (1991) disrupted the operation of the phonological loop in their subjects by articulatory suppression, the requirement continually to repeat an utterance, hence blocking rehearsal. This impaired the acquisition of foreign language vocabulary, while having little impact on native language paired-associate learning. Papagno and Vallar (1992) produced further evidence for the importance of the phonological loop in foreign language learning by showing that it was impaired by two variables known to have a major influence on the operation of the loop, namely phonological similarity and word length. Despite their interference with foreign vocabulary learning, neither of these phonological variables affected rate of learning pairs of native language words, again suggesting that learning new phonological forms depends on the loop.

2.2.3 Children with language impairment

All the work described so far has been concerned with the capacity for *second* language learning; the question of whether the phonological loop influences native language acquisition is, of course, of potentially greater biological significance. Susan Gathercole and I began to investigate this question using a sample of children who had been categorized as having Specific Language Impairment (SLI). They averaged eight years of age, and had normal non-verbal intelligence, but their level of language development was that of six-year-olds. We gave them a battery of verbal memory tests, and found that they had a particularly marked deficit in the capacity to repeat spoken nonwords, typically monosyllables such as *wux*, or *pij*. We developed a more extended nonword repetition test which, in its final version, involved items ranging from two syllables (e.g. *ballop*) to five (e.g. *pristoractional*) (Gathercole and Baddeley 1990). Each nonword was spoken to the child, who was asked to repeat it back. We compared our SLI group with children of the same age and non-verbal intelligence, and also with six-year-olds, who matched the eight year old SLI children in their level of language development.

The SLI children were substantially impaired in nonword repetition, even when compared to six-year-olds, scoring at a level that subsequently proved appropriate for children of four years (Gathercole and Baddeley 1990). We were able to rule out problems in hearing or articulation, and suggested that our test provided a measure of the capacity of the phonological loop, one that was even more appropriate than digit span for predicting language acquisition, since it demanded the processing of items resembling real words. We assumed that digit span would depend on the same system, but would be likely to rely more upon the existing knowledge of digits, for which our SLI children would have had two more years experience than their language-matched controls. As we shall see later, our hunch was correct, in that nonword repetition and digit span tend to be correlated, but with nonword repetition (NWR) proving a better predictor of language acquisition (Baddeley *et al.* 1998a).

2.2.4 Vocabulary acquisition in normal children

We also investigated the extent to which our new test was able to predict level of vocabulary in normal children (Gathercole and Baddeley 1989). Our basic design involved testing a range of children of a given age, measuring nonword repetition, non-verbal intelligence, typically with the Raven's Matrices test, and vocabulary level. This was measured using the British Picture Vocabulary Scale (BPVS) in which a word is spoken while the child looks at an array of four pictures, and is asked to point to the item specified. While non-verbal IQ was correlated with vocabulary at age 4 ($r = 0.388$) and 5 ($r = 0.164$), nonword repetition was more strongly associated with vocabulary level ($r = 0.525$ and 0.492 respectively). This correlation has now been replicated many times across a range of different age groups (see Table 2.1).

Table 2.1 The relationship between vocabulary, non-word repetition and digit span. Data from a range of studies, as reported by Baddeley, Gathercole and Papagno (1998).

Mean Age	n	Nonword repetition		Digit span	
		Simple	Partial*	Simple	Partial*
3.00	54	0.34	0.31	0.15	0.16
4.01	70	0.49	0.47	0.28	0.22
4.07	80	0.56	0.46	–	–
4.09	57	0.41	0.41	0.28	0.29
5.03	70	0.34	0.36	0.20	0.18
5.06	48	0.48	–	–	–
5.07	80	0.52	0.50	–	–
5.09	51	0.41	0.31	0.38	0.28
5.09	65	0.61	0.53	0.44	0.38
6.07	80	0.56	0.48	0.44	0.33
8.07	80	0.28	0.22	0.36	0.23
13.10	60	–	–	0.49	0.46

* With other potential predictors statistically removed.

Of course, correlation does not necessarily imply causation. It could, for example, plausibly be argued that subjects with large vocabularies are able to use this knowledge to help them perform the nonword task. Hence the observation by Papagno and Vallar (1995) that polyglots who speak a number of different languages have higher digit span might reflect the fact the loop can draw upon the more extensive language habits acquired in learning the non-native languages. Such a view was espoused by Brown and Hulme (1996), who proposed that a good vocabulary led to good verbal memory rather than vice versa. Support for such a view came from a study by Gathercole (1995) of the performance of children who have high or low scores on the nonword repetition test. She compared performance on items that were similar in phonotactic structure to English, such as *prindle* and *contramponist*, with performance on less word-like items, such as *ballop* and *skiticult*. Both high and low nonword repetition groups gained a clear and broadly equivalent advantage from word likeness, strongly supporting the idea that language habits contribute to nonword repetition performance.

A second feature of Gathercole's data, however, told a somewhat different story. When the children's vocabulary acquisition over the year *following* this test was recorded, it proved to be unrelated to performance on the word-like items, but clearly correlated with the capacity of the child to repeat the less word-like sequences. It seems likely, therefore, that there are two contributions to nonword repetition, one from existing language habits, which makes a broadly equivalent contribution across the two groups, and the other from a source that differs between the two groups. I suggest that this comprises the limited capacity phonological store. Language habits provide good support for both groups, but new learning depends on the capacity of the phonological store: children with higher phonological store capacity will be able to hold on to new words for longer, increasing the likelihood of long-term phonological learning.

Further evidence for the primacy of phonological storage came from a study using cross-lagged correlation to throw light on the causal link between existing vocabulary, nonword repetition and the capacity to acquire new words (Gathercole and Baddeley 1989). A group of children were tested at age four, and retested at five, on both vocabulary and nonword repetition. Using cross-lagged correlational logic, it was proposed that if the primary driving force was phonological memory, then nonword repetition at four years of age would predict vocabulary one year later significantly better than vocabulary at four would predict memory at five. On the other hand, if vocabulary were the driving factor, the reverse pattern should occur. The results were clear in indicating that nonword repetition predicted subsequent vocabulary acquisition rather than the reverse, although as children get older, the pattern becomes more reciprocal with both nonword repetition and vocabulary predicting subsequent performance (Baddeley *et al.* 1998a).

Sorting out clear causal links in cognitive development will inevitably be difficult, because a whole range of cognitive skills is likely to be developing in parallel, making it difficult to separate one from the other – the collinearity problem. The issue is further complicated by the tendency for cognitive development to involve a cyclic process whereby an initial capacity leads to the development of cognitive skills, which then further enhance that capacity which in turn enhances the developing skills. This has led to alternative accounts of our findings in terms of phonological processing rather than the phonological loop (Snowling *et al.* 1991, but see Gathercole *et al.* 1991). While one might argue for an unspecified phonological processing deficit as an explanation of the SLI results from children, the Snowling *et al.* interpretation can not readily account for our data from adults acquiring a second language. For example, it is implausible to suggest that PV's dramatic impairment in phonological STM results from a loss of language habits generally, as she has unimpaired vocabulary and syntax and speaks with perfectly normal speed and prosody (Basso *et al.* 1982). Similarly, while articulatory suppression, word length and phonological similarity all influence the phonological loop, and all interfere with the acquisition of novel vocabulary, it is hard to see how any of these could be regarded as temporarily removing the person's access to language habits.

2.2.5 Acquisition of syntax

The evidence for the role of the phonological loop in the acquisition of grammar is less strong than for vocabulary learning. It has been proposed that the capacity to store sequences of words plays an important role in syntactic development (Nelson 1987; Plunkett and Marchman 1993), a view supported by a study of two bilingual siblings by Speidel (1993). Both were of equivalent high general intellectual capacity, but one was slow to acquire individual words and made multiple syntactic errors, coupled with poor phonological memory. Daneman and Case (1981) showed that word span was a better predictor of performance on an artificial grammar learning task than chronological age. Studies by Blake *et al.* (1994) and Adams and Gathercole (1995; 1996) showed that phonological memory tests were able to predict mean length of utterance in spoken language while Ellis and Beaton (1993) implicated phonological memory in the acquisition of grammar in second language learning. We suggest, therefore, that the balance of evidence supports the idea that the phonological loop plays an important role in the acquisition of both native and second languages, a view that is discussed in detail by Baddeley *et al.* (1998a).

2.3 Sublexical short-term memory

As we have seen, the classic STM task is digit span, in which the subject remembers a sequence of digits, highly overlearned items from a very restricted set. In moving to word span, there has been a tendency, certainly on my own part, to keep to the repeated use of a limited set of words, explicitly to emphasize the need to store serial order and to minimize any contribution from long-term memory. This classic version of serial STM has indeed proved to be a surprisingly complex and empirically fruitful task, but if, as suggested by Baddeley *et al.* (1998a), the phonological loop has evolved to help acquire *novel* phonological sequences, then it seems paradoxical to study the process using components like digits that are already highly overlearned. For this reason, my colleagues have begun to move away from studying well-learned closed sets of items towards the study of nonwords, producing results that challenge and extend existing models of the phonological loop, as we shall see. The work focuses on two issues: a detailed analysis of error patterns, together with an analysis of the processes by which recall is influenced by lexicality, that is, by whether sequences of words or nonwords are to be remembered.

2.3.1 **Word and nonword error patterns**

A detailed analysis of errors has formed an important tool in developing and testing models of STM from its early days (Conrad 1960 1964; Sperling and Speelman 1970). For example, any precise model of digit span should be able to account for the observation that when sequence length exceeds span, subjects typically continue to recall most of the items, but do so in the wrong order. Such errors tend to move across relatively short distances within the sequence, with adjacent transpositions (e.g. *1, 2, 3, 4, 5, 6* to *1, 2, 3, 5, 4, 6*) being the most probable when all items are recalled (Aaronson 1968; Bjork and Healey 1974; Lee and Estes 1997). The fact that errors occur between adjacent items suggests that although order information may have become less accurate, it has not been totally lost.

A study of the retention of consonant-vowel-consonant (CVC) *nonwords* by Trieman and Danis (1988) however, produced a somewhat different picture. In this case, what appeared to be item errors predominated: that is, CVCs were produced that had not been presented in the sequence. However, closer inspection indicated that these apparent item errors themselves resulted from order errors within the sequence of *phonemes*, hence *wux caz* might become *cux waz*. One might therefore redescribe the apparent item errors as order errors resulting from the consonants and vowels becoming 'unglued' from the novel CVCs. Again, the transpositions occurred across relatively short distances, implying that some order information was still being stored.

Gathercole *et al.* (1999) studied serial recall of CVCs that varied in phonotactic frequency, that is in the likelihood that that combination of phonemes would occur in the language. High phonotactic items were better recalled than those comprising less familiar sound sequences. Like Trieman and Danis, they found that errors were predominantly due to migrations of individual phonemes, rather than of complete CVC syllables. Order errors were predominantly attributable to consonants, with the retention of order information in the vowels being substantially more robust. They suggest that the retention of order information principally depends upon the vowels, which have been demonstrated across a number of studies to be retained more reliably than the consonants. For example, Drewnowski (1980) showed that similarity across items in vowel sound (e.g. *dah, fah, gah*) led to poorer recall than consonant similarity (e.g. *dih, dah, doh*), suggesting that the vowels play a more central role in STM.

This pattern of results is consistent with the hypothesis that order information is principally carried by the vowel sounds, with consonants being more or less strongly attached to the individual vowels. In the case of a limited and closed set of phonologically dissimilar items such as digits or dissimilar consonants, retention of the order of the vowels is sufficient to allow the original string to be unambiguously regenerated, in contrast to a phonologically similar list, in which the common vowel would provide a relatively ineffective cue. Such an interpretation of the phonological similarity effect is common to a number of the computational models described later which separate the storage of order information from a later item selection stage. This process can be modelled relatively easily when the items already exist in some long-term lexicon, as in the case of digits and words, but presents more of a problem when, as in the present case, subjects are required to retrieve novel nonwords.

2.3.2 **Lexicality and redintegration**

Gathercole and colleagues found that the capacity to repeat nonwords was a good predictor of whether or not a child was likely to encounter reading problems (Baddeley and Gathercole 1992; Gathercole and Pickering 2001). However, although this *could* reflect a memory failure, the problem could be the plausible result of difficulty in either hearing or articulating the material. If hearing is the problem, errors should occur even on short sequences when presentation is auditory, allowing this possibility to be identified and the child's hearing then checked audiometrically. The complications of speech production may also be avoided by using recognition, rather than spoken recall, with the child hearing two nonword sequences varying in length, and detecting whether the order of the component sounds was the same or different. This, however, raises the further question of whether a nonword recognition measure would be comparable to the existing recall tasks as a predictor of vocabulary acquisition.

2.3.3 **Lexicality and recognition**

Gathercole *et al.* (2001) investigated this by measuring both recall and recognition span for words and nonwords. Their procedure was as follows: in the recall task, subjects would hear and attempt to repeat back sequences of monosyllabic words or nonwords of equivalent phonotactic frequency. Sequence length was increased to a point at which accurate recall broke down, i.e. span length for that type of material. Recognition was tested by presenting sequences of increasing length, and following each with a second sequence that was either identical, or had the order of two items switched (e.g. present *pig, hat, rug, day*; test *pig, rug, hat, day*). They found that words were substantially easier to *recall* than nonwords. Surprisingly however, there was little difference between word and nonword span when tested by recognition. This result was replicated across a range of studies by Gathercole *et al.* (2001), and further extended by Thorn and Gathercole (1999) in a study comparing span in monolingual and bilingual subjects for words in their first or second language.

They found a clear advantage for material in the subject's first language when tested by recall, whereas language type had little effect on recognition.

Returning to the practical issue that prompted the initial study, fortunately, nonword recognition did indeed prove to correlate with vocabulary acquisition (Gathercole *et al.* 2001), suggesting that it will provide a useful practical tool for testing children with speech production problems. This result also implies that it is the capacity to store novel phonological information, rather than existing language knowledge, that provides the predictive power of nonword repetition, at least during the earlier stages of language acquisition, and as such, it reinforces the earlier conclusions of Baddeley *et al.* (1998a) regarding the role of the phonological store in language acquisition.

2.3.4 Set size and recall

One final study will be described before attempting to pull together the evidence and consider its implications for the phonological loop model. In this study, Gathercole (In preparation) manipulated an important variable that distinguishes the standard memory span procedure from nonword repetition, namely that of whether a limited 'closed' set of items, for example the same ten words, is used repeatedly, or whether an 'open' set of words is used, with different words for every trial. As expected, she found an advantage to the closed set, in which the limited range of words made item recall much easier. Of more significance, however, was the pattern of errors obtained. She found that the closed set words behaved just as did digits, in that errors typically reflected the transposition of the order in which the words were recalled, with little tendency for the words themselves to be incorrect.

In contrast, words from the open sets were often incorrectly reported. On closer inspection, this proved to result from a tendency of consonants to switch their serial position. As in the case of nonwords, the typical pattern was for consonants to migrate to adjacent positions, for example, *hat-pen* to *pat-hen*. Combining the results from this and the Gathercole *et al.* (2001) study, she proposed that order information is stored at a sublexical level, with lexical knowledge being used at the later retrieval stage, at which the use of long-term knowledge to facilitate recall is often termed redintegration (Schweikert 1993; Brown and Hulme 1995). When a limited set of words is constantly reused, the range of potential candidates to match a given degraded memory trace is highly constrained, leading to better performance. When an open set of many potential CVC words is employed, however, the capacity for accurate redintegration is substantially reduced: although all items may be known to be real words, this is less helpful, as a large number of possible CVC items are real words, and are hence plausible candidates for recall.

If recall of order information depends principally on retention of the sequence of vowel sounds, phonologically similar lists having a common vowel will gain little from this redintegrative process, as the information retained will not differentiate between the possible candidate responses. This is likely to be the case regardless of whether memory is tested by recall or recognition, as is indeed the case (Gathercole *et al.* 2001). Redintegration could occur at either, or both of two levels. One involves the automatic use of language knowledge to enhance the encoding and/or retrieval of information within the phonological loop, a process analogous to pattern recognition. The other would involve intentional utilization of language-based or other knowledge, to interpret incomplete evidence in the process of active retrieval. The former automatic process should enhance the recall of words over nonwords, regardless of whether they are part of a list comprising only words, or form part of a mixed word/nonword list. The explicit strategic use of lexical knowledge on the other hand might be disrupted if words and nonwords are mixed. This is indeed the case with consonants tending to switch in mixed lists, just as in nonword recall. There is still an advantage to mixed over nonword lists, however, although the effect appears to be limited to item information, and not to enhance retention of order of information (Jefferies *et al.* 2006). It thus seems likely that order information is stored at a phonemic level, with lexical and other long-term knowledge occurring at a separate redintegrative stage. Further evidence for the role of lexical knowledge in immediate serial recall comes from studies of STM in patients suffering from semantic dementia, a progressive condition in which the patient loses access to the meaning of previously familiar words, when performance is poorer for sequences containing 'lost' words (Forde and Humphreys 2002; Jefferies *et al.* 2004a).

These recent developments continue to fit broadly within the initial phonological loop model although as proposed (Baddeley 1986) it faces one major problem, namely that it has no specified method of storing order information. It had already become clear (Baddeley 1968) that a simple chaining process, whereby each word acted as a stimulus for the next, could not account for the data, and that some form of more clearly specified serial ordering mechanism was necessary if the loop model was to develop. Fortunately, this issue was tackled by a number of very able computational modellers, with results that I describe below.

2.4 The problem of serial order

While the storage of serial order is trivial and easy for a traditional computer based on serial processing, this is not the case for the human brain, which appears to resemble parallel processing systems more closely. Obtaining serial recall from a parallel system is, as we shall see, a far from trivial task.

There are two basic ways of dealing with the storage and retrieval of serial order, namely chaining and contextual association, with the latter splitting into a number of subapproaches. Chaining assumes that each item is associatively linked with the next, with the result that presenting one item will cue the next which in turn will cue the next until the end of the sequence. The alternative is to associate each item with some form of context which then provides the ordinal cue. The simplest version of this is the 'slot model' in which the storage of items is based on a number of slots or locations which can be read off in the order of presentation (Conrad 1965). Other contextual models assume that order is determined by associating each item with a marker, usually the initial, and sometimes the terminal item, with these associations being used in order to retrieve the items in order. A third broad category of contextual model assumes that items are associated with a continually changing context, analogous to a temporal cue, and that this can then be used to cue the relevant items.

2.5 **Chaining models**

The assumption that items are stored and retrieved via a chain of associations extends back to Ebbinghaus (1885) and is still a popular one (Wickelgren 1965; Jordan 1986; Lewandowski and Murdock 1989; Murdock 1993; Meyer and Kieras 1999). The model is simple and intuitively plausible, proposing that a serial list may be regarded as a sequence of associated pairs, with the result that when the first item is cued, it will automatically call up the next and so forth. However, as Lashley (1951) pointed out, this approach has a number of problems. The first of these concerns the issue of repeated items. If each item is dependent on the prior item, then a sequence such as *7, 9, 6, 3, 9, 5* should be difficult to recall correctly, since the same item, *9* acts as a cue for two different pairs, namely *6* and *5*. The second problem concerns the effect of error on performance. A simple chaining model should predict that once the subject has made an error, then the chain will be broken, hence the subsequent sequence should also be erroneous, since the error will itself cue an inappropriate response, producing a cascade of errors. In fact, the most common form of errors in lists of around span length comprise transpositions, whereby two items switch positions, while leaving the rest of the sequence unaffected (e.g. *4, 5, 2, 8, 7* becomes *4, 2, 5, 8, 7*). One way of dealing with such problems is to postulate remote associations that go beyond the pair (Ebbinghaus 1885). In principle, these can be used to recover from errors induced by erroneous items, although whether such models provide an adequate account of the broader range of errors is open to question (Henson 1998).

An effect that does not appear to be resolvable by assuming remote associations was first pointed out by Baddeley (1968), and subsequently further explored by Henson *et al.* (1996). It was discovered serendipitously through an attempt to reduce the potential impact of phonological similarity on recall of consonant-based postal codes, with its theoretical significance only becoming apparent with Wickelgren's (1965) subsequent proposal of a chaining interpretation of immediate serial recall. Our subjects were presented with sequences of six letters under each of four conditions. The first involved six phonologically similar letters (e.g. *c, b, t, g, v, p*), the second, six dissimilar (*k, w, y, q, x, r*), while conditions three and four involved alternating similar and dissimilar items (*k, v, y, p, r, d* and *g, y, t, l, p, w*). As expected, the consistently similar lists were harder than the dissimilar, with the alternating lists falling between. A crucial question for the chaining hypothesis, however, concerns the location of the errors. From what is known of paired associate learning (Osgood 1949), errors arise because of *stimulus* similarity, hence, errors should occur *following* the similar letters rather than *on* the similar letters. Exactly the opposite was observed. The errors were much more likely to occur on the similar items themselves, rather than on the interpolated dissimilar items. This result was replicated and further extended by Henson *et al.* (1996), and the assumption that chaining models would predict otherwise has subsequently been confirmed from a number of simulations (Burgess and Hitch 1996; Henson 1998; Page and Norris 1998). To the best of my knowledge, this result presents a problem for all existing chaining models.

2.6 **Contextual models**

Conrad (1965) appears to have been the only recent theorist to suggest that human STM resembles that of a standard serial processing computer with a limited number of storage locations arranged in order. He did not however elaborate the model, leaving the number of slots unspecified. Also unspecified was the nature of the items; the fact that span differs widely between unconnected words and sentences suggests that what is stored is not individual words, but rather chunks of some sort. The slot model has thus simply not been sufficiently clearly specified or developed to represent a strong contender for a theory of serial order therefore, although as we shall see below, a slot-like mechanism does play an important role in the model proposed by Hartley and Houghton (1996).

A number of models have been proposed which determine serial order with reference to particular markers, notably the initial or the final item. Shiffrin and Cook (1978) proposed a model in which items were stored in terms of associations between nodes representing the beginning and end of the sequence, with the relative strength of the two associations providing a cue as to where in the sequence a given item had occurred. Lee and Estes (1981) proposed a model in which positional information was specified at a number of different levels, ranging from the position of the item within a segment of a single trial, through the position of that segment up to the position of that trial within the overall sequence of trials. However the model was developed and tested over twelve item lists and the contribution of the phonological loop to lists of this length tends to be minimal (Baddeley 1966b; Salame and Baddeley 1986).

2.6.1 **The primacy model**

A more recent model by Page and Norris (1998) proposes a mechanism within the phonological loop framework that is based on the assumption that order is generated by associating each successive item with the first item presented, hence its title, the *primacy model*. At the heart of the model is the mechanism known as *competitive queuing*, first proposed by Grossberg (1978; 1987) and subsequently developed by Houghton (1990). In the primacy model, the contextual cue is provided by a series of associations with the first item in the sequence, hence its name. Each item is represented in the model by a node. As each successive item is presented, its node is assumed to be associated with that of the first item, but with decreasing strength. As in the initial phonological loop hypothesis, the strength is assumed to decay over time, but to be potentially reactivated by cumulative rehearsal. At recall, the serial order of the constituent items is determined by reinstating the initial node, which will then activate all of the items presented in the list to a greater or lesser extent. Earlier nodes that have a stronger link with the first item will receive stronger activation than later. A competitive filter then selects the most active node, (the first in the queue), which will be that nearest to the start point, and feeds it on to a second stage, before suppressing that node. This second stage performs an output decision: only if the level of activation exceeds some criterion is a response made. Meanwhile, with the node representing second item in the sequence suppressed, the next most strongly associated node will be selected, and so forth.

Errors may occur because of noise at either the first stage, responsible for order information, or the second at which items are chosen. Errors may occur at the first stage as a result of 'noise' within the system, and are likely to lead to the next most strongly associated node. For example noise in the link between the start cue and item three would lead to the next strongest being selected, item four, probably followed by the somewhat weakened item three resulting in a transposition error whereby the order *1234* becomes *1243*. Such errors are indeed the most common when subjects are operating with lists that approximate to their digit span. Because of trace decay, the probability of error will increase with sequence length, and will tend to be greater during the latter parts of the list, resulting in the standard primacy effect which characterizes recall of visually presented digits.

The primacy model is further supported by a detailed examination of the pattern of errors observed. For each item in a sequence, the most likely response is that item itself, followed by adjacent items, with a very clear and marked tendency for nearer items to be more likely to occur as intrusions. This is not true of all STM models. As Nairne (1990) points out, for example, this presents a problem for the current version of his feature model.

Noise at the response selection stage leads to item errors, and it is at this stage that acoustic similarity is assumed to influence performance. Within the loop model, this stage relies upon phonological coding, with phonologically similar items having fewer features that distinguish the relevant items, making them more vulnerable to trace decay. Because the effect of acoustic similarity influences this later stage, the primacy model escapes the problem of predicting that errors should *follow* similar items, and the model is very successful in generating the sawtoothed curve produced by Baddeley (1968) and Henson *et al.* (1996). Page and Norris (1998) relate this latter response selection mechanism to data from speech production, suggesting that speech errors probably reflect the operation of this stage. Ellis (1980) had previously noted the similarity between errors in immediate verbal recall and speech errors.

It is possible however that memory and speech errors may reflect similar retrieval processes operating at different levels of the system. Saito and Baddeley (2004) investigated a method of inducing speech errors based on a traditional Japanese word game. An individual is asked to repeatedly utter a complex word, whereupon the tester speaks a second word. This will induce a speech error, but only if it is phonologically similar to the repeated target. As Saito and Baddeley point out, this differs from the standard effect of irrelevant speech on serial recall in two ways. First, unlike the memory effect (Jones and Macken 1995), it depends on the similarity between the spoken and heard items, and secondly because the timing is crucial, whereas irrelevant speech disrupts recall even when presented several seconds later (Norris *et al.* 2004). Saito and Baddeley interpret their results in terms of speech output buffer, which may utilize similar retrieval processes to the input-based phonological store.

There is no doubt that the primacy model provides a very simple and highly ingenious account of a wide range of data associated with the phonological loop. It can be criticized for not being more specific about how the initial item is cued, a problem for most of the theories in this area. There are also types of intrusion error which do not fit this pattern, but which can be explained by a somewhat more complex model such as Henson's *Start End Model* (SEM), which assumes both primacy and recency cues: Page and Norris suggest that such errors are attributable to factors outside the range of their model.

2.6.2 The start end model

As we saw, a detailed analysis of error patterns can be extremely informative. The phonological loop-based model that probably takes most advantage of this is Henson's model SEM, which assumes both a primacy gradient similar to that of Page and Norris, and also a recency gradient. This double cueing allows him to account for a number of error types that do not fit readily into the primacy model. It has been known for many years that grouping digits into triplets enhances recall, whether this is done by inserting brief pauses (Ryan 1969), by instruction (Wickelgren 1964), or spontaneously. The pattern of recall under these circumstances tends to reflect three-item mini serial position curves, with each triplet showing a higher error for the middle item than for the first and last. Under these circumstances, errors often represent switching between two items in the same serial position within its triplet (e.g. 123-456-789 becomes 123-756-489). A second characteristic error comprises what Henson calls 'protrusions', where an intrusion represents the item that was in that position on the previous list. The protrusion effect is weakened by long intertrial intervals (Conrad 1960; 1967), and only occurs when recall is required and the appropriate item was successfully retrieved (Henson 1998). There is no doubt that SEM does give a good account of a wide range of data, but does so at the expense of greater complexity. It will be interesting to see whether its subsequent development justifies the additional assumptions. There is no doubt that subjects can use recency as well as primacy cues, but whether they operate within the same mechanism or represent an additional strategic factor remains to be seen.

2.6.3 Temporal context models

Houghton's (1990) competitive queuing mechanism has stimulated a range of models that attempt to instantiate the contextual component in terms of some form of timing mechanism. The first and most developed of these is that proposed by Burgess and Hitch (1992) and subsequently modified (Burgess and Hitch 1999). Both versions of the model assume a series of overlapping temporal cues based on timing mechanisms that operate in parallel. As each item is presented, it is associated with the temporal pattern operative at that time. In the initial model, Burgess and Hitch (1992) assumed the parallel activation of one set of nodes representing phonemes, and a separate set representing words. The word nodes were assumed to be linked to the relevant contextual signal, and in the initial model also to interassociate through a chaining process.

However, as described earlier, chaining models have difficulty in accounting for the sawtoothed pattern of errors found when similar and dissimilar items are interleaved. The initial Burgess and Hitch model also had difficulty in giving an account of the interaction between long- and short-term components of the task, and of the effects of word frequency on performance.

In order to cope with these problems, a second version was proposed (Burgess and Hitch 1999). The new version abolished the chaining assumption and combined the input and output stages into a single layer. A further important modification was the assumption that the association between the context and the nodes operate at two levels, namely short-term faster weights which decay rapidly and long-term weights which are more durable, a mechanism previously introduced by Hinton and Plaut (1987). The slow weights provide a mechanism for long-term learning, while the fast weights allow the rapid registration of novel sequences. The process of inhibiting responses that have been emitted is now assumed to decay, producing a more realistic pattern of intrusion errors, while noise in the activation system is assumed to occur only at output.

The new model is capable of dealing with the phenomena explained by the first version, including the effects of sequence length, word length, phonemic similarity and the presence of frequent order errors, and in addition generates an appropriate sawtooth curve. Importantly, it also provides a mechanism that links the phonological loop with LTM, allowing both the enhancement of recall by prior knowledge and the gradual acquisition of new vocabulary as a result of learning. As with most models, it still does not give a good account of how the initial cue is selected so as to kick start the system, and in its Burgess and Hitch (1999) form, like the primacy and SEM models, does not handle memory for nonwords or the effects of modality. It also depends crucially on the plausibility of the temporal contextual cueing mechanism, a point we shall return to later. There is no doubt however that the model has been a very influential one, both because its first version was the first to explicitly try to model the phonological loop, and also because of its success in responding to the problems confronting the initial version. Current developments are focusing on the interface with LTM using the Hebb effect, whereby a repeated sequence within a serial STM paradigm is used to track the gradual build up of serial LTM (Hebb 1961).

However, while the Burgess and Hitch revised model does a reasonably good job of dealing with immediate memory for digits or words, where the subject is required to remember familiar lexical units, it cannot at present handle unfamiliar phonemic sequences such as occur in nonword repetition. While the model does have a phonemic level, this component of the system does not store serial order, and hence could not distinguish between *pat*, *tap* and *apt*.

If, as we propose, the principal function of the phonological loop is to assist in storing and learning novel phonological forms which will eventually form words in the child's vocabulary, this is a major limitation. There have been at least two attempts to remedy this problem, one by Glasspool (1995) and the other by Hartley and Houghton (1996).

2.6.4 Models for retention of nonwords

Hartley and Houghton (1996) proposed separate mechanisms for recall of sequences at the word and subword levels. The word level involves a competitive cueing model somewhat similar to that of Burgess and Hitch, while nonword sequencing is assumed to depend on a template or slot model in which sequencing is responsive to the phonological structure of the language.

Glasspool (1995) tackles the problem by assuming two separate short-term memory traces, one at the word and the other at the phonemic level. Each operates broadly according to the Burgess and Hitch (1996) model, and each has its own temporal context representing the different temporal grain of the phonemic and word-level processes. The word context steps on each time a new word is identified, while the phonemic level moves on every phoneme. Both systems then converge in order to produce a single output, with the word level only contributing if it is strongly activated. The model correctly predicts that span for words will be greater than for nonwords because of the long-term contribution from the existing temporal structure within the word, and that errors which represent the reordering of phonemes occur more frequently in memory for nonwords than for words (Aaronson 1968).

Glasspool's model could be criticized for being non-parsimonious by involving two systems rather than one, although the question of parsimony is always a difficult one to judge. You might for example argue that using the same principles over different levels is in principle a parsimonious strategy. It raises the interesting thought that perhaps a level above that of the word could be postulated, with similar systems for syntax, word level semantics and high-level world knowledge. Such a system could be seen as a form of the 'pandemonium' model proposed by Selfridge as long ago as 1955 as a way of conceptualizing the bottom-up processing of complex information, and might offer a possible solution to the problem of how immediate memory utilizes coding at so many different levels. Such a solution would also be very much in the spirit of Grossberg's (1987) proposal, that a limited number of mechanisms, such as competitive queuing, are utilized in many different biological roles. There may however, prove to be major problems in computationally implementing such a coordinated multilevel model.

The models described represent only a subset of the large number of attempts to produce computational or mathematical models of serial recall. They are selected because they specifically attempt to explain the data relevant to the phonological loop component of working memory, and are presented in a way that is intelligible to a mathematically limited experimentalist such as myself. It is important to bear in mind, however, that alternative models of serial order have been developed which explicitly reject the phonological loop hypothesis. Some, though not all of these, are discussed in the next chapter.

Chapter 3

The phonological loop

Challenges and growing points

Although the phonological loop forms only a relatively small part of working memory it is probably the most distinctive aspect of the Baddeley and Hitch (1974) multicomponent model, and the one that has been investigated in most detail. After more than 30 years it still generates controversy, and importantly, new and interesting data. The challenges occur at two main levels. The first and most general line of attack represents the classic objection made originally to the concept of short-term memory, that working memory is an unnecessary concept as the phenomena it explains simply reflect aspects of long-term memory. The second source of criticism comes from proposers of alternative models of STM which offer a different account of the various phenomena attributed to the phonological loop.

These challenges will be discussed in turn, beginning with a relatively recent attack on what is termed 'the standard model', which proves to be a simplified version of the phonological loop.

3.1 Nairne's critique

Although I have discussed working memory as if it were a generally accepted concept, there remains within the verbal learning and memory tradition a continuing commitment to a unitary view of memory. This was expressed most strongly in a relatively recent critique of the concept of working memory presented by James Nairne (2002), a distinguished memory researcher. It was published in an august and much cited journal, the *Annual Review of Psychology*, and entitled 'Remembering over the short-term: The case against the standard model'. I began to read it with some apprehension, but ended with a degree of puzzlement. I certainly disagreed with the tenor of the general conclusion that 'increasingly, researchers are recognising that short-term retention is cue driven, much like long-term memory, and that neither rehearsal nor decay is likely to explain the particulars of short-term forgetting' (Nairne 2002, p. 53). And yet, when I went through the individual points, I discovered that I agreed with most of them. How could that be?

I think the answer is given in the title, 'Remembering over the short-term'. Indeed, I remember hearing Jim Nairne present an invited conference address on the theme that short-term memory does not exist, describing his aim as explaining the memory processes that operate over the 30 seconds after a piece of information is presented. Recall over the first 30 seconds is likely to reflect an amalgam of behaviour based on several underlying systems, including both working memory and a substantial and more stable LTM contribution. The Peterson and Peterson (1959) short-term forgetting paradigm for example reflects a small STM component, together with a substantial contribution from LTM (see Baddeley 1998, pp. 31-37 for a discussion). Nairne and I agree on the probable interpretation of forgetting in the Peterson task, in terms of the discriminability of temporal cues (Baddeley 1976, p. 126-131), and we both propose that a similar mechanism can also be applied to the recency effect in both short- and long-term memory tasks (Baddeley and Hitch 1977; 1993).

Nairne goes on to raise a series of problems with the concept of subvocal rehearsal, which he regards as central to what he terms 'the standard model'. They include:

1 *Implementing a precise model of rehearsal is likely to be difficult.* I agree: within the phonological loop, at least, rehearsal is a covert activity under strategic control. Furthermore, it involves a form of subvocalization and hence an adequate theory will need to be related to a theory of speech production – not a simple matter. This is, I would suggest, both a necessary and worthwhile task.

2 *Individual differences in span occur when differences in rehearsal rate are ruled out.* That is certainly the case. I would, however, expect the capacity and/or durability of the phonological store to vary between individuals, and to be vulnerable to neurological damage, as in cases such as PV (Vallar and Baddeley 1984a).

3 *When rehearsal is controlled, different materials lead to differential memory performance.* For example, similar words are harder than dissimilar, and words are easier than nonwords. I entirely agree that neither of these effects is likely to be dependent on the articulatory process, and that they need a more complete model, as is provided by the phonological loop hypothesis.

4 *Word length effects are attributable to output delay, and may occur when presentation is too rapid to allow rehearsal.* I suggest that both covert rehearsal during presentation and overt speech during recall are time-based effects, with both fitting the phonological loop hypothesis.

5 *Patients who have lost the power to articulate may still show word length effects.* This is because rehearsal involves the running of an inner speech

programme, not overt articulation (Baddeley and Wilson 1985). Consistent with this view is the observation that dyspraxia, wherein such programmes can no longer be constructed, abolishes the word length effect (Caplan and Waters 1995).

In short, the issues Nairne raises are problematic only for a model that limits itself entirely to a very simple rehearsal loop that does not even involve a potentially separable phonological store. This was not true of the phonological loop hypothesis, even in its earliest form.

A substantial part of Nairne's thesis is based on the Brown-Peterson short-term forgetting task, wherein a small amount of material such as a consonant trigram is retained over a matter of seconds, during which rehearsal is prevented by a concurrent task. This paradigm does not involve the phonological loop, and is indeed unaffected by concurrent articulatory suppression (Baddeley *et al.* 1984a). I agree with Nairne that it is best explained in terms of the relative discriminability of temporal cues (Baddeley 1976, pp. 126-131; Nairne 2002), and that in this respect it resembles the recency effect in free recall (Baddeley and Hitch 1977). Both of these will be discussed in Chapter 6.

One point on which we do disagree concerns the relevance to current theory of McGeoch's (1932) quasi-philosophical claim that time per se cannot affect physical properties, and that such properties can only be influenced by actions that occur within that time, hence ruling out trace decay on logical grounds (McGeoch and Irion 1952). Nairne quotes this with approval. However, the brain is in constant activity, so genuinely unfilled time is unlikely to occur (before death at least). A more appropriate distinction would therefore be that between decay, seen as forgetting due to general neural activity (occurring during a delay), and forgetting due to specific interference. My own view is that both are likely.

I suggest therefore that most of Nairne's criticisms are based on his assumption of an excessively simplistic 'standard model', a model that is not held by any theorist I myself have encountered. It is certainly not an adequate representation of the current multicomponent working memory model, or indeed of the more limited phonological loop component. I was pleased to note that we now also appear to agree on this point. In a discussion of his more recent views, Nairne (2003) acknowledges that verbal/acoustic features play a distinctive role in STM tasks, and that our views are much more comparable than might appear (Nairne, personal communication, 2006).

That does not mean that there is now general agreement on the interpretation of the phenomena on which the phonological loop was based. As the next section will show, the phonological loop continues to generate vigorous, and I believe, fruitful controversy.

3.1.1 **The phonological loop hypothesis: interpreting the evidence**

Over the last 30 years, the phonological loop hypothesis has continued to stimulate empirical research. Some of this is generated by competing models such as those presented by Nairne (2002), who emphasizes similarities to LTM, or to Jones (1993), who attempts to explain the phenomena in perceptual terms. Furthermore as the Miyake and Shah (1999a) review of theoretical approaches to working memory indicates, many theorists accept the need for some kind of transient verbal or phonological memory, but are relatively neutral as to how closely such processes approximate to the phonological loop or the visuospatial sketch pad. Cowan (1999; 2005), for example is a major contributor to empirical research on phonological STM but concentrates his modelling on the role of attention, rather than the details of the phonological contribution. Verbal STM plays a role in the production system model developed by Meyer and Keiras (1999), which does indeed assume trace decay. It is not, however, essential to the model, which could accommodate change in this component without seriously threatening its usefulness as a tool for analysing performance on complex cognitive tasks, its principal aim. Finally, as will become clear later in this chapter, much of the research in the area has been carried out by investigators who have a commitment to answering the basic questions, but not to any particular overall theory.

All agree however, that deciding between competing theories must depend on a relatively detailed examination of the data. The next section gives an account of the phonological loop model and the new evidence that it has helped to generate, beginning with the topic that has probably stimulated the most extensive research and most vigorous controversy, the word length effect.

Before beginning the detailed analysis however, a very brief reminder of the phonological loop hypothesis might be useful for readers who are not in this field. Verbal material is assumed to be held in a limited capacity phonological store where traces decay relatively rapidly, but may be refreshed by subvocal articulation. Subvocal articulation can also be used to verbally recode visually presented material, hence allowing it to be registered in the phonological store. Blocking this process by articulatory suppression is assumed to prevent rehearsal. This will eliminate the phonological coding of *visually* presented material, but not to prevent *auditory* material from gaining access to the phonological store.

3.2 **The word length effect**

One of the most robust phenomena of verbal STM is the word length effect, the systematic decrease in memory span observed as the length of the remembered words increases (Baddeley *et al.* 1975). The effect was initially attributed to the effect of trace decay during rehearsal; longer words took longer to rehearse leading to greater decay. Consistent with this view was the observation that when rehearsal is prevented by the requirement to utter a sequence of irrelevant sounds such as the word 'the', performance declines, and the effect of length is removed (Baddeley *et al.* 1975). The absence of a word length effect in patients with impaired phonological STM also lent support to this view (Vallar and Baddeley 1984a), as did the discovery by Nicolson (1981) that the developmental increase in digit span in children was associated with a parallel increase in rate of articulation, and hence presumably of rehearsal. However, both word length and speed of articulation are complex variables, allowing a range of alternative interpretations that have challenged and modified the basic rehearsal-based explanation. Some of these are discussed below.

3.2.1 Trace decay or interference?

The question of whether forgetting over short intervals represents the fading of a temporary memory trace or its disruption by interference is one that has been present since the classic work of Brown (1958) and Peterson and Peterson (1959). Most theories of STM assume a system of limited capacity. That being the case, there is likely to be displacement of earlier items as new items are processed. The question remains however, as to whether at sub-span levels in the absence of such displacement, the memory trace will fade or not. Secondly, when span is exceeded, what is the nature of this displacement process? Both of these issue remain unresolved.

Our initial phonological loop model assumed trace decay, because this seemed to be the simplest assumption that was consistent with the data, avoiding the need for specifying the processes of displacement or interference. It subsequently appeared to be supported by detailed analysis of the word length effect which showed that when number of syllables was held constant, span for words with long vowel sounds such as *harpoon* and *Friday* was less than for more rapidly spoken words such as *bishop* and *wicket* (Baddeley *et al.* 1975).

Caplan *et al.* (1992) challenged this result, proposing instead that word complexity provided a better account of the determinants of span. Using a separate set of words from Baddeley *et al.* (1975), they reported no evidence that the words that were pronounced slowly were less well remembered; indeed, in one case their long words led to better recall. Baddeley and Andrade (1994) criticized this study on the grounds that the estimate of word length was based on the time taken by a separate speaker to utter the single words in isolation, not on rate of producing word sequences by their subjects. We also found that the two new sets differed in degree of phonological similarity, with the rapidly articulatable words being rated as more similar to each other. Both of these factors would militate against replicating the Baddeley *et al.* (1975) finding.

Caplan and Waters (1994) repeated their study, this time requiring their subjects to read out the words in order to measure articulation time and again finding no support for trace delay; they also report no difference in phonological similarity between the two sets when the words were rated by their own subjects. They suggested that the difference probably lay in the different pronunciation of the words between their US subjects and the UK group tested by Baddeley and Andrade. A later study by Lovatt *et al.* (2000) used English subjects and a third set of words presented both visually and auditorily. Although they found that one set of words was slower than the other when read from a list, they found no consistent difference in subsequent recall of their word sets, although they did observe an advantage for longer duration words in one condition, the opposite to the phonological loop prediction. They did however, replicate Baddeley *et al.* (1975) when using the original word set.

It therefore looked as though we had fallen foul of the language-as-a-fixed-effect fallacy, whereby general conclusions are drawn from a specific set of words, which subsequently prove to be atypical (Clark 1973). The duration effect was replicable using our own words (Lovatt *et al.* 2000), but did not appear to generalize to other sets. My own view was that the degree of the inconsistency simply reflected the insensitivity of this approach. There is a very limited set of words that allow spoken duration to vary while number of syllables is held constant, and many potential confounding variables which may influence recall. This paradigm thus seemed unlikely to provide a clear answer.

Mueller *et al.* (2003) apparently shared my doubts as to whether the methods currently used within the field were sufficient to test the hypothesis, but rather than accept this, set about to improve them. They argued that phonological similarity was likely to be an important variable, but were unhappy with simple subjective similarity ratings. Instead, they took the stimuli and broke them down into their basic phonological features, producing an algorithm that assigned in each case a measure of similarity that could be derived entirely objectively. Secondly, they took a much more thorough approach to measuring articulation time. For each of set words, they systematically presented sequences of each length, first of all practicing the subjects to ensure that they could recite the sequence, and then measuring speeded articulation time. They found, interestingly, that not only did the mean time to articulate vary with both the length of items and the number of items in the sequence, it also showed a somewhat different function depending on the particular set of words used.

Thirdly, they derived measures of verbal complexity. They then went on to test recall of the various sets of material used in all the earlier studies, in each case fitting functions relating performance to complexity, spoken duration and phonological similarity. They found no effect of complexity, while spoken duration and similarity variables were very clearly significant (see Fig. 3.1).

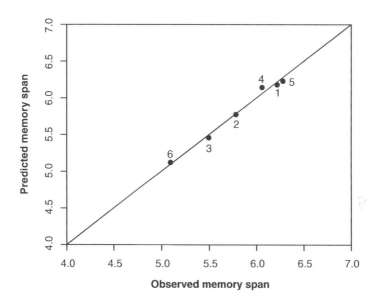

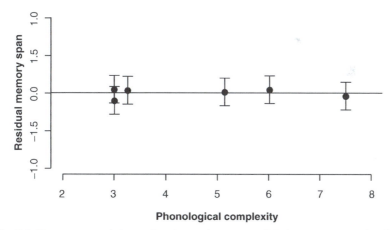

Fig. 3.1 The upper panel shows the observed versus predicted memory spans for six-word sets based on a multiple linear regression with mean articulatory durations and phonological dissimilarity as predictor variables. Numbers refer to different word sets. The lower panel shows the residual effect of phonological complexity after the estimated effects of duration and dissimilarity were removed. Data from Mueller *et al.* (2003).

Their results therefore appear to provide clear support for the importance of time-based forgetting as proposed by Baddeley *et al.* (1975). In doing so, their results suggest that, serendipitously, the set of words selected in the first study provide a more valid test of the decay hypothesis than did subsequent sets.

Mueller *et al.* conclude by emphasizing the careful methodology required if small differences in spoken word length are to be used as a basis for theoretical conclusions, stressing five caveats for testing hypotheses in this area. They include:

1 Articulatory durations may be mismeasured. It is necessary to measure articulation of sequences of items, bearing in mind that this will vary according to both the items and the sequence length.

2 Recall strategies are optional and the situation needs to be constrained so as to ensure a verbal strategy.

3 Even given rehearsal, strategies vary: for example, given strings of unrelated letters, subjects will use the vowels to produce multiletter syllabic chunks, rather than simply rehearse the letter names.

4 Even small differences in acoustic similarity may have big effects.

5 Such effects may interact with sequence length and strategy.

It seems unlikely that we have seen the end of this particular controversy, although the rigour suggested by the Mueller *et al.* study may discourage all but the most determined investigators. This may encourage concentration on other methods of varying time and complexity, such as those pioneered by Cowan and colleagues.

In one study, Cowan *et al.* (1992) tested the decay hypothesis by presenting a mixture of long and short words, varying the point in the sequence at which the long words occurred. In one condition, the long words were near the beginning of the sequence, in the other towards the end. They argued that placing the long words towards the beginning would mean that during the process of recall, saying or writing the early long words would delay the recall of the later short words. If the long words were towards the end of the test however, the short words would be spoken first, leading to a shorter *average* delay. As predicted, the latter condition led to better recall.

Another method of manipulating delay was used by Baddeley and Hull (1979): subjects heard a string of digits, described as a telephone number. The sequence was preceded or followed by the name of a town (this was in the days when one verbally gave the telephone operator a town name and a number). Two Welsh towns were used, one with a short name, *Rhyl* (pronounced *rill*), while the other was long, *Abergavenny*. The short name led to consistently better digit recall than the longer name, regardless of whether the interpolated

name was spoken by the experimenter as a suffix, or by the subject as a prefix to recall of the digits.

However, neither this nor the Cowan *et al.* (1992) study attempted to distinguish between an effect of time and one of number of interpolated syllables. Cowan (1992) therefore developed another technique whereby the items themselves were constant in length, but his subjects were required to recall the items either slowly or rapidly. He observed that rapid articulation led to better recall, a finding that has been challenged by Service (2000), with a rejoinder from Cowan *et al.* (2000). This issue remains unresolved, as does the whole question of whether trace decay will ultimately prove to be a satisfactory explanation of forgetting within the phonological loop, or whether a more complex interpretation is required. Alas this apparently straightforward question has, for over 40 years, proved very difficult to answer.

3.2.2 Does the word length operate through rehearsal or recall delay?

In their original study, Baddeley *et al.* (1975) attempted to rule out differential forgetting during the process of recall by requiring subjects to respond by writing only the first three letters of each recalled item, thus attempting to equate the written duration of long and short words. As Longoni *et al.* (1993) point out, however, it is entirely possible that subjects were subvocally pronouncing the words before writing them, leaving open the possibility that much of the effect observed might still be due to the output delay rather than slower rehearsal. Such an output delay effect was demonstrated by Cowan *et al.* (1992). Further support for this view came from a study by Henry (1991), who used a probe technique whereby a sequence of items was presented and then tested by giving one item from the sequence and requiring the production of the next. Under these circumstances which minimize the effect of output delay, a much reduced word length effect occurred. This finding was replicated and extended by Avons *et al.* (1994). Further support for the importance of output delay came from a study by Coltheart and Langdon (1998), using very rapid presentation to minimize the possibility of the use of rehearsal during input. Clear effects of both word length and phonological similarity were found.

However, while all of these investigators argued for the importance of forgetting during output, they did not deny the possibility that rehearsal also makes a contribution to the word length effect. Dosher and Ma (1998), however, did suggest that the word length effect might be entirely dependent on forgetting during recall. They employed a correlational approach in which several variables were measured and used to predict subsequent memory performance. The best of their predictors proved to be articulation time during output, a recall process that took considerably longer than the time needed by their subjects to rehearse items, typically averaging between four and six seconds. Since adding other measures such as rehearsal rate did not improve the fit to their data, they suggested that there was no necessity to assume any variable other than output delay.

The Dosher and Ma results were indeed consistent with their suggestion that slower output caused poorer recall, but they were also consistent with the reverse hypothesis. Hence, one might reasonably argue that if the memory traces were weak, they would take longer to retrieve. Such confounding is inevitably a problem when, as is common with studies in this area, the measure of articulation speed is based on speed of recall: any variable leading to poorer memory may lead to slower retrieval, resulting in a positive correlation. One might expect for example that sequences with a higher proportion of phonologically similar consonants would be remembered less well and be recalled more slowly. This would not, however, justify the conclusion that the similarity effect was due to the output delay.

Baddeley *et al.* (2002a) attempted to avoid this confound by controlling output time by using a recognition procedure. Subjects heard or saw a sequence of long or short words, followed by a second sequence that was either identical, or had two of the items reversed. Subjects were required to decide whether the sequence was the same or different. Hence time between presentation and test was controlled, and was held constant for long and short words. If, despite this, a word length effect was observed, then it would suggest an effect of word length on rehearsal. This recognition test was compared to the standard recall procedure, where the word length effect would be assumed to involve both rehearsal and output delay.

Clear word length effects were found with both recall and recognition, indicating an effect mediated by both rehearsal and output delay. This conclusion was reinforced by a second experiment in which articulatory suppression was required during the recognition stage, to eliminate the possibility that subjects might have been subvocalizing at their own rate while visually processing the recognition set. Again there was clear evidence for the role of word length during input, presumably reflecting subvocal rehearsal. In all our studies, however, a larger word length effect occurred with standard recall procedures which would be expected to involve *both* rehearsal and output delay effects.

To summarize, I would regard subvocal rehearsal during presentation and overt or covert articulation during recall as involving essentially the same processes, namely the serial retrieval and articulation of the remembered items. When these processes are slowed, by using longer words, more forgetting will occur.

3.2.3 **Articulation rate and memory span**

If the word length effect operates via its impact on speed of rehearsal and recall, then one might expect that subjects who articulate rapidly would tend to recall more than slow articulators, since faster rehearsal means less time for the trace to fade. Baddeley *et al.* (1975) found that this was the case. A subsequent developmental study by Nicolson (1981) showed that children's systematic increase in digit span with age was paralleled by an increase in the rate at which they articulate, a result that has often been replicated (Hitch *et al.* 1989; Hulme *et al.* 1984). Such robust results appeared to provide further reinforcement for the decay hypothesis.

However, the issue proved to be more complex than at first seemed likely. In a series of more detailed studies, Cowan and colleagues tackled this issue by analysing the articulation time of their subjects in more detail, dividing it into two components: the time taken to utter each item, and the gaps between successive utterances. They found that the gap length was more closely associated with individual differences in span than the time filled by the utterance (Cowan *et al.*1994). They suggest that this inter-item pause reflects the time taken to access the memory trace, suggesting in line with the earlier work of Sternberg (1966) that it may represent the speed with which a given individual can scan the items being stored. Hence, subjects who are rapid scanners have better spans. As children get older, their memory scanning rate increases, and it is this, they suggest, rather than articulation rate that predicts memory span.

However, despite its ingenuity, Sternberg's serial scanning hypothesis remains controversial, with a number of alternative hypotheses giving a better account of the data (see Baddeley 1990, pp. 199-202 for a review). One does not, however, need to accept the serial scanning mechanism to appreciate the general plausibility of Cowan's suggestion. It is possible that the interword gap may reflect the time taken to retrieve an item, regardless of the retrieval mechanism, and that differences in retrieval speed may thus influence the efficiency of the memory process. However, Cowan *et al.* based their measures on speed of articulation during sequence *recall*, which as we saw in discussing Dosher and Ma (1998) might be the *result* of a weak memory trace, rather than reflecting some underlying cause, such as a slower rate of memory scanning.

This issue was addressed by Jarrold *et al.* (2000) who measured articulation rate independently of recall performance, by using sequences well within span to study the process of articulation. Like Cowan *et al.* we found two separable components, one concerned with interspeech gaps, and the other with the duration of the spoken items. Both made independent contributions to explaining differences in memory span. Jarrold *et al.* found that the increase in memory span in children as they get older is best predicted by inter-item pauses, which they agree with Cowan probably reflects increasingly efficient retrieval as children develop. However, differences between long and short words when age was held constant were predicted by utterance duration, rather than interword pause time. This supports the view that the word length effect in adults reflects differences between long and short words in their impact on forgetting rather than on speed of retrieval. Such a view supports and extends that of Cowan *et al.* (1994), and is consistent with an elaborated version of the phonological loop hypothesis.

3.2.4 Are long words more fragile? A localist interpretation

Despite the fact that a temporal decay hypothesis seems to fit the data very well, other views have been proposed, notably by Brown and Hulme (1995), and Neath and Nairne (1995). Brown and Hulme suggest that long words lead to poorer recall not because they take longer to say, but because they are more complex, having more segments than short words. This gives a higher probability that at least one segment will be lost, leading to error or omission. They describe a model in which this does indeed prove to be the case. Of course, a five syllable word is not five times as likely to be forgotten as a one syllable word. This they attribute to a process of *redintegration*, whereby linguistic knowledge is used to correct errors in the word. Such a process also gives a plausible interpretation of why words are easier to recall than nonwords. As Brown and Hulme point out, the detailed nature of the redintegration process is currently unspecified. Their explanation therefore has two components: (1) Long words are more fragile, leading to more forgetting, and (2) The fact that words are redundant and familiar means that some forgetting can be repaired by redintergration. Two such opposing mechanisms do, of course, allow many results to be explained post hoc by assigning a greater or lesser influence to each of these competing factors.

3.2.5 Mixing long and short words

However, a crucial difference between the phonological loop and the complexity hypotheses concerns the question of whether the effect operates locally, at the level of the individual item, or is a global effect of the time taken to rehearse and/or output the whole sequence. If the effect is local, as the complexity hypothesis assumes, then regardless of the number or mix of words within the sequence, long words should tend to be recalled worse than short. The phonological loop hypothesis, however, predicts that performance should depend globally on the time to articulate the *whole* list, and hence accuracy on both long and short words should decrease as the number of long words in the sequence, and hence overall delay, increases. This issue was studied independently by

Cowan *et al.* (2003), and by Hulme *et al.* (2004), both using lists comprising different mixes of long and short words.

The results of the two studies provided no support for the localist prediction that the word length effect would survive presentation within a mixed list. Indeed when a single long word was included, it was particularly *well* recalled. This is, presumably, an example of the Von Restorff (1933) effect whereby an item that is dissimilar to the rest of a list, for example by being printed in a different colour or comprising a letter among digits, will be better recalled than the surrounding items. The presence of a Von Restorff effect in verbal STM was predicted and demonstrated by Conrad, in connection with the design of the British postal code. The initial code comprised several letters and a single digit (e.g. Norwich was NOR, followed by two letters and a digit). Conrad showed that placing the digit at the point of maximum error, just beyond the middle of the sequence for spoken codes, (e.g. NOR 2LK) optimized performance. The worst condition involved alternating letters and digits, as was adopted by the Canadian post office. This is probably because alternation discourages chunking. This pattern of results however, clearly necessitates a more complex interpretation of serial recall than is provided by the phonological loop alone.

To return to the theories; the localist interpretation of a clear word length decrement in mixed lists was clearly not supported, but did the total list duration prediction fare any better? Cowan *et al.* concluded that it did, whereas Hulme *et al.* found no such effect. A subsequent study by Bireta, Neath and Suprenant (in press) obtained the Cowan *et al.* result for Cowan's material, but found that it did not generalize to other sets of words, which tended to show that long and short words in mixed lists were as well recalled as short words in pure lists. Both Hulme *et al.* (2004) and Bireta *et al.* (in press) interpret their results as ruling out their earlier interpretations, accepting that neither the model proposed by Brown and Hulme (1995), nor the feature hypothesis proposed by Neath and Nairne (1995) could account for these results. I agree.

They propose instead to interpret the data in terms of a new hypothesis developed by Brown *et al.* (unpublished) which they term SIMPLE (Scale Invariant Memory, Perception and Learning). This is a highly ambitious model that attempts to explain virtually the whole of long-term and working memory in terms of the relative discriminability of items at retrieval. They make the assumption that the principal difference between long and short words lies in the greater discriminability of shorter words. It is not clear why this should be: one might equally plausibly argue that long words, having more features, would be more discriminable. Nor is there any attempt to measure discriminability independently. Instead the authors demonstrate that by making suitable assumptions, they can account for the data observed.

In a subsequent study, Hulme *et al.* (in press) use a simpler design in which pure lists of six long or short words are compared with lists comprising five short and one long, or five long and one short word. In these studies the long words accompanied by a single short item tend to be remembered only as well as pure long lists, while short words are well remembered regardless of whether they form part of a pure list or one containing a long word. They obtain a dramatic Von Restorff effect, however, with the long isolate being remembered significantly better than the short, and both dramatically better than words in any of the other conditions. A second study gave a broadly comparable picture, except that the Von Restorff effect was far less, with the isolated short word being remembered less well than in pure short word lists. Hulme *et al.* are able to fit most of the data to SIMPLE, but the model apparently makes the prediction that the isolated long and short words should be equally well recalled, which they are not. They suggest that the model may be made to fit the data by adding a further parameter, concluding that nevertheless, their results 'contradict the models that seek to explain word length effect in terms of list based accounts of rehearsal speed' (Hulme *et al.* in press).

How problematic are these data for the phonological loop hypothesis? It is certainly the case that the phonological loop model has not in the past attempted to give an account of the Von Restorff effect, and that an interpretation in terms of enhanced discriminability seems plausible, possibly along the lines of that proposed for the recency effect in Chapter 6. Like the recency effect, the Von Restorff effect has been shown to extend beyond immediate memory to delayed recall by Hendry and Tehan (2005), who offer a different interpretation from that of Hulme *et al.* having observed a somewhat different error pattern.

So what of the SIMPLE explanation? I should begin by admitting to a prejudice against models with multiple parameters that are then used to fit data post hoc, as in the case of Hulme *et al.* (in press). Furthermore, they appear to be proposing a number of other possible parameters that might be added to solve SIMPLE's problem. Finally, as discussed in Chapter 6, SIMPLE appears to fail when applied to data from immediate verbal recall that explicitly aims to test the discriminability assumption (Lewandowsky *et al.* in press; Nimmo and Lewandowsky in press).

So can the phonological loop do a better job? I think it can, first by accepting that the Von Restorff effect is a genuine and clear phenomenon that has not yet been adequately explored. One possibility is that the atypical item has its influence principally through an impact on phonology, for example by breaking up the prosody of the sequence, something that is known to have a marked effect on recall (Ryan 1969) Another possibility is an attentional effect whereby more processing is given to the atypical item. An important empirical question concerns what happens under articulatory suppression, when the word length effect disappears. Does the length-based Von Restorff effect also disappear? In the meantime however I would like to suggest an explanation for one of the effects that appears be creating problems for SIMPLE, namely, the observation that recall of a single long word embedded in short words is enhanced, while this is not the case for a short word among long neighbours. This would be predicted by a long word, being surrounded by short, rapidly spoken words, which formed part of a more rapidly spoken list. The opposite will be the case for an isolated short word embedded in long words, offering a simple list-based interpretation of the findings of Hulme *et al.* (in press).

It remains the case however that the mixed word length effect presents a challenge to all existing theories. None of the computational models of the phonological loop has yet been applied to this recently discovered effect. While the relative discriminability of items already plays a role in most theories, fitting the precise data may well present a problem, as it has done for SIMPLE. I anticipate some lively controversy.

3.3 Disrupting the phonological loop

One potentially powerful source of evidence regarding the nature of immediate verbal memory is provided by studies that attempt to interfere with its operation, generating new phenomena that place important constraints on underlying theory. Consequently this has been an extremely active and controversial research area. I will consider three types of interference with phonological memory, namely general interference from nonverbal sources such as concurrent manual tapping, more specific interference with the operation of the loop resulting from articulatory suppression, and finally disruption by irrelevant sound. In each case I will present first those phenomena that are generally accepted, then give the phonological loop account, followed by a more detailed discussion of those issues that are in dispute.

3.3.1 General interference effects

Virtually any concurrent activity may potentially interfere with performance through its demands on our limited attentional capacity. For that reason, a verbal task such as articulatory suppression, which is assumed to result in specific disruption to performance of the loop, is often accompanied by a control condition involving a nonverbal concurrent task such as regular manual tapping. Tapping is assumed to constitute a potentially attention-demanding secondary task, but one that does not involve the phonological loop, hence offering the potential to separate out the general effects of a concurrent load from modality-specific effects.

When compared to memory span performed alone, the effects of simple tapping may be minimal (e.g. Meiser and Klauer 1999), or more substantial (Larsen and Baddeley 2003). Increasing the complexity of the tapping clearly increased its disrupting ability in the Meiser and Klauer study, but had only a minimal additional effect in that of Larsen and Baddeley. In general, however, increasing complexity makes it more likely that there will be impairment in immediate memory, presumably resulting from increased attentional demand. It is therefore important to try to match the complexity of any control task with that of whichever modality-specific concurrent task is used, so as to ensure that any disruption observed can not be attributed to the general impact of the secondary task on the central executive (Baddeley and Andrade 2000; Baddeley *et al.* 2001; Meiser and Klauer 1999).

It is important to note that even manual tapping can have a specific disruption effect on the phonological loop when syncopation is involved, a phenomenon first noted by Saito when attempting to sing while playing the guitar, and subsequently confirmed experimentally (Saito 1994; Larsen and Baddeley 2003). The detailed effects of syncopated tapping are essentially equivalent to those of articulatory suppression (see below). Saito suggests that this disruption reflects the reliance of both speech and rhythm on a common prosodic timing process.

3.3.2 **Articulatory suppression**

3.3.2.1 **Visual presentation**

David Murray (1968), exploring the relationship between phonological STM and articulation, required his subjects to remember sequences of similar or dissimilar consonants, while at the same time repeatedly uttering an irrelevant sound, the word 'the'. This impaired recall, but also removed the influence of phonological similarity. The finding is readily replicable (Levy 1971; Peterson and Johnson 1971), leading to the use of articulatory suppression as a common means of interrupting the process of subvocal rehearsal (Baddeley 1986).

The assumption has often been made, at least implicitly, that the suppression effect is all-or-none, since a wide range of concurrent articulations have been used, ranging from the ominous 'double double' through a cheery 'hiyah' to a possibly commercially sponsored 'Cola Cola', and for children, a comforting 'teddy bear, teddy bear'. In fact, the nature of the articulation does make a difference, particularly when the concurrent activity might itself be relatively demanding, such as reciting the months of the year (Baddeley *et al.* 2001).

Repeating a single item has a marked effect, especially when memory items are presented visually. Increasing the number of articulated items within a highly practised sequence, such as counting from one to nine, typically has relatively little further effect (e.g. Larsen and Baddeley 2003; Meiser and Klauer 1999).

However, the disruptive effect can show a slight increase when articulatory complexity is increased (Jones and Macken 1995; Saito 1997).

The suppression effect appears to depend on the need to modulate articulation. Hence a single continuous vowel sound such as 'aahh' has no effect on performance, while a repeated 'ah', 'ah', 'ah' disrupts performance and removes the phonological similarity effect (Saito 1997). A similar result is found for continuous versus repetitive whistling (Saito 1998), suggesting that vocal articulation is not necessary for disruption to occur.

In conclusion, there is no doubt that articulatory suppression does seriously disrupt the immediate serial verbal recall of visually presented material. Larsen and Baddeley, for example, find disruptions of 37 per cent when suppression involves repeating the digit 'two' at a regular two per second rate, 41 per cent when repeating it in a syncopated pattern, and 42 per cent from repeating the counting sequence one to six, with all three conditions totally removing the phonological similarity effect.

3.3.2.2 Auditory presentation

In contrast to visual presentation, when sequences are presented auditorily the phonological similarity effect remains. This result is predicted by the phonological loop hypothesis on the grounds that auditory presentation leads to direct registration of the stimuli within the phonological store without the need for subvocal articulation. Suppression does, however, reduce performance by interfering with rehearsal. Finally, it is important to note that even in the most seriously disrupted condition in which presentation is visual and phonological recoding apparently avoided by articulatory suppression, subjects still recall an average of three or four digits, suggesting the need to assume a substantial contribution to digit span from one or more other sources. We return to this issue in Chapter 8.

3.4 The irrelevant speech effect

3.4.1 A case of mnemonic masking?

Colle and Welsh (1976) appear to be have been the first to note that immediate memory for visually presented digits may be disrupted by the simultaneous presentation of irrelevant speech, in this case, prose spoken in German, an unfamiliar foreign language to his student subjects. In this and a subsequent study, Colle (1980) observed that the effect did not appear to be the result of simple distraction, since no effect of white noise was observed, the concurrent speech was in an unfamiliar language, and its loudness had no impact on its capacity to disrupt, causing him to describe his findings as 'acoustic masking in primary memory' (Colle 1978).

These findings were extended by Salamé and Baddeley (1982), who, in this and subsequent studies, also found no effect of sound level, or white noise even when pulsated within the same intensity envelope as the speech. We also found no difference between the disrupting effect on digit recall of meaningful words, nonsense syllables, or even irrelevant spoken digits (Salamé and Baddeley 1982; 1986; 1989). We did, however, observe that performance was disrupted by vocal music, and in our studies at least, to a lesser extent by instrumental music (Salamé and Baddeley 1989), and by fluctuating complex sounds (Salamé 1990).

At a more theoretical level, we ruled out the possibility that the effect operated at a lexical level by our demonstration that remembering a digit sequence was no more disrupted by irrelevant spoken digit sequences, than it was by words made up from the same phonemes (e.g. instead of *one-two*, etc. *tun-woo, etc.*). We also observed that with visual presentation, articulatory suppression removed the irrelevant speech effect. We interpreted this result as suggesting that the irrelevant speech effect operated via the phonological store, which was not utilized under suppression, which prevented the visual items from being registered within the store (Salamé and Baddeley 1982). One feature of our results appeared to support something analogous to the mnemonic masking hypothesis first suggested by Colle (1980), since there was slightly but significantly less interference from disyllabic than from monosyllabic words, a finding that we suggested could be attributed to disyllabic words being less phonologically similar to monosyllabic digits, hence leading to less acoustic masking.

This tentative speculation proved erroneous. Extensive further research specifically targeted at this issue has shown no evidence for any effect of similarity between the material being remembered and the auditory material being ignored (Jones and Macken 1995; Larsen *et al.* 2000; Le Compte and Shaibe 1997), nor did the initial finding of less disruption from disyllabic words replicate (Le Compte and Shaibe 1997). A simple mnemonic masking interpretation of the irrelevant speech effect is thus not supported. A similar conclusion was drawn from a study (Salamé and Baddeley 1990) which attempted to test mnemonic masking more directly, by combining phonological similarity with irrelevant speech. We argued that if irrelevant speech added 'masking noise' to the trace, then this should have a particularly marked effect on phonologically similar sequences, which were assumed to be difficult precisely because they had fewer distinguishing features, and were hence more vulnerable to disruption. Subjects recalled sequences of consonants selected from either an acoustically similar set or a distinctive set. They performed this task either silence or irrelevant speech.

Two important results emerged from this study. First, that the effects of phonological similarity disappeared at long sequence lengths, a finding that had been observed in other contexts, and interpreted as suggesting that when the phonological loop is no longer able to cope with the amount of material presented, subjects seek alternative strategies (Baddeley 2000; Hall *et al.*1983; Johnston *et al.* 1987). This implies that long sequences are inappropriate for studying the phonological loop, a point that recurs throughout this review. The principal result of the study, however, was that over intermediate lengths, when ceiling and floor effects were avoided, phonological similarity and irrelevant speech produced additive effects, a result that was entirely inconsistent with the mnemonic-masking prediction that irrelevant speech should be more disruptive with similar sequences.

By this point, however, it was clear that any adequate interpretation of the irrelevant speech effect would require a more complete model than that provided by the purely verbally specified phonological loop. In particular, any adequate model needed to provide a convincing account of how serial order is stored and retrieved. Sadly, this recantation of the mnemonic masking hypothesis (Salame and Baddeley 1986) appears to have registered much less firmly in the collective mind than the original speculation, which has now been enshrined as a clear prediction of the phonological loop hypothesis (Jones and Macken 1995; Neath 2000). This failure of the simple mnemonic masking hypothesis is important in providing a valuable theoretical constraint on models of STM. As we shall see later, however, it is open to a number of interpretations, several of which fall within the broad scope of the phonological loop hypothesis. These will be discussed later.

3.4.2 The changing state hypothesis

While I waited hopefully for a more sophisticated computationally explicit model of the phonological loop, a new group entered the field of irrelevant speech, and dominated it for the next few years. Dylan Jones (1993) began systematically to investigate which features of sound determined whether or not it would interfere with immediate verbal recall. He and his colleagues showed very clearly that even a sound as simple as a fluctuating pure tone was sufficient to disrupt memory, causing him very reasonably to suggest that the phenomenon should be termed the irrelevant *sound* effect. They showed that a single repeated tone often caused no reliable disruption of memory (Jones and Macken 1993; Jones *et al.* 1993). Exactly the same pattern appeared to operate for spoken sounds, with a single item typically having little or no effect (Jones *et al.* 1997; Tremblay *et al.* 2000; Larsen and Baddeley 2003). Tremblay and Jones (1998) investigated the effect on digit recall of increasing the number of irrelevant spoken letters, finding a marked increase between one and two irrelevant spoken items with a diminishing effect of adding further items.

Jones (1993) proposed the *changing state hypothesis* as an explanation of this range of findings. He linked his findings to auditory scene analysis (Bregman 1990), arguing that those features that caused disruption were those that one would expect to signify a single 'auditory object', whereas conditions that did not create disruption, such as the repetition of a single item or white noise, would not give rise to the perception of an integrated auditory object, and hence would not disrupt memory for sequences, in contrast with a spoken word or fluctuating to which would. Such irrelevant sounds would, like the sequence to be recalled, be represented by a trajectory across a multidimensional sensory field which he terms the Object-Oriented Episodic Record (O-OER). The presence of an irrelevant trajectory will then disrupt retrieval of the remembered items.

3.4.3 The object-orientate episodic record model

Jones rejects the assumption of separate visuospatial and verbal STM systems, supporting his view by showing the disruption by irrelevant speech of a task involving short-term sequential visual recall (Jones *et al.* 1995). More recently, Meiser and Klauer (1999) performed a study contrasting the standard digit recall task with a conventional spatial memory task, the Corsi blocks procedure in which subjects watch and attempt to reproduce a tapped sequence on a spatial array of blocks. They found a very clear double dissociation, with the visuospatial task being interfered with principally by spatial tapping rather than articulatory suppression, while digit span showed the opposite pattern, just as the working memory theory would predict. In addition, some general interference was found across modalities, increasing with the complexity of the concurrent task. It was shown by the authors to be most readily interpreted as an effect of disrupting the central executive.

Despite the claims that Jones makes for a single multimodal STM system, there is, of course, abundant further evidence of separate visuospatial and phonological STM systems (see Chapters 4, 5 and 10). Sources include data from neuropsychological patients (Della Sala and Logie 2002; Vallar and Papagno 2002), from normal subjects (e.g. Brooks 1967; Logie *et al.* 1990) and from functional imaging studies (Smith *et al.* 1996). It is not clear, furthermore, that the O-OER hypothesis actually needs to assume a common surface for visual and verbal memory, although Jones does appear to continue to hold this position. It is, of course possible to present a case for an *additional* multimodal short-term store. The recently proposed episodic buffer represents just such a store (see Chapter 8), but Jones (personal communication) maintains that this should not be identified with his concept of an object-oriented episodic record.

A further question then arises as to whether, as both Neath (2000) and Jones *et al.* (1996) propose, articulatory suppression and irrelevant speech have a common origin. There would appear to be a number of clear differences. First, whereas repeating a single item is virtually as disruptive as repeating six items, this is not the case with irrelevant speech, where one item has virtually no effect, two items have a very clear effect, with six having little more (Larsen and Baddeley 2003; Tremblay *et al.* 2000). The phonological loop hypothesis is able to give a simple account of conditions under which irrelevant speech, articulatory suppression under constant and syncopated conditions, phonological similarity and word length all interact. The O-OER model has not so far devoted very much attention to phenomena other than irrelevant sound, so it is possible that it could present a simple and coherent account, but it does not yet appear to have done so.

For the most part, Jones and his group have concentrated largely on the irrelevant sound effect, pointing out with some justification that the current phonological loop model does not attempt to specify exactly what acoustic features determine whether sound will interfere. Furthermore, computational models of the phonological loop have tended to ignore the effects of irrelevant sound, although there is an indication that this is beginning to change with an interpretation proposed within the primacy hypothesis offered by Page and Norris (2003).

3.4.4 **The phonological loop unmasked?**

The area has been enlivened by a series of experiments by Jones and colleagues (Jones *et al.* 2004; 2006) which they suggest undermine the whole concept of phonological short-term storage. Instead of a phonological loop, which they describe as 'perceptual organization masquerading as phonological storage', they propose a 'perceptual-gestural view' of short term memory (Jones *et al.* 2006). Their attack is based on an interesting alternative interpretation of a three-way interaction between the effects of similarity, presentation modality and articulatory suppression on STM performance, which they rightly identify as an important source of evidence for the loop hypothesis.

It may be recalled that phonologically similar items such as letters impair performance whether presented visually or auditorily, except when the subject is suppressing articulation, when the effect disappears for the visual but not the auditory items. The phonological similarity effect is assumed to be at the signature of storage within the phonological store. When presentation is visual suppression prevents the phonological code being registered within the store: when presentation is auditory it gains direct access to the store, so that in this latter condition one would still expect the find a phonological similarity effect, although overall level of performance would be likely to be impaired by the prevention of rehearsal.

Jones *et al.* (2004), studying immediate recall for sequences of seven similar or dissimilar letters, observed in their study that the preservation of the phonological similarity effect under conditions of suppression and auditory presentation was largely limited to performance on the last two items (see Fig. 3.2). They suggest that this is a purely sensory effect of the type previously studied and attributed by Crowder and Morton (1969) to what they term Precategorical Acoustic Storage (PAS). In line with this interpretation, they show that the effect is largely moved by following the sequence with a spoken suffix. This interpretation was followed up in a subsequent study (Jones *et al.* 2006) using five-item lists and showing that phonological similarity with spoken presentation can be removed by combining articulatory suppression with a spoken prefix and suffix in the same voice as the items to be remembered. They propose that the concept of a phonological store be replaced by the concept of perceptual organization, coupled with a rehearsal process based on 'gestural planning', which is assumed to be the basis of the phonological similarity effect.

There is no doubt that the effect identified by Jones and colleagues offers a challenge to the existing hypothesis, especially given that most of the previous research in this area has not provided serial position data. The exception is

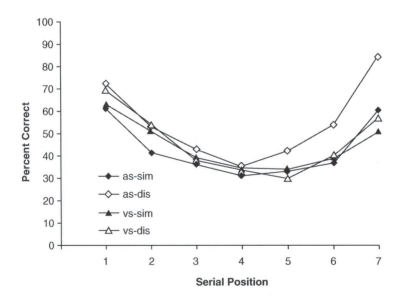

Fig. 3.2 Effects of phonological similarity on the recall of consonant sequences under articulatory suppression. The similarity effect predicted by the phonological loop hypothesis with auditory presentation is found, but only across the recency component. Data from Jones *et al.* (2006).

Murray (1968) who finds the crucial effect throughout the serial position curve, but whose data are rejected by Jones *et al.* as based on an atypical method. A major reason for doubting the generality of findings reported by Jones, however, concerns the fact that they represent performance under conditions where the phonological loop is likely to be heavily stressed, and where considerable research indicates that phonological coding tends to be abandoned. This phenomenon was as the heart of a major controversy concerning the utilization of phonological coding by good and poor readers, with the Haskins group (e.g. Shankweiler *et al.* 1979) observing clear phonological similarity effects in STM for good readers, but not for those who are reading poorly. It subsequently proved to be the case that this was because poor readers had lower spans than good readers, with both groups using phonological coding at lengths when performance was good, but apparently abandoning it when performance dropped below a particular level (Hall *et al.* 1983; Johnston *et al.* 1987). This is related to the previously described study by Salame and Baddeley (1986) found clear and additive effects of irrelevant speech and phonological similarity at immediate list lengths, with both tending to disappear when performance dropped below around 50 per cent. All the instances in which Jones *et al.* (2004; 2006) show a complete absence of phonological coding on earlier parts of the list are in conditions where performance is around 50 per cent or less.[1]

Fortunately Jan Larsen and I had independently been carrying out a number of experiments in which we systematically studied a range of variables under both visual and auditory presentation. These included retention of phonologically similar and dissimilar sequences of six consonants presented with and without articulatory suppression (Baddeley and Larsen, in press *a*). We have several sets of data, all of which are broadly consistent in suggesting a substantial effect of phonological similarity on recall with auditory presentation. In one study we used articulatory suppression, while in another we used silent mouthing, shown by Murray (1967) to be effective in suppressing articulation, without being open to the objection that the stimuli may have been masked by the subjects vocalization. The results of this latter study are shown in Fig. 3.3 from which it is clear that, whereas the similarity effect is absent with visual presentation and suppression, a robust effect is observed throughout the list

---

[1] The suggestion of a 50 per cent cut off simply represents a rough rule of thumb based on empirical observation. If, as I suspect, this represents a strategic effect, then it seems likely that this breakpoint is open to change. It is important to note that the 50 per cent suggestion is not a theoretical prediction based on the phonological loop model.

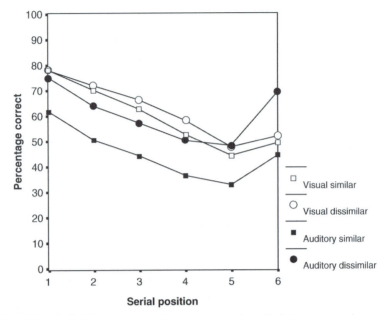

Fig. 3.3 Recall of six-letter consonant sequences under articulatory suppression. With auditory presentation, an effect of similarity is found throughout the list. Data from Larsen and Baddeley (in press *a*).

when presentation is auditory. The effect is clearly not limited to the final two items, as Jones *et al.* claim. (But see Jones *et al,* in press, for a contrary view.)

Like Jones *et al.* we do find an additional modality effect for dissimilar but not similar items, which in our case survives a ten second pre-recall delay filled by the repetitive mouthing of a single item, 'ma'. Both the survival of the effect over a delay (Crowder 1978a) and the absence of auditory recency for similar materials have been reported previously (Crowder 1978b; Darwin and Baddeley 1974). This latter finding has interesting implications for any attempt to provide a unitary hypothesis to cover immediate serial verbal recall. As noted earlier, the irrelevant sound effect is not influenced by any phonological similarity between the items remembered and the disrupting sounds, in contrast to the modality effect as reported by Jones *et al.* (2006), whereas similarity does influence the final stages of speech production as demonstrated by Saito and Baddeley (2004). In short, although I am sure this controversy will continue, and prove fruitful in establishing when the loop is and when it is not employed, I do not see any reason to change the basic phonological loop model (Baddeley and Larsen, in press *b*).

In conclusion, while there is no doubt that Jones and colleagues have made a substantial empirical contribution, particularly towards mapping the characteristics of sounds that cause interference with phonological storage, their theory has major limitations which include:

1 It assumes a chaining interpretation of serial recall, which is inconsistent with a range of evidence (see Chapter 2, p. 26).

2 Its development is largely based on the irrelevant sound effect, and has little to say on other phenomena.

3 Its assumption of a single multi-modal system is inconsistent with the data from other groups, and

4 With data from neuropsychology and neuroimaging.

5 It remains a loosely specified verbal account that does not seem to lend itself to more precise modelling, and

6 Unlike the phonological loop, it has had little impact beyond the psychological laboratory.

However, within the area of irrelevant sound, there is no doubt that the O-OER model and the changing state hypothesis have proved extremely fruitful. Furthermore, there are clear advantages to the assumption of some form of short-term multimodal storage, as reflected in my own assumption of an episodic buffer (Baddeley 2000), a concept which may well have been influenced by discussions with Dylan Jones, although Dylan himself denies any such responsibility. Happily, I think I see a convergence of views. Despite the differences he specifies between his own approach and the working memory model (Jones *et al.* 2006, p. 278), his current views can be seen as having much in common with the phonological loop, although expressed in terms that favour perception over memory, dismissing the phonological loop concept as 'reification'. I plead guilty as charged; I believe that functions depend on structures at a theoretical and conceptual level, and that these map on to the operation of a physical object, the brain.

3.4.5 Irrelevant speech and the feature hypothesis

The feature hypothesis was initially designed to give an account of brief sensory memory effects, together with immediate recall of lists, sometimes extending to eight or nine words, unlike the phonological loop which does not address sensory memory, or the substantial LTM component likely to be employed with word lists beyond five or six items. Neath (2000) produced a stimulating article in which he applied the feature hypothesis to data from irrelevant speech, noting that the hypothesis predicted a number of interactions that did not appear to be predicted by the phonological loop or O-OER hypotheses. These include predicting an interaction with word length such that the effects of irrelevant speech are absent with long words. In contrast, the phonological loop hypothesis predicts a clear effect, provided the lists are short enough to make a phonological strategy effective, although not at the longer lengths used by Neath *et al.* (1998).

A similar prediction was made in the case of phonological similarity, which was assumed by Neath (2000) to eliminate the effect of irrelevant speech. However, as Salamé and Baddeley (1986) showed, provided ceiling and floor effects are avoided, irrelevant speech and phonological similarity effects are additive. The effects only disappear when list length increases (Hanley and Broadbent 1987; Hanley 1997). A further prediction by Neath (2000) was that there should be no irrelevant speech effect with auditory presentation. However, studies by Hanley and Broadbent (1987) showed that at moderate list lengths, clear irrelevant speech effects occur. In a later study, Hanley and Bakopoulou (2003) showed an irrelevant speech effect can occur even with longer lists, provided subjects are explicitly instructed to use articulatory rehearsal. Such effects disappear when semantic coding is encouraged.

Finally, the feature interpretation of the irrelevant speech effect requires that the disrupting speech occurs at the same time as the material to be recalled is presented. There is, however, clear evidence of disruption by irrelevant speech that occurs only after the memory items have been presented (Macken and Jones 1995), an effect that occurs even when rehearsal is prevented so as to prevent any possibility of the co-occurrence of memory items and irrelevant speech (Norris *et al.* 2004).

The feature hypothesis thus appears to make erroneous predictions about the effects of auditory presentation, word length, phonological similarity and simultaneity. As discussed earlier, the feature hypothesis also has difficulty in accounting for the absence of an effect of word length in lists of mixed long and short words (Cowan *et al.* 2003; Hulme *et al.* 2004). The feature hypothesis may perhaps prove more successful in tackling other components of working memory such as the episodic buffer (see Chapter 8) which, given its complexity and multidimensional nature, is likely to have more in common with the LTM mechanisms that appear to have influenced the development of the feature hypothesis.

3.5 The phonological loop: an overview

One of the advantages in studying the phonological loop is that theorization is constrained by a rich array of robust empirical data. Attempting to give a plausible account of each provides some idea as to where the strengths and weaknesses of the phonological loop model lie, and hence as to whether it should be extended or abandoned. The various phenomena will be discussed in turn.

1 *Phonological similarity effect.* I assume that sequences of words or consonants are registered in the phonological store, a sublexical temporary storage system. Items are linked to a series of contextual cues, either time-based

(Brown and Hulme 1995; Burgess and Hitch 1999) or based on serial position cues (Henson 1998; Page and Norris 1998). Items are stored as a series of phonological features, with vowel sounds being dominant. Phonologically similar items will have many common features, with the result that miscueing is more likely. I continue to assume trace decay, which so far appears to offer the simplest account regardless of whether forgetting is assumed to result from spontaneous decay or from some form of displacement or interference, although the detail would of course change in important ways. Effects of lexicality, semantic coding and the process or processes of redintegration are assumed to operate during retrieval from the phonological store, probably automatically, and/or as a post-retrieval checking stage which is likely to be accessible to executive control.

2 *Word length effect.* I continue to maintain that this results from forgetting due to delay in rehearsal and output. This occurs because the phonologically encoded information dissipates either over time (trace decay) or as a result of interference from intervening activity. The question of deciding between decay and displacement continues to offer a difficult challenge.

3 *Articulatory suppression.* I continue to propose that this prevents both subvocal rehearsal, and the registration in the phonological store of visually presented material. As discussed earlier, even simple repetition involves adding a concurrent task, hence there is also a potential additional central executive load which will depend on the complexity and degree of overlearning of the suppression task (see Baddeley *et al.* 2001). Unlike its specific effect, which is limited to phonological/verbal tasks, such executive disruption may influence visual memory, and indeed any task that places demands on attentional control. Suppression interacts with phonological similarity only under visual presentation, when it prevents the phonological recoding of the visual stimuli. Auditory material gains direct access to the phonological store without requiring subvocalization. Phonological similarity will thus continue to impair memory performance.

4 *Irrelevant sound effect.* This presents two separate but related questions. First, what determines whether a given sound will or will not disrupt serial recall, and secondly, how does this disruption occur? I am broadly in agreement with the changing state hypothesis proposed by Jones (e.g. Jones 1993; Jones *et al.* 1996) as providing a good account of what sounds do and do not disrupt memory, and am also sympathetic to his attempt to link that hypothesis to auditory scene perception. As discussed earlier, however, I do not regard either the O-OER hypothesis proposed by Jones (1993), or Neath's (2000) feature hypothesis, as providing a convincing account of the whole gamut of memory data. A more likely interpretation seems to be that proposed by Page

and Norris (2003), who propose that irrelevant sound disrupts the process linking items to serial order cues, either by adding 'noise', or by the need to inhibit or 'damp-down' the system so as to prevent spoken items automatically accessing the phonological memory system (Gisselgard *et al.* 2003).

5 *Redintegration and the influence of LTM* Virtually all the phenomena discussed so far have depended upon the sublexical phonemic store. There are, of course, many phenomena that indicate the impact of long-term factors on immediate memory span, including the advantage of words over nonwords (Gathercole *et al.* 2003), high frequency over low frequency words (Hulme *et al.* 1997) and positive effects of rated concreteness (Walker and Hume 1999), as well as long-term sublexical factors such as word likeness (Gathercole 1995). These clearly influence the output of immediate memory tasks, and could reasonably be regarded as part of the mechanism involved in retrieval from the phonological loop. They do, however, extend well beyond the territory that is unique to the phonological loop system, and will be discussed in Chapter 8.

3.6 Conclusion

Although the phonological loop hypothesis continues, after more than 30 years, to be controversial, it still gives a relatively simple account of a very wide range of robust findings from carefully designed laboratory studies. It has proved to be a fruitful testbed for computational modelling. Finally, as the previous chapter illustrated, it has provided an easily understood basic model, accompanied by a toolkit of flexible but robust tasks that have allowed it to be applied beyond the laboratory to a range of developmental, educational, neuropsychological and neuroimaging applications.

However, there are still major areas of the phonological loop model that require further development, including

1 We need to know more about the conditions under which the loop is used, and whether its apparent abandonment with increased sequence length and difficulty represents a strategic choice, or is simply a breakdown in its operation due to overload.

2 The question of how serial order is stored and retrieved is still not fully understood.

3 Can existing computational models be modified to handle the process of chunking at both sublexical and supralexical levels? and

4 How does this relates to the role of the phonological loop in acquiring and using language?

Chapter 4

Visuospatial short-term memory

The visuospatial sketchpad (VSSP) has been described as the most neglected component of working memory (Pearson 2001). This may seem surprising, given that it is assumed to operate at the interface between vision, attention and action. Vision research is one of the most extensive and well-established fields of psychology, and its interface with attention is an area of considerable sustained interest, drawing heavily both on cognitive psychology and neuroimaging and neurobiological studies using animals. This represents a distinct advantage when compared to the language-based phonological loop, which does not feature prominently within the animal kingdom. Although iconic memory formed one of the classic areas from which cognitive psychology developed, its brief peripheral visual storage processes have tended to be regarded as more relevant to perception than to memory. Furthermore, memory researchers have typically found it easier to manipulate material and to test theories using verbal items, rather than become involved in the niceties of precisely controlling visual stimuli. Consequently, while there have been a number of relatively well-developed areas of relevance to the VSSP, they tend until recently to have operated largely in isolation from the psychophysical approaches that characterize much mainstream vision research.

4.1 The case for a separating visuospatial and verbal working memory

A logical starting point is the question of whether there is any need to assume a specific system that is responsible for the short-term retention of visual or spatial information. While it is generally accepted that temporary storage of visuospatial and verbal information employ different systems, this view is not universally held. As discussed earlier, Jones and colleagues have proposed a single unitary system, principally on the basis of detecting similarities between the way in which visuospatial and verbal items are retained over short intervals (Farrand and Jones 1996; Jones *et al.* 1995). As discussed earlier, their suggestion that irrelevant sound has a similar effect on verbal and spatial immediate recall proved not to be readily replicable (Meisser and Klauer 1999), and as we shall see below, articulatory suppression, despite having a major effect on verbal serial recall, has little or no effect on its visuospatial equivalent (Smyth and Pendleton 1989).

Some of the strongest evidence for separate phonological and visuospatial STM comes from the study of neuropsychological patients. For example, DeRenzi and Nichelli (1975) identified two separate groups of patients, one of which had preserved digit span and impaired performance on the Corsi block-tapping measure of spatial span, in which the tester taps a sequence of locations which the subject attempts to initiate, gradually increasing the number of locations until errors are made. The other group of patients showed the reverse pattern of impaired digit and preserved Corsi span. Such a double dissociation is readily explained by the assumption of separate visuospatial and verbal systems. A more detailed analysis of individual patients showing these differential patterns is provided by Hanley *et al.* (1991) for a patient with preserved verbal but impaired visuospatial span, while a patient studied by Basso *et al.* (1982) showed the reverse pattern (see Della Sala and Logie [2002] and Vallar and Papagno [2002] for a detailed account of such patients). Not only is it clear that visuospatial and verbal STM are differentiable, but as we shall see below, there is very good evidence for further fractionation within the visuospatial domain.

The VSSP concept that was proposed to account for this pattern of data (Baddeley 1986; Baddeley and Hitch 1974) assumes that the sketchpad serves as a storage system capable of integrating visual and spatial information, whether acquired from vision, touch, language or LTM, into a unitary visuospatial representation. Note that the sketchpad is not in itself modality-specific, although the question of whether visual and spatial information might also be stored separately was initially left unspecified. It was assumed that some form of rehearsal occurred, but its nature was unclear, implicit eye movements being considered as one possibility but not receiving unequivocal support (Baddeley 1986).

What has changed? As in the case of the phonological loop, the principal weakness of the VSSP concept lay not in what it got wrong so much as in what was left unspecified. Although progress in this area has not been rapid, there are some very welcome signs that this is changing, with increasing evidence that previously separate research traditions are converging to study the interface between attention, perception and memory. I will begin by discussing visuospatial STM, leaving the role of the VSSP in visual imagery until the next chapter.

4.2 **Fractionating visuospatial working memory**

Our visual world comprises objects that may be present in specific locations. The objects may move, with locations changing over time, or we may encounter a sequence of different objects appearing sequentially at the same location. Studies of visuospatial working memory have used a wide range of methods that typically combine two or more of these variables. An object must be presented at a location, even if this is not a critical feature of the test, and objects typically comprise a particular spatial pattern of features. Furthermore, experimental visual memory procedures typically involve a stimulus followed by a visual test, requiring at least minimal sequential memory storage. As we shall see, it has become increasingly clear that memory for objects, spatial location and temporal sequence may involve different memory processes, which may of course interact with each other, and with other components of working and long-term memory. Despite its complexity I believe we are making good progress. I shall try to demonstrate this, first by giving a separate account of spatial, object and sequential visual STM, before discussing the complex issue of separating these various components of the VSSP.

4.3 Memory for spatial location

Imagine you are in a room one evening, when a power cut plunges it into darkness. How good would you be at remembering where the door was, or perhaps where you might have happened to see a box of matches? There have been a number of studies along these lines over the years, with the evidence suggesting that the capacity for whole-body motion in an appropriate direction remains modestly accurate anything up to 30 seconds after the lights have been turned off (Steenhuis and Goodale 1988; Thomson 1983), whereas the capacity for accurate manual reaching appears to disappear rather more rapidly (Elliot and Madalena 1987). We appear to register the location of a number of objects relatively automatically (Andrade and Meudell 1993; Hasher and Zacks 1979), although attention to the scene does increase accuracy (Naveh-Benjamin 1987; 1988). The capacity to remember the locations at which objects have appeared appears to be almost as good in children as in adults, although the capacity to associate a particular object with its location shows a clear developmental trend (Schumann-Hengsteler 1992; Walker *et al.* 1994). Such a task thus appears to have two components, remembering where and remembering what, which are differentially influenced by cognitive development. We will begin by considering memory for location, beginning with the simplest case of remembering a single location, and considering separately memory for visual and kinaesthetic input.

Posner and Konick (1966) asked their subjects to remember the position of a dot located along a straight line, testing them after a brief interval that was either unfilled, or was filled by one of a series of digit processing tasks that varied in cognitive demand. They found no forgetting during the unfilled delay, but with a filled delay, amount of forgetting increased with the demand of the intervening task. Posner and Konick (1966) interpreted their results as suggesting that some form of rehearsal was possible, but was disrupted by their concurrent cognitive task. The fact that performance increased with the attentional demand of these tasks suggests that the process was not simply one of subvocal rehearsal, as all of their verbal tasks should have prevented articulation. This is also the pattern shown in the standard verbal version of the Peterson short-term forgetting task, in which an attentionally demanding task results in forgetting, while articulatory suppression does not (Baddeley *et al.* 1984a).

Dale (1973) tested retention of the location of a dot which appeared briefly at a random location within a one foot square open field and observed clear forgetting when the delay was filled by a digit processing task. Warrington and Baddeley (1974) showed that amnesic patients with grossly impaired LTM were able to perform this visual STM task normally, but were impaired on a long-term memory version in which they were required to learn and retain a pattern comprising an array of dots.

The above studies were all based on the Peterson and Peterson short-term forgetting paradigm, which raises the possibility that the forgetting observed may be principally based on proactive interference, which in turn reflects the capacity of the subject to discriminate the memory trace of the test item from earlier items. In the case of verbal memory, recall on the first trial is excellent but declines rapidly on subsequent trials, unless an intertrial delay is interposed (Keppel and Underwood 1962; Loess and Waugh 1967). However, Warrington and Baddeley (1974) found no evidence of build up of PI, in contrast to the picture for verbal short-term forgetting where both amnesic patients and control subjects showed the standard rapid build up of PI across successive test trials (Baddeley and Warrington 1970).

When the open field on which the stimulus appears contains potential landmarks such as a drawn circle or square, subjects tend to use these (Nelson and Chaiklin 1980). A later study by Igel and Harvey (1991) varied the number of dots between one and ten, presenting them simultaneously or sequentially, with or without a square framework. All three factors influenced performance, which deteriorated as the number of dots increased, was better for simultaneous than for sequential performance, and improved with the presence of landmarks. Huttenlocher *et al.* (1991) suggest two types of locational coding, one that is coarse and categorical – for example, which quadrant the stimulus occupied – while the other is more fine-grained and appears to use something analogous to polar coordinates.

To summarize: STM for visual location shows little loss over brief unfilled intervals, either because the stimuli are rehearsed or possibly because forgetting only occurs in the presence of interference from interpolated stimuli. A rehearsal interpretation is favoured by the fact that apparently nonvisual tasks such as digit processing increase forgetting, with the amount of forgetting being related to the difficulty of the intervening task. Unlike verbal STM, the little evidence available suggests that PI does not play a major role.

4.4 **Object-based short-term memory**

Classic work on the cognitive psychology of visual attention highlighted the fact that our visual system takes in information through a number of separate sensory channels, independently coding features such as shape, location, size and colour, and hence giving rise to the question of how the different channels combine to yield an integrated percept (Treisman 1993). The visual system is clearly informationally limited, but according to Duncan (1984) is capable of combining and encoding two features such as orientation and texture, just as readily as a single feature, provided the two are combined within a single object. Egly *et al.* (1994) went on to demonstrate that attending to one component of an object, such as a rectangle, results in the automatic spread of attention across the whole object.

Irwin and Andrews (1996) demonstrated a similar phenomenon in immediate memory. Their subjects viewed an array of six letters, all in different colours, after which they were required to move their eyes to an object in the periphery. At this point the letters disappeared, being replaced by an asterisk coinciding with the location of one of the letters. The subject's task was to report the letter, its colour, or both. Performance was studied across set sizes ranging from one to twelve letters. Subjects proved able to retain three to four letters, performing just as well when *both* colour and letter form were required as they did when only one feature was demanded.

Although this might appear to suggest that visual STM is limited in terms of number of objects, not features, it is of course possible that subjects may have been using verbal coding for the letter names, as suggested by Walker and Cuthbert (1998). This problem was avoided by Luck and Vogel (1997) by using as stimuli bars presented at different orientations, not an easy feature to encode verbally. They combined the oriented bars with up to four different stimulus features such as colour and texture. Again they found that subjects were able to retain about four objects, regardless of whether this involved storing one, two or four features.

In a subsequent study, Vogel *et al.* (2001) carefully explored a range of possible alternative explanations of these findings. They ruled out a verbal coding interpretation by using rapid presentation which would allow little time for naming, coupled with the use of shapes that are not readily nameable. Neither of these manipulations impaired performance. A further study required subjects to maintain an ongoing verbal load of two digits. This was sufficient to disrupt an equivalent verbal memory task based on letters, but had no influence on their visual memory task.

A further experiment extended their investigation of the number of features that can be maintained, showing that subjects were able to recall up to 16 features, provided they were distributed across four objects. A final study examined the effects of delay on performance, with the array of objects tested after retention intervals of 900, 2900, or 4900 msec. They found the standard effect of number of objects, with accuracy declining as set size increased from four to eight to twelve items. There was, however, no effect of delay, and no interaction between delay and number of objects. In short, they found no evidence of forgetting, a point that we shall return to later.

In discussing their results, Vogel *et al.* point to a similar capacity of three to four items in Sperling's study of visually presented letters (Sperling 1960), noting also that span for visually presented digits is at about this level when phonological coding is disrupted by articulatory suppression (Baddeley *et al.* 1984a). Finally, it is noteworthy that Cowan (2001; 2005); in an extensive review of the existing literature across many modalities and paradigms, argues strongly for a working memory capacity of about four chunks, as observed by Vogel *et al.*

4.4.1 A model of visual working memory

Vogel *et al.* (2001) propose a model that draws upon neurophysiologically based theories of feature binding in visual attention. They suggest that encoding a visual object results in increased firing of those neurons that code the object's features, an assumption that is consistent with both single unit recording studies (Fuster and Jervey 1981; Miller *et al.* 1996), and with neuroimaging evidence (Cohen, Perlstein *et al.* 1997). This then raises the question of how to encode two objects that have different values of the same features, for example, a red vertical bar and a green horizontal bar. This problem could potentially be solved by also encoding the locations of the two objects. However, we know that recognition memory for patterns is *not* dependent on the recognition pattern appearing in precisely the same location as the original stimulus (Phillips 1974), suggesting that location is not the crucial disambiguating cue.

An alternative solution to the feature binding problem is to use synchronous firing, with the relevant features of each object, including location, firing in synchrony, leading to the integration of the features that fire together. In the case of such a model, the limit is likely to be set not by the number of features, but by the risk of accidental synchrony as the number of objects increases. The idea of binding features by synchronous firing is not of course a novel one, and has received reasonable support at both a neurophysiological and a computational level (e.g. Singer and Gray 1995; von der Malsburg 1995). Finally Raffone and Wolters (2001) have proposed a detailed computational model giving a more precise account of the results described by Luck and Vogel (1997) and Vogel *et al.* (2001).

4.4.2 **Limitations of the Vogel *et al.* model**

What are the shortcomings of the model at this point? As Vogel *et al.* point out, it seems implausible to assume that our memory at any given time can only contain four objects, given the apparent richness of our subjectively experienced visual world. They argue that this is not a reflection of the stability of our memories but of the world itself, citing as evidence the phenomenon of *change-blindness*. The change-blindness paradigm is one in which a complex scene is viewed, followed by a brief blank interval after which the scene is shown again but with one critical feature changed. Subjects are remarkably bad at detecting such changes, either in the laboratory or in the real world where there have been some remarkably dramatic demonstrations. For example, a subject is stopped and asked a question in the street. Before he or she can reply, two people carrying a screening object such as a door pass between the subject and the questioner. During this brief masking period the questioner is replaced by someone else. The subject rarely notices (Rensink 2000). Rensink *et al.* (1997) suggest that our perceptual selection from the environment is guided by LTM which focuses on points of current importance ignoring other features, a view supported by Wagar and Dixon (2005). Using a categorization task, they found that those features that were most diagnostic were least liable to change blindness.

While the phenomenon of change-blindness certainly demonstrates that visual working memory is highly selective, and that we do rely on continuities in the world, the fact that the world *appears* continuous implies that we are storing information about it somewhere, albeit in transformed and reduced form. The fact that we can remember a sequence of movements, as in the Corsi block-tapping test, would seem to demand a mechanism that extends beyond the retention of four objects. Finally, the fact that we can create a visuospatial image based on auditory input (Baddeley and Lieberman 1980; Brooks 1967; 1968) suggests that although the link between visual working memory and visual attention is an important one, it reflects only part of a complex visuospatial storage and manipulation system.

4.4.3 The role of attention in visual working memory

One attractive feature of the Vogel *et al.* model is that it provides a link between visual memory and the classic issues of visual attention, such as object perception (Duncan 1984), visual search (Duncan and Humphreys 1989), and the classic binding problem (Singer and Gray 1995). Other studies have further supported this link, resulting in the emergence of a number of general principles. These include:

1 *Attentional factors may influence working memory encoding*: Schmidt *et al.* (2002) presented their subjects with an array of six coloured squares, one of which was followed by a cue indicating that a probe would follow. Attention is automatically drawn towards a change within the field. Even when there is no relationship between the location of the change and the item to be probed, the square associated with the change cue is better recalled if it is subsequently probed. A second study by Woodman *et al.* (2003) used detection of change after a brief delay as a measure of which items had been encoded. They found that those items that were linked by Gestalt principles such as continuity, were more likely to be attended to and encoded, with a result that changes to such patterns were more readily detected than changes to gestalt-unrelated items.

2 *Holding an item in working memory can bias attention*: Downing (2000) presented subjects with a single face which they were required to remember. The display was replaced by two faces, one new and one old, and followed by the requirement to judge the location of a gap in a bracket. When the bracket appeared at the same location as the face being held in working memory, judgements were more rapid and accurate than when it appeared in the location just vacated by the novel face. This is particularly striking since there is a natural tendency for eye movements to move *towards* a novel stimulus. Holding an item in working memory thus appears to be a sufficiently powerful determinant of attentional location as to override this tendency.

3 *Attention-demanding tasks do not necessarily disrupt visual working memory*: This is supported by the finding by Vogel *et al.* (2001) that filling a delay with an attention-demanding task does not increase forgetting. Cocchini *et al.* (2002) studied the retention of a random matrix pattern over a delay that was either unfilled, or occupied by the retention of a sequence of digits of span length. They found no reliable difference between the two conditions. That is not to claim that nonvisual activity during the retention interval never impairs retention. Morey and Cowan (2005) for example find that the need to retain and overtly articulate a digit sequence can impair

visual recall, attributing the effect to competition between attentionally based retrieval processes in visuospatial maintenance and overt verbal recall.

In general, attempts to link research on visual attention with the study of working memory appear to have been successful in suggesting (1) That the capacity of the system is reflected in number of *objects* rather than *features*, (2) That the system does indeed interact with attention in a coherent way. (3) There is a surprising lack of forgetting over brief delays, together with clear evidence of response interference effects. This suggests a range of new questions that promise to throw considerably more light on the underlying mechanisms. Finally, (4) the model proposed by Vogel *et al.* (2001) ties in very neatly with existing theorizing on attention and on possible solutions to the binding problem in perception and awareness, again providing a welcome link between working memory and attention.

4.4.4 Visual search and STM

The absence of any sign of forgetting in many of these studies may seem somewhat surprising, given the abundant evidence in the literature for short-term visuospatial forgetting over a filled delay (Dale 1973; Phillips 1974; Phillips and Baddeley 1971; Phillips and Christie 1977a, b). A possible solution to this problem is however, suggested by a series of recent studies, concerned with the interaction between visual search and visual and spatial STM.

Woodman *et al.* (2001) required their subjects to retain the visual features of *objects* while performing a spatial search task. They found no disruption of retention, or of the search task. However, when Woodman and Luck (2004) combined a *spatial* memory task with visual search, they found an increase in both slope and intercept of the scanning task. Oh and Kim (2004) report a similar result: remembering the colour of four squares had no effect on visual search, while requirement to remembering their location influenced both the slope and intercept of the scanning task. It appears to be the case therefore, that spatial memory is disrupted by visual search, but visual or object memory is not. Why should this be?

4.4.5 The role of eye movements

Searching through a visual array for a target will typically involve moving the eyes, a process that was shown to disrupt performance on the Brooks (1967) spatial imagery task in a study by Christopher Idzikowski and myself, reported briefly in Baddeley (1986), and finally published with a further study some 20 years later (Postle *et al.* 2006). The task, which will be described in more detail in the next chapter, was somewhat complex: however subsequent studies have shown similar disruptive effects of eye movements on simpler tasks. Hale *et al.* (1996) studied STM for letters and their location within a matrix. They found significant disruption of spatial STM when either eye movements or a pointing response was required, whereas a spoken response disrupted memory for letters, which presumably reflected phonological loop involvement.

Eye movements are, however, likely to be associated with movement of attentional focus. In an extension to the studies subsequently reported in Postle *et al.* (2006), Idzikowski and I carried out a study aimed at separating these effects, and somewhat to our surprise found eye movements to be *more* disruptive than attentional movements. However, given the difficulty we had encountered with referees over our somewhat basic eye-movement technology in our attempt to publish the paper that became Postle *et al.* (2006), we put this result on one side for possible later investigation. Such a study was carried out by Pearson and Sahraie (2003), who found that shifts of attention involving eye movements were significantly more disruptive of spatial STM that were attentional shifts alone, a result that they attributed to the role of oculomotor activity in visuospatial rehearsal. Lawrence *et al.* (2004) combined spatial and verbal STM tasks with interpolated eye movements. In one condition attention and eyes were centrally focused. A second involved attentional movement with eyes fixated; a third required attentional focus with eyes moving, while both moved in a fourth condition. Both types of interpolated movement impaired spatial STM, with eye movements having the greater effect.

It thus appears to be the case that eye movements can disrupt spatial STM, giving one possible explanation of the pattern of results linking spatial STM with visual search. Such results are also consistent with the hypothesis proposed by Hebb (1968) and revived by Baddeley (1986), that visuospatial rehearsal may be based on implicit eye-movement control processes. It is important at this point to note that many other spatial activities also appear to disrupt visuospatial memory, including pointing (Brooks 1968) arm movement (Lawrence *et al.* 2001; Quinn and Ralston 1986), and spatial tapping (Della Sala *et al.* 1999). It seems unlikely that all of these are attributable to eye movements, suggesting that eye movements are simply one of a range of ways in which concurrent active movement may disrupt spatial memory.

Why should spatial but not visual activity be so disruptive? One speculation is that spatial memory depends on maintaining spatial coordinates over time, possibly using attentional focus to counter a tendency to drift. Other disruptive interpolated spatial activities such voluntary eye and hand movements are likely to have their own spatial coordinates that must be maintained if accurate responses are to be made. It may perhaps be the conflict between the coordinates of the memory task and interpolated activity that disrupts spatial memory. Another feature of such disruptive interpolated tasks, whether based on eye movements, arm movements or manual tapping is that they involve the active performance of *sequences* of responses. Before going on to discuss the basis of the interference, we should consider the more basic issue of the capacity of the VSSP to retain sequential information.

4.5 Sequential storage in visuospatial short-term memory

One of the earliest measures of visual STM was developed by Corsi and popularized by Milner (1971) as a visuospatial analogue of digit span. It involves a quasi-random array of nine blocks; the tester begins by tapping two blocks and asking the patient to imitate, gradually increasing the length of sequence until performance breaks down, typically at lengths of about five blocks or about two items less than digit span. Neuropsychological evidence points to a clear distinction between Corsi and digit span, and a classic double dissociation with some patients impaired on digit span with normal Corsi span, while others show the reverse (De Renzi and Nichelli 1975; Hanley *et al.* 1991; Vallar and Baddeley 1982). Consistent with this pattern is the observation that articulatory suppression disrupts verbal span but has no effect on Corsi span (Smyth and Pendleton 1989).

Dissociation from verbal span is clearly important, but leaves open the nature of the visuospatial memory processes underpinning Corsi span. Performing the sequence of taps clearly involves *spatial* coordinates, but it is equally plausible to envisage the sequence being stored as an overall *pattern* of actions, perhaps making retention more visual than spatial. Further light was thrown on this by the development of a second visual span task that does not require retention of sequential information.

Development of the paradigm was prompted by one of the earliest studies of visual memory (Posner and Keele 1967). This study attempted to use RT measures to separate storage of the phonological representation of a letter from its visual code (Posner and Keele 1967), concluding that the visual code survived for about 1.5 sec. Phillips and Baddeley (1971) took issue with this conclusion on the grounds that the method confounds the rate of the loss of the visual code with the rate of development of the alternative verbal code. They suggested that a better approach was to use material that was not readily verbalized, hence allowing a purer measure of visual STM. Phillips and Baddeley developed a set of stimuli based on a 5 × 5 matrix of cells, half of which were randomly filled, followed by a pattern mask to disrupt iconic memory (Sperling, 1960b). After an unfilled delay ranging from 0.3 to 9 sec, a test matrix was presented that was either identical or had one cell changed. Subjects then made a same/different judgement. Performance levelled out at about 9 sec, whether measured by RT or accuracy, in contrast to the 1.5 sec delay rate suggested by the Posner and Keele experiment. Phillips (1974) went on to show that performance was a function of pattern complexity, as determined by matrix size. By gradually increasing the matrix size, it is possible to establish the visual 'pattern span' for a given individual, the point at which virtually perfect performance breaks down.

Della Sala *et al.* (1999) describe the development and validation of a pattern span measure based on recall rather than recognition. This involves viewing a matrix in which half the cells are randomly filled. The subject is then given an empty matrix and asked to mark the previously filled cells. Testing begins with a simple 2×2 matrix, gradually expanding the matrix size to a point at which performance breaks down, typically at a level of approximately 16 cells. Della Sala *et al.* suggest that pattern span is separable from the Corsi sequential span, reporting a study by Grossi *et al.* (1993) which identified two patients suffering from Alzheimer's disease, one showing very poor performance on Corsi span, with preserved pattern span, while the other showed the opposite. Della Sala *et al.* themselves describe two patients who are impaired on the Corsi task, but above the median on pattern span, together with a further patient showing the opposite. They also describe a study involving normal subjects, indicating that pattern span is disrupted by presentation of irrelevant visual stimuli to a greater extent than by spatial tapping, while the Corsi task shows the opposite pattern, of disruption by subsequent spatial, rather than visual, processing. This double dissociation suggests that Corsi span is not simply encoded as a spatial pattern, and that its sequential character is important.

Can sequences of patterns be stored? The initial answer seemed to be negative. A series of experiments by Phillips and Christie (1977a, b) presented sequence of matrix patterns of the type just described for recognition which were then probed. They found excellent performance on the last item, but only when it was probed first. When probed second it showed the same low recognition level as all earlier items did, regardless of their probe order. Performance on the last item was unaffected by subsequent visual stimuli, but was disrupted by a more demanding executive task. This result influenced my own initial conceptualization of the VSSP as a parallel storage system that was not equipped to retain sequences of items. As we shall see, that may not be the case when less complex visual stimuli are used.

A number of studies have explored this issue by studying the retention of somewhat simpler stimuli presented sequentially in the same spatial location.

While retention of serial order tends to encourage reliance on verbal coding, a good deal of evidence points to the capacity to retain the serial order of visually presented items that are *not* readily verbalizable, ranging from wallpaper patterns (Broadbent and Broadbent 1981) through unfamiliar Chinese ideograms (Wolford and Hollingsworth 1974) to faces (Smyth *et al.* 2005). Logie *et al.* (2000) reviewed these studies, observing that the evidence is often somewhat equivocal because of the problem of being certain of completely ruling out any form of verbal coding. Logie and Marchetti (1991) attempted to solve this problem by using stimuli for which naming would be of little value. They presented subjects with an array of squares, all of the same nameable colour, for example, red, but varying in their particular shade. Since presentation was rapid, and the basic colours used varied from trial to trial, verbal coding was extremely difficult. Testing was by recognition, with each sequence being followed by a recognition sequence that was identical except for a single change in either shade or presentation order. Recognition was tested after a ten second delay that was either unfilled, filled by unseen arm movements, or by irrelevant pictures. Arm movements disrupted retention of sequential information, whereas pictures interfered with memory for colour, suggesting a distinction between visual and colour memory on one hand and memory for serial order and spatial information on the other, a result that is consistent with previously described dissociation between Corsi and pattern span.

4.5.1 STM for action sequences

The sequential tasks described so far all require the reproduction of an arbitrary sequence of visual stimuli or spatial locations. There is, however, another important class of visuospatially specified activities for which serial order is often crucial, namely the performance of sequences of actions as in acquiring a new motor skill or in communication through gesture or dance. Smyth and Pendleton (1989) were concerned with the capacity to remember sequences of such actions. They compared memory for spatial locations with the capacity to remember and repeat a sequence of seen hand gestures. Two potentially interfering tasks were used: one was spatial and involved a series of movements to specified locations, while the other employed a more purely kinaesthetic task requiring the subject to squeeze a bulb during encoding. As expected, spatial span was impaired by concurrent movement, but not by the kinaesthetic squeezing. However, memory for gestures showed exactly the opposite pattern, being disrupted by the kinaesthetic, but not by the spatial interpolated task (see Fig. 4.1). Note that both memory tasks involved recall of serial order, suggesting separable spatial and kinaesthetic STM, both having the capacity to hold sequential information.

		Concurrent task	
		Move to location	Squeeze
Memory task	Movements	Impaired	0
	Spatial	0	Impaired

Fig. 4.1 The impact of concurrent movement and squeezing on retention of sequences of movements or spatial locations. 0 = No impairment. Data from Smyth and Pendleton (1989).

A similar dissociation was shown by Smyth *et al.* (1988), in a study which required the subject to watch the experimenter perform a series of movements such as raising the left arm above the head, stepping forward onto the right leg, tilting the head back, and so forth, and then imitate this sequence. Subjects had a span of about four such movements (cf. Cowan 2005). Subjects were also tested on Corsi spatial span and on verbal STM. These three tasks were then combined with three potentially interfering activities, namely articulatory suppression, tapping out a repeated spatial pattern, and a movement task. This involved the subject repeatedly raising both hands in the air, moving them to the shoulders and then to the hips, continually repeating these actions. The latter task disrupted memory for movements, but not Corsi or verbal span. Spatial tapping affected only the Corsi task, while articulatory suppression had no effect on Corsi performance, but significantly reduced both verbal and movement span (see Fig. 4.2).

		Concurrent task		
		Movements	Spatial tapping	Articulatory suppression
	Body actions	Impaired	0	Impaired
Memory task	Corsi	0	Impaired	0
	Digits	0	0	Impaired

Fig. 4.2 Memory for sequences of actions, locations or digits as a function of three concurrent tasks, involving movements, spatial tapping or articulatory suppression. 0 = No impairment. Data from Smyth *et al.* (1988).

The combined pattern of results from Smyth *et al*'s two studies reinforces the distinction between the Corsi spatial span task and memory for sequences of gestures, presenting further evidence for a separate kinaesthetic system. It could, however, be argued that these studies did not include an object-based STM task. It seems unlikely that the visual-object system is equipped to store sequences of gestures and actions, but this should be checked. One surprising finding is that articulatory suppression interfered with retention of movement sequences, although movement did not interfere with verbal span. This could suggest that subjects were using a verbal code to supplement memory for gestures.

Kinaesthetic STM is clearly of considerable potential relevance to the acquisition and performance of a wide range of skills ranging from dance (Smyth *et al.* 1988), through rock climbing (Smyth and Waller 1998) to rowing (Woodin *et al.* 1996). While it is important to study ecologically relevant tasks, the complexity of many such activities make it very difficult to separate the possible role of kinaesthetic STM from those of spatial, visual and verbal memory. This is an interesting and important aspect of working memory, but one which is still largely unexplored.

4.5.2 Modelling serial order in visuospatial short-term memory

In contrast to the verbal domain, there appear to have been few attempts to model visuospatial serial order retention, perhaps unsurprisingly, given the relative paucity and complexity of available data. There are clear similarities with verbal serial position effects, including the classic bowed serial position curve (Logie and Marchetti 1991; Smyth *et al.* 2005), and the recency effect (Phillips and Christie 1977a, b), although in this case recency was limited to one item and is undisturbed by a non-demanding interpolated task.

A useful starting point therefore may be to hypothesize that the models developed for verbal STM and described in Chapter 3 may also be applicable to the visuospatial domain. Should that prove to be the case, it would not of course undermine the extensive evidence for separate verbal, visual and spatial systems, but would suggest that the same problem, namely that of storing serial order, had been solved in comparable ways across systems. This could imply a simple unitary system for maintaining serial order, but this seems unlikely, given that serial verbal recall does not interfere with spatial recall in the Corsi task, and serial spatial tapping does not interfere with recalling sequences of body movements.

4.6 Separating the threads

We began this chapter with the case for separating visuospatial and verbal STM. By this point we have concluded not only that a separate visuospatial system must be assumed, but also that object-based visual storage involves a different subsystem from the storage of information regarding spatial location, which in turn appears to be separable from the system storing movement through space, possibly on a kinaesthetic basis. But are we in fact justified in making these distinctions? The classic evidence for the need to assume two separate systems involves a crossover double dissociation whereby for example, Task A is disrupted by Activity 1 but not Activity 2, whereas Task B shows the opposite, with Task 2 but not Task 1 disrupting performance. However, while such a result would place valuable constraints on theoretical interpretation, it does not guarantee that the two systems are separate. This issue is discussed at length by a number of contributors to the February 2003 issue of *Cortex* (Volume 399, pp. 1-202). These potential objections include:

1 Differential processing, whereby the two memory tasks differ in more than one dimension. For example, Corsi and pattern differ both the visual-spatial and the unitary-sequential dimensions, making interpretation difficult.

2 The observed difference may stem from any point in the processing and memory tasks, for example reflecting the capacity to perceive or register the two sets of stimuli rather than their retention.

3 The dissociation may stem from different degrees of similarity between the memory and processing tasks across the two systems, hence being explicable if one assumes for example a single multi dimensional LTM system subject to classic interference effects, as in the feature hypothesis proposed by Nairne (1990) and described in Chapter 3.

4 Given certain assumptions of non-linearity, it is possible to generate data that appear to reflect a double dissociation on the basis of a single parameter (Kello 2003).

5 Perhaps the most serious objection to a reliance on double dissociation is the possibility that the two systems may not be equated on a third or fourth determinant of performance. This is particularly telling in the case of a system such as the multicomponent model of working memory, which assumes that a range of subsystems may be brought to bear upon the performance of any task. Some of these such as the phonological loop may be reasonably easy to eliminate, but others such as the central executive are more complex and much harder to rule out. The problem becomes even more challenging when, as in the case of the sketchpad, the subsystem itself appears to fractionate into two, or probably three potentially different subcomponents. In theory, one could search for triple or quadruple dissociations. This would demand 9 and 16 conditions respectively, all balanced on every dimension except those being studied. Not a tempting way to proceed.

My own view is that the only way to tackle such complexity is through the classic method of converging operations. This involves using a range of different tasks that are thought to reflect the various hypothetical underlying systems. The tasks should be chosen to attempt to rule out alternative hypothesis, fully accepting that no single experiment will be crucial, but banking on the assumption that a sufficiently rich and coherent body of data will place major constraints that will rule out most of the rival hypotheses. This is the method that we have used to tackle the phonological loop. As we saw, the result is not 'proof', which I myself regard as an appropriate criterion for mathematics but not for science, but rather, a gradually accumulating body of evidence for a particular way of conceptualizing the world. Like most theories, it will of course be expanded and probably in due course replaced. In the meantime I would suggest that both the method and the resulting model have proved fruitful. But what of the sketchpad, which is almost certainly more complex than the phonological loop? I suggest a conclusion reinforced in the case of the dissociation between visual and spatial STM by an impressively thorough series of experiments carried out by Klauer and Zhao (2004).

Klauer and Zhao begin by discussing the previously described potential pitfalls in interpreting double dissociations, going on to analyse 11 studies that argue for a dissociation between visual and spatial STM, pointing out that none escapes all the potential objections. They then go on to describe a series of six experiments that attempt to rule out such alternative interpretations and begin by developing simple spatial and visual tasks, based an earlier study by Tresch *et al.* (1993). The Klauer and Zhao spatial task involves remembering the location of a white dot on a black visual background, while their visual task involves memory for Chinese ideographs. An ideograph was shown, followed after a 10 second retention interval by a set of eight items, with the subject required to pick the one that had been presented earlier. During the 10 second delay interval, subjects performed either a spatial task in which 12 asterisks were presented, with 11 moving randomly, and the twelfth stationary. The subject's task was to identify the stationary item. The task chosen to disrupt visual memory involved colour discrimination. During the interval, the screen would be flooded by a series of monochromatic colours, seven of which would be categorized as belonging to the 'red family' and seven to the blue range. The basic paradigm thus involved spatial or visual stimuli followed by colour or movement judgement tasks to form four interference conditions, to which were added two baseline control conditions in which each of the memory tasks was performed alone. It was predicted that the movement judgement would disrupt the spatial dot memory task, while colour judgement would impair the visual task of ideogram recognition.

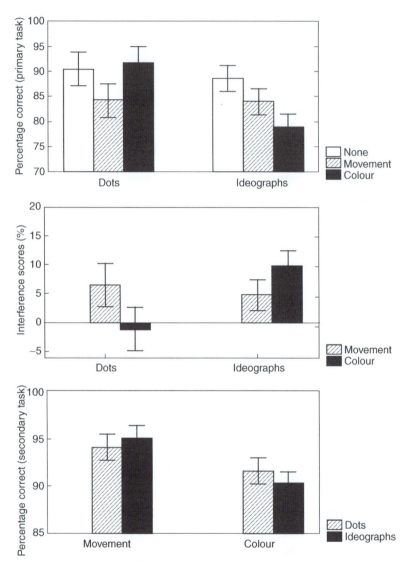

Fig. 4.3 Memory for dot location and ideographs as a function of task presented during a ten second retention interval. The upper panel represents memory performance, the middle panel, the degree of interference, and the lower performance on the secondary tasks. See text for details. Data from Klauer and Zhao (2004) Figure 2.

The results of this basic paradigm are shown in Figure 4.3. The upper panel shows primary task performance, the degree of interference observed is shown in the middle panel, and performance on the concurrent task is shown in the bottom panel. Considering first primary task performance, it is clear that the concurrent movement task disrupts retention of the spatial location of dots, whereas the colour judgement task does not. In the case of the ideographs both concurrent tasks impair performance with the colour judgement being significantly greater. This differential pattern of disruption is shown more clearly in the middle panel, while the lower panel indicates that both tasks were being performed conscientiously and that this pattern of results does not reflect a differential trade-off between the primary and secondary tasks. The data therefore provide a classic demonstration of the predicted double dissociation. Klauer and Zhao then go on to confront this interpretation with the potential objections discussed earlier.

Their next experiment tests the hypothesis that their results might be due to the influence of the secondary tasks on perception or encoding, rather than storage. They test this hypothesis by delaying the onset of the secondary tasks up to a point at which encoding will have been completed. The pattern of results remains the same.

They noted that some subjects reported using verbal coding of the dot locations, which had been presented at the eight cardinal compass points on a circular array. To avoid this they used a range of dot locations that differed on each trial, coupled with articulatory suppression. Klauer and Zhao were also concerned that the repeated use of a limited number of ideographs might have led to a major contribution from LTM. They therefore changed the ideographs on every trial, sampling at random from a pool of 512. The overall pattern of results remained unchanged, suggesting that neither the phonological loop, nor LTM were responsible for their previous findings.

Their fourth experiment was concerned with the argument that their findings might simply reflect degree of similarity between the sets of tasks rather than indicating separate storage systems. While it is hard to argue that Chinese ideographs and colour are very similar, one can make a reasonable case for similarity-based interference between the location of a visually presented dot and an array of asterisks. They therefore replaced their movement task with the requirement to tap out a spatial sequence on a hidden keypad. Once again, the broad pattern of results remained, tapping had little effect on retention of ideographs but clearly disrupted dot retention, whereas colour processing again showed the reverse pattern.

Their final two experiments were concerned with the possible role of the central executive: could the observed pattern reflect the differential executive loading of the various tasks? This was tested by requiring the subjects to attempt to generate random numbers at a rate of one per second throughout the task. Overall performance was reduced, but the interference pattern remained the same. A final experiment also included a third primary task, arithmetic, that was assumed to be dependent on executive processing. On this occasion in addition to spatial tapping and colour judgement, they included a task in which subjects were required to respond as rapidly as possible to randomly occurring stimuli, a task that they assumed would disrupt executive processing. Their assumptions proved justified, with the random interval task disrupting arithmetic more than colour or tapping, while the overall pattern of results remained the same, with dot retention disrupted by spatial tapping, and ideograph memory by colour processing.

Klauer and Zhao (2004) conclude that their evidence provides strong support for a fractionation of visuospatial memory into separate visual and spatial components, which are not readily interpreted in terms of trade offs in resource allocation, differences in storage-processing similarity, effects of long-term memory, or of the executive processing.

There is no doubt that the ingenuity and thoroughness with which Klauer and Zhao pursue this important issue is something of a tour de force. I suspect that it might however evoke one of two conflicting responses in the reader, both, in my view, mistaken. One view might be to note that after all this substantial effort, the conclusions reached are consistent with those of the 11 imperfect studies reviewed by the authors, implying that this series of experiments was unnecessary. I strongly disagree with this: the potential dissociation between visual and spatial working memory is important and basic, both for cognitive psychology, and as we shall see later, for cognitive neuroscience. It is therefore appropriate that it be established as firmly as possible, using the best available current methodology. It would be highly desirable if all such proposed distinctions were at some point subject to an investigation as careful and thorough as that provided by Klauer and Zhao.

A second response might be to suggest that this should become the paradigm for future research, with papers only being published if they live up to the rigorous methodological standards set by Klauer and Zhao. I believe this to be an equally mistaken view. The series of experiments described were possible only because they took advantage of many years of earlier investigation, developing concepts and methods, which then fed into the 11 studies they cite, which in turn allowed Klauer and Zhao to select appropriate tasks and conditions. Always requiring such rigorous standards would simply shackle the field, discouraging new lines of research that form the seed corn of future theoretical development. It would also be likely to limit research to those tasks that can be tightly constrained within the laboratory. As we will see in the next chapter, many important features of the VSSP are represented by its application to complex tasks that are of considerable practical importance, but which may not, currently at least, be amenable to the elegant and detailed analysis represented by the Klauer and Zhao study.

4.7 **Conclusions**

The evidence suggests a clear difference between the short-term storage of features representing visual objects, and of their spatial location. Visual memory appears able to hold up to four objects, each of which may comprise multiple features. This system does not typically show short-term forgetting, even when a visual search task is interposed between presentation and test, whereas spatial STM is sensitive to the demands of any interpolated task. Both systems appear able to store serial order, provided relatively simple stimuli are used. There is some evidence, though it is less extensive, for a third subsystem concerned with the storage of actions, which may rely on a motor or kinaesthetic code. All three temporary storage components are assumed to be coordinated within the visuospatial sketch pad, a system that is capable of manipulating visuospatial information as part of the overall working memory system, providing a basis for complex cognitive processing, as will be described in Chapter 5.

Chapter 5

Imagery and visuospatial working memory

The evidence we have discussed so far could be described as representing short-term rather than working memory, since virtually all the paradigms simply involve encoding limited amounts of material which must then be held briefly and either recalled or recognized, without any need for further processing or transformation. For a task to be regarded as going beyond simple storage, and meriting the term working memory rather than STM, one might expect a number of additional features. First of all, working memory is assumed to be able to manipulate the material being stored. It should also, in my view at least, be able to register and incorporate information indirectly, either from long-term memory, or by allowing cross-modal encoding, as when, for example, a visually presented consonant sequence is phonologically recoded. Working memory is typically assumed to be dependent upon a limited capacity attentional control system, not simply on limited storage capacity. Finally, underpinning the whole concept of working memory is the assumption that it serves a useful general function in providing a basis for complex real-world cognitive activities.

It was for that reason that my earlier account of the visuospatial sketchpad (Baddeley 1986) began with the ingenious but complex paradigms developed by Brooks, rather than, as in the case of the phonological loop, beginning with simple short-term storage. Having on this occasion begun with basic storage, we are now in a position to analyse more complex tasks, and ask whether they can reasonably be regarded as based upon storage within the systems captured by the more basic STM paradigms. What might these systems comprise?

As we have seen, the picture is less clear than is the case for phonological STM. The influence of variables such as similarity are less clear-cut, and the mechanism, or mechanisms, for visuospatial rehearsal appear to be less obvious and easy to study than subvocal rehearsal. Furthermore, while it seems likely that visual, spatial and possibly kinaesthetic information is stored in potentially independent subsystems, separating such systems is often very difficult in practice. Consequently, in many of the studies to be described, it will be far from clear whether the visuospatial code is primarily visual, spatial, or indeed kinaesthetic.

Furthermore, the precise paradigms on which our knowledge is based vary quite substantially, often making it unclear as to whether the disruptive effects of concurrent tasks operate through impairment of encoding, storage or retrieval. Finally, there is no simple and obvious interpretation of the nature of visuospatial rehearsal, with attempts to argue for a visuospatial analogue of the word length effect receiving little support (Smyth and Pendleton 1990). Despite these limitations, however, there is considerable evidence for a visuospatial system that acts in parallel with the phonological loop as a subcomponent of working memory, a system that I shall continue to refer to as the visuospatial sketchpad.

5.1 **Visuospatial coding and verbal memory**

Allen Paivio (1969; 1971) is principally responsible for reintroducing the concept of visual imagery into the study of verbal learning and memory. He was able to demonstrate that words that were judged as likely to evoke sensory images were much easier to learn than low-imagery words; he interpreted his results in terms of the *dual coding hypothesis*. This proposed that imageable words could be remembered, not only in terms of such verbal characteristics as sound and meaning, but also in terms of imagery, as reflected in their capacity to evoke quasi sensory associations. Given the neo-behaviourist climate in which he was initially operating, it is perhaps unsurprising that he made no claims as to whether the subjects actually *experienced* the visuospatial images, defining his measure purely operationally in terms of the ratings that were given when subjects were instructed 'To rate a list of words as to the ease or difficulty with which they arouse mental images i.e. a mental picture of sound or other sensory experience' (Paivio *et al.* 1968, p. 4).

We thus have the paradox of a measure that is based on instructions that assume conscious experience in the raters subsequently being used as if it were an objective measure that simply happened to work. This allowed Paivio to escape being accused of the sin of introspectionism, by defining imagery operationally and treating it simply as a further encoding dimension that enhanced memory performance.

In the case of STM, while semantic coding in general and imageability in particular do have some influence on verbal span (Baddeley 1966a), the effects tend to be small, at least in the case of the standard span-based procedure in which a limited set of words is used repeatedly, placing the principal emphasis on recall of serial order, while being greater for open sets of words and longer sequences, in which item memory places a larger role (Hulme *et al.* 1997).

5.1.1 **Imagery and verbal short-term memory**

The strongest evidence for a major role of imagery in immediate verbal recall came initially from an ingenious technique developed by Brooks (1967), in which subjects were required to use visual imagery to store verbal material. It involved presenting the subject with the task of hearing and repeating back a sequence of sentences. In the crucial condition, it was possible to use a 4 × 4 matrix to support the visual recoding of the sequences since they could all be mapped onto the matrix. One square was identified as the starting point, and the subjects were then instructed to remember and repeat back a sequence of sentences such as the following: *In the starting square put a 1. In the next square to the right put a 2. In the next square beneath put a 3. In the next square to the right put a 4*, etc. The sequence always ran from one upwards, and could always be recoded as a path through the matrix. Such recoding was prevented in a second condition by replacing the spatial adjectives with non-spatial bipolar equivalents to produce sequences such as: *In the starting square put a 1. In the next square to the good put a 2. In the next square to the strong put a 3. In the next square to the good put a 4. In the next square to the bad put a 5*, etc. Subjects proved able to remember an average of eight sentences using the spatial version, but only about five using the formally equivalent non-spatial task for which they appeared to rely on phonological coding.

Brooks (1967) showed that performance interacted with modality of presentation, with auditory presentation favouring the visuospatial code, and reading the non-spatial sequence. He interpreted this result in terms of interference between the mode of presentation and the mode of storage; reading the visually presented sentences interfered with the visuospatial matrix code and vice versa.

My own involvement in this are was influenced by the personal experience of listening to the UCLA-Stanford American football game while driving along a freeway. I had a very good image of the game, but noticed that I was weaving from lane to lane, and rapidly switched to music. On returning to Britain, I decided to investigate the effect by combining the Brooks matrix task with visuospatial tracking (Baddeley *et al.* 1973). We required our subjects to perform the verbal and spatial versions of the Brooks task while carrying out a tracking task in which the subject had to keep a stylus in contact with a moving spot of light. Tracking greatly disrupted the visuospatial version of the task, but had no effect on the non-spatial version.

In a later study (Baddeley and Lieberman 1980), we tackled the question of whether subjects were using a visual or a spatial code. We devised a purely visual secondary task in which subjects were asked to judge the brightness of a large screen, pressing a key when brightness increased. The non-visuospatial task required blindfolded subjects to track a moving sound source with a flashlamp; when the lamp was on target, the sound emitted by the target changed. We found that this spatial but non-visual auditory tracking task disrupted the visual imagery-based Brooks tasks, while the visual brightness judgement task did not. The verbal version of the Brooks task showed the opposite pattern, being more disrupted by brightness judgement than by auditory tracking. We concluded that we were studying spatial rather than visual imagery.

Despite its ingenuity, the Brooks matrix task has the drawback that both conditions are very demanding of general attentional resources. This was shown by Salway and Logie (1995) in a study combining the visuospatial and verbal Brooks tasks with articulatory suppression, spatial tapping, and with verbal random generation, a task that is known to place a heavy load on executive processing (Baddeley 1966c; Baddeley *et al.* 1998b). As predicted, spatial tapping disrupted the spatial version more than the Brooks verbal matrix task, while the opposite pattern was shown for articulatory suppression. However, verbal random generation had an even more dramatic impact on both, with the visuospatial suffering more than the verbal matrix task, even though the random generation was itself verbal. This suggests that the use of the visuospatial mnemonic is highly demanding of executive resources.

Further evidence of the potentially greater vulnerability of visuospatial tasks comes from a study by Farmer *et al.* (1986) who combined articulatory suppression and spatial tapping with a verbal reasoning task and a task involving spatial transformation. Neither concurrent task significantly impaired verbal reasoning, while both affected the spatial task, although with a greater effect from the spatial tapping. As the individual difference studies to be described in Chapter 11 show, there is a tendency for central executive measures to be more closely linked to tasks assumed to reflect the sketchpad, than they are to phonological loop measures.

We went on to study the role of visuospatial imagery in more conventional verbal memory tasks, teaching our subjects to use a spatial imagery mnemonic based on locating the items to be remembered on a prespecified route through the campus (Baddeley and Lieberman 1980). We contrasted this with a learning method based on rote verbal rehearsal, finding, as expected, a clear advantage to the imagery mnemonic. When combined with tracking using a pursuit rotor however, the imagery group's performance declined to the level of the rote learning group, who showed no effect of concurrent tracking. However, tracking had little effect on a less spatial mnemonic in which pairs of items were associated by imagining them interacting visually, for example, associating *lion* and *pipe* by imagining a lion smoking a pipe (Baddeley and Lieberman 1980). On the basis of these studies, we concluded that the visuospatial sketchpad was principally a spatial system.

This prompted Logie (1986) to present an alternative view. He suggested that our observation of spatial rather than visual interference resulted from the use of a spatial rather than a visual memory task. Using the paired associate task that we had claimed to be insensitive to disruption, Logie demonstrated that forgetting would occur if auditory presentation of the word pairs was accompanied by the presentation of *visual*, rather than spatial material, that the subject was instructed to look at but otherwise ignore. Line drawings and even colour patches were sufficient to disrupt the use of imagery.

A subsequent series of studies by Quinn and McConnell (1996a; b; 1999) also used either rote rehearsal or an imagery mnemonic to learn pairs of words. They showed that simply requiring the subject to look at a screen containing a twinkling visual noise pattern made up from multiple pixels randomly flickering on and off was sufficient to disrupt the imagery mnemonic, while having no effect on rote performance. Irrelevant speech had the opposite effect of disrupting rote learning, but leaving the imagery mnemonic unaffected. It should, however, be noted that although the visual noise effect has been replicated on a number of occasions (e.g. Baddeley and Andrade 2000; McConnell and Quinn 2000), there have been failures to find a robust effect (e.g. Andrade *et al*. 2002), suggesting that this phenomenon is not yet well understood.

5.1.2 Functions of the visuospatial sketchpad

We have so far limited discussion of the potential use of visuospatial working memory largely to its value as a mnemonic aid. It is, of course, used much more widely.

Hatano and Osawa (1983a; b) showed that expert abacus users were able to perform calculations by simply imagining the abacus, and were moreover able to use the imagined abacus to help remember number sequences. Performance was disrupted by a concurrent visuospatial task, suggesting that it depended on the use of the sketchpad. As with the phonological loop, utilization of the sketchpad is an optional strategy. A study by Garden *et al*. (2002), for example, examined the capacity of their subjects to learn an unfamiliar route through the streets of a medieval Italian city. While doing so, they either performed a spatial tapping task on a hidden keyboard, or suppressed articulation. Subjects had previously been questioned about their method of finding their way around in an unfamiliar city. Those who reported using a mental map proved to be more disrupted by the visuospatial task, while those who relied on landmarks were more influenced by articulatory suppression.

5.1.3 **Image manipulation and mental synthesis**

Visuospatial skills can, of course, be very important in certain occupations, such as architecture and engineering. There also tends to be a gender difference, with men being somewhat better at spatial manipulation and mental rotation than women, and being more likely to use a holistic strategy, while women are more likely to employ a more piecemeal, analytic and slower approach (Linn and Petersen 1985). A later study by Hsi *et al.* (1997) observed a similar gender difference among engineering students, together with a significant correlation between spatial manipulation and performance on the first year engineering graphics course, a difficult course for which 25 per cent of students obtained either a D or a Fail grade. Hsi *et al.* attempted to tackle this problem by talking to experienced engineers about strategies of spatial manipulation, then using this information to produce a one-day intensive course on spatial manipulation strategies. This resulted in improvement in performance to a point at which hardly any failures occurred, together with elimination of the gender difference.

A number of studies have attempted to analyse the processes underlying such visuospatial manipulation, and in particular those involved in discovering relationships through a process of mental synthesis. Finke and Slayton (1988) developed a task in which subjects were required to form images of letters, which must then be manipulated, at which point the subject should report the object depicted. For example, 'Imagine a capital J, then a capital D. Rotate the D through 90 degrees to the left, and place on top of the J. What does it look like?' The answer is an umbrella. Brandimonte *et al.* (1992) developed a related task in which subjects were given a stimulus comprising several parts, and asked mentally to remove one and label the result. For example, they may be shown an oval with a triangle at each end which resembled a wrapped sweet or candy. They were then required mentally to remove one of the triangles and redescribe it, the correct answer being a fish. Interestingly, performance was better when subjects were suppressing articulation, presumably because then they were forced to rely on the visuospatial code, rather than a verbal label.

Pearson *et al.* (1999) attempted to analyse the processes underlying mental synthesis, requiring their subjects to manipulate either four, six or eight symbols (e.g. square, triangle, circle, rectangle) so as to create a nameable object. If subjects produced a name, they were later required to draw the object. If they had not succeeded after two minutes, they were asked to recall the constituent symbols. Retention of the symbols decreased with set size, but was always at a higher level than successful completions, indicating that forgetting was not the only factor leading to failure. In order to gain some idea as to the underlying processes, subjects were asked to perform under control conditions or accompanied by either articulatory suppression or spatial tapping.

Articulatory suppression reduced the number of objects retained, but had no effect on capacity to combine them, whereas spatial tapping had the opposite effect, influencing combination but not memory. Under these circumstances, the phonological loop appears to support performance by holding items in readiness for revisualization, while the process of combination depends on the sketchpad.

5.2 Modelling the visuospatial sketchpad

5.2.1 Logie's model of the sketchpad

Baddeley (1986) had little to say about the detailed structure of the sketchpad, simply speculating that it may comprise separable visual, spatial and possibly lexical components, and that it probably serves to maintain images by some unspecified form of rehearsal. Logie (1995) has proposed a more detailed model in which he differentiates between a passive store, the *visual cache*, and an active component, the *inner scribe*, analogue to the phonological storage and articulatory rehearsal components of the phonological loop. Logie suggests that the scribe underpins the spatial as opposed to the visual aspects of the system, that it is involved in storing sequential information, and that it is responsible for actively maintaining information in the passive visual store cache. He suggests that spatial movement, or indeed the internal planning necessary for movement, is sufficient to interfere with the operation of the inner scribe, and hence to disrupt visual STM.

Two studies throw light on Logie's conceptualization of the sketchpad. Bruyer and Scailquin (1998) applied dual task methodology to analyse the processes underpinning visual imagery. They use the Kosslyn (1994) model to differentiate between generating an image, maintaining it, and image manipulation, utilizing a set of tasks devised for this purpose by Dror and Kosslyn (1994). They study the effect on these stages of secondary tasks that have been shown to disrupt either the phonological loop (articulatory suppression), the spatial component of the VSSP (categorizing the action of tones as presented on the left or the right) or the central executive (random generation). They also manipulated the complexity of the imagery task, to ensure that they were replicating the basic phenomena expected from prior imagery research; the relevant effects were indeed replicated. As expected, articulatory suppression had no effect on any of the three stages of imagery, nor however did any of the concurrent tasks influence image maintenance. Both image generation and image rotation were however disrupted by the spatial task, and even more impaired by random generation.

This pattern of results is consistent with Logie's model, provided one assumes that the generated images may be maintained without rehearsal.

Active maintenance by the inner scribe should have been disrupted by both the visuospatial and executive secondary tasks. The disruption to image generation and manipulation observed from these latter tasks is consistent with data from memory for chess positions and capacity to select the optimal next move, both tasks likely to depend on visuospatial imagery (Robbins *et al.* 1996).

One feature of Logie's model is that the visual cache is passive, and only the inner scribe is capable of active rehearsal and image manipulation. A recent study by Mohr and Linden (2005) focuses on the visual-spatial distinction, using tasks that allow both maintenance and manipulation to be studied under a range of task combinations. The basic paradigm involved two objects whose colour and orientation was critical either for simple recall, or for manipulation, in which case the subject was required to combine and average the colours and/or orientations, responding to a subsequent test stimulus accordingly. These tasks were combined with articulatory suppression or random letter generation. Two principle results emerged. First, random generation impaired both colour and orientation manipulation, consistent with Bruyer and Scailquin's (1998) observation that image rotation appears to demand executive resources. Mohr and Linden's second finding was more surprising; their subjects were just as good at manipulating orientation and colour simultaneously as they were when manipulating only one dimension. This would seem to suggest separate independent manipulative processes for the visual and spatial systems, rather than a single limited capacity inner scribe serving both. The evidence on this issue is still sparse, however, and does not yet fully justify abandoning Logie's concept of a single rehearsal process.

A second important feature of the model proposed by Logie is the assumption that information enters the sketchpad via long-term memory, rather than directly from sensory input. This is very different from the assumption implicit in much of the earlier work on visual and spatial STM, or the more recent work stemming from the visual attention tradition (see Chapter 4), and is linked to the proposal that the sketchpad should be regarded as a mental workspace.

5.2.2 Perceptual and representational neglect

The case for regarding the sketchpad as a workspace rather than a perceptual gateway is discussed by Della Sala and Logie (2002) in a chapter that makes extensive use of neuropsychological evidence. Of particular relevance is the phenomenon of *representational neglect*. Bisiach and Luzzatti (1978) report the case of two patients who were asked to describe from memory the cathedral square in Milan, their native city. In both cases they gave a good description, except that the left side of the square was hardly mentioned. They were then told to imagine walking across the square, turning round, and again giving a description. This time the previously neglected part of the square was on their right, and was now described in detail; the side that was previously well-described was now ignored. Baddeley and Lieberman (1980) suggested that this might represent the impairment of a system for representing information within the visuospatial sketchpad, a position that was also taken by Bisiach (1993) in a later review of the area.

An alternative explanation, of course, is to suggest that the patients were suffering from an attentional deficit, rather than a storage or representational limitation that is specific to the sketchpad. A tendency to ignore the left visual field is often found in patients with damage to the right hemisphere. However, patients have since been identified who show this form of *mnemonic* neglect with no evidence of its *perceptual* equivalent (Beschin *et al.* 1997; Coslett 1997), while others show perceptual neglect in the absence of any sign of neglect when required to describe mental representations. One patient studied by Beschin *et al.* (2000) had suffered from two consecutive strokes, one in the left parietal/occipital lobes, the other in the right thalamus. The former resulted in severe perceptual neglect for material presented in the right hemispace, but with no right representational neglect, while the right thalamic injury, in contrast, produced left representational neglect, in the absence of left perceptual neglect.

Such data clearly argue for a visuospatial working memory system that does not simply act as a perceptual gateway. Furthermore, the fact that the sketchpad can be activated by spoken words, as in the case of the Brooks matrix task, or of visual imagery-based verbal mnemonics, clearly makes a similar point, since both depend on the use of long-term knowledge to convert the auditorily presented words into a visuospatial code.

I am, however, less comfortable with Logie's suggestion that all information passes through LTM before reaching the sketchpad. First of all, it seems to imply a strict serial flow of information, although unconventionally from LTM to STM. A fixed serial processing in either direction seems simplistic. It would appear to imply the same status for a meaningless shape seen on an open field and a complex meaningful image created in response to a verbal description. Of course, the shape is not processed by a totally naive system, but the evidence for the importance of LTM in this context is far from clear. My own preference remains that of assuming that visuospatial information may be encoded in the sketchpad either through perception, from LTM, or via a combination of both. Thus, while I fully accept the claim that the sketchpad is, or at least forms part of a mental workspace, I can see no advantage in proposing that access must inevitably be through long-term memory.

5.3 **Visual imagery**

Virtually all the work described so far has involved memory for visuospatial material. In terms of publications, however, it is probably the case that far more work has been done on the study of visual imagery, much of it concentrating on the issue of whether or not imagery can be regarded as closely analogous to perception. As I regard this work as related to working memory, I will describe it, albeit briefly. A more detailed historical overview is given by Richardson (1999).

5.3.1 **Mental rotation**

Much of the research on imagery was initially stimulated by the classic demonstration by Shepard and Metzler (1971) who required subjects to judge whether two representations of three-dimensional objects were identical or whether one was the mirror image of another. The two were presented in different relative orientations. Response time proved to be a linear function of the difference in orientation between the two, just as if the subjects were mentally rotating one of the objects until it lined up with the other, and then making the judgement. Similar results were obtained from familiar letter stimuli (Shepard and Cooper 1982) and from a task that involved mentally folding a two-dimensional pattern so as to create a three dimensional object (Shepard and Feng 1972). Shepard noted the close analogy with actually performing the acts, referring to it as 'mental rotation', observing that it appeared to resemble a continuous analogue process, rather than a series of discrete steps. He did not, however, relate his findings to the experience of conscious awareness.

5.3.2 **Scanning the mental image**

A similarly agnostic view on conscious awareness was taken by Kosslyn (1978; 1980) who suggested that subjects are able to scan visual images in a way that closely resembles overtly scanning a visual scene. For example, when the subject was given a picture of a dog which was then removed, and asked questions about it, it took longer if a question about the nose was followed by a question about the tail, than it would to respond to a question about a closer feature to the nose, such as the dog's ears, just as if attention had further to move to reach the tail. In another study, subjects were taught the geography of an imaginary island, and then required to answer questions about its various locations. Once again, time to answer was a function of distance from one location to the next (Kosslyn 1980). Kosslyn describes many ways in which he found such 'internal scanning' to exactly resemble its external form, interpreting his results through a highly complex model. This involved five separate 'productions', each of which involved transforming input to produce a new data structure. Each of the five was capable of 'alteration transformations' which changed the basic data structure, which was then made available to a comparison process. The model was computationally simulated, and used to give an account of a wide range of results (Kosslyn and Shwartz 1977).

Kosslyn's methods have, however, been strongly criticized. In particular, it was suggested that his subjects were simply using their knowledge of perception to simulate perception using a strategy which may or may not be relevant to the processes actually underlying their judgements. Intons-Peterson (1996) showed that the speed of 'visual scanning' varied depending on semantically relevant but non-visual factors such as whether the subject was imagining herself carrying a weight or not. A later study showed that subjects were influenced by non-visual expectations, even when such expectations were false (Jeannerod et al. 1994). Equally problematic for Kosslyn's interpretation was a study by Hinton and Parsons (1988), who asked their subjects to imagine a wire cube sitting on a shelf in front of them. They were then asked to take hold of the nearest lower right-hand corner, and the furthest left-hand corner, and then orient the cube such that their left hand was immediately above their right. The task then was to describe the location of the remaining corners. Almost everyone reports that they lay upon a horizontal line, like a cubic equator. In fact, they form a crown shape. Hinton and Parsons suggest that rather than actually manipulating the representation as Shepard or Kosslyn might suggest, subjects attempt to simulate it. When the problem is complex, they simply fail.

5.3.3 Kosslyn's proto-model

Kosslyn (1994) has since switched his attention away from his original image scanning procedure, concentrating instead on a detailed analysis of the neuro-biology of perception, using this to drive what he describes as 'a proto-model' for both perception and imagery. The model has some 15 components, but as in the case of his first model, imagery is assumed to depend upon an attentional window operating on a visual buffer. This is assumed to be located in the primary visual cortex, a conclusion that initially appeared to be well supported by neuroimaging data (Kosslyn et al. 1993). However, while some subsequent studies support this view (Kosslyn et al. 1999), others reject it (e.g. Cohen et al. 1996; Mellet et al. 1995).

Such disagreements about localization are readily explicable if one accepts that visuospatial imagery has at least two separate components with separate anatomical locations. Existing neuropsychological evidence suggests that the visual component is most likely to be located primarily in the occipital lobes, and the spatial in the parietal lobes, with executive control likely to depend upon frontal areas (Smith and Jonides 1997; 1999). This pattern of activation has been shown on a number of occasions for visual working memory (see Chapter 12).

Further evidence for such a distinction comes from the neuropsychological literature, with some patients showing an impaired capacity to perform spatial tasks, with visual imagery preserved, while others show the opposite pattern. Luzzatti *et al.* (1998) describe E.P., a patient with right temporal and hippocampal damage who performs badly on spatial tasks such as mental rotation, or the Brooks matrix or Corsi block tasks, but is able to perform tasks that require visual rather than spatial imagery, for example retrieving an image from long-term memory in order to describe the ears of a dachshund, the colour of a banana, or the shape of the state of California. Other patients with a similar pattern of impaired spatial and preserved visual imagery are described by Hanley and Davies (1995) and by Carlesimo *et al.* (2001).

Wilson *et al.* (1999) report the case of a sculptress (L.E.) who showed the opposite pattern. She demonstrated good spatial processing and motor activity, performing within the normal range on the Corsi blocks test and having no difficulty finding her way along the complex route involved in driving to and from the neuropsychological laboratory. However, she appeared to have lost her capacity to form visual images. She performed poorly on pattern span, and although she had been a very good sculptress in a realistic style, reported that she could not remember what any of her work looked like. Her current style had become very abstract, and her capacity to draw realistically from memory was almost nonexistent. Farah *et al.* (1988) describe a similar case of a patient (L.H.) with preserved spatial processing, good performance on mental rotation, mental scanning and memory for locations, while showing impaired memory for the colours, sizes and shapes of remembered objects.

5.3.4 Working memory and the experience of imagery

Although not explicitly stated, I have always thought of our experiments using the Brooks task as tapping imagery as phenomenologically experienced. However, attempts to study the phenomenology of imagery have in the past proved surprisingly frustrating. There is no doubt that some people report having quasi-visual experiences when remembering a scene. Galton (1880) requested a range of eminent Victorian gentlemen to report on their recollected breakfast tables, finding that people differ dramatically in how vivid they think their imagery is, from a vividness that resembles perceptual experience to a denial of any quasi-visual experience. There is a long tradition of working with subjective estimates of imagery, much of it using one or other questionnaires such as that of Betts (1909). However, there is little evidence that such measures predict actual behaviour. DiVesta *et al.* (1971) tested a large sample of participants on subjective measurements of imagery and on a wide range of memory tasks. The only measure that correlated with rated strength of imagery was social desirability, a measure of the extent to which the subject likes to please. Later studies have sometimes found associations between self-ratings and visual memory, but these are low, and tend to be negative (Heuer *et al.* 1986; Reisberg *et al.* 1986).

My own involvement in exploring the phenomenological aspects of working memory stemmed from an invitation to contribute to a book on auditory imagery (Baddeley and Logie 1992). I began to realize how weakly supported was my implicit assumption that imagery represented activation within the relevant working memory slave systems. Jackie Andrade and I decided to tackle the question directly (Baddeley and Andrade 2000).

5.3.5 What makes an image vivid?

Our basic hypothesis was very simple, namely that auditory imagery represents activation within the phonological loop, and visual imagery the equivalent in the sketchpad. We assumed that articulatory and spatial suppression would differentially influence the two. We assumed in addition, that both types of imagery would depend partially on the central executive. However, by always combining visual and spatial imagery, we hoped to use the *interaction* between mode of image and mode of disruption as an indication of the specific contribution of the two subsystems, over and above any general attentional effect resulting from the requirement to combine the imagery and concurrent tasks. Hence, if articulatory suppression reduces the vividness of auditory imaging more than visual, and if the opposite is the case for visual imagery, then our results can not be readily interpreted in terms of a single system such as the central executive.

We had one further problem: how to measure vividness. We argued that the problem with earlier work on individual differences was that the questionnaires that were used implicitly required subjects to compare their own experience with that of others. We proposed to use a within-subjects design, in which subjects judged the vividness of their images under a series of different conditions, hence implicitly using perceived vividness in the control condition as a personal baseline. We hoped in this way to produce a more sensitive measure.

Our method, therefore, involved inducing an image, either by visual or auditory perception, or based on the subjects' long-term knowledge. They were to hold the image for ten seconds during which time they were to evaluate its vividness and then respond on the five-point scale, ranging from 1 (no image at all) to 5 (as vivid as perception).

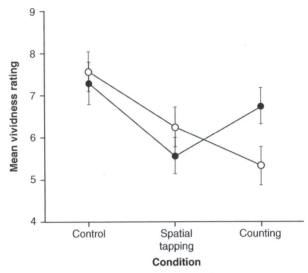

Fig. 5.1 Influence of visuospatial and verbal secondary tasks on the rated vividness of images for recently presented arrays of shapes and patterns of tones. Open circles represent auditory stimuli, closed circles represent visual stimuli. Data from Baddeley and Andrade (2000).

Our initial studies involved presenting either an array of standard shapes, circles, squares, hearts, etc., or a sequence of tones. During the ten second interval, the subject was either left free, or required to perform an intervening articulatory suppression or spatial tapping task. Figure 5.1 shows the method and results of our initial study, from which a number of points emerged. First, all our subjects appeared to find the task a natural one, and no-one in this or later studies declined to take part on the grounds that they had no visual imagery. Secondly, both tasks caused a decrement on both types of imagery, suggesting a general dual task effect which we assumed was attributable to the role of the central executive. Most crucially, however, we obtained a clear interaction, with articulatory suppression leading subjects to rate their auditory images as less vivid, while spatial tapping reduced the subjective vividness of visual images.

5.3.6 The role of long-term memory

In a series of further studies, we verbally cued subjects to form images from LTM, for example, an auditory image of someone talking on the telephone or walking on gravel, or a visual image of some local scene such as Kings College Chapel or Cambridge Market. Under these circumstances we continued to get a sizeable overall secondary task deficit, suggesting the continued importance of the central executive, together with a significant interaction, although the magnitude of the interaction was much weaker. Over a series of experiments, we detected the influence of a number of variables on rated overall vividness of verbally cued images. Hence, moving images were less vivid than static, and bizarre images, such as a swan shopping, were rated less vivid than more normal scenes such as a woman shopping. This does not seem to have resulted from subjects simply obliging by providing the popularly expected response, since naive subjects *predict* that bizarre images will be more vivid, but actually rated them in our study as less vivid than more conventional episodes.

These verbally generated images were presumably based on retrieving information from LTM. They did not fit into our initial hypothesis, which would have continued to predict a strong interaction between secondary task and image mode. Instead, we obtained large effects of LTM variables such as complexity and bizarreness that were not predicted. We suggested that our results might be interpreted as follows. We began by rejecting the idea that was implicit in our initial hypothesis, that an image is like a picture, with a vivid image being a rich and detailed picture, maintained by the sketchpad or loop. We proposed instead that an image represents quasi-sensory information retrieved from either the relevant subsystem of working memory or from LTM. Hence, when I myself say that I have a vivid image of Cambridge market, I mean that I can imagine a particular flower stall, the man who habitually ran it, and produce an internally convincing array of the sorts of flowers that might be displayed. It is almost certainly not an accurate record of one of the many experiences of this scene, but rather is something built up from my personal semantic memory, a generic representation resulting from many different encounters with the stall and with flowers. Degree of vividness, then, on this view would reflect the amount of potentially available quasi-sensory detail that can be retrieved from either working memory or LTM.

Evidence for this interpretation came from our final study in which we presented our subjects with coloured pictures of British birds, providing the name of the bird and some basic facts. We subsequently cued the bird's name, asking the subject to form an image and judge its vividness. We had already determined the self-rated knowledge of birds in our subject group, which fortunately fell into two approximately equal subgroups, those with at least moderate knowledge and those with rather little. We found that knowledge of birds was closely associated with rated vividness of the image of the picture that had been shown. This could, of course, simply reflect the way in which people habitually respond to questionnaires; people who are cautious in rating their knowledge of birds may also be cautious about rating the vividness of their images. Fortunately we were able to rule this out through a second study using the same subjects. We reverted to our earlier procedure of presenting a novel array of circles, squares and triangles, immediately followed by a judgement of the vividness of the recollection. On this occasion, the array was presented either briefly, or for a longer exposure. We predicted that a longer exposure would allow better encoding of the novel pattern, resulting in a more durable trace, more quasi-sensory information, and a higher level of perceived vividness. There was a clear difference in subsequent vividness ratings, with the longer exposure leading to more vivid images. Furthermore, we found no correlation between average level of rated vividness across the two experiments, ruling out the suggested interpretation in terms of differences among subjects in the degree of caution they apply to the task of rating their subjective experience, and supporting our interpretations of the previous experiment in terms of degree of knowledge.

5.3.7 Implications for the working memory model

How did our results leave the working memory interpretation of imagery? In some ways it was very encouraging. We had shown that it is possible to obtain coherent and consistent data using self-ratings of vividness. Furthermore, we consistently found our predicted interaction. However, the magnitude of this effect was really very small in cases where imagery depended on information retrieved from LTM, suggesting our revised interpretation. Most significantly, however, we were left with the question of how subjects were maintaining the images while they judged their vividness? Clearly not in the slave systems, since the modality-dependent effects were far too small. Could it be in the central executive? However, by this stage we had abandoned the assumption that the executive had the capacity to store information, proposing that it functioned simply as an attentional control system (Baddeley and Logie 1999). This left us in the position of either assuming that this all happened in LTM, or postulating a fourth working memory system. I shall return to this issue in Chapter 8 in which a fourth working memory component, the episodic buffer, is proposed and discussed.

5.4 Conclusions

So where does this leave the concept of a visuospatial sketch pad? Is it a form of attentionally enhanced perception, as the previous chapter might suggest? Or perhaps a post-LTM workspace, as suggested by Della Sala and Logie (2002). These are not, of course, mutually exclusive, but differ in emphasis, with investigators from the visual attention field stressing attentional and encoding factors and those from a working memory tradition placing more emphasis on manipulation and executive processes. It seems likely that these approaches will soon begin to interact and coalesce increasingly drawing on evidence from neuroimaging (see Chapter 10), and on studies based on single-unit recording in animals (Goldman-Rakic 1996). Links with the classic lines of research on visual imagery are less straightforward, for a number of reasons. First because this area is itself fragmented. Much of the most influential work such as that of Shepard and of Kosslyn has not been concerned with memory, and has explicitly avoided any direct link with phenomenological experience, both features of the approach associated with the working memory model. The VSSP approach to visual imagery has also drawn heavily on neuropsychological single-case studies and unlike much of the mainstream experimental work, has been strongly committed to issues of practical applications, whether clinical, ergonomic or educational (Andrade *et al.* 1997; Logie 1995; Della Sala and Logie 2002).

In summary, I assume that the sketchpad is a subsystem that has evolved to provide a way of integrating visuospatial information from multiple sources, visual, tactile and kinaesthetic, as well as from both episodic and semantic LTM. As such I assume access from both perception and LTM. Readers of Chapter 8 will note similarities between this view and the characteristics attributed to the proposed episodic buffer. A major theoretical and empirical challenge for the WM model is to explore this hypothetical sketchpad-episodic buffer interface. There does seem to be a system that specifically deals with integrating visuospatial information. Does this then feed into a higher level integrative system, and if so is this part of a more extended hierarchy? We return to this issue in Chapter 8. Finally as Chapter 10 will illustrate, the rapid development of neuroimaging provides a potentially powerful tool that may help integration of diverse approaches to visuospatial working memory.

Chapter 6

Recency, retrieval and the constant ratio rule

During the 1960s, the term STM was applied to any paradigm that involved presenting material and then testing it from zero to 30 seconds later. This was a very active research area, with investigators coming from two rather distinct traditions. One, associative interference theory, was committed to a unitary concept of memory which was to be studied by carefully mapping the variables that controlled learning and forgetting, typically then going on to give an account in terms of a limited range of stimulus-response associationist principles. The term verbal learning was often applied to this approach, with its principal protagonists being Arthur Melton (1963) and Leo Postman and Benton Underwood (Postman and Underwood, 1973).

The second approach, in contrast, assumed separate long- and short-term memory systems. It was much more willing to speculate on possible mechanisms, in particular using the computer as a metaphor, and taking its terminology from information processing. It formed an important component of the newly developing cognitive psychology, and was represented by such figures as Broadbent (1958) and Conrad (1967), in the UK, and Miller (1956), Neisser (1967) and Posner (1967) and in the US.

6.1 Recency in free recall

6.1.1 Recency as short-term memory

One of the principal sources used as evidence of a distinction between STM and LTM was the recency effect in free recall, the tendency for the last few items presented to be well recalled. The effect is abolished by a filled delay of a few seconds (Glanzer and Cunitz 1966), regardless of whether the material filling the delay is or is not similar to items to be remembered. Recency is found in densely amnesic patients, despite their impaired LTM (Baddeley and Warrington 1970), but is absent or greatly reduced in patients with impaired STM (Shallice and Warrington 1970). Furthermore, the recency effect is insensitive to a wide range of variable such as rate of presentation, word concreteness, attentional distraction and aging that have a marked effect on the recall of earlier items in the free recall list (Glanzer 1972). Recency thus appeared to represent one of the strongest sources of evidence for the STM-LTM distinction.

6.1.2 Long-term recency

However, it gradually became clear that the recency effect extends beyond STM. Bjork and Whitten (1974) and Tzeng (1973) showed a clear recency effect in recall after a filled delay, provided the items to be recalled were themselves each separated by a filled delay. Baddeley and Hitch (1977) found recency extending over several weeks in the recall of rugby games. Evidence for a distinction between the processes involved in recency in verbal free recall and verbal memory span was provided by the observation by Baddeley and Hitch (1974) that recency was unaffected by a concurrent digit span recall task. Had they depended on the same limited-capacity short-term store, as assumed for example by the Atkinson and Shiffrin (1968) model, the concurrent digits should have eliminated recency. It is now generally agreed (e.g. Baddeley 1998b; Nairne 2002) that the recency effect is a robust phenomenon of considerable generality, and that it is not limited to STM.

The recency effect can be described briefly and precisely. Over a very wide range of situations extending from seconds to years, the probability of recalling a given item is a constant function of two variables, the temporal distance between that item and its nearest competitor (Δt) divided by the interval between item presentation and test (t). This is termed the discrimination ratio, and has been demonstrated to hold constant under a very wide range of circumstances. With immediate recall, this favours the more recent items, an advantage that is eroded as recall is delayed.

6.1.3 Trace decay or interference?

The recency effect is shown most clearly in the classic free recall paradigm in which subjects attempt to recall a list, typically of 15-20 words in any order they choose. The effect is not, however, limited to free recall. Consider, for example, the Peterson and Peterson (1959) short-term forgetting paradigm, whereby subjects attempt to recall a consonant trigram after a filled delay ranging from 3 to 18 seconds. Recall declines rapidly as a function of delay. The Petersons ruled out an interpretation in terms of stimulus-response associative interference on the grounds that the intervening task, counting, was quite dissimilar to the letter-based memory task; studies of LTM have shown similarity to be essential for interference to occur (McGeoch and Irion 1952). While accepting the importance of similarity in LTM, the Petersons suggested that their results reflected the spontaneous decay of a separate *short-term* memory trace. This conclusion proved premature. As Keppel and Underwood (1962) elegantly demonstrated, the degree of forgetting of the very first letter sequence tested is minimal. The forgetting function develops rapidly over the subsequent sequences to reach a plateau within four or five tests. They suggested that such forgetting was therefore the result of proactive interference, whereby earlier items interfere with the retention of later material, just as occurs in LTM (Underwood 1957).

Subsequent research reinforced the conclusion that interference between items was a crucial variable, although Baddeley and Scott (1971) provided evidence that even when testing is limited to a single item, significant though modest forgetting occurs, but is complete within about 5 seconds. It has been suggested that forgetting might be due to mutual interference between items within the sequence (Nairne 2002). This interpretation would predict that rate of forgetting would increase with the number of items retained. Baddeley and Scott found no evidence for such a relationship.

However, although a small contribution from trace decay cannot be ruled out, it is clear that the bulk of the forgetting seen in the Brown-Peterson paradigm is due to some form of interference, although not necessarily one that conforms to the classic SR associationist assumptions (see Baddeley 1976, pp. 124–131 for a further discussion). An elegant paper by Turvey *et al.* (1970) cast light on this question in a study that moved away from the standard design whereby each subject is tested for retention over a range of delay intervals, with the order in which the different intervals were tested being randomized. Instead, Turvey *et al.* limited each of several groups to a single delay. For example, one group always recalled after 5 seconds, another after 10 seconds, another after 25 seconds. Under these conditions, somewhat surprisingly, delay did not affect amount recalled, with subjects tested after 25 seconds remembering as much as those tested after 5 seconds. However, regardless of the delay that they had previously experienced, Turvey *et al.* included one final test that involved the same delay for all groups, namely 15 seconds. Under these circumstances, large differences occurred between groups, with those subjects who had previously had a short delay showing much poorer performance than those who had previously experienced long delays.

6.2 The constant ratio rule

These results are readily explained in terms of the constant ratio hypothesis (Baddeley 1976). If the subject's problem is to discriminate between the item that has just been presented (the target item) and the immediately prior item, then subjects encountering a regular 5 second delay will have to discriminate each 5 second target item from a prior competing items that occurred 5 seconds before the target, a 5 versus 10 second ratio (i.e. 0.5). Subjects given a regular 25 second delay will need discriminate a target after 25 seconds from a competing prior item at 50 seconds, giving exacting the same 0.5 target-competitor ratio, and hence equal performance. However, when subjects switch from a 5 second to a 15 second delay will have to discriminate a 15 second target from a 20 second prior competitor, a more difficult 0.75 discrimination, while switching from a 25 to a 15 second discrimination given an easier 15:40 target to competitor ratio.

The area in which the discrimination ratio has been used most widely, however, is in free recall, in which a sequence of items is presented and the subject asked to recall as many items as possible in any order. When recall is immediate, there is clear tendency for the last few items presented to show a high level of recall, the recency effect. The effect does not depend on an explicit strategy during *learning*, as it is found to be equally prominent under incidental learning, when the subject is not aware that recall will be required (Baddeley and Hitch 1977; Pinto and Baddeley 1991).

The idea that our capacity to discriminate amongst our memories becomes less as delay increases goes back at least to the British psychologist James Sully (1892), but was put most cogently by Crowder:

> Items in a memory list presented at a constant rate pass by with the same regularity as do telegraph poles when one is on a moving train. Just as each telegraph pole in the receding distance becomes less distinctive from its neighbours, likewise each item in memory becomes less distinctive as the presentation episode recedes to the past.
>
> (Crowder 1976, p. 462).

A number of investigators have produced evidence supporting the constant ratio rule in free recall, in studies ranging from laboratory tasks that test the recall of verbal material over intervals of seconds, to memory for real-world events such as rugby games tested after delays of up to a matter of weeks (Baddeley and Hitch 1977).

Whereas the standard recency effect in immediate free recall can be obliterated by a mere five seconds of counting (Glanzer 1972), under appropriate circumstances much more robust recency effects can be found. For example, Bjork and Whitten (1974) required their subjects to remember lists of unrelated words. In order to eliminate any contribution from short-term or primary memory, they preceded and followed each word with arithmetic, with a similar arithmetically filled delay occurring between the end of the list and free recall. Despite the filled delay, they found a marked recency effect. Furthermore, having performed on several such lists, the experimenters concluded by asking the subjects to recall as many of the items as possible from any of the lists. The previously observed *within-list* recency effect disappeared in this final free recall, but there was an advantage for the most recent list, an advantage that disappeared when subjects were tested again the following day. Bjork and Whitten interpret the recency advantage observed to the use of a recency-based retrieval strategy, rather than to any difference in degree of encoding of the words within the lists. This result was reinforced by the absence of recency in a later study in which recall was replaced by recognition, a procedure that was assumed to facilitate the retrieval phase, and by controlling test order, to prevent the utilization of a recency-based strategy.

Evidence of the constant ratio rule was demonstrated over a wide range of recall intervals by Glenberg *et al.* (1980) under laboratory conditions, while Baddeley and Hitch (1977) demonstrated recency effects in the recall of opponent teams by rugby players extending over a matter of weeks, when the players were asked which teams they had played against. As the discrimination ratio hypothesis would predict, the function reflected the number of interpolated games rather than amount of elapsed time.

More direct quantitative evidence for the discrimination ratio hypothesis came from another real-world study in which Pinto and Baddeley (1991) tested the capacity of their colleagues at the Applied Psychology Unit in Cambridge to remember where they had parked their car across a two-week period. Under these conditions, a clear recency effect occurred. However, experimental subjects who had visited the Unit on only a single occasion remembered where they had parked equally well whether their visit had been two hours before (72 per cent), one week before (73 per cent) or one month before (72 per cent). There was, however, one difference between the three groups. Because there were no markings on the car park, subjects were allowed to choose just one location on the sketch map, or if uncertain, to opt for two adjacent places. In fact, very few people parked across more than one location, but the number taking the less precise option rose from 14 per cent after two hours, to 30 per cent after one week and 60 per cent after a month, suggesting that something was changing, although possibly only degree of confidence.

In a final experiment, groups of subjects came to the laboratory twice, separated by an interval of about two weeks. They were subsequently tested by being sent two envelopes, with strict instructions as to which to open first. The first envelope specifically asked them where they had parked four weeks earlier. For half the subjects (the Proactive Interference or PI group) this was their second visit, while for the other group (the Retroactive Interference or RI group) the four-week recall was their first visit. The results indicated that a second visit did decrease recall from 72 per cent observed in the previous experiment for subjects who had only made one visit, to 47 per cent in the PI group, and a significantly poorer 39 per cent in the RI group. As the discrimination ratio hypothesis would predict, having two competing events reduced overall performance. The second envelope tested memory for their other visit. The RI group, for which this had occurred two weeks before recalled correctly at a rate of 61 per cent, significantly more than the recall of the PI group whose other visit occurred six weeks before (20 per cent). Finally, plotting percentage recall for each of these conditions showed that the results followed the constant ratio rule. In conclusion, the study showed first that degree of forgetting of a *single* event showed relatively little increase over time per se, whereas when *two* events were retrieved, recall dropped from 60 per cent after two weeks to approximately 40 per cent after four, and 20 per cent after six weeks.

6.3 **Theories of the recency effect**

6.3.1 **Context and recency**

Let us provisionally agree then with Glenberg *et al.* (1980), Nairne (2002) and Brown *et al.* (Unpublished) that the constant ratio rule is a widespread phenomenon within memory. How should we explain it? Glenberg *et al.* (1980) suggest that each item is encoded against an ever-changing contextual background, which in due course serves as a recall cue. They suggest that the greater the elapsed time, the greater the degree of change, hence there will be fewer cues in common between the encoding and retrieval contexts and recall will be poorer. Unfortunately, they provide no empirical evidence in support of their context assumption. Indeed, their study itself gives evidence against it. In their first experiment, the difficulty of an arithmetic task is varied, with level of difficulty either remaining the same during both presentation and the period immediately preceding recall, or changing between presentation and pretest. This change in difficulty level, and hence of context between learning and recall, however, had no effect. It appears then that within the Glenberg model, context is not distinguishable from elapsed time. Given McGeoch's oft-quoted rejection of decay theory on the grounds that time per se can have no effect (Nairne 2002), it is understandable that Glenberg *et al.* might wish to clothe it in a more respectable guise. Others such as Nairne (2002) – who cites the McGeoch dictum with approval – and Bjork (2000) emphasize the importance of the temporal discrimination ratio, and hence implicitly of time, but do not directly address the question of how time might serve as a cue.

6.3.2 **Trace decay**

Another possible explanation is a decay hypothesis of LTM, such as that suggested by Baddeley (1976, pp. 95–99). This proposed that retrieval involved two stages, first accessing the general cluster of memory traces, and then discriminating among them. This latter process is likely to be determined by a range of factors including degree of learning and similarity between the desired trace and potential competitors. In addition, all traces would be subject to some decay which might, in the interests of peace and harmony with the shade of McGeoch, be relabelled 'general interference'. Such non-specific interference might plausibly result from the fact that the nervous system is in constant activity and change, and as such could potentially add noise to the memory trace; a longer delay leading to more noise.

Clearly such a proposal would require much more precise definition within a general interference theory framework. It would be necessary to make assumptions about such basic issues as whether a simple response competition hypothesis will work, or as seems more likely, one needs to assume some degree of unlearning, with the learning and unlearning processes reflecting temporal variables, as for example proposed by Anderson and Bjork (1994). The model would also require assumptions regarding the relative contribution of general and item-specific interference. It would in short, require a well worked out theory of forgetting, an important topic that has received less attention than it deserves in recent years, although happily there are signs that this is changing (Anderson *et al.* 2000; Rubin and Wenzel 1996).

6.3.3 Working memory and recency

What then are the implications of the discrimination ratio hypothesis, and theories of forgetting in general for the concept of working memory? The suggestion made by Nairne (2002), Ward, (2001) and Brown *et al.* (unpublished) is that the presence of common principles across different types of memory implies that there is no need to assume that the memory systems are different. However, although the presence of common principles across systems may be *necessary* for a claim of identity, it is surely not sufficient. Otherwise one might conclude from the fact that Weber's law applies to vision, sound and smell, that they comprise a single unitary system. All memory systems need to solve the problems of encoding, storage and retrieval. The fact that analogous solutions to these problems might occur across different systems is of considerable interest, but unless the systems are equivalent in all other ways, such findings do not imply a simple unity. Given the range of evidence discussed earlier, from psychological, neuropsychological and neuroimaging studies, it would surely be a highly retrograde step to return to the 1950s view of a single unitary system. But in that case, how can we explain the presence of very similar principles determining recency effects in long- and short-term memory?

Baddeley and Hitch (1974) studied the immediate free recall of lists of unrelated words, under control conditions, or concurrent with a second task, repeatedly hearing and recalling sequences of six random digits. While the concurrent memory load impaired performance on words across the earlier serial positions, assumed to reflect LTM, they had no influence on the recency effect. We concluded that recency did not depend upon the phonological loop system, which would have been fully occupied by the concurrent digit task. On the other hand, densely amnesic patients appeared to show normal recency in the immediate free recall of word lists (Baddeley and Warrington 1970), suggesting recency in free recall is not attributable in any simple way to LTM. Furthermore, Shallice and Warrington (1970) showed that recency is grossly impaired in patients with a phonological STM deficiency. Could it be that such patients are simply unable to use a recency strategy? Vallar *et al.* (1991) tested this possibility by studying the recency effect in a patient, P.V., who had a very pure deficit of phonological STM. We used two free recall tasks, one involving the standard immediate recall of a word list, known to produce a recency effect that can be eliminated by a few seconds of interpolated activity (Glanzer 1972). As expected, even without any intervening task, P.V. showed little evidence of a recency effect. The second task involved attempting to solve simple anagrams, and then unexpectedly being asked to recall the anagram solution words, a task known to result in a robust recency effect Baddeley (1963). Under these conditions, P.V. showed normal long-term recency.

How can we explain this rather complex pattern of results? Baddeley and Hitch (1977; 1993) proposed the following. When an item or situation is encoded, those representations involved in the processing will automatically be activated, resulting in the priming of that representation, making it subsequently easier to reactivate. Total available capacity of activation within a given category is limited, hence the presentation and priming of each successive item will reduce the activation level of previously primed items within the relevant category. The recency effect then results from a retrieval strategy that capitalizes on the fact that the most recently primed items will be most readily accessible. A simple analogy is to view the internal representation of each item as acting like an electric light bulb, with activation being analogous to illuminating the bulb. Once illuminated it will retain heat, which will make that bulb somewhat easier to illuminate again. Each subsequent bulb illumination will however drain some of that heat. Retrieval is seen as gradually increasing the amount of current to the relevant bank of light bulbs, causing the most recent to be illuminated first. The retrieval process of increasing current depends on the capacity to isolate the appropriate and separable bank of bulbs. It should be emphasized that the simple light bulb analogy is intended to give a flavour of a type of model. For example, given that recency effects may extend over many months, something other than a simple time-based heat analogy is clearly called for.

6.3.4 **The SIMPLE hypothesis**

One possible candidate is the SIMPLE (Scale Invariant Memory, Perception and Learning) model cited by Hulme *et al.* (2004) as a submitted paper by Brown, Neath and Chater. This is a highly ambitious general model that stresses discriminability as the main determinant of recall, emphasizing *temporal* discriminability as particularly important for serial recall (Hulme *et al.* 2004, p. 103). Time has the methodological advantage of being a dimension in which similarity can be specified objectively for the items to be recalled. However, as mentioned in Chapter 3, this model has difficulty accounting for data on temporal spacing in immediate serial verbal recall (Lewandowsky *et al.* in press; Nimmo and Lewandowsky, in press a, b).

The ubiquity of the constant ratio rule suggests that SIMPLE will probably do a better job for free recall. In so far as I can tell however, SIMPLE seems to be a rather complex model, involving an unspecified number of stimulus dimensions of variable weights, leading to a danger that it may become a means of post hoc curve fitting, rather than a fruitful conceptual tool for increasingly our knowledge. Time will tell.

Suppose, however, we return to our basic verbal model and try to apply it to the various recency phenomena: how good a job will it do? We assume that the process of priming is automatic, and unlike episodic LTM is not reduced by the imposition of an attentionally demanding secondary task, such as concurrent digit span; hence the preserved recency in the Baddeley and Hitch (1974) free recall experiment. Priming may operate at a number of different representational levels, including the phonological, hence the preservation of recency in immediate verbal free recall in amnesic patients (Baddeley and Warrington 1970), and its absence in patients with STM deficits (Shallice and Warrington 1970). As expected, therefore, P.V. fails to show a recency effect in the classic immediate free recall situation because that typically relies on a phonologically activated lexical system. Because her phonological store is impaired, this system tends not to be used. On the other hand, given that long-term semantic coding is normal, it can show normal priming and hence unimpaired long-term recency.

6.3.5 **Multiple concurrent recency effects**

This, of course, implies the possibility that one may potentially have a large number of simultaneous recency effects reflecting different aspects of long-term memory. For example, the last party you went to and the last time you went to the cinema or travelled abroad are all probably quite readily accessible, in ways that the penultimate or earlier items are not. This possibility was studied by Watkins and Peynircioglu (1983), who presented their subjects with tasks selected from clearly different conceptual domains, for example, solving riddles, performing simple actions or stating favourites from specified categories such as foods, or singers. Hence a subject might be asked about favourite foods, followed by solving riddles which in turn was followed by performance of specified actions. Subjects were then asked to recall as many items as possible from the three tasks in any order. This led to three simultaneous and apparently equivalent recency effects, for riddles, actions and favourites. It is important to note, however, that identifying sufficiently separate domains was not a straightforward task. For example, interleaving semantic categories such as animals, colours and flowers, results in a single recency effect. This contrasts with the build up and release from PI in the Peterson short-term forgetting task, where switching from animals to colours, for example, produces a complete release from the prior interference. It seems likely, therefore, that recency and the Peterson task have a somewhat different basis. We will return to this point later.

By this point, Crowder's telephone pole analogy needs to be extended, at least to include more than one railway line. Perhaps a better analogy is to suggest that the attempt to retrieve experiences involves setting up retrieval cues that will evoke appropriate instances, of trips to the theatre or journeys abroad for example. Each of these sets of cues will produce an array of potentially retrievable and discriminable events. An alternative analogy is to clusters of buildings, comprising farms, villages and towns, scattered across a plain. A task like free recall essentially involves identifying and reporting as many buildings as possible. The nearest buildings to the observer will be more readily accessed and identified. When it is necessary to attempt to identify and name a specific distant building, then success will depend first of all on identifying the appropriate cluster and secondly on separating that building from any potentially confusable neighbours. The recency effect reflects the relative accessibility as a function of competing buildings, while the constant ratio rule concerns the process of differentiating between competing targets. The Watkins and Peynircioglou (1983) result suggests that if the relevant targets are distinctly separate, they will not mutually interfere.

Needless to say, such a model requires adequate specification, including not only the decision rules, but also how time is represented, and the question of whether interference occurs as a simple result of competition between items, or involves some further inhibitory or unlearning processes (Anderson and Bjork 1994). The question of what constitutes a distinct and separable retrieval domain is also an important one that, as yet, does not appear to have been explored. Hence, while many theorists agree on the importance and generality of the constant ratio rule, this represents simply the first step towards what needs to be a much more elaborated theory.

6.3.6 **Recency and rehearsal**

Before concluding, we should consider an ambitious attempt by Ward (2001) to base an entire theory of working memory on recency. He describes a series of experiments using the technique devised by Rundus (1971) to study the role of rote verbal rehearsal in free recall. Subjects are presented with a list of unrelated words, and required to rehearse them aloud during presentation, after which free recall is required. Performance is then plotted as a function of number of overt rehearsals for each given item, and their recency. A combination of these measures gives a good account of both primacy and recency effects (Tam and Ward 2000). Ward proposes a unitary General Episodic Memory model (GEM), which he argues provides a good general account of both long- and short-term memory data.

I agree that rehearsal often plays an important role in the primacy effect, but am far from convinced of the importance of rehearsal in the wide range of recency effects observed in free recall. The account provided by Ward (2001) rests on the correlation he observes between number of rehearsals and recall probability. This could reflect either an influence of rehearsal on subsequent recall, as he suggests or a tendency for items to be selected for rehearsal that are, for whatever reason, more readily retrievable. The potential confounding of retrievability and rehearsal frequency makes such correlations difficult to interpret unequivocally. The fact that the Rundus method adopted by Ward forces a rote rehearsal strategy on the subject also raises problems as to the generality of such results, given that the preferred strategy for most subjects in free recall is to rely on semantic rather than phonological coding (Kintsch and Bushke 1969; Tulving 1962).

Finally, an interpretation in terms of rehearsal has difficulty in accounting for the fact that recency effects are prominent under incidental learning conditions, where the subject has no cause to rehearse. For example Baddeley and Hitch (1977) required their subjects to categorize names as belonging to boys, girls, or both. One group was aware of the fact that they would subsequently have to recall the names, while a second was not. Both showed equivalent recency. Similarly, in the case of our study of long-term recency in remembering parking locations (Pinto and Baddeley 1991), there is no reason to assume that subjects who had attended the Applied Psychology Unit for testing would need to continue to rehearse the place in which they had parked days or weeks before.

Hence, although Ward (2001) and I agree on the importance of the recency effect, and on the role of discrimination in retrieval, we disagree on the value of the Rundus overt rehearsal technique, and the generality of conclusions based on simple measures of rote rehearsal.

6.4 **The evolutionary function of recency**

Given the breadth of application of the constant ratio rule, it is obviously of theoretical significance, but is it of any practical importance? I suggest that it is, for two related reasons. First of all, the statistics of events within the world is not random but clustered. Having encountered one sheep, we are more likely to encounter other sheep rather than zebras or penguins, while references to football in the newspapers tend to cluster together as do references to holidays or a prominent figure such as the Pope. It therefore makes sense to have a system that is biased towards expecting something that has happened recently, namely a system that is primed. Such priming is, however, very probably entirely passive, whereas the recency effect is based on an active strategy that may be used or avoided. Why might such a strategy be useful, other than for subjects in psychological experiments?

In modern life, as we saw earlier, remembering where you parked your car appears to benefit from recency, as does remembering your hotel room when travelling; it is not much help when returning to your room to know that over the last week you have stayed in rooms 236, 119, 501 and 402, unless it is clear which one was last. More fundamentally, when you wake up next morning in the hotel room in a city you have never visited before, how do you know where you are? In all cases I suggest that one uses a recency strategy, probably beginning by recalling the previous evening and using that to construct the pattern of your activities over the past few days. That in turn can be fitted into a nested set of frameworks, extending at a whole series of levels, both specific, such as the reason for your journey, and more general, your career, family and indeed whole life history.

We also appear to carry with us expectations as to what is likely to happen next. In the hotel example, the anticipated activities of getting up, finding breakfast, locating a meeting and ensuring that you subsequently catch your plane, all reflect planning that is almost certainly guided in part by long-term recency-based retrieval. It is as if we carry around a nested set of frameworks. All are based on past experience, some episodic such as where we were last night, and some semantic, such as our knowledge of how hotels function. If we have normal semantic and episodic memory, then we can use these to guide our immediate actions, and to plan for the future. This process almost certainly involves working memory as well as LTM, and reflects a capacity that is typically impaired in dysexecutive patients with frontal lobe damage (see Chapters 7 and 8).

Preserved working memory is, however, not sufficient. Amnesic patients with good working memory capacity, but who lack adequate episodic memory, are unable to build up an ongoing structure that represents their lives.

A densely amnesic relative of mine, for example, who lived in the same room in the same residential home for well over a year, still asked where she was on returning to her room, and, as is characteristic of amnesic patients, had no idea what she would be doing in even a few minutes time. Tulving (2002) suggests that episodic memory provides the means of achieving 'mental time travel', allowing us to move back into the past and recollect earlier experiences, and to use this to formulate plans and expectations for the future. I suggest that the recency effect is what allows us to orient ourselves in time and space, and as such provides the rock on which our location in the present and projection into the future can be founded. Without the recency mechanism, I suggest that we would have great difficulty knowing where we are in time, and once outside our normal routine, in place. If we do not know where we are now, we have little chance of knowing where we will be in the future, and hence will be doomed to live in the permanent present, as tragically illustrated by the case of Clive Wearing, a very talented musician who became profoundly amnesic following a brain infection which left him unable to remember for more than a few seconds, locked in the present with little memory of the past and no capacity to anticipate the future (Wilson *et al.*).

In conclusion, there is no doubt that the recency effect is one of the most stable and reliable phenomena within the study of human memory. There is also widespread agreement that it broadly follows the constant ratio rule. There is, however, much less agreement about its interpretation, with some theorists such as Nairne (2002) regarding it as evidence for a unitary memory system. Others, including myself, see it as a mechanism that can operate across a range of different memory stores, reflecting one of a range of general principles, but not itself implying a unitary system. Indeed, I would regard the recency effect as typically involving two types of memory; an *implicit* priming effect and an *explicit* retrieval strategy. Such priming may occur in any of a range of memory systems, from a very brief quasi-sensory echoic store (Glucksberg and Cowan 1970) to both episodic (Pinto and Baddeley 1991) and semantic memory (Watkins and Peynircioglu 1983). Selection and operation of the strategy will depend on the central executive, the component of working memory that will be considered next.

Chapter 7

Fractionating the central executive

There is no doubt that the component we labelled the central executive is the most important subsystem of the three-component working memory model, and the one that presents the most difficult challenge. My first attempt to analyse the executive (Baddeley 1986), comprised a rather tentative single chapter. My current attempt impinges upon at least half of the present book. It would be nice to be able to claim that this is because we now understand how the central executive functions. Sadly, but not surprisingly, this is not the case. However, there have been considerable strides made in a range of areas pertinent to an understanding of the central executive. Covering even a fraction of this work, however, would represent a major task extending well beyond my own relatively modest contribution to the topic. Of particular relevance to the concept of a limited capacity central executive is Cowan's (2005) assumption of a limited-capacity focus of attention capable of holding about four chunks of information, a view which we both regard as entirely compatible with the multicomponent model of working memory. Although Cowan and I are fundamentally in broad agreement, we differ in emphasis. Perhaps for historical reasons, I have tended to emphasize short-term storage, and to be influenced by neuropsychological evidence, while Cowan stresses the role of the focus of attention, and developmental approaches. His excellent book (Cowan 2005) is recommended as providing a much fuller account of the role of attentional capacity in working memory than that provided here. The work of Shallice (Shallice 2002; Shallice and Burgess 1996) is also broadly compatible, although it attempts a much more detailed fractionation than my own, and relies more heavily on neuropsychological, neuroimaging and computational approaches. Finally, there is a large and growing neurobiological literature on executive control, well represented by Stuss and Knight's (2002) *Principles of frontal lobe function*.

The next three chapters, however, have the much more modest aim of describing my own attempts to put more flesh on the concept of a central executive. They are based on an approach (Baddeley 1996), which identified four candidates as important executive component processes, namely the capacity to focus attention, to divide attention, to switch attention and to provide a link between working memory and long-term memory. The first three of these will be covered in the present chapter and the fourth in Chapters 8 and 9. Before beginning this survey, I will summarize some of the background evidence for the basic assumption of a central executive.

I have previously pleaded guilty to creating an executive that is virtually a homunculus, a little man in the head who takes all the important but difficult decisions. My justification for this is the same as that proposed by Attneave (1960). Provided we attempt to describe the functions performed by our homunculus, we can then set out on a policy of divide and rule, attempting systematically to give a plausible account of how each of these processes might be performed. This strategy of making the homunculus increasingly redundant will, one hopes, end by allowing us to dispense with him altogether. We are certainly not in a position to do that at present. However, I think it is becoming increasingly clear just how this might potentially be achieved. The chapters that follow, therefore, could be seen as providing tentative steps towards a pension plan for the homunculus.

7.1 The central executive as rag-bag

For at least the first decade after the Baddeley and Hitch (1974) paper, we concentrated principally on the phonological and visuospatial subsystems, simply because they appeared to offer much more tractable challenges than did the executive. Although not a particularly bold strategy, I would claim that it worked reasonably well over the short term. However, as acknowledged in Baddeley (1986), repeated referrals of problems to the executive, without even speculation as to how they might be dealt with, was becoming an embarrassment. This led me to adopt of the Norman and Shallice (1986) supervisory attentional system (SAS) model as a potential framework for the executive. However, unless this framework is used constructively within the WM model, it can still be argued that any appeal to the central executive concept does little more than indicate that the phenomenon in question probably depends upon some form of relatively flexible attentionally limited control system. One problem with the absence of a clearly formulated model of the executive is the danger that others will invent such a structure, labelling it the central executive, and then going on to argue against its plausibility. The assumed monolithic status of the executive is a popular example, despite the claim that 'It seems unlikely that the central executive will prove to be a simple unitary system.' (Baddeley 1986, p. 253). Kimberg *et al.* declare that 'by definition the central executive is unitary' (Kimberg *et al.* 1997, p. 187), presumably on the grounds that executive is a singular noun. A similar line of reasoning would lead one to conclude that the term government being singular by definition implies a dictatorship.

A similar line to that of Kimberg was taken by Parkin (1998) and is refuted by Baddeley (1998). I assume that the central executive can in common with the other components of working memory, be fractionated into subcomponents. However, if the multicomponent model is to continue to develop, it is essential that the nature and function of the central executive be addressed.

7.2 Executive processes and the frontal lobes

In recent years, much of the research carried out on executive function has related it to its putative anatomical locus within the frontal lobes. Data from patients with frontal lobe damage played a crucial role in the development of the SAS model (Shallice 1988), and in its adoption as part of the working memory model (Baddeley 1986). The assumption that executive processes depend critically upon frontal lobe function has since received overwhelming support (for review, see Roberts *et al.* 1998; Kane and Engle 2002; Stuss and Knight 2002).

7.2.1 The dysexecutive syndrome

Single case studies of patients with bilateral frontal lobe damage provide some of the strongest evidence. Consider R.J., for example (Baddeley and Wilson 1988), who suffered substantial bilateral frontal damage after driving into the back of a horse van. After being unconscious for several days, he gradually recovered. R.J. was a civil engineer with an estimated premorbid IQ of 120. His language was well preserved, as was his visual and verbal memory span. He had good social skills and an excellent sense of humour. His LTM was impaired, and subject to extensive confabulation. He gave an elaborate and totally false recollection of his accident, and in a test of autobiographical memory, produced a number of bizarre 'recollections'. For example, he described writing to an aunt about the death of his brother Robin. When further questioned, he accepted that his brother Robin continued to visit him, but suggested that this was a later child who had also been called Robin. Although his confabulations changed from day to day, he gave every evidence of believing them strongly. For example, one weekend at home, he turned to his wife in bed and asked why she kept telling people they were married. When she protested that they were and had several children, he pointed out that that did not necessarily mean they were married. On being shown the wedding photographs, he conceded that the bridegroom did look like him, but denied that it actually was him. This was not a persistent delusion, but a single episode of confabulation, which he later denied.

One feature of frontal lobe patients is a tendency to perseverate. In giving an account of the accident in which he had sustained his head injury, R.J. included a lengthy conversation with a lorry driver with whom he had collided, in which each politely accepted responsibility.

R.J.: 'I am afraid it was my fault.'
Lorry driver: 'No, I was certainly to blame.'
R.J.: 'Yes but it really was me.'
Lorry driver: 'No. I insist that it was me to blame.'
R.J.: 'But I definitely made a mistake' etc.

After about ten of these, he eventually broke out of the loop and continued the narrative. Paradoxically, as well as tending to perseverate, such patients are readily distractible, showing evidence of what is sometimes termed utilization behaviour, whereby seeing an object is enough to encourage them to utilize it, regardless of how socially appropriate it might be, for example, picking up and using a comb that happens to be lying on the desk, or leaning over and drinking the examiner's cup of tea (see also Chapter 17).

The Norman and Shallice model captured this pattern of deficits by assuming that action is controlled at two levels. Much of our behaviour is dependent on overlearned existing schemata, which are largely under stimulus control. Novel behaviour or actions in emergency are dependent on a second process, the supervisory attentional system (SAS) which is normally capable of overruling any habitual action which appears to be leading to undesirable behaviour. The SAS is also capable of searching for possible solutions under circumstances where there is no available habitual response. We will return to this model and its subsequent extension later in the chapter. Before doing so, however, it is perhaps worth briefly describing some of the many alternative formulations that have been presented, usually based on speculation about the structure and function of the frontal lobes.

7.2.2 Neuroanatomical approaches

One influential account of executive control in working memory is presented by Goldman-Rakic (1988), and based on experiments using single cell recording to study working memory in awake monkeys (Fuster and Bauer 1974; Funahashi *et al.* 1989). She identified certain cells in the frontal lobes which are active only when the monkey is successfully remembering a cued location prior to a delayed response. She found other cells that code other types of sensory information, for example, shape versus location, proposing a model of working memory as a system for the online processing of information or behaviour in the service of a wide range of cognitive functions. She proposes that working memory is iteratively represented across a number of autonomous subdivisions, each with its own executive control system. This allows the system to integrate attentional, memorial, motor and very possibly affective dimensions of behaviour.

If extended to humans this model would appear to propose that the articulatory loop, for example, has its own central executive. This simply does not seem to fit either the neuropsychological data nor that based on normal function, both of which suggest a clear separation between phonological and executive processes, although of course the two do interact. I suspect the difference in emphasis between Goldman-Rakic's proposal and my own stems from the level of analysis, single cell recording versus complex behaviour analysed at a system level.

In general, both neuropsychological and neuroimaging evidence appears to support an organization based on function rather than modality (Tulving *et al.* 1994; Owen 1997; Smith and Jonides 1997). The separation of modality of presentation from the nature of the processing is particularly clearly illustrated in the case of language processing, where for example visually presented letters tend to be encoded phonologically (Conrad 1964) and where spoken sequences may be encoded visuospatially (Brooks 1967; Baddeley and Lieberman 1980). Goldman-Rakic's single unit recording studies were, of course, carried out on monkeys whose phonological loop, if it exists, is unlikely to play a major role in their memory performance.

There is no doubt however that Goldman-Rakic's work has had a major positive influence on the study of working memory, linking elegant neuro-physiolgical studies on monkeys with concepts and techniques from human cognitive psychology and neurospsychology. Considerable progress is being made in understanding the functions of the frontal lobes based on animal studies, neuropsychological research and work using neuroimaging techniques (see Roberts, Robbins and Weiskrantz [1998] for some excellent examples of such progress).

7.2.3 Computational modelling of executive control

One approach is to continue to refine and develop earlier models by combining neuropsychological data and computational modelling. A good example of this is the continued development of the Norman and Shallice (1983) model which was computationally simulated by Cooper, Shallice and Farringdon (1995). They showed that adding 'noise' to the system simulates the effect of damage to the frontal lobes producing behaviour analogous to the neuropsychological syndromes of action disorganization and utilization behaviour found in patients with frontal lobe damage (L'Hermite, 1983). Shallice (2002) attempts to specify in greater detail the way in which the supervisory component might operate, providing a complex model involving three principal stages involving four temporally distinct phases and some eight different processes. At the core of the system is the generation and implementation of new temporary schemata that correspond phenomenologically to what we think of as strategies. As such they correspond to what Miller *et al.* (1960) refer to as 'plans'.

A broad outline of the Shallice (2002) model is shown in Figure 7.1 in which Stage 1 is responsible for the construction of temporary new schemata. Its subprocesses involve setting goals, generating schemata, which in turn may be influenced by retrieval from episodic memory, and by longer-term strategies. Stage 2 involves implementing new schemata that are held in what is termed a 'special purpose working memory'. This is followed by a third stage of assessment and verification of the new schema, which may result either in its verification and use, or in its rejection and a repetition of the schema generation phase.

The operation of the model may be illustrated by performance on the Brixton spatial anticipation test (Burgess and Shallice 1996c), a non-verbal analogue of the Wisconsin Card Sorting task which is sensitive to the effects of frontal lobe damage. It comprises a 5×2 array of circles, of which one is filled and the remainder unfilled. The subject has to decide which circle will be filled next, a process that is determined by one of eight different abstract rules, for example, the next circle beneath, or possibly an alternation between two circles. The task produces three scores, (a) number of correct responses, (b) number of bizarre responses of a type never given by control subjects, and (c) number of occasions on which the subject switches from a rule at a point when it is still operating successfully. Measures a and b correlate highly with each other ($r = 0.6$) whereas c correlates with neither a ($r = 0.13$) nor b ($r = 0.13$). All three measures, however, show impairment when patients with frontal lobe damage are compared with patients with matched WAIS intelligence performance, but whose lesions are more posterior. Shallice and Burgess suggest that both number correct and number of bizarre responses reflect failures of strategy generation, implicating impairment at Stage 1, while score c reflects a failure of Stage 2 to implement the schema.

7.3 Working memory and executive processes

As a cognitive psychologist, I feel I ought to be able to contribute to an understanding of executive processes in a way that is complementary to that of more neurobiological or computational approaches. In my own case, since I have not had good access to patients with clearly delimited frontal lobe lesions, or to convenient local neuroimaging facilities, I have concentrated principally on normal subjects, together with research on patients suffering from Alzheimer's disease (AD). One approach (Baddeley 1996) was to attempt to go back to first principles and identify processes that any executive system would require if it is to function effectively. Having identified such subprocesses, I then attempted to find a range of tasks on which they might reasonably be expected to depend. If the executive processes postulated were indeed fundamental, then

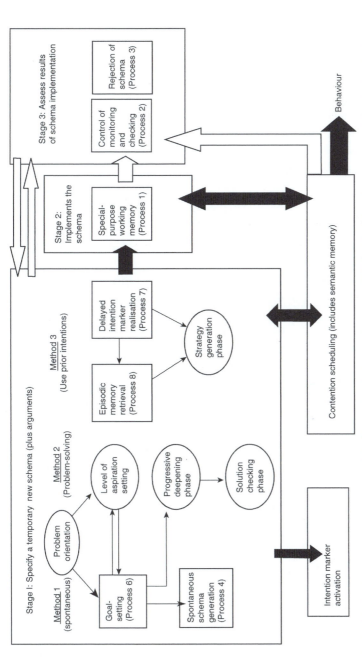

Fig. 7.1 The Mark II Supervisory System model developed by Shallice and Burgess (1996). All of the diagram (except for the Contention Scheduling component) concerns supervisory system processing. Within the large rectangle representing different stages of Supervisory System operation, temporally distinct phases of Supervisory System operation are represented by ellipses (reprinted from Shallice (2002), Fractionation of the Supervisory System in D. T. Stuss and R. T. Knight (eds) *Principles of frontal lobe function*, p. 263: New York, Oxford University Press). Reproduced with permission from Oxford University Press and the Royal Society.

they should operate across modalities and be applicable to a range of situations and tasks. I identified four candidate processes, namely the capacity to focus attention, the capacity to divide attention between two concurrent tasks, the capacity to switch attention from one task to another, and finally the capacity to integrate working memory and LTM (Baddeley 1996c). The first three are discussed below, and the fourth postponed until the next chapter. The study of attention is, of course, a field that has been extensively investigated (see Pashler [1998] for a recent overview). What follows is not intended as a review of this extensive and highly developed field, but simply as an account of my own attempt to form a much needed bridge between the study of attention and the analysis of the central executive.

7.4 **Focusing the limited capacity**

The capacity to direct and focus attention is perhaps the most crucial feature of working memory. The evidence that the system has a limited capacity is in general overwhelming, which is not to deny that under certain highly constrained conditions, two complex tasks may be performed simultaneously. A good example of this is the demonstration by Allport *et al.* (1972) of the capacity of an expert pianist to sight read and play a musical score and shadow prose at the same time with little or no apparent interference. Considered from the viewpoint of the Norman and Shallice model, one assumes that both of these tasks could, for this subject at least, be run using highly practised existing schemata, which can be interleaved with relatively little demand on the SAS system. There seems little doubt that a less accomplished pianist would show interference.

7.4.1 **Attentional control of complex tasks**

Of the many demonstrations of limited attentional control capacity, let us consider one, the study by Robbins *et al.* (1996) of the performance of moderate and highly skilled chess players. The work was prompted by a study by Holding (1989), who demonstrated that counting backwards in threes interfered with the retention of chess positions, and concluded that this reflected the importance of verbal coding. We challenged this interpretation, using dual task methodology to test other hypothesis. Both moderate and highly skilled players attempted to retain a briefly exposed position, either under control conditions, or while performing a series of concurrent secondary tasks designed to interfere with each of three components of working memory. Articulatory suppression was used to disrupt the phonological loop, a spatial tapping task was employed to disrupt the sketchpad, and randomly generating sequences of numbers were used to disrupt the central executive.

As expected, memory performance was highly correlated with chess skill. However, both expert and novice groups showed the same pattern of disruption from the secondary tasks, namely no impairment from articulatory suppression, a moderate disruption from spatial tapping, and a substantial drop when verbal random generation was required, suggesting that Holding's earlier result reflected the executive demand of backward counting, rather than disruption of verbal processing as he proposed.

A second experiment presented our novices and experts with a position from a middle game, requiring them to choose the best next move. Again, performance correlated with chess skill rating, and was again uninfluenced by articulatory suppression, but impaired by both spatial tapping and random generation. Indeed, the required rate of concurrent random generation had to be reduced in order to allow the subjects to perform at all adequately. Broadly equivalent results, namely little evidence of verbal coding, together with reliance on visuospatial and executive skills, are also reported as part of an extensive study of the cognitive psychology of chess by Saariluomo (1995).

The concept of a limited capacity attentional system is at least as old as cognitive psychology (Miller 1956; Welford 1956; Broadbent 1958; Fitts and Posner 1967; Neisser 1967). However, it is not simply the case that the more difficult the task, the greater its attentional demand (Allport *et al.* 1972; Logie *et al.* 2004). In a continuation of our chess studies, for example (Baddeley and Robbins, unpublished data), we gave our subjects the task of briefly viewing a middle game and deciding whether white or black had the advantage. This is quite a difficult task, which correlated with chess expertise. However, performance was not impaired by a demanding concurrent load. We assumed that this was because there was insufficient time to perform a systematic analysis of the position, hence forcing the subjects to rely on a relatively automatic pattern recognition-based positional judgement. Consistent with this was our observation that reducing the amount of available time for the judgement had no impact on performance.

7.4.2 **Practice and automaticity**

A second variable that interacts with ongoing executive demand is degree of practice. In a study of stimulus-independent thoughts, the tendency to let the mind wander, Teasdale *et al.* (1995) demonstrated that performing an unfamiliar task was sufficient to disrupt such thoughts, whereas performing the same task after a number of further practice trials had no such effect. Such a result is consistent with the classic demonstration of Schneider and Shiffrin (1977) that repeated experience of a limited set of stimulus-response mappings will reduce the attentional demand of the task in question. In a task using prisoners, who presumably had time on their hands to practice, Mowbray and Rhoades (1959) investigated the effect of prolonged practice on Hick's Law. This states that, given a task that involves reacting as quickly as possible, for example by pressing a key in response to an associated light, reaction time increases logarithmically with the number of stimulus-response alternatives. Hick proposed that the slope of the function indicates the rate at which the subject is able to process information. After sufficient practice however, the prisoners achieved zero slopes. Given sufficient practice, it seems that the demand for attentional control becomes minimal, as habit-based automatic processes become ever more efficient.

Yet another complicating factor is the strategy adopted. The capacity to generate examples from a semantic category such as animals appears to be an executively demanding task. It is highly sensitive to frontal lobe damage (Milner 1964) and is readily disrupted by a concurrent task such as choice reaction time (Baddeley *et al.* 1984b), or random generation (Baddeley *et al.* 1998b). Rosen and Engle (1997) found, as one might expect, that subjects with high working memory spans scored well on this task, and showed clear impairment when required to perform a concurrent task. Paradoxically, however, low span subjects showed no secondary task disruption, presumably because unlike high span subjects, they were not using an attentionally demanding strategy, even under control conditions. The question of strategy is one that pervades the working memory literature, since the essence of the working memory system is its flexibility. However, the strategy explanation can be criticized as potentially allowing a post hoc explanation of virtually any unwanted experimental findings. Such explanations are much more convincing when they are supported by subsequent studies that explicitly control strategy (e.g. Hanley and Bakopoulou 2003).

7.4.3 Random generation

One of the unexpected benefits from adopting the Norman and Shallice SAS model was its capacity to give an account of earlier data on the capacity for generating random sequences. This proves to be a very demanding task. When asked to produce a random sequence of letters, for example, subjects tend to favour some letters over others, to produce too many sequences in alphabetic order such as *AB*, *RS* and *XYZ*, and to avoid immediate repetitions such as *AA* and *RR* (Towse 1998; Tune 1964). Such deviations from randomness increase both with rate of generation, and in dual task conditions, with the demands of the secondary task (Baddeley 1966c). Random generation resisted earlier attempts at interpretation within a more conventional stimulus-response framework, but appeared to lend itself to interpretation with the Norman and

Shallice model, based on the distinction between responding on the basis of ingrained habits, and the capacity of the SAS to intervene. Hence, given the instruction to produce a stream of letters, the natural tendency would be to use the alphabet recitation schema, or to produce common acronyms such as *USA* and *CIA*. Given the instruction to make the sequence random, however, there would clearly be a need to avoid such stereotyped sequences, producing a tension between what is easy to retrieve, and what is optimal. Exploring the nature of random generation, therefore, seemed to offer the possibility of throwing light on the fundamental processes involved in the executive control of action.

In a subsequent series of experiments, we chose to tackle the problem by moving away from the verbal generation of alpha-numeric information to the requirement to press an array of ten keys at random (Baddeley, *et al.* 1998b). There were two reasons for this. The first was practical, since it meant that subjects entered their responses directly into the computer, thereby simplifying analysis. The second was more theoretically oriented, and related to our assumption that executive processes were relatively modality-free. If so, we should observe broadly similar phenomena regardless of whether the subject was uttering a sequence of numbers or letters, or pressing a sequence of keys.

Our first experiment, therefore, studied the influence of rate of randomization on the redundancy of the resulting response sequence, using either the digits 0-9, or ten keys, arrayed to match the shape of the two hands. Although verbal generation was somewhat more random, the effect of generation rate was equivalent, with faster generation leading to statistically less random sequences. As in the earlier study (Baddeley 1966c), we also found that as speed increased, the number of stereotyped responses became greater. In the case of key pressing, the preferred sequences comprised first of all the homologous key on the other hand, followed by adjacent keys on the same hand, and then adjacent on the opposite hand. We combined our randomized key-pressing task with concurrent verbal tasks, to see if degree of randomness was sensitive to concurrent task demand. This indeed proved to be the case. The requirement to generate items from semantic categories is known to be both attentionally demanding (Baddeley *et al.* 1984) and sensitive to frontal lobe damage (Milner 1982). As a concurrent task, it substantially reduced the randomness of key pressing. Even more disruptive was the requirement to perform a concurrent intelligence test (Baddeley *et al.* 1998).

At this point we were thinking rather generally in terms of some specific executive component which was required both for generation and for other important cognitive tasks. In an attempt to test this rather vague hypothesis, we decided to combine random keyboard generation with the requirement to verbally produce random digit sequences. We expected this to lead to the dramatic overload of the assumed specific component, and the breakdown of performance. We were in for a surprise. When combined, keyboard randomization was impaired, to about the same extent as would occur if it were combined with verbal category generation, but random number generation was only minimally disturbed.

In order to account for this unexpected result, we were forced to think in more detail about the processes involved. We suggested that random generation involved at least four processes, selecting a 'retrieval plan', operating it, checking the output to avoid stereotypes or repetitions, and if necessary switching to another retrieval plan. There is evidence to suggest that once a retrieval plan is specified, the retrieval process itself is relatively undemanding (Baddeley *et al.* 1984; Craik *et al.* 1996; Naveh-Benjamin *et al.* 2000). Furthermore, if we assume that verbal and motor retrieval plans do not mutually interfere to any great extent, then it seemed likely that the imposed load must have had effect on either the switching or the checking stage, or perhaps both. Both these stages occur after a response has been emitted. Impairment of either of these processes would therefore not produce a dramatic immediate disruption, but would simply increase the redundancy of the output by not switching sufficiently frequently. Comments by subjects suggested that stereotyped sequences and deviations from randomness in verbal generation are much more noticeable than in key pressing. Indeed, some subjects claimed (wrongly) that the requirement to perform a demanding concurrent task made keyboard generation *easier*, something that was not ever claimed with verbal generation. It seems likely therefore that our subjects were monitoring and maintaining verbal generation at the expense of deterioration of the less salient manual task.

We decided to test our switching hypothesis by combining keyboard generation with a task that itself involved frequent switching, arguing that this would disrupt the switching component, and hence dramatically impair performance, even though the switch itself was highly predictable. We opted for a task that was based on a commonly used neuropsychological task, the Trails Test, which is assumed to measure task switching. It involves an array of numbers or letters scattered across a sheet of paper. In the basic condition, Trails A, the subject is presented with either numbers or letters, and instructed to start with the first item, for example, number 1, join it to number 2 by pencil, continuing to trace the path and connecting the numbers in ascending order. In the case of letters, the subject begins with A and moves through the alphabet. In Trails B, the switching condition, the subject is shown a mixed array of numbers and letters, and required to alternate, beginning with A, joining it to 1, which then is joined to B, then to 2, etc. As we were studying manual generation, we devised a verbal equivalent of the Trails Test. In the Trails analogue, the subject either recited the letters of the alphabet, or counted. In the crucial Trails switching condition they were asked to produce alternating spoken sequences such as A, 1, B, 2, C, 3, etc. When we combined this verbal alternation task with manual random generation, we found a very substantial decrease in randomness, a result that we regarded as consistent with our assumption that the switching component of the trails task was disrupting the switching stage of random generation. This in turn led us to the hypothesis that the capacity to switch attention might represent a basic and separable executive function. We set out to test this hypothesis: again using dual task methodology.

7.5 Task switching and the central executive

In 1927, Jersild published an extensive series of experiments that attempted to measure the attentional cost of switching from one task to another. A typical experiment involved a list of pairs of digits, with subjects asked either to add the two digits in one condition, to subtract the second digit from the first, or to alternate addition and subtraction from one digit pair to the next. He found that switching led to substantial slowing of performance. Somewhat surprisingly, his work was neglected for almost half a century, until Spector and Biederman (1976) reintroduced the arithmetic task switching paradigm, demonstrating among other things that the cost of switching was substantially reduced, if not removed, by providing the appropriate plus and minus cues on the response sheet, rather than simply instructing the subject to alternate.

7.5.1 Switching and the central executive

Almost 20 years then went by before the issue was raised again in an influential paper by Allport *et al.* (1994), which directly challenged the widely held view that task switching was an attentionally demanding process, dependent on a limited capacity executive control system. This view was in turn challenged by Rodgers and Monsell (1995) who found that their subjects could reduce the cost of switching given an appropriate cue and sufficient time to process this information. This has subsequently become an extremely active research area, in which the proposal that switching might reflect the operation of the unitary executive function has proved over-optimistic (see Monsell [2005] for a recent review). For present purposes, however, rather than review this complex and developing literature, I will focus on a series of our own experiments that, although unsuccessful in throwing great light on the mechanisms underpinning task switching, caused a valuable modification in my own conception of working memory.

Our attempt to investigate the possibility of a specific switching component within the central executive used the very basic Jersild paradigm in which alternation is required within a printed list of items. We wanted a task that could be used clinically, involving minimal equipment and a task that could easily be understood and readily be performed by both normal subjects and patients suffering from dementia. We opted for a simple paper and pencil task that we found to give robust results, even though it did not allow the detailed measurement of individual responses that would have been possible with more sophisticated techniques. The task involved simply presenting the subject with a column of single digits. In one condition, the requirement was to add 1 to each digit, a second condition involved subtracting 1 from each, while the crucial switching condition required alternation between addition and subtraction. We found clear evidence of switch cost, even when the appropriate plus and minus signs were provided with each sum. We found that the cost of switching was particularly high for AD patients. We decided to explore the task in more detail using normal subjects, studying switching while performing a range of secondary tasks (Baddeley *et al.* 2001b).

Our first experiment studied the effect of omitting or including the plus and minus signs, combining this with simultaneous performance of the verbal trails task described previously. We reasoned that if there is indeed an executive component specialized for switching, then it should be dramatically overloaded by the need to switch on both arithmetic and verbal trails tasks at the same time.

We chose not to use our previous 1-A-2-B-3-C task, since we were concerned that the counting component might well interfere directly with the addition or subtraction involved in the main task. Instead, we required the recitation of items from two other familiar sets, namely days of the week and months of the year. Hence, subjects would either recite the days or the months, or would alternate (e.g. *January-Monday-February-Tuesday-March-Wednesday*, etc.). We did, however, need one further control. It seemed possible, though unlikely, that simply suppressing articulation might impair performance. We therefore included an articulatory suppression condition in which subjects repeatedly recited in canonical order either the days of the week or the months of the year.

Our results fell into two categories. When plus and minus signs were provided, offering a direct cue as to whether that specific item required addition or subtraction, there was a modest but highly reliable effect of switching, which was slightly increased by the addition of the verbal trails task, but not by articulatory suppression. Switching did, therefore, seem to place something of a load on executive processes, but the effects were far from dramatic, and hence not supportive of the idea of a specific switching subprocess that might have been greatly disrupted by the requirement to perform two concurrent switching tasks.

When signs were absent, however, much more dramatic impairment was found. Somewhat surprisingly, there was substantial disruption even from the articulatory suppression condition, suggesting an important role for the phonological loop in controlling action. It was however, suggested by a referee of our submitted paper, that reciting months of the year, or even days of the week, might not be so easy a task as we had assumed. This proved to be the case, since the effects observed were indeed reduced when articulatory suppression involved simply repeating the word 'the', although the overall pattern remained (Baddeley *et al.* 2001b).

7.5.2 An executive role for the phonological loop?

In a subsequent study Emerson and Miyake (2003) have extended this result, varying the difficulty of the addition and subtraction task, and comparing switching between two and three operations. They replicated the substantial effect of articulatory suppression. Increasing either difficulty level or number of switching operations increased overall processing time, but these factors did not interact with the effect of articulatory suppression. A further experiment varied the degree of cueing of the switched arithmetic operation. Each item was either presented without a cue, with a clear plus or minus cue, or in an intermediate condition presented in a colour which indicated either addition or subtraction. Switch cost depended on the strength of the cue, being greatest in the no-cue condition, and least with the arithmetic signs, but again the effect did not interact with the presence or absence of articulatory suppression.

Emerson and Miyake interpret their results in terms of the use of speech cues to control behaviour: 'Because (inner or private) speech allows generation of serial performances that have reliable properties such as duration, repeatability, and evocation of related information, private speech is well suited to serve a variety of control functions' (Carlson 1997, p. 168). Its advantages include the fact that it is inherently sequential, and hence good for keeping track of ordered actions. The phonological loop holds a limited number of items which it keeps readily available to conscious awareness. The verbal content of the phonological loop readily triggers other responses, including both semantic associations and task relevant intentions. Subvocal articulation is highly practised and resistant to interference. Finally, it has the advantage of being maintained with relatively little attentional demand.

Further evidence for the use of verbal control in task switching comes from clinical studies using the Wisconsin Card Sorting Task in which patients have to sort cards into categories, working out the correct categorization from feedback presented by the tester. Once a category has been achieved, the tester switches, leaving the patient to detect the switch and identify the next category (Milner 1964). Patients with frontal lobe damage tend to have difficulty in switching from one category to the next, suggesting a dependence on executive processes. Dunbar and Sussman (1995) found that switching was also impaired by articulatory suppression while Perry *et al.* (2001) noted that instructing schizophrenic patients to verbalize their hypotheses improved their performance. Finally, there is evidence that switch costs may be increased in aphasic patients, with degree of disruption correlating with extent of speech impairment (Mecklinger *et al.* 1999).

The proposal that speech may play an important role in the control of action is not of course a new one. It formed an important component of Vygotsky's (1962) approach to cognitive development, emphasizing the role of speech in the development of thought processes. Luria (1959) further developed these ideas, carrying out an ingenious series of experiments on the role of speech in the control of action. He employed a task in which a child is instructed to squeeze a bulb when a red light flashes, but not to squeeze to a blue light. Below the age of three, children tend to press in response to both lights even though they are able to report the instruction correctly, and to perform the task if the tester gives the instruction 'press' when the red light comes on, and 'don't' to the blue light. By three-and-a-half, children begin to be able to make the appropriate verbal responses, but still do not perform the action. Between four and five, children finally learn to accompany their speech with the appropriate action, and in due course to perform the action without speech. Luria (1959) went on to show similar phenomena in neuropsychological patients with frontal lobe damage, resulting in the subsequent development of an approach to neurological rehabilitation in which the patient is encouraged to control action by overt self instruction.

Returning to the role of attention in task switching, there is some indication that concurrent executive demand from such tasks as verbal trails or random generation can interact with switching, suggesting that under certain circumstances at least, switching may be attentionally demanding. However, there is no strong evidence for a specific component of the executive that is exclusively devoted to switching. Indeed, switching under certain circumstances actually appears to enhance performance. Subjects required to write sequences of letters as rapidly as possible respond more slowly when the same letter is repeated (*A*, *A*, *A*, *A*, etc.) than when alternating (*A*, *B*, *A*, *B*, etc.), which in turn is slightly slower than longer repeated sequences (such as *A*, *B*, *C*, *D*, *A*, *B*, *C*, *D*, etc.), a result that appears to reflect the build up of some kind of inhibition (Nohara 1965; Wing *et al.* 1979). Hence, although there are growing numbers of hypotheses as to the factors underlying task switching, I myself am inclined to agree with Rubenstein *et al.* (2001), who suggest that switching is not a general function, but a process whose costs or benefits are likely to vary depending on the precise situation and the strategy adopted by the subject to deal with it.

7.6 **Division of attention as an executive skill**

It is clearly the case that we need, on occasion, to split our attention across more than one task. For example, I am currently walking in the rain along a narrow road, dictating while holding an umbrella which I attempt to avoid skagging in the brambles, meanwhile listening for approaching cars which might just possibly not notice me. The latter activity is relatively undemanding, but given the possible consequences, potentially important. A similar potential multitask conflict occurs in driving while telephoning, an activity that has been shown to be dangerous, not principally because of the potential need to use one hand to hold the telephone, but because of the potential division of attention. As long ago as 1969, Brown *et al.* for example, showed that the need to perform a demanding verbal reasoning test had little or no effect on manual skill in steering between two markers, but had a substantial impact on the driver's capacity to judge whether the gap was wide enough. Difficulty in performing two tasks at the same time is consistent with the assumption of a specific cognitive capacity for sharing attention, but by no means forces this interpretation (see Bourke *et al.* [1996] for a discussion).

7.6.1 **Dual task performance in Alzheimer's Disease**

My own involvement with studying the capacity for dividing attention stemmed from collaborative research on the cognitive deficits associated with Alzheimer's disease. An initial study indicated that in addition to the well-established marked impairment in episodic LTM, our patients also showed deficits in both visual and verbal immediate memory (Spinnler *et al.* 1988). We speculated as to the possibility that this might reflect an underlying deficit in the central executive component that contributed to both our STM tasks, a conclusion that was consistent with a more detailed analysis of verbal STM in such patients by Morris (1984; 1986). The question arose, however, as to how to measure the proposed executive deficit.

Using the basic tripartite model of working memory, it seemed plausible to assume that the executive would be required if it were necessary to coordinate two or more separate activities. Furthermore, if one activity relied principally on the phonological loop, and the other on the sketchpad, then we should be able to avoid more peripheral sources of perceptual or motor disruption. Our first study used visuospatial tracking, in which subjects had to keep a stylus in contact with a moving spot of light. By varying rate of target movement, we could equate the level of performance of our three groups, namely patients suffering from the early stages of Alzheimer's disease (AD), elderly normal subjects matched for age, and young subjects. In each case, we set tracking performance at about 70per cent time on target. We combined tracking with each of three secondary tasks, one involving articulatory suppression, a second requiring the subject to press a foot pedal in response to an auditory stimulus, while a third required subjects to hear and repeat back sequences of random digits. In the case of the memory span task, by pre-testing, we were able to ensure that digit sequence length was set at span level for all three groups. Each of the three tasks was then combined with tracking.

We found no significant impairment in any group as a result of simple articulatory suppression. The two control groups showed a modest degree of decrement from concurrent reaction time and digit span tasks that was broadly equivalent for normal young and elderly subjects. The AD patients, however, showed a substantially greater disruption from the need to combine tasks (Baddeley et al. 1986). A subsequent study (Baddeley et al. 1991) involved a longitudinal study of patients. We found that as the disease progressed, their capacity to perform the tasks alone showed little change, whereas dual task performance declined systematically. Could it be the case that the dual task condition was just more difficult, and hence more sensitive to the effects of AD? This seemed unlikely, since increasing the level of difficulty of a unitary semantic judgement task did not make it more sensitive to the disease (Baddeley et al. 1991).

We interpreted our results in terms of a specific component of the central executive concerned with dual task coordination, which we argued was disrupted in AD. Unlike other cognitive capacities such as episodic memory, however, the capacity to divide attention appears to be comparatively preserved in normal ageing (see also Salthouse et al. 1998). If we could establish this firmly, then we would have achieved two things, theoretical progress in fractionating the central executive, together with a potentially useful clinical test that might be useful in deciding whether a forgetful patient was or was not likely to be suffering from AD.

In a review of the attentional deficits associated with AD, Perry and Hodges (1999) identified the capacity to divide attention as one of the strongest candidates for a separable deficit. As they pointed out, however, alternative interpretations could be offered, for example, in terms of level of difficulty or as just one example of a more general speed of processing deficit. Decline in speed of processing has been proposed as the principal deficit in normal ageing (Salthouse 1992; 1996), while a similar argument has been presented in the case of AD (Nebes and Brady 1985).

Two subsequent studies have addressed this issue. Baddeley *et al.* (2001a) again demonstrated that increasing level of difficulty did not necessarily make a task increasingly sensitive to AD. We compared simple and choice reaction time (RT), finding that young subjects, normal elderly and early AD patients all respond more rapidly when a single stimulus, a triangle, requires a single key press response (Simple RT) than when required to make separate responses to triangles and circles (Choice RT). Choice RT was also more sensitive to the effect of age, with elderly subjects more disrupted by increasing set size than young. There was, however, no evidence for this increase in RT to be disproportionately greater in patients than in elderly controls. In contrast, as predicted, we did find a disproportionate deficit in each of two dual task paradigms. One involved a manual box-crossing task analogous to tracking, in which subjects marked a chain of boxes on a response sheet, working as rapidly as possible while remembering and repeating back span length digit sequences.

The other task moved away from memory altogether. Subjects were given a visual search task comprising lines of pictograms. Each line was preceded by a target pictogram, and the subject was required to cross out any matching items on that line, before moving on to the next target and line. The concurrent task was analogous to that of a traveller sitting on a railway station and listening for the announcement of his destination. We chose the name *Bristol*, the city in which the study was run, embedding this among other familiar town names, and requiring the subject to call out 'Bristol' whenever the name was detected. The visual search and 'Bristol' tasks were performed singly and in combination. Both of our dual task procedures showed the standard effect, namely no significant decrement as a result of age, but a very clear dual task impairment in AD patients. This result emphasized both the replicability of our earlier finding, together with its generalization to tasks without any direct memory requirement.

A study by Logie *et al.* (2004) tackled the level of difficulty hypothesis more directly. Using the concurrent tracking and digit span paradigm, we titrated both tracking speed and digit sequence length to a point at which our young, elderly and patient groups were matched on performance when these tasks were performed individually. For each task, we then systematically varied the level of difficulty. In the case of tracking, we substantially reduced target speed to make it easier, or made it more difficult by increasing speed. We similarly varied the difficulty of the digit span task, either presenting fewer digits than span, or more than span. When the tasks were performed singly, all three subject groups behaved in the same way, with performance improving when the task was made easier, and deteriorating when it was made harder. The three functions, having been matched at span level or baseline tracking level, showed totally superimposed performance across our three subject groups, providing no support for the suggestion that simply increasing difficulty will make a task more sensitive to AD. In another study using the same subjects, the task was set at the easiest level for both tasks, and both single and dual task performance observed. Even under the easiest conditions, AD patients showed a significant dual task decrement, whereas control subjects showed no sign of impairment.

7.6.2 Is task-combination an executive skill?

We would claim, therefore, that our results show a prima facie case for regarding the capacity to combine tasks as being a potentially dissociable executive skill, one that is surprisingly well-preserved in the normal elderly, provided one matches young and old on individual task performance, but which is consistently impaired in AD patients. We do not wish to claim that it will not prove possible to detect an age effect; many studies have indeed claimed such an effect (see Riby *et al.* 2004 for a review). However, studies often fail to equate performance across groups on the individual tasks. It is therefore unsurprising that requiring the elderly to combine two tasks on which their performance is inferior causes even greater decrement than is found on either of the single tasks alone. Even when individual tasks are equated, an age effect may be detectable. Our results across a series of studies suggest, however, that any such effects appear to be, at most, slight, compared to the robust dual task deficit found in AD patients. We therefore suggest that the capacity to divide attention is a candidate component of the central executive, while accepting that only time will tell how widely our results can be generalized.

Fortunately, there already exists evidence of some generality, and of potential practical significance. Hartman *et al.* (1992), for example, applied our findings to the task of a physiotherapist treating an individual patient recovering from head injury. They compared the patient's capacity to perform a motor task alone with performance when accompanied by general verbal encouragement, or when accompanied by friendly conversation. Normal subjects were able to perform the task regardless of distraction. Head injured patients also showed no effect of general encouragement, but performance deteriorated when accompanied by conversation, an effect that was particularly marked in patients with frontal lobe damage. In another study, Alberoni *et al.* (1992) studied the capacity of AD patients to remember the content of videoed conversations, as a function of number of participants. We found a substantial effect of increasing number of speakers on the capacity of AD patients, but not controls, to follow a conversation. This finding is not of great theoretical significance, since overall conversational difficulty would be likely to increase with group size.

However, this result was selected by a publication for AD carers as being of clear practical relevance to relatives arranging visits to AD patients.

7.6.3 Does social behaviour involve multitasking?

Dual task performance measures were included in a study by Alderman (1969), who was concerned to understand why certain patients derived no benefit from a rehabilitation scheme for head injured patients with severe behavioural problems. He found that patients who did not benefit showed slightly poorer performance on a range of frontal lobe tests, but performed consistently badly on a series of dual task measures.

Further evidence for an association between behavioural disturbance and impaired dual task performance came from a study of patients with frontal lobe lesions (Baddeley et al. 1997). Patients were tested on the previously described task involving box-crossing and digit span. They were also tested on two measures that are commonly associated with frontal lobe damage, namely verbal fluency in which the subject must generate items from semantic categories, and the Wisconsin Card Sorting Test (WCST), in which patients must learn to sort on the basis of each of six specified stimulus dimensions, and then switch when that dimension is no longer treated as correct. In addition, patients were assessed independently for signs of dysexecutive behaviour, using both an interview and assessment of the patient's medical records to judge whether they showed the attentional deficits and disinhibited behaviour that is often associated with frontal lobe damage. The patients showed clear evidence of impairment on all three cognitive tests, and about half showed evidence of dysexecutive symptoms in their behaviour. These behavioural symptoms were significantly associated with poor dual task performance, but not with degree of deficit in either capacity to perform the WCST, or the verbal fluency tests, for which impairment was equally likely in dysexecutive and non-dysexecutive patients. It appears to be the case therefore that although impaired verbal fluency and WCST performance were, as expected, associated with frontal lobe damage, a separate frontally based capacity was reflected in both dysexecutive behaviour and impaired dual task performance. Why should this be?

One possibility is that adequate social behaviour requires a capacity for dual task performance, balancing one's own needs and desires with those of the people you are interacting with. It is equally possible, however, that the area of the frontal lobes involved in dual task performance and those required for adequate social interaction just happen to be anatomically adjacent. Whichever proves to be the case, this clearly appears to be an interesting area to investigate further, from both a theoretical and practical viewpoint.

7.7 **Conclusions**

To summarize, we began by proposing a general attentionally limited control system, the central executive, basing a good deal of our case on neuropsychological evidence, principally from patients with frontal lobe damage. This was followed by the consideration of three candidates for component executive processes. The first, a capacity to focus a limited capacity system, is quite broadly accepted as a feature of most current attentional theories (Pashler 1998). The second, a capacity to switch attention, on closer examination seemed unlikely to be based on a single executive subprocess. The third, the capacity to divide attention, appears more promising, though by no means firmly established. The fourth function proposed for the executive (Baddeley 1996), namely the capacity to link long-term and working memory, will be discussed in the next chapter.

Chapter 8

Long-term memory and the episodic buffer

Of the four functions that I suggested might be desirable in a central executive, three were characteristics of attentional control, namely the capacity to focus, to divide and to switch attention, while the fourth capacity was qualitatively different, namely that of interfacing working memory with long-term memory (Baddeley, 1996). Implicit in the first three is the idea of the central executive as an *attentional control system*, something that was made explicit by Baddeley and Logie (1999). Such a view differs from the initial concept, which regarded the central executive as comprising a limited capacity pool of *general* processing capacity that could be used for a range of functions including both attentional control and temporary storage. The modification to our original view stemmed from the fear that a general processing concept was simply too powerful, with too few constraints to generate tractable and useful questions. By treating the executive as a purely attentional system, it became easier to frame potentially fruitful questions, although as we have just seen, not necessarily to answer them at this stage with any degree of completeness. However, having banished storage from the executive, it became increasingly clear that we were left with a number of problems in tackling the fourth question raised, namely that of how working memory and long-term memory interact.

8.1 Some reductionist views

Before beginning the search for a link between working memory and long-term memory, we should consider a number of alternative views that would largely dispense with the question. One of these is the suggestion that WM is simply part of the system for processing language. This view tends to be taken by investigators whose primary interest is in language, and who regard temporary storage simply as a secondary feature of the systems involved. This is therefore partly a question of focus rather than content. However, it may lead to a neglect of those features of WM that are not language-based, as in the case of Allport's (1984) proposal that STM deficits in patients are caused by a subtle deficit in speech perception.

8.1.1 **Working memory as language processing**

It seems very probable that the phonological loop has evolved from systems that were specialized for speech perception (the phonological store) and production (the articulatory rehearsal system). The evidence suggests however that the loop provides a separate offline system for storing and manipulating language-related material that goes beyond a basic capacity to perceive and produce speech (Vallar and Papagno 2002). This conclusion is based on the observation that although language processing and phonological STM are often both impaired in patients with left hemisphere damage (Vallar *et al.* 1992), speech processing and phonological STM can show a clear dissociation. For example, patients such as P.V. have grossly impaired phonological STM but normal perception and production of language (Basso *et al.* 1982; Martin and Breedin 1992). Conversely, patients may show relatively well-preserved verbal STM, despite a major auditory perceptual deficit (Baddeley and Wilson 1993a). Furthermore, even if such peripheralist views of working memory might in principle provide an account of phonological STM, they say nothing concerning the crucial capacity of the system to serve as a working memory, to manipulate information in order to solve problems, or indeed about the capacity to interface with LTM. This is not, of course, to argue against a range of more complex accounts of working memory that emphasize language processing which I would regard variants on a multicomponent model (e.g. N. Martin). They differ from my own approach in focusing on patients who may have relatively complex language deficits, rather than searching for cases who show isolated deficits in a specific component: in this case, the phonological loop. Both styles of theorising tend to accept the need to assume some form of temporary storage within a multicomponent working memory.

8.1.2 **Working memory as activated long-term memory**

A much more widely held view of WM is that it simply represents the currently active components of LTM. This was of course the dominant view in North America up to the late 1960s (e.g. Melton 1963), and was proposed more recently by Nairne (2002) and by Ruchkin *et al.* (2003). My objection to this view is not that it is incorrect, but rather that it appears to give a clear answer without actually doing so (Baddeley 2003a). WM is certainly dependent on LTM, but in so many different ways as to make a simple identification of WM with activated LTM quite unhelpful. Such a view might reasonably, for example, be taken to imply that if one understands LTM, then an understanding of WM will naturally follow. There is little evidence for this. Although we certainly know a great deal more about WM than we did 30 years ago, I would suggest that almost all of this has resulted from treating the system as *separate* from LTM.

Advocates of a single memory system have often relied on demonstrating *analogies* between WM and LTM, an approach that began with Melton's (1963) classic attack on the concept of STM, was continued by Postman (1975) and more recently by Nairne (2002) and Ruchkin *et al.* (2003). Such analogies are almost always based on experimental paradigms that involve both long- and short-term components. It is therefore not surprising that such hybrid paradigms show similarities to explicitly long-term tasks. Examples of such tasks include the Peterson short-term forgetting test, free recall and running memory span. However, similarities do not demonstrate identity; the fact that both lizards and elephants have four legs, an absence of fur, two eyes and a mouth does not make them the same species. This issue has already been covered in relation to Nairne's (2002) advocacy of a unitary memory system, and hence will not be discussed further.

However, while resisting the view that WM is simply part of LTM, I would certainly agree that there are several quite different ways in which WM and LTM interact. If we consider the phonological loop, for example, it is clear that pseudo words are easier to recall if they are word-like, phonotactically similar in structure to the subjects' native language (Baddeley 1971; Gathercole *et al.* 2001). Hence a nonword such as *monage* is likely to be better recalled than *luzok*, despite the fact that both are unfamiliar and meaningless. More explicit influences of long-term knowledge can, of course, also influence performance, which is presumably why subjects in digit span experiments virtually never respond with anything other than digits. Semantic knowledge at the level of individual words, concepts and general world knowledge also influences immediate verbal recall, again probably relying on both implicit and explicit processes.

I agree, therefore, that working memory does involve activated LTM in a range of different ways, but then, so do most aspects of human cognition. For example, much perception also involves activated LTM; we tend to see the world in terms of tables, chairs and sunsets, not as purely sensory features. Such links with prior experience are, of course, important, but would not lead us to suggest that perception, or even something more heavily dependent on learning, such as language, is *simply* activated LTM. So having agreed that the undoubted link between WM and LTM presents a problem, or probably a series of problems, rather than a solution, what else can one say about it?

8.2 **Some skeletons in the working memory cupboard**

Our decision to postulate a central executive devoid of memory capacity led to a number of problems. Initially I chose to set such difficulties aside, to be reconsidered in due course. Although I regarded such issues as simply 'on the back burner', given their potential threat to the adequacy of our model of WM, a more accurate metaphor might be skeletons in the cupboard. Eventually, we attempted to put one skeleton too many into the cupboard: they all fell out, emphasising the need for a rather fundamental rethink of the structure of WM. The problems broadly fell into three categories: (1) Evidence for the short-term storage of information that could not readily be explained by the phonological loop or the sketchpad; (2) The problem of how the visuospatial and phonological systems might interact; and (3) The unresolved problem of the interface between WM and LTM. They will be discussed in turn.

8.2.1 A back-up store for STM?

We have tended to treat the phonological loop as though it were the sole source of digit span performance. If that were the case, then with visual presentation and articulatory suppression, span should drop virtually to zero. In fact, span typically drops from six or seven to four or five digits (e.g. Larsen and Baddeley 2003b), suggesting the need to assume some kind of additional 'back-up' store (Page and Norris 1998). Could this simply reflect the contribution of LTM to span? If so, patients with a pure phonological STM deficit showing normal LTM should have spans of four or five digits, rather than the spans of one or two items typically reported (Vallar and Shallice 1990b).

8.2.2 Preserved recall in STM patients

When STM patients recall auditorily presented digits, their span is about one item. With visual presentation it rises to around four digits (Shallice and Warrington 1970; Basso *et al.* 1982). An obvious way out of this dilemma is to attribute the increase to the visuospatial sketchpad. However, the sketchpad had typically been assumed to hold information in parallel, and to be inappropriate for serial recall. A series of studies by Phillips using matrix patterns suggests that only the final item is held in STM (Phillips and Christie 1977). A possible solution is to postulate a further system, possibly lexically based, that is specialized for serial recall. However, while there is good evidence for the retention of visual features of verbally coded sequences (see Logie *et al.* [2000] for a review), it is less clear if, and how the sequential order of items that are not verbally codable is maintained (though see Chapter 4 for a further discussion of this issue).

8.2.3 Semantic coding in STM

Although my initial study showed that immediate serial recall of five-word sequences principally reflected phonological coding, a small but significant effect of semantic coding was also found (Baddeley 1966a). Other studies have shown much more powerful semantic effects, (e.g. Brener, 1940; Hulme, Roodenrys *et al.* 1997). Semantic factors tend to be more influential when the difficulty of retaining item rather than order information increases, for example as a result of using longer sequences or larger sets of potential items. The fact that semantic factors contribute to STM paradigms was not a problem for the initial Baddeley and Hitch working memory model. It did however become a problem once the executive was stripped of its storage capacity, leading to the question of how these phonological and semantic codes were stored and how they were combined to enhance recall.

8.2.4 Sentence span

Immediate memory for sentential material is typically substantially greater than span for unrelated words (Brener 1940). Baddeley *et al.* (1987) found spans of around five for unrelated words and 15 for sentences. Should one suggest, therefore, that LTM contributes 10 words to span, and WM five? Suppose then that we test a patient with a phonological STM deficit resulting in an unrelated word span of one item, but with normal LTM; what might we expect? Sentence span should presumably be around 11 words, comprising ten from LTM and one from STM. The span observed was five (Baddeley *et al.* 1987). This suggests an interactive process whereby a basic phonological core is amplified by contributions from LTM. If the basic span is grossly restricted, then overall performance will also be severely limited.

Such a view is broadly consistent with the recent work by Gathercole (unpublished) who suggests that memory span in general relies upon the phonological storage of information at the syllabic or sub-syllabic level, which is then interpreted using redintegrative processes. As observed earlier, however, the current WM model remains silent on exactly how these processes might operate, or indeed where any intermediate products might be stored during redintegration.

8.2.5 Prose recall

The issues raised by sentence span are even more acute when considering recall of prose passages comprising a paragraph or more. The issue was presented particularly clearly by K.J., a highly intelligent patient with a dense, but very pure amnesia (Wilson and Baddeley 1988). When tested on retention of the paragraph comprising the prose recall subtest of the Wechsler Memory Scale, he performed normally on immediate test, while totally failing to recall anything 20 minutes later. His lack of delayed recall was expected, but how did he manage to do so well on immediate test? The passage in question, a brief newspaper-like story about a lady losing her purse and being helped by the police, comprised around 20 'idea units', each several words long. This is sub-stantially beyond the capacity of the phonological loop; nor was it plausible to assume that this amount of detail could be stored in the sketchpad. So how was such good performance achieved?

Fortunately, the prose recall test was included as part of a routine clinical battery given by my colleague, Barbara Wilson, who had, over the years, tested many patients with memory deficits. We therefore decided to see how typical K.J.'s performance might be, and if, as we were reasonably certain, it proved to be atypical, to try to assess what allowed him to do so well (Baddeley and Wilson 2002). All our amnesic patients performed badly on delayed recall, as, of course, we expected. We found that most amnesic patients also performed relatively badly on immediate recall. There was, however, a small number of patients like K.J., whose immediate level of performance ranged from moder-ate to excellent. When we examined their clinical profile, two features stood out; they tended to have a high level of intelligence as measured by the Wechsler Adult Intelligence Scale, and in most cases to have well-preserved executive capacities, characteristics that, unsurprisingly, tended to correlate.

We interpreted our results as follows. We assumed that comprehending a coherent prose passage involves activating and combining representations within LTM. These range from the meanings of individual words, through concepts and up to higher order structures such as story grammars and scripts, reflecting shared social knowledge (Kintsch and van Dyck 1977; Schank and Abelson 1977). In subjects with normal episodic memory, we assume that such structures will be consolidated within LTM and hence can form a basis for retrieval after a delay. Patients with defective episodic LTM, however, regardless of how well the structure representing the passage is built and maintained in WM, will fail to consolidate the trace, and hence will not remember it after a brief filled delay.

Our second assumption is that while the task of constructing an overall representation of the paragraph in WM may be relatively straightforward given normal episodic memory, in the absence of this it becomes a highly attentionally demanding task, requiring the constant active maintenance and updating of the memory structure if it is not to collapse. Amnesic patients who are able and willing to do this can demonstrate good immediate recall, but nevertheless remain incapable of longer term storage and retrieval of the story. A particularly striking example of the capacity to maintain information in WM over time despite dense amnesia was described to me by Endel Tulving (personal communication, 1999). The patient in question claimed to still be able to play bridge, despite extremely dense amnesia. Tulving decided to test this and set up a game. Not only was the patient able to keep track of the bidding and the resultant trump suit, but was able to remember the fall of cards well enough to allow him and his partner to win the rubber.

Our interpretation of preserved prose recall despite amnesia has considerable similarity to the concept of long-term working memory put forward by Ericsson and Kintsch (1995). It differs, however, in stressing the temporary nature of the retrieval structures built by our amnesic patients, in contrast to the emphasis by Ericsson and Kintsch on the prior development within LTM of the necessary retrieval structures, as for example, in the case of mnemonists who are capable of demonstrating remarkable immediate recall only because of many hours of practice building up the necessary structures in LTM. As we shall see later, I also assume a more active and flexible role of working memory, in addition to the utilization of the activated structures and representations within LTM assumed by Ericsson and Kintsch.

8.2.6 Chunking

Perhaps the most powerful single observation about the functioning of STM was the demonstration by Miller (1956) of the importance of chunking, enhancing span by combining several items into a single integrated chunk. The recall advantage of prose over unrelated words presumably stems from the capacity of subjects to bind together individual words within the prose material into meaningful chunks. Miller's suggestion that our capacity for processing information might be determined by *number* of chunks rather than items has continued to be influential, although current opinion tends to favour a capacity nearer four than Miller's magical number seven (Cowan 2001; 2005).

In the initial WM model, chunking was implicitly assigned to the processing and storage capacities of the central executive. However, given its new truncated form, with its lack of storage capacity, the executive seems ill-equipped to perform this important task. Could chunking perhaps be assigned to LTM? Since our densely amnesic patient K.J. appears to be able to chunk perfectly adequately, as shown by his capacity for immediate prose recall, it would seem to suggest that chunking does not depend on intact episodic LTM. Furthermore, he appears to be able to utilize some system or process that maintains the chunked representations over short delays. Finally, the very flexibility of our capacity to combine information into chunks seems to suggest that the process goes beyond the simple coactivation of existing structures in LTM.

8.2.7 Working memory span

As we shall see in Chapter 10, one of the most extensively investigated features of working memory concerns individual differences in its overall capacity. In a classic study, Daneman and Carpenter (1980) required their subjects to process a series of sentences, and afterwards recall the last word in each. They measured the maximum number of sentences that could accurately be processed and recalled in this way, terming it working memory span. They demonstrated a substantial correlation between span and reading comprehension in college students, while subsequent studies have shown it to predict performance on a wide range of cognitive tasks, including measures of general intelligence, and practical cognitive skills such as learning to programme or understand electronics (Kyllonen and Christal 1990; Daneman and Merikle 1996; Engle *et al.* 1999;). Once again, this task clearly demands storage processes that exceed the capacity of the verbal and visuospatial subsystems. Working memory span also predicts cognitive functioning much more effectively than measures of either simple word span or episodic LTM (see Chapter 11). The question arises once more as to how the Baddeley and Logie version of WM can account for these important results.

8.2.8 Conscious awareness

As discussed in the section on imagery, Baddeley and Andrade (2000) attempted to give an account of the processes underpinning the conscious awareness of visuospatial and auditory images, purely in terms of the visuospatial and phonological subsystems. While our results indicated that these subsystems formed a plausible part of the story, particularly for recently encoded novel stimuli, we had difficulty in using them to give an account of images based on LTM. Although WM was clearly involved, the apparent contribution from the loop and sketchpad to images deriving from LTM was rather modest. Our revised interpretation of these results involved combining information from LTM and from the relevant WM subsystems, but left completely unspecified *how* such information was integrated (Baddeley and Andrade 2000). Attentional capacity appeared to be necessary, since a demanding secondary task tended to reduce ratings of vividness for all image types, but we had no suggestions as to what this system might be.

The problem of integrating information from more than one source also arises in other more standard procedures. For example, Logie *et al.* (2000) were able to demonstrate visual similarity effects in immediate serial consonant recall. The visual effects were small compared to those based on phonology, but were reliable, operating across all serial positions and occurring both with and without articulatory suppression. These results imply some common point at which visual and verbal information can interact.

To summarize, although the simple Baddeley and Hitch (1974) model is capable of accounting for a good deal of data, the attempt to limit its storage capacity to the visuospatial and verbal subsystems has created a number of significant problems. These appear to suggest that the capacity of WM to store information exceeds that of the existing subsystems. We also need a mechanism for allowing verbal and visuospatial subsystems to interact with each other, and with LTM. Finally, the system appears to be related to conscious awareness and to be attentionally limited.

In response to these problems, I proposed the concept of an *episodic buffer*, identifying it as a fourth component of working memory (Baddeley 2000). In retrospect, it could equally well be regarded as a fractionation of the initial central executive into an attentional control component as proposed by Baddeley and Logie (1999), and an additional storage component. Such a conceptualization has the attraction of neatness, since the loop and sketchpad can also be separated into processing and storage components. This may, however, have the drawback of suggesting closer similarities than proves to be the case. For present purposes, therefore, we will treat the episodic buffer as a separate subsystem, as shown in Fig. 8.1.

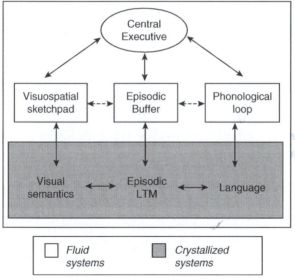

Fig. 8.1 The revised model of working memory proposed by Baddeley (2000). It includes a representation of links to long-term memory, and includes a fourth component, the episodic buffer. In this initial version, links between the subsystems and the buffer operated via the central executive. It now seems likely that there are also direct links (shown here as dotted lines). From Baddeley, A.D. (2000). The episodic buffer: a new component of working memory? In: Trends in Cognitive Sciences 4(11), 417–423. Reproduced with permission from Elsevier.

8.3 **The episodic buffer**

I will start by attempting to justify the name, since it was the name that crystallized my somewhat inchoate thoughts on the need for a further component of WM. The system is episodic, in the sense that it integrates information into coherent episodes; it is a buffer in that it comprises a limited capacity storage system that enables information coded using different dimensions to interact. Its capacity is set in terms of chunks, a chunk being a package of information bound by strong associative links within a chunk, and relatively weak links between chunks. A central feature of the buffer therefore is its role in *binding* information from diverse sources into unified chunks.

Hummel (1999) distinguishes between *static* and *dynamic* binding. Static binding occurs when two features co-occur, a perceptual example, would be yellowness and bananas. Repeated observation of yellowness and bananas may result in binding of these in semantic memory. This binding can be based either on the basic structure of the underlying perceptual system, or on learning. Examples of structural factors that facilitate perceptual binding are offered by the gestalt principles such as continuity and closure which help to parse the visual array into objects and into scenes. Binding based on learning occurs when long-term knowledge helps us chunk familiar objects in complex scenes such as a car parked in front of a house. In both cases binding would appear to occur at comparatively little attentional cost. Dynamic binding involves the novel combination of items which may be combined in many different ways, potentially involving the integration of a number of apparently arbitrary objects and features, for example, a red banana floating in a lake of blue porridge. Hummel suggests that such dynamic binding places considerably higher computational demands on the system. This issue will be addressed in the next chapter.

To summarize. The episodic buffer is assumed to be a temporary storage system that is able to combine information from the loop, the sketchpad, long-term memory, or indeed from perceptual input, into a coherent episode. This process may be attentionally demanding, whereas direct retrieval from LTM is assumed to be relatively undemanding (Baddeley *et al.* 1984b; Craik *et al.* 1996). As Fig. 8.1 (see p. 147) shows, the buffer provides a link between the executive and LTM. In the initial (Baddeley 2000) version shown, the flow of information from the phonological loop and the visuospatial sketchpad occurs indirectly through the executive. I did not assume a direct link with these subsystems, preferring to leave this question open to empirical investigation. As the next chapter indicates, the evidence tends to favour such a link.

The episodic buffer is assumed to be the basis of conscious awareness. A number of theorists have suggested that a principal function of consciousness is to bind together information gleaned from separate perceptual channels such as colour, shape and location, into coherent objects (Baars 1997; Dehaene and Naccache 2001). The reflexive character of conscious awareness, the fact that we can be aware of our experience and reflect upon it, implies a system that has both temporary storage and manipulative processes. Both are, of course, at the centre of the concept of WM. These issues are discussed further in Chapter 16.

A possible criticism of the concept of an episodic buffer is that I am simply replacing a cupboard full of skeletons with a single insubstantial ghost. I propose three methods of fleshing out my potential apparition. The first is to go through the list of problems outlined, and say how I think the concept of an episodic buffer offers a potential solution. Secondly, I shall apply the concept to a series of questions proposed by Miyake and Shah (1999b) as central to any model of working memory. The third is to attempt to use the concept of an episodic buffer as a framework for empirical studies. If it proves capable of generating experiments that are fruitful in helping understand more about the processes and systems of working memory, then it will have succeeded, even if the findings result in substantial modification, or even the abandonment of the initial concept. In short, the episodic buffer is a conceptual tool, not a specified model. None of these stratagems should, of course, be regarded as intrinsically capable of *demonstrating* the validity of the episodic buffer. What they should do, I hope, is to illustrate its potential heuristic value as a means of tackling the comparatively neglected question of how the subsystems of working memory are integrated and interfaced with LTM.

8.3.1 Burying the skeletons

How might the concept of an episodic buffer help in tackling our nine problems? Possible approaches to each of these may be summarized as follows:

1 *The back-up store.* The episodic buffer offers one way of supplementing the limited capacity of the phonological loop by utilising a multimodal code to provide additional storage capacity.

2 *STM patients.* Show grossly impaired performance only when auditory presentation results in information entering the episodic buffer through the impaired phonological store. With visual presentation, a more adequate route into the buffer is available.

3 *Semantic coding in STM.* Because of its capacity for linking with LTM and providing a multidimensional code, it allows the phonological loop to capitalize on semantic information. This may be unnecessary for short sequences but becomes increasingly valuable for long sequences and for those for which item information is critical.

4 *The multidimensional episodic buffer store.* Might plausibly be assumed to be capable of storing serial order in a way that is not open to the sketchpad.

5 *Recall of sentential and prose material.* Enhanced span results from the capacity of the buffer to use and integrate information from both the WM subsystems and LTM, allowing span to be increased by chunking.

6 *Chunking.* It is assumed that the active chunking of previously unrelated items may occur within the episodic buffer, utilising the attentional capacity of the executive to capitalize on prior learning, and to combine information from separate sources in novel ways.

7 *Redintegration.* Is assumed to be a process whereby the executive takes advantage of information available in LTM in order to optimize interpretation of the contents of the episodic buffer. There may however be other more automatic processes whereby long-term knowledge facilitates both chunking and retrieval from STM.

8 *Working memory span.* Is assumed to reflect the storage capacity of the buffer, together with the efficiency with which the executive can use this capacity.

9 *Conscious awareness.* Provides one mode of retrieval of information from the buffer. It is particularly effective in allowing multiple sources of information to be processed in parallel (see Chapter 16).

8.3.2 How might the buffer work?

At this stage, it is clearly inappropriate to expect a precise and detailed model. What follows, therefore, should be regarded as a basis for generating testable hypotheses about the way in which information from LTM may be held and manipulated in WM. They are essentially guesses which aim to facilitate investigation of an important but neglected area, not firm predictions which if unsuccessful would necessarily imply that the whole model be discarded. I shall again use the Miyake and Shah (1999b) questions as a convenient framework. The questions and my tentative answers are as follows:

8.3.3 Basic mechanisms and representations

This breaks down into a series of subquestions.

1 *How is information encoded and maintained?* I initially assumed as a working hypothesis that encoding would depend heavily on the operation of the central executive, that it may operate through the phonological loop, sketchpad, or from LTM, and be maintained by rehearsal. While the phonological component may be maintained through subvocalization, I suspect that this is atypical of most types of rehearsal. Whereas the phonological

code can literally be regenerated, this is not the case for a visual, or I suspect a semantic code. It seems likely, therefore, that rehearsal within the buffer is more analogous to continued attention to a particular representation.

2 *What is the retrieval mechanism?* I would regard conscious awareness as the principal retrieval mode. Whether it is the only mode I am less certain. Consider an instruction such as 'press the right-hand button when the red light appears'. It clearly seems to be the case that we can set up a temporary 'program' that allows us to perform such an operation. Is this maintained in the episodic buffer, on in some parallel system? If in the buffer, I suspect that it is not necessary to become aware of the instruction in order to obey it. So far, however, we know remarkably little about this important capacity (Monsell 1996), so suggesting that such temporary programs are stored in the buffer at least offers a potentially useful starting hypothesis.

3 *How is information represented: is the format different for different types of information?* I assume a single multidimensional code which provides an interface for information from many different sources. These are likely to include LTM and the subsystems of WM, together with information from sensory systems, including those such as smell and taste, that do not themselves have an active means of control and manipulation. Again, this is a highly speculative assumption that at least has the advantage of encouraging consideration of an intriguing but relatively unresearched area.

8.3.4 Control and regulation

1 *How is the information controlled and regulated?* I assume that control depends both on the systems feeding into the buffer, and on the central executive. Hence, phonological information would be controlled in part by the process of subvocalization, while information from LTM would be substantially more influenced by habits and experience. The flow of information would, however, be determined by the supervisory component of the central executive, which in turn would be influenced by higher-level goals.

2 *What determines which information is stored and which ignored?* Both existing habits and higher-level goals determine the flow of information, as discussed in the chapters that follow.

3 *Is control handled by a central structure?* Yes, the central executive, although the extent to which this represents a single hierarchical structure with one basic controller or a more heterarchical alliance of multiple executive processes remains to be decided. The way in which this system might operate is discussed in subsequent chapters.

8.3.5 **Is the episodic buffer unitary or non-unitary?**

1 *Does it consist of multiple separable subsystems?* At this stage of theorising, the buffer is regarded as a unitary subsystem within multicomponent working memory. It seems probable that as a result of empirical exploration, the buffer may be fractionated, as has proved to be the case with the loop and sketchpad.

8.3.6 **The nature of the buffer's limitations**

1 *What mechanisms constrain capacity?* Capacity is limited in a number of different ways. First of all, the buffer will be constrained by the fact that its sources of information, namely LTM and the various subsystems, themselves have limits. The buffer itself is limited in the number of chunks that can be maintained (Cowan 2005), and by the efficiency with which the central executive can operate the system. This in turn will depend upon the overall attentional capacity of the executive.

At a more neurobiological level, such limits will themselves tend to reflect a number of parameters including measures of excitation and inhibition, rates of decay within the relevant stores, and interference effects depending upon the precise character of the material being maintained. While there will be similarities in the mechanisms operating within the various subsystems that feed into the episodic buffer, these mechanisms are unlikely to be identical, given the differential constraints imposed by the need to process sound, vision and meaning.

8.3.7 **The role of the buffer in complex cognitive activities**

1 *A role in language comprehension?* I assume that the buffer plays a role in dealing with the comprehension of complex episodes, although the extent to which the buffer is heavily involved in routine comprehension is uncertain (see below). It is possible that most access to long-term memory representations may be relatively automatic, given the evidence that retrieval from LTM appears not to be heavily dependent on working memory capacity (Baddeley *et al.* 1984; Craik *et al.* 1996).

2 *Spatial thinking?* I see the episodic buffer as offering a cognitive workspace, and hence as playing a central role in spatial thinking, backed up by the visuospatial sketchpad. I assume the same would apply to a number of other problem-solving activities, except that emphasis would be placed on other subsystems than the sketchpad. In particular, flexible access to LTM, and the capacity to pick up and utilize analogies across different contexts

and modalities is likely to be important. Performance will be influenced by the number of chunks that can be maintained, and by the attentional capacity of the central executive. I return to this issue in the next chapter.

8.3.8 Relationship of the buffer to LTM and knowledge

1 *Relation to episodic LTM.* The episodic buffer is the principal link between working memory and LTM. It resembles episodic LTM in that it is concerned with integrating and maintaining specific individual episodes. It differs, however, in that such maintenance is temporary, and attentionally limited. Entry of new material into episodic long-term memory is assumed to be dependent on the buffer, which is also assumed to play an important role in episodic retrieval. The buffer may, however, be well-preserved in densely amnesic patients, and conversely, possibly disrupted in patients whose LTM is otherwise unimpaired. Such patients would, of course, experience secondary problems with new learning of a type that is often encountered in dysexecutive patients, who typically show poor attentional and strategic control of both learning and retrieval (Stuss and Knight 2002).

2 *Relationship to semantic memory.* The buffer will frequently utilize semantic information in representing episodes, and such episodes will in due course contribute to semantic memory, as part of the normal process of accrual of knowledge.

3 *Relation to procedural skills.* Such skills would not be assumed to play a particularly important role in the episodic buffer, although as discussed earlier, it is conceivable that action plans such as instructions to perform a specified task in a particular way might be stored temporarily within the buffer.

8.3.9 What is the relationship to attention and consciousness?

The episodic buffer is assumed to be controlled by the central executive, a system whose capacity is attentionally limited. Retrieval from the buffer is assumed to operate principally through the process of conscious awareness, allowing information from multiple sources to be combined into a coherent overall representation.

8.3.10 How is the episodic buffer biologically implemented?

It seems unlikely that the episodic buffer reflects the operation of a single area of the brain. Given that its function is to pull together information from many different subsystems, it will potentially be influenced by all of these, to a greater or lesser extent. Nevertheless, it seems highly probable that the frontal lobes will be heavily involved, given their extensive links throughout the brain, and their involvement in 'higher-level' functions that coordinate processes such as perception and memory (Stuss and Knight 2002). It is also possible that the hippocampus may play a role in binding new information within the buffer with existing information in LTM.

The processes involved in such integration are essentially those that are required for any theory of binding. Hypotheses currently fall into two broad categories. At the individual cell level, there is evidence to suggest that particular neurons may be specialized for detecting specific features, while others detect conjunctions of features (Fuster 2002). It is possible in principle that a hierarchy of such neurons could provide a binding mechanism, broadly along the lines advocated by Goldman-Rakic (1998).

A second approach is to suggest that components of a single scene are integrated through the synchronous firing of the relevant units (Gray and Singer 1989; Hummel 1999; Singer 1999). Vogel *et al.* (2001) propose such an interpretation for their observation that the capacity of visual working memory is limited to about four objects, regardless of how many features each object comprises. They suggest that the limit is set by the interference due to overlap of firing as the number of objects increases.

Neuroimaging research is beginning to tackle the question of feature integration, with a study by Prabakharan *et al.* (2000) being particularly relevant. This study was concerned with the short-term retention of consonants, and of locations. Four conditions were used. In one, subjects were shown four consonants, with recognition tested after a brief delay by presentation of a probe consonant. A second condition involved four spatial locations which were likewise probed. The third condition combined these: as in the single task, the consonants were presented in the centre of the screen, and the locations arrayed across the screen. The final condition integrated the two tasks by presenting each consonant at one of the relevant locations. Degree and location of functional magnetic resonance imaging (fMRI) activation was studied, with the consonants activating the areas in the left hemisphere typically associated with the phonological loop, while the locations typically activated the visual equivalents, principally in the right hemisphere (see Chapter 12). Presenting both the line of consonants and the array of locations activated both sets of areas. However, when the consonants were placed in the specific locations, the overall level of activation was reduced, and its principal focus moved to the right frontal cortex, leading them to conclude that 'the present fMRI results provide evidence for another buffer, namely one that allows for temporary retention of integrated information' (Prabakharan *et al.* 2000, p. 89).

A similar conclusion was reached by Bor *et al.* (2003) in a study concerned with spatial working memory. They selected matrix patterns which varied in the ease with which they could be chunked and found that the greater the degree of chunking, the greater the extent of frontal fMRI activation.

8.3.11 Relationship to other models

One of the advantages of the episodic buffer concept is that it provides a bridge between the Baddeley and Hitch working memory model, with its emphasis on separating and identifying the phonological and visuospatial subsystems, and other approaches focusing on either executive processes or links to LTM. It may be helpful to compare the revised multicomponent working memory model with some of these.

My approach has much in common with that of Cowan (2001; 2005), although at first sight our models may seem to be very different. He tends to focus on attentional limitations, and to be less specific about the visuospatial and verbal subsystems. This appears to me to be a matter of emphasis. Indeed, the one major difference that I would make between our approaches is his emphasis on working memory as activated LTM, which seems to me to risk underemphasising the capacity of WM to combine and manipulate information in novel and creative ways.

The concept of working memory as activated LTM features even more prominently in the long-term working memory model of Ericsson and Kintsch (1995). The episodic buffer differs from their approach in assuming a temporary and flexible workspace that draws upon working memory; it thus proposes a much more dynamic system than that of Ericsson and Kintsch, which appears to depend on the simple activation of representations in LTM.

The assumption of an active, creative system is supported by the fact that one can readily set up a totally novel combination of concepts, such as an ice hockey-playing female elephant, and then go on to solve problems such as to how this new player might best be used, as a defender, perhaps, capable of delivering a mean body check? Or perhaps even better as a goalkeeper? Such manipulation of newly created complex representations would appear to go beyond simple activation, and to require something like a temporary workspace. Cowan (2001) comes close to this in proposing that the 'addresses' of the items that have been activated in long-term memory are maintained in a temporary store. Such an assumption does not appear to offer any advantage over the buffer concept, since it still requires storage, and specification as to how these addresses might be combined.

More generally, by allowing multidimensional coding, the episodic buffer concept becomes more readily comparable to a range of models of short-term and working memory that assume the system to be based on a wider range of memory coding than did the original model. While differences between my own model and the above remain, the greater breadth resulting from the episodic buffer concept makes it easier to address common problems, notably that of how WM relates to LTM.

The concept of an episodic buffer does therefore appear to offer a potential interpretation of the wide range of data that proved problematic for a working memory model that assumed a purely attentional central executive. A critic might complain that I have simply reverted to the old concept of an all-powerful executive. I would suggest that separating attentional and storage capacities is an important development for the model. Whether I am justified in this claim will depend on how successful the concept of an episodic buffer is in going beyond an account of existing data to generate new studies that succeed in expanding our knowledge in new and fruitful ways. The next chapter describes our first steps in trying to meet this challenge.

Chapter 9

Exploring the episodic buffer

In the short time since the concept was proposed, the episodic buffer appears to have created interest, and so far at least, to have met with more approval than criticism. Whilst this is encouraging more than this is needed if the concept is to be other than a convenient label for a range of unsolved problems. For me, that involves providing a framework that allows potentially important questions to be asked in a way that leads to new empirical findings. We have just begun that process, selecting as our initial question the role of executive processes in binding, the process of combining information from two or more sources into unitized chunks.

We have focused on two potentially contrasting paradigms, one concerned with visuospatial working memory, and the other with memory for prose. In both cases we continue to use the secondary task procedures that have proved productive throughout our development of the working memory model. We provisionally accept a distinction between two broad classes of binding: one is relatively passive, dependent on automatic processes, while the other is active and attentionally demanding. An example of automatic binding would be the influence of gestalt perceptual principles such as proximity and continuity on structuring a visual scene, while active binding might involve combining an arbitrary set of features into a single chunk, such as would be involved in creating an image of a rugby-playing nun with a pink hat, for example. As will become clear, our investigations are still at an early stage, but I will conclude with speculations about their impact on my current views of the concept of an episodic buffer.

9.1 Binding in visual working memory

As described in the chapter on the visuospatial sketchpad, a very welcome recent development in the field has been the growing interest in working memory from established investigators who have previously concentrated on visual attention. A series of studies by Luck, Vogel, Woodman and colleagues concludes that it is possible to hold some four objects in working memory, with each object potentially comprising an extensive range of features (Luck and

Vogel 1997; Vogel *et al.* 2001). They propose that the binding of features into objects is an automatic process and does not require attention.

Wheeler and Triesman (2002) extended and modified the approach of Luck and Vogel, and while in broad agreement, suggest that feature binding is not automatic. They base this conclusion on a condition in which an array of shapes differing in colour is presented, with memory tested by presenting an equivalent array in which the shape and/or colour of one item may or may not be changed. They find poorer performance when subjects are required to retain the *combination* of both features, for example colour and shape, rather than one or other feature. However when a single probe rather than an array of items is used to test retention of the array, there is no evidence that binding and retaining two features into a single object is any more demanding than remembering one feature such as shape. They argue that the difference between their two studies stems from the greater attentional demand of having several features presented simultaneously at retrieval. While this could reflect the greater attentional demand of binding per se, the single probe evidence suggests that it is more likely to result from the influence of the attentional demand of searching through the visual array on maintenance or retrieval, rather than binding at encoding.

We decided to investigate this issue using a dual task paradigm. If the binding together of two features is attentionally demanding, then it should be more readily disrupted by a secondary task than is the encoding of individual features (Allen *et al.* in press). Our first experiment attempted to replicate the findings of Wheeler and Triesman using a single probe. Subjects were briefly shown four shapes, four patches of colour, or four coloured shapes. Retention was tested after a brief delay by presenting a single item and requiring the subject to decide whether it had or had not just been presented. Under these conditions, our results suggested that our subjects were virtually as good at detecting whether a *combined* colour and shape had occurred as they were at detecting the individual features. Like Wheeler and Triesman, when testing with a single probe, we found no extra cost of binding the two features into a single object.

We then went on to combine our visual memory task with an attentionally demanding concurrent activity. If binding is attentionally demanding, then we might expect that it would be more sensitive to the effect of the additional load. We began by asking our subjects to count backwards in threes, finding that this disrupted overall performance. The disruption, however, was no greater for the retention of bound features than it was for single features, again suggesting that the process of binding was not especially demanding of general attentional resources. A third study replicated this and checked for possible strategic complications, this time using a concurrent digit span task. Our additional guessing correction suggest a small additional cost of binding over individual feature retention. We again found a clear general effect of the secondary task, but the effect was no greater for binding than for retention of individual features. A final experiment presented the memory items sequentially, before probing memory by presenting a test item from the sequence. Again we studied the effect of a concurrent backword counting task. When the final item was probed, we again found no clear evidence for greater disruption of binding. However, earlier items did show a differential disruption, with the decrement increasing with the number of items interposed between presentation and test. This suggests that binding may be automatic, but is more readily disrupted than is information from individual features.

Our results so far have supported the Luck and Vogel position of relatively automatic binding of features, as least when no more than four objects are presented. We regarded this as a baseline, and proposed to extend our investigations, expecting at some point to find that the binding of features does become attentionally demanding. In an attempt to increase the difficulty of binding, our next series of studies presented shape and colour in separate locations. The task proved more difficult, but once again, a concurrent load had no greater effect on encoding of separated features than on the encoding the features presented as a coloured shape (Karlson *et al.* in preparation).

Our work so far has principally concerned the binding of features into objects. We would however expect similar processes to operate at the level of binding objects into chunks, with gestalt principles such as symmetry, continuity and completion facilitating binding. Evidence for this comes from a study by Rossi-Arnaud *et al.* (2006), in which subjects attempted to remember the location of filled squares within a matrix. The experimenter indicated a series of locations in sequence, a task that was similar to the Corsi block tapping task, except that the array of targets comprised a regular 5×5 matrix. The locations were random or symmetrical about the vertical, horizontal or diagonal axis. Subjects were able to benefit when the pattern was symmetrical about a vertical axis, but not from horizontal or diagonal symmetry. An attention-demanding concurrent task reduced level of performance, but did not interact with the presence of vertical symmetry, suggesting that utilization of this gestalt property was automatic. A subsequent study used simultaneous rather than sequential presentation, a task resembling pattern-rather Corsi-span. A clear effect of vertical symmetry was found, a weaker horizontal effect, and no effect of diagonal symmetry. A concurrent attentional load impaired performance, but again did not interact with symmetry. We concluded that the gestalt principle of symmetry was encoded automatically and readily in the vertical plane, an effect that also occurs for the perception of symmetry, possible reflecting the frequency and importance in the environment of vertically symmetrical objects (Rossi-Arnaud *et al.* 2006; Pieroni *et al.* submitted).

9.2 Binding in memory for prose

Our second line of investigation uses the much more complex situation offered by prose recall. There is of course extensive research in this area, though relatively little of it is directly applicable to the question of the attentional demands of binding. What evidence there is, is far from consistent. Poulton (1958) for example, required his subjects to read passages of text at rates ranging from 37 to 293 words per minute. He found that a forced increase in reading rate impaired subsequent recognition of statements about the meaning of the passage to a greater extent than recognition of individual words. This suggests that the binding of the individual words into higher level semantic chunks may have been disrupted by the demand for faster reading.

Our own research (Baddeley and Hitch 1974) found that the comprehension and retention of prose was impaired when subjects were concurrently required to rehearse a sequence of six random digits. In the same series, we showed that a concurrent digit load impaired the speed, though typically not the accuracy, of reading and verifying or rejecting sentences that varied in syntactic complexity, each of which purported to describe the order of two following letters (e.g. *B* is not preceded by *A-AB*). The greater the digit load, the slower the verification (Baddeley and Hitch 1974). Size of concurrent digit load also influenced the speed at which subjects could verify syntactically simple statements about the world such as 'Shoes are sold in pairs', or 'Nuns are sold in pairs' (Baddeley *et al.* 1984b). As discussed in Chapter 10, there is also abundant evidence to suggest that individual differences in working memory span, as measured by the capacity to simultaneously store and manipulate information, correlates highly with reading comprehension (Daneman and Carpenter 1980; Daneman and Merikle 1996).

However, prose comprehension is a complex activity which involves considerably more that simply binding together features in working memory. Many studies have involved subsequent retention of the meaning of the passage, which in turn is likely to depend upon episodic memory. There is considerable evidence to suggest that input to episodic memory is highly dependent upon available attention (Murdock 1965; Baddeley *et al.* 1984b). Hence it might not be binding per se but rather the *retention* of such bindings that is impaired by the various secondary tasks.

A second possibility is that the attentional demand of retrieval is crucial. This is a less probable interpretation for two reasons. The studies described typically impose an attentional load during encoding, but not at retrieval (Murdock 1965; Baddeley and Hitch 1974). Secondly, a good deal of evidence suggests that the effect of a concurrent attentional task on retrieval is much less pronounced than its effect on learning (Baddeley *et al.* 1984b; Craik *et al.* 1996b; Naveh-Benjamin *et al.* 2003). Finally, although the abundant evidence based on working memory span might at first sight seems to make an obvious case for the role of attention in binding (Daneman and Carpenter 1980; Just and Carpenter 1992), later studies suggest a more complex picture. A series of studies by Caplan and Waters (1999; Waters and Caplan 2004) suggest that the contribution of *syntax* to comprehension, appears to be relatively automatic. Furthermore, although Baddeley and Wilson (2002) found preserved capacity to temporarily retain a prose paragraph in a small sample of highly intelligent but densely amnesic patients, a subsequent study has emphasized that such use of executive processes to maintain prose material may be relatively unusual (Gooding *et al.* 2005) probably reflecting a strategy that depends on a combination of dense amnesia and high intelligence.

In our own case, seeds of doubt as to the importance of attention in prose comprehension came from a series of attempts to develop a secondary task based on the capacity of subjects to generate random sequences of key presses, a task we had shown to be a measure of attentional demand (Baddeley *et al.* 1998b). We required our subjects to press keys at random while performing a range of concurrent tasks. As the demand of the concurrent task was increased, the randomness typically decreased. The decrement was greatest for tasks known to be executively demanding, such as semantic category fluency or performing a concurrent intelligence test.

In a subsequent unpublished series of studies we decided to apply this technique to the analysis of prose comprehension, requiring our subjects to press keys as randomly as possible at a one per second rate, either alone, or in combination with reading each of three prose passages, varying in level of difficulty. Subjects were then required to answer questions on the content of the passage. The easiest passage was taken from a fairy story written for young children, a second intermediate passage gave an account of a tropical disease, while the hardest passage was taken from a philosophy text. The three were clearly different on standard readability norms, and although equivalent in length, they took different amounts of time to read under unpaced conditions. We fully expected the level of difficulty to be reflected in the randomness of the key presses, but to our surprise found no evidence of this. There was a significant reduction in randomness when reading, but this was no greater for the hard philosophy passage than it was for the easy fairy story.

We assumed that the absence of an effect of passage complexity occurred because subjects were compensating for difficulty by reducing their reading rate. To avoid this we equated the rate of presentation, in one study using paced visual and in another paced auditory presentation. We obtained exactly the same results, concurrent reading reduced randomness, but the reduction was no greater for the philosophy passage than for the fairy story. Furthermore, there was no difference across passages in the effect of concurrent keyboard generation on the ability to answer questions about their contents.

Our unexpected negative results were, however, based on the relatively novel keyboard generation technique, so in due course we moved to the tried and trusted method of concurrent reaction time (Posner and Mitchell 1967). We required the subject to read the various passages at the same time as responding as rapidly as possible to an auditory stimulus. Two levels of concurrent task were used, simple reaction time in which a single tone occurred and choice reaction time in which the subject had to make a differential response to a higher or lower tone. As expected, choice reaction was slower than simple, and concurrent reading slowed down performance. There was no interaction between readability and the effect of concurrent task demand: philosophy and fairy story were equally disrupted and had an equal effect on reaction time.

In a last desperate effort to demonstrate an effect of task difficulty, we increased the number of alternatives in the concurrent RT task to eight. The results are shown in Fig. 9.1. Our secondary task had certainly increased in difficulty as reflected in RT performance, but as in previous studies we found virtually no evidence for the greater vulnerability of the more demanding passage, whether measured in terms of the impact of the passages on reaction time, or of the concurrent task on subsequent passage recall.

This whole series of experiments seemed to point to a system in which the difference between the passages was real, as measured by standard readability measures or speed of reading. It was also clear from its effect on random generation that the activity of reading or listening was attentionally demanding. However, the amount of attention devoted to comprehension appeared to be relatively constant. It suggested a process of comprehension in which the level of performance was principally set by some other factor such as existing knowledge, rather than by the capacity to bring attentional resources to bear. Comprehension appeared to be much nearer to an automatic process than to one of continuous hypothesis-generating or problem-solving.

However, our approach had at least one major weakness. We had begun the series assuming that the concurrent task would be our main measure, using

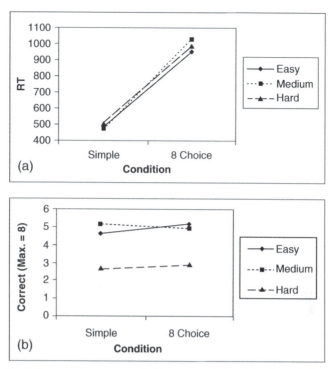

Fig. 9.1 The influence of prose complexity on a concurrent simple or choice reaction time task. Subjects heard prose from a fairy story, a descriptive passage or a philosophy text at the same time as performing a two choice or eight choice reaction time task. (a) indicates that reaction time was not influenced by passage difficulty, and (b) that subsequent level of recall did not depend on the difficulty of the RT task. Data from Baddeley and Anderson (unpublished).

only a relatively small number of subsequent questions about the passage to ensure that subjects would pay attention to its contents. Our results did not suggest that the level of subsequent retention declined with the addition of a demanding concurrent task, but this could simply have reflected the crudeness of our memory measure. Furthermore, even if we had obtained an effect on retention of the meaning of the passages this could have reflected the influence of attention on episodic memory, rather than on binding per se. This distinction is well illustrated by Cermak and O'Connor's (1983) amnesic patient who was an expert on laser technology. He was able to read an article on laser developments that had occurred since his illness, explaining them to the tester, but subsequently had no memory for the content of the passage. He appeared to able to bind the material into a comprehensible structure, but not to bind that structure into LTM.

We therefore decided to minimize demand on long-term episodic memory, instead using immediate recall as our measure of binding. While this is far from ideal, since performance is likely to be strongly influenced by the phonological loop, such effects can be manipulated by means of articulatory suppression. We chose to study the effects of prior language habits on binding by systematically varying the structure of the material to be recalled so as to allow the impact of linguistic and semantic factors to be detected. If the binding together of the words in a sentence into larger chunks is more attentionally demanding than the rote retention of unrelated words, then we would expect it to be more susceptible to concurrent task demands.

Existing evidence on this issue remains equivocal. There was a slight suggestion in our early results (Baddeley and Hitch 1974: Hitch and Baddeley 1976) that more complex syntactic structures, which certainly take longer to verify, may be more susceptible to concurrent demand, although the results were far from convincing, while subsequent work by Waters and Caplan (1996; 2004) suggests that syntactic processing is relatively automatic. However, we were not specifically concerned with the role of syntax in binding, opting instead to use sentence-based material that was likely to benefit from language habits at a range of levels including syntactic, semantic and pragmatic. We hoped that our secondary task technique would tell us if, and when, binding in prose retention is dependent upon attentional capacity. Two sets of experiments will be described, one manipulating sequences of simple sentences, and the other using a within-sentence manipulation.

Jefferies *et al.* (2004a) required their subjects to hear and repeat back sequences that comprised either a number of simple active declarative sentences. Hence, a sentence sequence might be *Mice like to eat cheese; The weather in summer is often hot; The road was long and dusty* while a length three random word test might comprised the same words in scrambled order, for examples *like to mice eat cheese; summer often in hot is weather the* and *long dusty road the was*. The level of performance was equated by first measuring span, the number of sentences and scrambled word sequences, that can be accurately recalled. We then tested subjects using sequences that were 50 per cent above span. Subjects were given three successive repetitions, allowing us to study both immediate recall on trial one and learning on trials two and three. Finally, our subjects were tested either at baseline when unencumbered by a concurrent task, or were required continuously to press one of four keys in response to one of four spatially located visual stimuli. As soon as the subject responded, the next stimulus appeared, a procedure that has been used extensively by Craik and colleagues, and found to influence encoding in episodic LTM and itself be influenced by episodic retrieval (Craik *et al.* 1996; Naveh Benjamin *et al.* 2003).

The concurrent RT task did impair performance, although the size of the effect was modest, and the pattern somewhat complex. Retention of the strings of unrelated words showed little impairment on trial one, but an increase in disruption was found in this scrambled word condition across subsequent learning trials. In contrast, retention of the sequences of sentences showed a maximum effect on trial one which then declined. While both scrambled words and scrambled sentences showed learning, this was more rapid in the case of the sentences.

This picture was broadly replicated in a second study which included rather longer sequences of lists or sentences. The first study had selected lists that were 50 per cent above span: this study went up to 200 per cent above. If anything, the longer sequences tended to show less of an impact of the concurrent task. Once again, rate of learning across trials was greater for sentences than wordlists.

A final study included a third type of material. In addition to strings of random words and sequences of unrelated sentences, we used sentences that were thematically related, hence making the material approximate more closely to normal prose. Once again the scrambled words showed an increasing effect of concurrent demand over successive learning trials, while scrambled sentences showed the opposite trend. However, the prose-like thematically linked sentences showed very little effect of concurrent task, regardless of stage of learning.

How should we interpret our pattern of results? As expected, the greater constraint provided by sentential form and semantic compatibility enhances memory, with scrambled sentences being easier than scrambled words, and coherent sets of sentences being easiest. Less predictable was the effect of the concurrent RT task, which had somewhat different effects on Trial 1 and on subsequent learning. On Trial 1, immediate recall of sentences was clearly impaired by the concurrent task, whereas neither scrambled words nor coherent prose sequences showed very much initial disruption.

We interpret these results in terms of the attentional demand imposed by chunking. The scrambled words are effectively equivalent to a single list of unrelated words with a low level of sequential constraint. As Tulving (1962) has shown, subjectively organized chunks do form in such random lists, but typically only with repeated presentation. This process of gradually building up subjectively organized chunks is presumably attentionally demanding, as reflected in the increasing effects of the secondary task over successive trials. In the case of thematically related sentences, it seems that the binding of words within simple sentences into chunks may be attentionally relatively undemanding, as is the binding of the sentences into a single coherent chunk in the thematically organized material. In the case of the unrelated sentences there is no overall thematic link, and hence, it is necessary to create some form of binding between sentences. Our data suggest that this occurs principally on trial one, with the impact of the concurrent task declining on subsequent trials, presumably because this attentionally demanding stage has been largely completed.

This, admittedly post hoc account, provides an explanation of both the effect of concurrent RT on memory performance, and of the comparable effects of memory on RT that we also observed. However, these effects are relatively small, compared to the influence on both recall and rate of learning of within- and between-sentence redundancy, effects that are presumably based on syntactic and semantic constraints. The relatively minor effects of a continuous concurrent RT task on these variables suggests that the influence of language habits may be largely automatic. As such, this series of experiments provides results resembling those of our studies varying passage difficulty. However, in this set of experiments, the concurrent task does appear to have some impact on the additional chunking required for binding together sentences that are not thematically coherent. We did in addition have a further concern. Subjects seemed to find the concurrent visual task relatively undemanding. Furthermore, they were free to use the phonological loop to boost their immediate recall performance. We tackled these issues in a second series of experiments which focused on the immediate retention of single sentences (Baddeley *et al.* In preparation).

One problem with sentential material is that it can vary greatly in level of difficulty, depending on the syntactic structure of the sentence and the knowledge required to comprehend it. This latter point is made very strongly in a study by Hambrick and Engle (2002) in which they required their subjects to recall excerpts from a baseball commentary. Their US subjects all understood baseball, but varied substantially in their degree of interest and knowledge. Their subjects comprised equal numbers of elderly and young participants, half of high working memory span capacity and half of low. Hambrick and Engle observed a major effect of baseball knowledge on subsequent recall, together with very much smaller effects of age and WM span, again suggesting a large relatively automatic contribution of knowledge to recall, together with a significant but small contribution from attentional processes.

In an attempt to limit the influence of such individual differences in prior knowledge, we devised a task which we termed *constrained sentence span*. This involves using a limited set of nouns, verbs, adjectives and adverbs that are repeatedly used across successive sentences, resulting in sequences that are entirely meaningful but very bland in semantic and syntactic content. Examples might be *The old sailor sold the red bicycle to the blonde lawyer*, or *The tall lawyer bought the red car from the old sailor* or *The blonde sailor bought the green bicycle from the tall priest*. Sentences could be increased in length by adding adjectives and adverbs, also taken from a constrained set. We assumed that these would be substantially more difficult than 'wild' sentences taken from normal discourse, as we thought proactive interference from earlier sentences would force the subject to rely on the most recent active binding. As expected, the constrained sentences were somewhat easier than the same words in scrambled order, with spans around six and eight respectively, but were substantially harder than 'wild' sentences culled from a daily newspaper for which span averaged around 12 words but was highly variable, depending on the particular sentences used. A series of pilot studies using this material suggested little difference in constrained sentence span depending on whether the same set of words was repeatedly used, or whether each trial involved totally different items, suggesting that PI may play a smaller role than we anticipated, possibly because of heavy reliance on the phonological loop. We opted to use the constrained sentence set based on the limited word pool for reasons of operational simplicity in producing large numbers of sentences approximately matched in terms of word frequency, imageability, and difficulty.

We began by testing the immediate recall of scrambled words, constrained sentences and wild sentences, under baseline conditions, and combined with the four-alternative visual RT task we and Craik *et al.* (1996) had used previously. We found little impact of the secondary task on performance, reinforcing our suspicion that the phonological loop may have been playing an important intermediary role, and leading to our next study, which attempted to systematically explore the roles of the phonological loop, the visuospatial sketchpad and the central executive in the retention of the sentences and scrambled words.

We began by titrating the length of the constrained sentences and sequences of scrambled words to achieve a percentage recall that was matched across the two. We then developed verbal and visual forms of the N-back memory task in which the subject is required to process a stream of items, responding when an item is repeated after a specified delay. Level of difficulty can then be varied by means of this delay, with zero-back, the detection of an immediate repetition, being easy, and two-back being possible but very difficult for both our verbal material, digits and our visuospatial material. This involved retaining the location of a series of dots, each presented in one of the cells of a 3 × 3 matrix. Subjects either pressed a key corresponding to the cell that had just been presented (zero-back), or one that matched the cell presented two items earlier. We assumed that the zero-backed tasks would involve the phonological loop and the sketchpad respectively, but would require minimal executive processing,

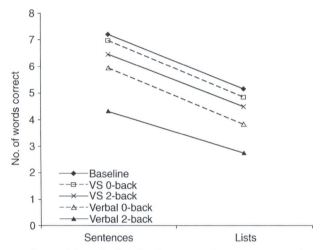

Fig. 9.2 Immediate serial recall of auditorily presented sentences or random word sequences as a function of concurrent task. Data from Baddeley *et al.* in preparation.

whereas two-back tasks are known to be highly demanding of executive resources, placing heavy demands on the frontal lobes (see Chapter 12).

Our next study involved auditory presentation of constrained sentences or scrambled word sequences. The results are shown in Fig. 9.2. Consider first the zero-back tasks which are assumed to place a load principally on the phonological and visuospatial subsystems. There is a clear effect of the zero-back digit task, indicating a role for the phonological loop, but little effect of the visuospatial zero-back task. This confirms our suspicion that the visuospatial sketchpad plays little role in the immediate retention of material of this type. In contrast, both two-back tasks impair performance, suggesting a role for executive processes in recall. Crucially however, there is no significant interaction between concurrent task and type of material. While executive processes do enhance performance, they do so just as effectively for unrelated words as for sentences, again suggesting that under our conditions of immediate recall, much if not all of the benefit obtained from using chunkable sentential material occurs automatically.

However, the constrained sentence studies so far described have used auditory presentation. Even with articulatory suppression, this allows access to the phonological loop, although not to subvocal rehearsal. Our next experiment aimed to prevent all use of the loop by combining suppression with visual presentation of the material to be recalled. We used the same material, except that each sentence or list was presented visually. This precluded use of the visual N-back task, but not the verbal task. Our results are shown in Fig. 9.3.

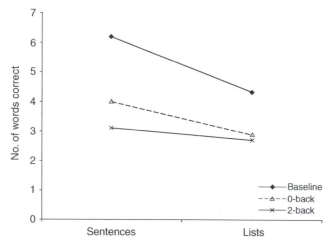

Fig. 9.3 Immediate serial recall of visually presented sentences and word lists as a function of concurrent task. Data from Baddeley *et al*. in preparation.

On this occasion we do obtain an interaction between concurrent task and material, with the sentences showing a greater degree of disruption than the scrambled words. We were concerned that some kind of floor effect might have been responsible and replicated our study using a less demanding concurrent task. The pattern of results was the same.

To summarize, our initial experiment demonstrated that when extra storage is provided by access to the loop, even when verbal rehearsal is prevented, chunking appears to occur with little apparent demand being placed on executive processes. When access to the loop is blocked completely by combining suppression with visual presentation, executive processes are required to utilize fully the sequential redundancy provided by well-formed meaningful sentences.

9.3 **Some implications**

In proposing that an additional component – the episodic buffer – should be added to the three component working memory model, I hoped for two things. The first was that it would extend the scope of the model, allowing it to address a wider range of issues. The second was that it should prove empirically fruitful in suggesting tractable but important questions and yield novel findings. This chapter has described some initial steps towards this latter goal. How successful has it been?

We chose to tackle a central feature of the buffer, namely its capacity to bind together information from a number of sources, both within and between modalities. In the case of visual working memory, we have begun by investigating within-modality binding, in the expectation that this would be most likely to reflect an automatic rather than executive process. Our findings broadly support this view, providing a baseline for exploring more demanding binding tasks both within and across modalities, and between perceptual stimuli and long-term semantic and episodic memory. We see our work as connecting with that of colleagues such as Luck, Vogel and Triesman who come from the perspective of visual attention. We regard this link between the two fields as important, but suspect that their work is likely to continue to focus on the binding of objects in vision, whereas ours is likely to move into more cognitively complex paradigms.

Our second line of study was concerned with analysing the contribution of language habits to prose comprehension and retention. Again we found a smaller effect of executive processes than expected. In the immediate recall paradigm, this is partly because of the role played by the phonological loop, which appears to provide enough temporary storage to allow subjects to make full use of the redundancy within the prose material, with little need for additional executive support. However, it is clear that such redundancy has a substantial impact on performance independent of either the phonological loop, or a major involvement of the executive. Again this suggests a clear role for relatively automatic linguistic processes. When the phonological loop is blocked however, by using visual presentation and articulatory suppression, then executive processes are needed to take full advantage of language-based chunking.

Our results also raises some interesting questions for current models of immediate verbal serial recall. This is particularly clear in the case of some of the computational models of serial order described in Chapter 2. As we saw, chaining models in which each item serves as a cue for the next did not give a good account of the evidence (Baddeley 1968; Henson *et al.* 1996). This led to a series of models (Burgess and Hitch 1999; Henson 1998; Page and Norris 1998) in which order was stored by associating each item with either a serial position cue, or with a developing context. However, the essence of the sequential redundancy within sentences lies in associations *between* successive items, a phenomenon readily accommodated by a chaining mechanism, but not easily fitted into positional or context-based models. Furthermore, this is exactly the type of mechanism that would seem to be required if the phonological loop is to serve as a language acquisition device which needs to bind sequences of novel but phonotactically constrained phonemes into words (Baddeley *et al.* 1998a).

There would seem to be at least two ways of tackling this problem. The first is to assume that the serial recall process proposed by such models operates upon representations at an item level, as the models do indeed assume, as they operate using a limited set of familiar items such as digits. Let us then suppose that instead of assuming that only existing lexical items may be selected, chunks comprising phonological sequences of varying degrees of complexity may become increasingly available as learning proceeds. The process of learning new words will benefit if the words resemble one's natural language in structure, as they are likely to offer more and larger existing chunks. This still leaves the question of how serial order is maintained within these chunks. One possibility is that the same mechanism operates as at the lexical level – a primacy cue for example. Another possibility is that some form of chaining operates at this level, though not at the previously studied lexical level.

A rather different interpretation is to explain the redundancy effect in terms of a Bayesian retrieval process that takes advantage of differential phonotactic probabilities. Such a mechanism might operate at a number of possible levels, including the early, relatively automatic retrieval processes, and/or later less automatic checking stage. We are beginning to investigate these various options.

At a more strategic level, our results have led to a modification of our original acceptance of a simple dichotomy between active and automatic binding, proposing instead three broad categories of binding. You may recall that one study that strongly influenced the development of the episodic buffer model was the observation that some densely amnesic patients were able to show excellent immediate recall of prose passages that clearly exceeded the capacity of the loop and sketchpad. Such patients appeared to have high intelligence and good executive skills, prompting us to conclude that that the central executive was a crucial factor in their preserved prose recall (Baddeley and Wilson 2002). However, our subsequent research on prose suggests that executive processes play a relatively small part in prose recall by most subjects. The crucial difference would seem to be their possession of normal episodic LTM. I suggest therefore that we accept a third important source of binding, namely that provided by long-term episodic memory.

A good example of the binding capacity of episodic memory comes from two studies by Naveh-Benjamin and colleagues. The first of these studied the recognition memory of elderly and young subjects using pairs of words that were either highly or remotely semantically associated (Naveh-Benjamin et al. 2003). Retention was tested by the capacity to recognize either individual words as having just been presented, or pairs, which comprised two presented words that might or might not have been presented as a pair. The elderly subjects performed just as well as the young on both the individual and on the seman-tically pairs of associated items, but much more poorly on the pairs that were remotely linked. Naveh-Benjamin *et al.* (2003) suggested that this might reflect the effect of age on attentional capacity.

This hypothesis was tested in a later study (Naveh-Benjamin *et al.* 2004) in which the experiment was repeated except that instead of having young and elderly subjects, two groups of young subjects were used, with one group required to perform a concurrent attentionally demanding task. The prediction was that this group, given their reduction in available attention, should perform in a similar way to the elderly. This did not occur. There was an impact of concurrent task on performance, but it did not interact with the nature of the pairs of items being retained. In short, the binding deficit shown by the elderly group was not the result of attentional loss but rather of the episodic memory deficit that is unfortunately a prominent feature of ageing.

The third type of binding is what we refer to as active binding, and within the multicomponent working memory model is assumed to depend on the central executive. We have so far found little evidence for this type of binding in our visual memory studies, although we have begun by studying tasks in which automatic binding seemed most probable. We have found some evidence of attentionally based active binding in our sentence recall studies, though less than we anticipated.

9.3.1 Implications for the episodic buffer model

I must confess to being somewhat surprised by our results, as I had imagined that the comprehension and encoding of prose would be a much more active and demanding process than appears to be the case. It would seem that 'effort after meaning', stressed by Bartlett (1932), may not be so effortful after all. Our results have some theoretical implications for the initial episodic buffer model. It may be recalled that the model explicitly omits any direct connection between the episodic buffer and the phonological and visuospatial subsystems, routing information through the central executive. How would this model handle our results?

Consider first the visuospatial working memory binding studies. The fact that the concurrent attentional task does not differentially disrupt binding suggests that the binding of features does not require executive resources. However, provided one accepts that passive binding may occur at the more peripheral level, this result is not problematic, although it would certainly be consistent with a direct link between the visuospatial sketchpad and the episodic buffer. The results of the sentence material are more challenging so, in that binding appears to involve both the phonological loop and information from semantic memory in the case of the constrained sentences, while memory for unrelated words appears to depend principally on simple phonological coding (Baddeley 1966a; b). With auditory presentation, disruption of the central executive had an equivalent effect on both sets of material, which would seem to suggest that the utilization of semantic and syntactic knowledge does not rely upon the operation of the executive. As such, it presents preliminary evidence for a direct link between the phonological loop and the episodic buffer. In my view, the evidence is now tipping in the direction of assuming direct links between the visuospatial and phonological subsystems and the multidimensional episodic buffer.

So where does that lead the episodic buffer hypothesis? First of all, the hypothesis has already proved to be a useful one in provoking questions, and coming up with clear answers. As in the case of the questions that prompted the initial Baddeley and Hitch experiments in 1974, the answers are not quite what we expected, but none the less provide a clear framework for further developing the model. As we shall see later, working memory is starting to emerge as simply one of a range of important systems underlying complex cognition, many of which operate relatively automatically. If we are to understand working memory, then it will be important to not only understand what the system does, but also what it does not need to do.

Chapter 10

Individual differences and working memory span

The possibility that people might differ in their cognitive abilities, and that these differences might be studied scientifically, extends back at least to Sir Francis Galton, who invented the technique of correlation specifically to study such differences (Galton 1883). John McKeen Cattell, a young American visitor to Wundt's laboratory in Leipzig, chose to study differences between individuals in such basic capacities as sensory sensitivity and speed of reaction, typically finding positive but rather low correlations between the performance of an individual on these various measures (Boring 1929).

10.1 The psychometric tradition

10.1.1 Early developments

The modern approach to individual differences, however, sprang from a practical problem. The French psychologist Alfred Binet, in collaboration with André Simon, the headmaster of a school for handicapped children, was asked to develop methods that would allow children who had particular educational needs to be identified. The idea was that such children would then be given a special form of education. However, since evaluation at the time depended on teachers' judgements, there was a fear that this might be an unreliable method, with the result that children who needed the extra help would not receive it, whereas other children might be placed in inappropriately unchallenging educational environments.

Binet used a very pragmatic approach. He developed a series of small readily measured tasks which, through observation and trial and error, appeared consistently to distinguish between children who had obvious intellectual problems, and those who clearly did not. Furthermore, it was noted that level of performance on these tests improved steadily as the child got older, typically reaching a plateau at about age 16. By expressing a child's score as a proportion of the average score of children at that chronological age, a simple but powerful measure was produced, the Intelligence Quotient or IQ.

A visiting US educationist, H. H. Goddard, saw the potential of this approach, and continued to develop and promulgate it on his return to the US. Over the next century, this approach developed into a major industry, psychometrics, widely used in both education and employment decisions, backed by an increasingly sophisticated armoury of statistical techniques. The approach has, however, also generated some major and hotly contested controversies regarding the nature of intelligence, the underlying construct that many of the tests are assumed to measure. These include the issue of the relative extent to which intelligence is dependent on heredity or environment, the question of whether racial differences exist, and more generally the role of cultural factors in performance on such tests (for an excellent review, see Mackintosh [1998]).

Despite the controversy, there does seem to be clear evidence of substantial achievements resulting from the psychometric approach to the measurement of intelligence. The American Psychological Association set up a committee chaired by a cognitive psychologist, Ulric Neisser, tasked with evaluating what we do and what we do not know about intelligence. The committee concluded that although much remains to be further investigated, intelligence tests do perform a useful function in predicting with reasonable accuracy, who will be likely to function most effectively within current Western society. That does not of course mean that these characteristics will necessarily be optimal across other societies, or indeed across the whole range of jobs within our society. Furthermore, it is clearly the case that such tests do not measure many other important personal and emotional qualities, or predict likely performance on a range of other activities such as music or painting. Nonetheless, the psychometric industry has had a considerable amount of practical success in predicting educational and occupational achievement (Neisser *et al.* 1996).

10.2 The concept of intelligence

The psychometric approach has had considerably less success in generating a theoretical understanding of the processes underlying high or low performance on intelligence tests. During the early years of last century, Spearman (1927) noted that all the constituent tests that made up batteries such as that proposed by Binet tended to correlate positively with each other. He interpreted this as suggesting that they all drew upon a single component which he referred to as general intelligence, or G. He developed the statistical method known as exploratory factor analysis in order to investigate this relationship, supporting his argument by identifying both G and a number of more specific subsidiary factors. This view was contested by the American psychologist Louis Thurstone (1940) who pointed out with some justification that any selection of tests might tend to have a group that were similar to each other, and that would therefore produce a central factor. For example, investigator A might tend to have rather a lot of tasks based on verbal reasoning, while B might tend to choose several visuospatial tasks. Each would expect to come up with a G factor, but they would not be the same.

One obvious way of trying to tackle this is to look across a wide range of different studies in order to decide whether the pattern looks more like Spearman's G, or like Thurstone's multiplicity of separate factors. Such an analysis was performed by John Carroll (1993), who analysed no fewer than 400 such studies, producing the result that is summarized in Fig. 10.1, taken from a brief but excellent survey of intelligence by Ian Deary (2001). As Fig. 10.1 suggests, there does seem to be support for a general factor, together with rather a mixed array of subsidiary processes, which in turn can be analysed into yet smaller components. A study of motor skill by Edwin Fleishman (1965) and Fleishman and Parker (1962), for example, identified no fewer than 14 subfactors of motor behaviour including control precision, response orientation reaction time, speed of arm movement and wrist-finger speed, in addition to nine other abilities that relate to physical or structural aspects of the body such as static and dynamic flexibility and strength, gross body co-ordination and trunk strength.

To a cognitive psychologist like myself, the subcomponents seem to represent a very large and somewhat incoherent list that does little to advance our basic understanding. I suspect that a basic problem is that of reliance on correlation as the principal analytic tool. Two tests may correlate, or fail to correlate, for a number of different reasons. It seems likely, for example, that Binet's selection of a wide range of complex tasks was more effective than the earlier attempt by Cattell because the latter focused on simple unitary measures. Binet, on the other hand, used complex tasks that were presumably able to tap many different underlying processes, potentially providing a measure reflecting many different capacities. From the practical viewpoint of selecting children who are likely to have difficulty in normal schools this does not matter, but if one wishes to know exactly what underpins differences between children, then the multiple complex test approach has clear limitations.

Investigators have, of course, attempted to target tests on particular functions, but in the absence of an independent theoretical basis, new tests will simply reflect the intuitions of the test designer, coupled with a rejection of those tests which tend not to correlate with factors proposed. This may be an unfair criticism, given that any theoretical approach needs to bootstrap itself up using its initial assumptions. However, for whatever reason, the psychometric

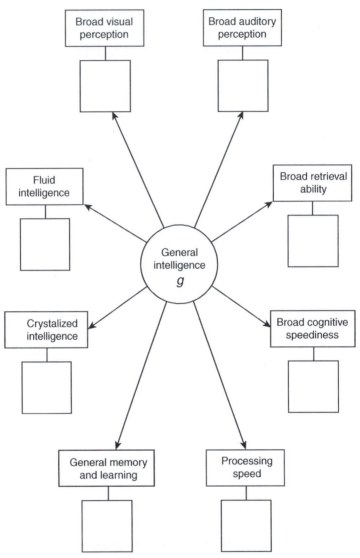

Fig. 10.1 A hierarchical representation of the associations among mental ability test scores. This diagram was the result of decades of work by John B. Carroll who re-analysed over 400 large, classic databases on human intelligence research. Reproduced from I. J. Deary Intelligence: A Very Short Introduction, Oxford University Press, with permission.

approach appears to have had considerably less success in developing theory than in its practical aims. Mackintosh summarises the situation as follows:

> Factor analysis can do no more than describe the relationships between different IQ tests. This is not the same as uncovering the structure of human abilities. That will only be achieved by the development and testing of psychological theory. Thus the fact that a general factor can always be extracted from a battery of IQ tests does not mean that there is a single underlying cognitive process tapped by all IQ tests. It is equally possible that all IQ tests tap a larger number of different processes, but there is some overlap in the set of processes tapped by the different groups of tests. Decision between these alternative possibilities will require experimental and theoretical analysis.

> (Mackintosh 1998, p. 230)

An interesting example of the problems of applying the psychometric approach to the analysis of cognition is shown in recent studies of cognitive ageing.

10.2.1 The psychometric approach to ageing and cognition

There has in recent years been a very substantial growth in the number of cognitive psychologists working in the general field of ageing. With an ageing Western population, it is of course very appropriate that governments should be concerned with how effectively people will cope in a technological society that changes rapidly and hence makes constant intellectual demands on young and old. This naturally leads to the question what cognitive changes occur as we grow older? The obvious answer is that many things change, and an obvious solution is an attempt to reduce the large array of cognitive measures that change with age to something more manageable, perhaps even to a single crucial factor, the G factor of ageing, A perhaps?

One can approach this problem by sampling subjects across a range of ages, testing them on a broad sample of tasks, then going on to produce clusters of tasks using factor analysis or some related technique. The next step is to see how well each of these correlates with age, and to what extent they correlate with each other. Let us assume that both correlate with age, factor X highly and factor Y, less so. It is conceivable that the link with age comes in both cases from a common component shared by X and Y. If that is the case, then statistically allowing for this correlation, there may be little additional variance contributed by Y, which can thus be discarded as a major determinant of age-related cognitive decline. Consider a third factor, Z. This might be less highly correlated with age than Y, but if it is relatively independent of X, then allowing for X would not substantially change the correlation, leading one to conclude that factor Z did indeed reflect a component of cognitive ageing that differs from that contributed by X.

A large number of studies of cognitive ageing in recent years have used this or other related approaches. The most extensive and carefully argued example of this comes from the work of Tim Salthouse (1992; 1996) who, reviewing many studies, concluded that most if not all of the variance in cognitive function resulting from age can be captured by a single factor, speed of processing. Hence, while a very wide range of measures decline with age, those based on speed of processing appear to be the best predictors of overall decline, leaving little or no variance to be explained by other factors such as memory performance or attentional control. Clearly, memory does decline with age, and is not typically measured by speeded tasks. However, it can be argued that it depends upon the speed of operation of underlying processes such as encoding and retrieval, with slow processing resulting in less complete and elaborated encoding, and slower, and hence less effective, retrieval (Salthouse 1996). Although developed by Salthouse to account for the decline of cognitive function in the elderly, speed of processing has been applied as an explanation much more widely, in particular to the development of cognitive capacity in children (Fry and Hale 1996; 2000; Kail 1988; 1992; Kail and Park 1994).

There are, however, problems in conceptualizing speed as a unitary psychological function. In general, all our psychological measures depend on measuring either speed or accuracy. It would, of course, be interesting if only the speed measure were sensitive to ageing effects. This does not, however, appear to be the case.

At the same time as Salthouse was conducting his programme in Atlanta, a German psychologist, Paul Baltes, was conducting an extensive parallel study in Berlin. Over a period of years, he repeatedly tested subjects of a wide age range on many different tasks, going on to conduct a statistical analysis similar to that of Salthouse. What Baltes and his group found was that their best predictors of age differences were two sensory measures – auditory and visual sensitivity – measured in terms of accuracy, not speed (Baltes and Lindenberger 1997). While it is plausible to argue that all cognition reflects the speed of basic operations, it is harder to argue that having poor vision causes you to do poorly on an auditory memory task, or that poor hearing results in slowed visual reaction time, or that either is causally related to the observed decline in memory or reasoning ability. A further problem for a simple speed hypothesis came from their observation that an equally good predictor of cognitive decline with age was offered by a measure of grip strength, lending new meaning to the expression 'He's losing his grip' (Baltes and Lindenberger 1997). A direct causal link between perceptual sensitivity and general cognition was not, of course, what the Baltes group proposed. As Lindenberger and Pötter (1998) points out, there has been a tendency in theoretical accounts of cognitive ageing to neglect the basic fact that correlation does not demonstrate causation.

It seems likely that many different functions decline in parallel as we grow older. Depending on the particular strengths of the test battery used, one or other test may prove more sensitive and/or more reliable as a measure of this underlying multicomponent process, and will hence be able statistically to overshadow further indicators of the many other processes that are declining in parallel, which happen to be less well detected by the particular methods employed. This is not a problem if one's aim is to predict the probable performance of an elderly individual, or to draw general conclusions about the likely overall performance of a population, both purposes for which psychometric methods were initially developed. It is a problem, however, if one wishes to give a *causal* account of the nature of the change. Speed measures may provide powerful predictors of performance decline, but we need to know whether their success results from their convenient averaging of many declining processes, or from a single crucial process. If the latter, then it is important to specify its nature and investigate it directly.

The view of ageing as reflecting the parallel decline of multiple systems is sometimes referred to as the Ford car hypothesis (or, in Britain, as the Woolworth's bicycle pump theory). Both of these devices are assumed to have been designed using components built to a common minimal level of durability, so as to avoid unnecessary expenditure in making any part last longer than it needs. This could perhaps be regarded as the null hypothesis of cognitive ageing, the simple theory that needs to be disproved before we accept an alternative and perhaps more interesting hypothesis. The multiple parallel decline hypothesis may indeed prove inadequate; demonstrating this will, however, require stronger evidence than that provided thus far by the correlational approach to cognitive ageing.

10.3 Individual differences in working memory

10.3.1 Working memory span

The approach to the study of working memory favoured by Baddeley and Hitch (1974) was based on the classic methods of experimental cognitive psychology, supplemented by evidence from neuropsychological cases. Within North America, however, much of the research in this area has relied upon psychometric methods using individual differences between groups of normal subjects, investigated using correlational methods. This line of research was initiated by a highly influential study concerned not so much with the analysis of working memory per se, but with its potential role in language comprehension. Daneman and Carpenter (1980), accepting the Baddeley and Hitch (1974) proposal that working memory involved a combination of the storage and processing of information, combined these processes in a task that became known as *working memory span*. Their subjects were required to read a series of sentences out loud, subsequently recalling the last word of each, with span being determined by the maximum number of sentences that could be processed and accurately remembered in this way. For example a subject might be required to read:

> For several hours the battle for the farmhouse raged.
> Under no circumstances would he allow the young man to purchase his ticket,

whereupon the correct response was 'raged' and 'ticket'. Performance differs reliably across subjects, who are typically able to recall between two and five terminal words.

Daneman and Carpenter (1980) found that this simple measure correlated highly significantly with the reading comprehension scores of their subjects, students at Carnegie-Mellon University, whether measured in terms of verbal scores on the Scholastic Aptitude Test or prose comprehension as measured by the Nelson-Denny Reading Test. They went on to demonstrate that students with high spans were consistently better at carrying relevant information over from one sentence to the next in a prose passage, as indicated by pronominal reference (Daneman and Carpenter 1983). High span subjects also show more efficient use of contextual information to interpret unfamiliar words within a complex text (Daneman and Green 1986). McDonald *et al.* (1992) and King and Just (1991) showed that high span subjects were better at parsing and disambiguating potentially ambiguous texts, and were able to hold multiple potential meanings of a given word such as 'bank' (river or financial) for longer periods. These authors tended to regard their measure as broadly consistent with the working memory model, regarding it as reflecting a system that was more complex than the phonological loop, but somewhat more language-specific than the central executive (Daneman and Tardif 1987). We will return to this issue later.

10.3.2 Is working memory span language-specific?

In subsequent years, many studies have replicated the strong association between working memory span and reading comprehension. Daneman and Merikle (1996) identified some 74 studies showing broadly similar results, with correlations between working memory span and comprehension averaging 0.41 for global comprehension (N = 38), and 0.52 for more specific comprehension measures (N = 36). For STM tasks involving storage but not processing correlations were lower, 0.28 for global and 0.40 for specific comprehension measures.

The predictive power of working memory span, however, is by no means limited to language comprehension. Engle *et al.* (1991) showed that children with high spans are better able to follow and obey complex sequences of directions, with the influence of span being higher for longer sequences, and for older children. Benton *et al.* (1984) assessed the capacity of their subjects to compose passages of prose, finding that subjects with high spans produced better prose composition. In a similar vein, Kiewra and Benton (1988) found that working memory span was a better predictor than the American College Test, or their overall grade point average, and of the capacity of students to take notes, and to benefit from them on a subsequent test.

It could be argued that virtually all the tasks described so far are essentially measures of the comprehension and use of language, and that predicting language comprehension from a test of sentence processing is hardly a surprising result. There are a number of reasons for not agreeing with this criticism. First of all, given the brevity and apparent simplicity of the span measure, it is remarkable that it can predict such a range of language processing tasks, and do so with such apparent replicability. More importantly, as we shall see, although Daneman and Carpenter themselves were principally concerned with language processing, working memory span has proved to predict a much wider range of tasks. Kyllonen and Stephens (1990), for example, were interested in the capacity of working memory span to predict the performance of US Air Force recruits on the complex tasks that might be required of them. They found a high correlation between span and the performance of students undertaking a course on logic gates. Shute (1991) performed a similar study in which subjects participated in a 40-hour-long course on the PASCAL programming language. The outcome of a subsequent programming test correlated more highly with span than with either general knowledge or an algebra test.

Perhaps the broadest claim for working memory span was made by Kyllonen and Christal (1990), who statistically combined measures from a number of tasks that required the simultaneous storage and manipulation of material into a single working memory span factor, demonstrating that it correlated very highly with reasoning ability, as measured by tests taken from standard intelligence batteries. A similar result was obtained by Engle *et al.* (1999a) in a study indicating a high correlation between working memory span and measures of fluid intelligence. Kyllonen and Christal suggest that the main difference between working memory and IQ. measures reflects the greater susceptibility of reasoning tests to cultural and educational experience. Working memory measures tend to be less culturally influenced, but more dependent on processing speed. This would seem to suggest that such measures would have advantages in attempting to select candidates from varied cultural backgrounds, as indeed is the task facing US Navy recruiters. It is perhaps also significant that the most recent version of the Wechsler Adult Intelligence Scale (WAIS) now incorporates a subgroup of tests that are labelled as measures of working memory, although I myself would regard them as a compromise between tasks based on working memory research and existing tests.

10.4 **What does working memory span measure?**

10.4.1 **Correlational approaches**

Given the wide range of important functions that can be predicted on the basis of working memory span, it clearly has practical value, but exactly what is it measuring? Could it simply be a short and neat way of combining estimates of many different functions, or does it reflect the capacity of a single crucial component of cognition? Although the bulk of research using the measure has simply used it as a marker of some hypothetical working memory system, an increasing number of studies are concerned with attempting to understand what it is that gives this simple measure its power. They have used a range of different techniques. Perhaps the simplest is to manipulate variables that might conceivably be assumed to increase or decrease span. For example LaPointe and Engle (1990) showed that span was smaller when the words to be remembered were longer, suggesting a possible contribution from the phonological loop. Lobley *et al.* (2005) observed that acoustic similarity among the words also reduced span, although this depended on the particular response processes required, raising the potentially important issue of strategy. Finally, Tehan *et al.* (2001) obtained effects of both word length and phonological similarity on both simple and complex span tasks.

Despite the popularity of working memory span as a measure, there are no generally agreed precise procedures, or indeed sets of material, which makes it difficult to draw clear conclusions that generalize across different studies. In view of this, it is remarkable that so many investigators have succeeded in broadly replicating the original Daneman and Carpenter (1980) findings. The situation is, however, less reassuring when we begin to examine more subtle effects. For example, Baddeley *et al.* (1985), using a group testing procedure that required subjects to verify sentences, but not to articulate them, replicated the association between span and reading comprehension. However, they found no effect of age upon performance, while Lustig *et al.* (2001) find an effect of age under some, but not all, conditions.

Experimental studies demonstrating that one variable or another may influence overall working memory span are valuable in giving hints as to how the task is performed; important when comparing studies using somewhat different paradigms. Furthermore experimental methods can provide a more direct test of a causal hypothesis than correlational methods.

Demonstration that a given variable can influence complex span performance may provide one possible interpretation of the correlation observed between span and other cognitive measures. However, it is entirely possible that a variable could influence span, but not be crucial to its correlation with a complex task performance. Within the multicomponent working memory model, for example, it could be that span is influenced by both the central executive and the phonological loop, but that its capacity to predict complex cognition rests entirely upon the executive component. Hence, a patient with a very pure phonological loop deficit might do poorly on working memory span, but have few problems in language comprehension (see Caplan and Waters [1999] for a review of the neuropsychological concomitants of span).

10.4.2 Combining experimental with correlation methods

A second and more promising approach to the analysis of working memory span involves combining correlational and experimental methods (Engle *et al.* 1999a; Miyake *et al.* 2001; Bayliss *et al.* 2003). This approach begins by testing a large sample of subjects on the working memory span task. Two groups are then formed from the best and worst performers, and are then compared on the task being investigated. For example, Rosen and Engle (1994) studied the capacity to generate items from semantic categories, for example requiring their subjects to produce as many animals as possible within a specified time. This task is known to be reliant on executive capacity, being impaired in patients suffering from frontal lobe damage (Milner 1982), and readily disrupted by a concurrent task that absorbs the capacity of the central executive (Baddeley *et al.* 1984b). As predicted, high span subjects generated more category members. Rosen and Engle then required their subjects to perform a demanding secondary task while generating items. Somewhat counter-intuitively, although this impaired the performance of the high span subjects, it had no impact on those with low span. A plausible suggestion is made that high span subjects normally use attention-demanding strategies to enhance performance. Such strategies are abandoned when subjects are required to perform the concurrent task, resulting in their producing fewer items. Low span participants show no concurrent task effect. Rosen and Engle suggest that this is because such subjects do not have sufficient working memory capacity to develop and utilize complex strategies. A secondary task that disrupts such strategies will thus have little effect on their performance.

It is, however, possible to suggest other interpretations. For example some other factor, such as lack of motivation, may lead these subjects to put less effort into the span task, and hence not bother to develop strategies, even though they may be perfectly capable of doing so. Indeed, if the low span subjects are capable of performing both the category generation task and the secondary task with no decrement, then when performing category generation alone, they would seem to have been under-using their available attentional capacity.

If the greater secondary task decrement in high span subjects were the result of a single isolated experiment, it would be less worrying, However, the effect has been demonstrated by Engle and colleagues across a range of different tasks (Engle *et al.* 1999b). Hence, although the strategy of selecting extreme groups might seem to be an economical one that maximizes the possibility of detecting an effect, it would also appear to maximize the likelihood of strategic differences. This is, of course, still a possible confounding factor even when studies use the whole range of the population, rather than its extremes, since the different levels of span performance could, in principle, represent different proportions of subjects using one or other strategy. This does, however, seem inherently less likely than the occurrence of a single aberrant group of poor performers. However, as we saw in the discussion of ageing and cognition, psychometric problems may remain, even when using the full population range.

Fortunately, techniques are developing that appear to allow specific hypotheses to be tested using individual difference measures. The most basic level of analysis is simply to look for correlations amongst various potential predictors of working memory span, possibly using multiple regression to decide which measures predict the greatest proportion of unique variance, when the contribution from the other variables are removed. As we saw in the case of age effects, this tends to favour functions that can be measured reliably, regardless of whether these are inherently the most important. This creates problems for measures of executive processing, which typically involve novel situations that are less likely to yield a score that is reliably consistent from one trial to the next, whereas a simple repetitive task such as choice reaction time is more likely to yield a consistent and reliable score. Furthermore, measures such as speed of processing, which can be based on a large range of tasks, may gain yet further in reliability. Finally, multiple regression is not easy to map onto specific models of the underlying processes, something that is clearly desirable in any area as complex as working memory.

This latter problem is addressed by the various forms of structural equation modelling, whereby a series of specific hypotheses may be proposed; provided that adequate measures of the underlying components can be made, the competing models can be compared as to how well they account for the resulting data. This still leaves the problem of the tendency for the executive measures to be unreliable. Fortunately this can be tackled using the technique of *latent variable analysis*, a promising way of teasing apart the potential components of the central executive that will be discussed in the next chapter.

However, regardless of any future success in analysing working memory span, there is no doubt that it has proved to be a very powerful predictor of a wide range of cognitive activities. Considered purely as a pragmatic psychometric measure, it has a number of advantages over more traditional tests. It offers a series of brief tests that do not rely heavily on prior knowledge, and as such is beginning to influence more traditional psychometric approaches. In addition, it has a much closer link to current cognitive psychology than does the classic approach to intelligence. If this link is to be fruitful however, we need to know why and how WM span tasks work. This is considered in the next chapter.

Chapter 11

What limits working memory span?

Working memory span, typically measured by tasks requiring the combined short-term storage and manipulation of information, is capable of predicting a remarkably wide range of complex cognitive tasks. As such, it must be capturing one or more very important cognitive processes. What might these be? In recent years, a number of research groups have attempted to move beyond the simple demonstration of the predictive power of WM span and to analyse its components, beginning with unitary hypotheses emphasizing such general factors as speed and inhibition, followed by more complex interpretations that are of direct relevance to the multicomponent model of WM. These will be discussed in turn, followed by an account of the application of the concept of WM to the analysis of individual differences in school achievement.

11.1 The speed hypothesis

As we saw in the previous chapter, the concept of speed of processing has played a very prominent role in attempts to explain the effects of ageing, and has also been proposed as a possible basic determinant of working memory capacity. Case *et al.* (1982) developed a measure they termed counting span. This involved presenting a series of cards, each containing a number of objects. The subject's task was to count the items on each card and then recall the various totals, with span being set as the largest number of cards that could be processed accurately and the totals remembered. Case *et al.* found that span increased systematically with age, as did speed of counting. They suggested a trade-off between the demands of processing and of remembering. As processing became more fluent, more attention was available for remembering. Finally, they taught their adult subjects to count using new names for numbers, an activity that, with practice, they could perform perfectly, but slowly. Under these circumstances their span was equivalent to that of children who counted at that speed when using normal digits. Case *et al.* assumed that basic mental capacities are constant during development, but that learned skills such as counting steadily improve with practice, resulting in the improvement in performance with age.

Subsequent studies using more conventional measures of working memory span have attempted to test the speed hypothesis directly. Using a step-wise regression design, Engle *et al.* (1992) showed that the correlation between speed and reading comprehension vanished when working memory span was covaried, while the correlation between span and comprehension remained significant after the effects of speed were controlled. This result rules out processing speed as the basis of the correlation between working memory and comprehension. A similar conclusion was also reached by Kyllonen and Stephens (1990). Bayliss *et al.* (2005a) studied the development of working memory span between the ages of 6 and 10, using tasks that were specifically designed to allow separate measures of speed and storage capacity to be made. We found evidence for separate general processing speed and storage components, both of which increased in capacity with age. In addition, we found a third factor that shared variance with both speed and storage and correlated more highly then either speed or complex storage measures with reading and mathematics and with intelligence as measured by Raven's Matrices test. We rejected interpretations based on speed alone.

11.2 The resource pool hypothesis

11.2.1 Is processing capacity general?

An assumption made by Case *et al.* and shared by Daneman and Carpenter (1980) and indeed a large number of contributors to this field, was that memory and processing draw on a common pool of general attentional resources. If so, then the better the subject is at sentence processing, the more capacity will be left to devote to memory, and vice versa. In recent years, this assumption has been increasingly questioned. One of the first suggestions that this plausible assumption might be false came from a study by Hitch and Baddeley (1976). They performed a detailed analysis of a study in which a verbal reasoning task was combined with concurrent serial digit recall. An implicit assumption of the Baddeley and Hitch (1974) model was that both of these draw upon the same limited capacity executive system. For a given level of difficulty, subjects could devote more attention to reasoning, resulting in a more rapid response at the expense of a higher memory error rate, or vice versa. Hence, when level of difficulty is held constant, there should be a negative correlation between the two subtasks, with higher error rates being associated with more rapid reasoning. In fact, exactly the opposite was found. This was interpreted as suggesting that when processing was running smoothly, both tasks would be performed without error. However, when one of them ran into difficulty, for whatever reason, attention was switched from the other, leading to impairment on both, and to a positive correlation.

Further evidence for the potential independence of storage and processing comes from a study by Duff and Logie (2001). They manipulated independently both these aspects of a task in which subjects were required to perform arithmetic operations varying in difficulty, while retaining sequences of unrelated words. In contrast to the resource-sharing hypothesis, they found no evidence that word retention was influenced by the difficulty of the arithmetic, as opposed to an effect of length of the delay imposed between word presentations and test. Nor was there any evidence that increasing the word load made the arithmetic task slower or less accurate. A subsequent study by Cocchini et al. (2002) showed that the capacity of subjects to retain a sequence of digits was unaffected by the requirement to encode and recall a visual matrix pattern between word presentation and test. Similarly, retaining a visual pattern was unaffected by the requirement to encode and recall a digit sequence between visual presentation and test. Such results imply that the performance on these tasks principally reflects the operation of independent visuospatial and phonological subsystems, rather than on a common pool of executive capacity. They do not, of course, imply that this will necessarily be the case for other tasks for which performance is limited by executive, rather than storage capacity.

11.2.2 **Storage or processing?**

Towse and Hitch (1995; Towse et al.1998) attempted to separate the processing and storage components of the Case et al. counting span task, independently manipulating the speed with which subjects could perform the counting task, and the elapsed delay before recall. They found that counting span was sensitive to delay, but not to attentional load. In a later study, Hitch et al. (2001) compared two conditions, both of which involved the same mix of easy, and hence fast, and hard (slow) components. In one condition the short delays occurred at the beginning of the sequence of operations, which ended with the long delay, while the other condition had the reverse order. Note that when a long delay item comes last, all the items will suffer from the delay it imposes, whereas in the reverse order, later items will not suffer a long delay, hence the average length of delay across the whole sequence will be less. This time-based prediction contrasts with that of a processing hypothesis, since total amount of processing is the same regardless of order. As predicted by the storage hypothesis, span was consistently higher when the long delays come first and the mean storage time per item is minimized. Hitch et al. therefore reject the limited attentional pool interpretation, suggesting instead that subjects switch between memory and counting tasks, with span being determined by the amount of forgetting that occurs during counting.

Saito and Miyake (2004) challenge this interpretation. They first replicated the basic findings of Towse *et al.* (1998) using adults rather than the children used in the initial study. They performed two further experiments. In one, delay was held constant, but amount of processing varied by using experimenter-paced item presentation. In the second, amount of processing was held constant while time was varied. In both cases performance was related to amount of intervening processing rather than elapsed time. They interpret their results as consistent with the importance of item retention, but suggesting that forgetting results from interference rather than delay.

The picture is further complicated by a recent study by Lépine *et al.* (2005) which compared the capacity of two types of measure to predict literacy and mathematics scores. They used two standard complex span measures, reading span and operation span, together with two novel tasks that were apparently simple, but were presented at a rapid paced rate. One task involved remembering a series of numbers each of which was followed by reading sequences of either four, five or six letters. The second task involved the presentation of sequences of letters to be remembered, with each being followed by a very simple paced arithmetic task which they required their subjects to read out and then report the sum (e.g. *W*. 9, +1, −1, +1, +1: subject reports *10*: *K* 7, −1, −1 etc). They found a higher correlation between academic performance and their simple paced tasks than they found with their conventional complex span measures. The apparent simplicity of their basic tasks, together with the strict control of processing, led them to reject strategic factors and interpret their result in terms of basic processing capacity. However, the problem with rapid pacing as used in both this and the Saito and Miyake (2004) study, is how subjects cope when performance begins to break down – a highly complex issue. This controversy is far from resolution.

A number of similar caveats should also be borne in mind. First of all, the particular role of switching between tasks as opposed to genuine simultaneous performance may vary substantially, depending on the precise experimental conditions. Within the working memory model, a complex task like sentence span is likely to depend on both the phonological loop and the central executive. It is, however, entirely plausible that the predictive capacity for cognitive function is mainly carried by its executive loading. Such an interpretation was proposed by Engle (1996) with the one modification that he emphasized the importance of attention for the capacity to *inhibit* irrelevant material.

11.3 **The inhibition hypothesis**

The idea that inhibition may be an important component of working memory capacity is not a new one. It is certainly the case that patients with frontal lobe damage often exhibit both executive problems and disinhibited behaviour (Shallice 1988; Stuss and Knight 2002). Furthermore, Norman and Shallice (1986) propose that their SAS system controls behaviour through its inhibitory capacities. One of the strongest claims for the importance of inhibition as a determinant of cognitive performance more generally is that of Lynn Hasher and Rose Zacks (1988), who have suggested that much of the cognitive decline associated with ageing may reflect a reduced capacity for inhibition. Lustig *et al.* (2001) use this framework to interpret the decrement in performance on working memory span tasks that is sometimes reported in the elderly. They suggest that the difficulty in inhibiting irrelevant information in the elderly might make them particularly subject to proactive interference. The standard way of testing span is to begin with one or two sentences, gradually increasing the number of sentences to a point that performance breaks down. By this point in the experiment, Lustig *et al.* argue that considerable PI will have built up from earlier successful trials. On the other hand, if testing begins at a level just above span, then subjects will be tested on their maximum performance before a great deal of PI has built up. As predicted, elderly subjects did indeed perform better when testing began with long sequences. Young subjects did not derive any advantage from this manipulation, but were helped when each trial was separated by a short break, a situation that has been shown to minimize proactive interference in the Peterson short-term forgetting task (Loess and Waugh 1967).

11.3.1 Interference effects in working memory

The role of inhibition was explored by Cantor and Engle (1993), who had high and low span subjects perform a fact verification task employing the *fan effect*. This effect involves teaching the subject a series of invented facts, for example, *the sailor is in the park, the priest is sleeping, the mayor is on the boat*. Under the fan condition, a number of such facts are attached to the same person, for example, *the soldier is on the boat, the soldier is in the park, the soldier is sleeping*. Subjects are then presented with a sentence and asked if it is true or false. Verification time increases with the size of fan, that is with the number of facts associated with the same subject. Cantor and Engle (1993) showed that the fan effect was greater in low span subjects, presumably because of their lower executive capacity.

A more detailed account of the processes underlying this result was sought by Conway and Engle (1994), who noted the similarity between the fan effect, where verification time increases with number of linked sentences, and Sternberg's (1966) observation that reaction time increases linearly with number of items to be remembered. In Sternberg's paradigm, subjects are shown a list of digits, and then tested by being required as rapidly as possible to decide whether a subsequent probe digit did or did not come from the recently presented set. When tested using this procedure, low span subjects showed a steeper slope relating set size to reaction time. This suggests that their reduced capacity made them more susceptible to the cost of storing and/or retrieving the digits. A further experiment, however, placed important constraints on this interpretation. The Sternberg task typically uses digits, with the same digits used repeatedly in sequences of any length. This was the procedure used in Conway and Engle's initial study. In a later study, however, they ensured that each set size involved different items, for example set size one might be the digit 5, set two, the digits 1 and 8, and set size four, digits 2, 4, 7 and 9. Under these circumstances, the slopes were equivalent for high and low span subjects. Conway and Engle concluded that the crucial factor that made the task differentially difficult for low span participants was the need to avoid potential competition from the occurrence of the target digit in other sets. In short, low span subjects were more susceptible to proactive interference, a difficulty in deciding whether a test item came from the target set, or from an earlier set of digits.

Kane and Engle (2000) tested this hypothesis in a memory study using a classical PI design. Three different lists of ten words were presented and recalled. Each of the lists was of ten items comprising one item from each of ten semantic categories such as animals or occupations. High and low span subjects were tested, and as expected, all showed progressively poorer recall across the three lists, the classic PI effect. However, while the two groups were equivalent on List 1 recall, low span subjects showed a greater decline across successive lists as predicted, demonstrating greater susceptibility to interference.

Conway *et al.* (2001) went on to show that this susceptibility to interference was not limited to memory. They required their subjects to shadow a continuous spoken message, repeating the words that were presented to one ear, and attempting to ignore the message in the other ear. Embedded in this unwanted message, however, were a number of repetitions of the subject's own name, a stimulus that Moray (1959) had shown is particularly likely to break through from the unattended ear and be noticed. When questioned afterwards, 65 per cent of the low span subjects reported hearing their name, compared to 20 per cent for those with high spans, who were presumably more successful in inhibiting the unwanted message and keeping it from conscious awareness.

A similar illustration of the greater capacity of high span individuals to inhibit unwanted information comes from a study of the Stroop task by Kane and Engle (2000). The Stroop effect occurs when the response required of the subject is in direct conflict with a strong habitual response. In the classic case, colour words are printed in different coloured inks. When the subject is asked to name the colour of the ink, for example, of the word 'blue' printed in red. The correct response (*red*) is slower and less accurate than when a neutral word or a line of x's is used instead of an incongruous colour name. Under this standard paradigm, there was a modest, but significant correlation between working memory span and speed. However, when the pattern changed so that name and ink colour were consistent for 75 per cent of the time, low span subjects showed a much more marked tendency to make errors on the 25 per cent of occasions that an inconsistent Stroop stimulus occurred. They found the task of inhibiting the dominant but inappropriate response particularly hard when the dominant response was usually appropriate.

In response to this substantial body of evidence, Engle (1996) proposed the *inhibition resource hypothesis*. This suggests that a very wide range of cognitive activity depends on the capacity to inhibit competing or unwanted streams of information or response habits. This process is assumed to be attentionally demanding. The various working memory span tasks are assumed to work because they place a heavy load upon the subject's capacity to maintain the relevant remembered items against the competing demands of processing and resisting competition from earlier items. However, while Engle and colleagues have made a strong case for the potential importance of inhibitory processes, at least two further questions remain. To what extent can inhibition be regarded as a unitary function, and even if this is the case, is it solely responsible for the predictive capacity of working span measures? These two questions will be considered next.

11.3.2 Is inhibition unitary?

Despite the popularity of the concept of inhibition, and the many measures and phenomena that are assumed to reflect it, there is little agreement as to either its definition or measurement. The situation is aptly summed up by Rabbitt:

> In our laboratory we have been unable to find any commonality of individual differences in 'inhibition' between each of a wide variety of logically identical, but superficially dissimilar Stroop-like tasks. That is, we can find no evidence that the ability to inhibit responses across a range of different tasks is consistently greater in some individuals than in others.

(Rabbitt 1997, pp. 12-13)

The term inhibition is used in many ways. In the area of vision, for example, lateral inhibition refers to a sensory mechanism that enables the perception of a boundary to be sharpened by suppressing activation in cells adjacent to maximally activated cells. On the other hand, inhibition of return refers to an entirely different phenomenon whereby eye movements typically do not return to a location that has just been fixated. Within the cognitively more complex area of random generation, at least two effects occur that appear to be inhibition-dependent.

One of these comprises a powerful tendency to avoid immediately repeating the same item, an effect that appears to be implicit, and is uninfluenced by either the rate of generation required or the size of a concurrent cognitive load (Baddeley *et al.* 1998). Repeating an item typically facilitates processing, an effect known as positive priming. There is however a danger of creating a positive feedback loop whereby the organism would become locked into a response cycle whereby each response primed itself, presenting an ever-greater difficulty of breaking out of the repetition loop. An automatic inhibition of immediate repetition would avoid this problem.

A further feature of random generation is the need to inhibit stereotyped responses, alphabetic sequences such as *a b*, or *q r s*, for letters, counting sequences for digits, and in the case of key pressing, producing the analogous finger of the other hand (Baddeley *et al.* 1998). Unlike repetition avoidance, these effects increase with speed of generation and with concurrent load, suggesting that inhibiting them requires active attention. It is an open question whether the inhibition involved in this situation draws on the same capacity as that involved in focusing on a single stimulus in a noisy environment, or of recalling items from the last list, under conditions of PI from earlier similar lists.

11.3.3 A multivariate approach to inhibition

The question of whether inhibition is a unitary function has been addressed in a recent study by Friedman and Miyake (2004) that makes excellent use of *latent variable analysis,* a statistical procedure that is more attuned than earlier correlational methods to test more complex hypotheses. Friedman *et al.* begin by identifying three potentially separable types of inhibition. The first of these concerns the capacity to inhibit a prepotent response, based on an established prior habit. They study this using three tasks, each of which is assumed to reflect prepotent inhibition. The first involves the classic Stroop paradigm, as described above. The second tests the capacity to respond appropriately to a stop signal that instructs the subject to inhibit a previously planned response, while the third involves the anti-saccade task. This apparently simple but powerful measure relies on the automatic tendency for the eye to move towards a new stimulus. It contrasts two conditions: one is the pro-saccade in which subjects are required to move their eyes towards a visual stimulus, the other an anti-saccade condition which requires the eyes to move in the opposite direction as rapidly as possible (Hallett 1978). In order to do so, the subject must inhibit the natural tendency to fixate the cue, rather than the instructed response location. Roberts *et al.* (1994), showed that the anti-saccade condition was differentially impaired by a concurrent task, suggesting that it depended upon a process with limited attentional capacity. This conclusion is further supported by the demonstration of Guitton *et al.* (1985) that anti-saccade performance is impaired in patients with frontal lobe damage, and by the observation by Sweeney *et al.* (1996) that anti-saccade performance is accompanied by increased activity in the dorsolateral prefrontal cortex. Finally, Kane *et al.* (2001) found that high and low working memory span subjects performed equivalently on the pro-saccade, but that low span subjects responded more slowly and less accurately to anti-saccade signals.

A second category of tasks used by Friedman and Miyake (2004) was that of *distractor inhibition.* This was also measured using three separate measures. The first was the Eriksen and Eriksen (1974) flanker task whereby the subject must identify a visually presented item, either on its own, or when flanked by potentially distracting irrelevant items. A second distractor inhibition task involved word naming, while a third required the subject to match shapes, both under distracting conditions.

Proactive interference was the variable assumed to link the third cluster of tasks. One of these involved the Brown-Peterson task in which subjects remember a short sequence of items over a filled delay, in which performance decrement has been shown to depend crucially on PI from earlier items (Keppel and Underwood 1962a; Wickens *et al.*1963). A second task involved the classic PI paradigm from verbal learning, in which the subject learns pairs of items (the A-B condition), followed by other pairs in which the same stimuli are paired with different responses (A-C). The final condition involved a cued recall task which again involved an interference condition.

Friedman and Miyake's first step was to confirm that the various tasks did indeed intercorrelate with other members of a proposed category, so as to ensure that it was plausible to assume that each cluster could be combined into a single latent variable. Although intercorrelation between the various tests was relatively low, latent variables were successfully identified. The next step was to test the hypothesis that these did indeed represent three separable types of inhibition. In fact, they proved to fall into two rather than three categories, with both prepotent response inhibition and distractor inhibition being best accounted for through a single latent variable. Both were clearly separable from the variable underlying the PI tasks.

The next stage of the analysis was to investigate the relationship between the two types of inhibition identified, and a range of other capacities that might plausibly be thought to be influenced by inhibitory factors. One of these involved task switching, where a latent variable was derived from three different switching tasks, one involving switching between number and letter processing, another requiring switching between the local and global features of a complex array, while the third involved switching between semantic categories. Depending on the precise measure used, switching correlated between 0.73 and 0.55 with prepotent response inhibition, but was unrelated to PI. This result did not simply reflect a reduced sensitivity of the PI measures, since this latent variable showed a significant association with a questionnaire measure of susceptibility to intrusive thoughts (r 0.36), whereas the prepotent response measure did not correlate (r −0.11). Prepotent response inhibition did however show a significant, although weak correlation with Broadbent's Cognitive Failures Questionnaire (Broadbent *et al.* 1982) in which subjects are asked to report everyday slips of action and attention, whereas PI was not significantly related.

These results appear to suggest that at least two forms of inhibition can be identified, and that they play interestingly different roles in a range of potentially important tasks. Does that therefore mean that Engle and Hasher are justified in placing so much emphasis on the role of inhibition in working memory span? Fortunately, Friedman and Miyake had tested their subjects on reading span. They found that performance was significantly related to both measures of inhibition, though to a relatively modest extent, for prepotent response, r −0.23, for PI, $r = 0.33$. There was no reliable association between the inhibitory measures and intrusion errors.

The Friedman and Miyake study is potentially a very important piece of work which if replicated, indicates the possibility of using latent variable analysis to test relatively subtle hypotheses. The pattern of results observed is complex but coherent, suggesting that it is unlikely that working memory span, with its capacity to predict performance on a rich array of cognitive tasks, can be adequately interpreted in terms of a single variable.

11.4 Components of working memory

11.4.1 Is working memory domain-specific?

In their initial paper, Daneman and Carpenter (1980) assumed that the system they were measuring was specific to language processing, a point that was made more explicitly by Daneman and Tardif (1987) in a paper that claimed to present evidence for separate language-based and visuospatial working memories. A stronger case for this dichotomous view was presented by Shah and Miyake (1996). In addition to the standard reading span working memory measure, they also tested performance on a second span measure based on

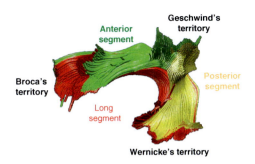

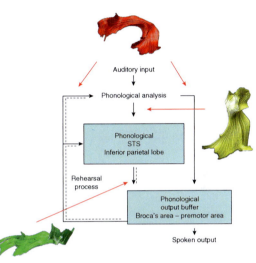

Plate 1 The upper figure represents a reconstruction of the arcuate tract which connects Broca's and Werinicke's centres. (Data from Catani *et al*. 2005). The lower panel represents a possible mapping onto the phonological loop model (Catani *et al*. 2005 modified). See also Figure 12.1.

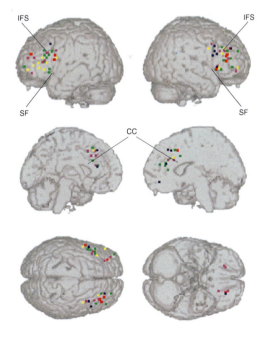

Plate 2 Systematic comparison of frontal activations associated with five cognitive demands. Activations are from studies of response conflict (green) task novelty (pink) number of elements in working memory (yellow) working memory delay (red) and perceptual difficulty (blue). Shown are lateral (top row) and medial (middle row) views of each hemisphere, along with the whole brain views from above, (bottom left) and below (bottom right). (CC: Corpus collosum; IFS: Inferior frontal sulcus; SF: Silvian fissure). (Figure 2 from Duncan and Owen 2000). See also Figure 12.5.

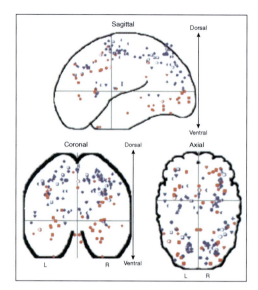

Plate 3 Combined data for studies involving STM for visual objects (pink) or spatial location (blue). The distinction is principally between ventral locations for objects, and dorsal for locations. Data from Smith and Jonides 1999. Figure 4. See also Figure 12.2.

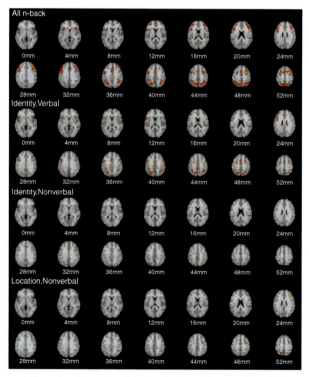

Plate 4 Meta-analytic activation maps for all n-back studies combined (top panel), tasks involving verbal memory (second panel), those involving non verbal retention of identity (third panel), and those involving retention of location (bottom panel). (From Owen *et al*. 2005 Figure 1). See also Figure 12.4.

combined spatial manipulation and memory, finding that reading span predicted reading comprehension, but not measures of spatial ability, while the spatial span showed the opposite pattern.

The case for a more general concept of working memory capacity was argued by Turner and Engle (1989) who developed a task they termed operation span, in which the subject is required to perform a sequence of simple arithmetic operations, each followed by an unrelated word, which was subsequently to be recalled. As in the reading span task, span is determined by the maximum length at which all the words can be recalled correctly. Turner and Engle found that this task predicted reading comprehension virtually as well as the standard reading span task, arguing that since it depended on arithmetic, not language comprehension, it implied that working memory span reflects a general, rather than language-specific executive capacity. A similar view was taken by Kyllonen and Christal (1990), reviewing a range of working memory tasks, by Kane *et al.* (2001), and by Engle *et al.* (1999), who showed a strong association between working memory span and performance on the anti-saccade task, in which the subjects have to respond by moving their eyes *away* from the location of a visual cue. It would appear therefore that the two tasks from the totally dissimilar verbal and visuospatial domains have a substantial common component. Engle *et al.* summarize their position as follows:

> Just as in intelligence research, general working memory factors appear to account for too much variance (in individual differences in cognition) to be ignored. However, in some studies (e.g. Shah and Miyake 1996), significant variance is left to be explained beyond that accounted for by a general factor. We suggest that the behavioural, neuropsychological, and neuroanatomical evidence support such a hierarchical view of working memory/attention. The specific factors correspond primarily to the domain of to-be-stored information, but the general factor transcends the domain of processing.
>
> (Engle *et al.* 1999a, p.125)

The Baddeley and Hitch (1974) working memory model does, of course, represent one example of such a model. This multicomponent model has, however, emerged principally from experimental studies using dual task methods, coupled with neuropsychological evidence. To what extent does the initial Baddeley and Hitch (1974) framework survive a more detailed examination using an approach based on individual differences? As is clear from the above review, the individual difference-based approach to working memory has tended to focus on more executive aspects of the system, in addition to utilizing mainly correlational rather than experimental methods, combining data from multiple tests and employing statistical analyses based on structural equation modelling. However, it is increasingly the case that such studies take into account verbal and visuospatial STM as well as more general executive processes.

11.4.2 **Structural equation modelling of working memory**

Engle *et al.* (1999) tested 133 subjects on a set of working memory span tasks, short-term verbal memory tasks, and standard measures of intelligence. Verbal STM was measured using word span for similar and dissimilar items, while further verbal memory tasks included backward word span and free recall, which was split into long-term and recency components. Working memory measures included operation span in which a series of simple arithmetic problems are each followed by words that are subsequently recalled, and the standard reading span test. They also included a measure of random generation performance. Finally, non-verbal intelligence was measured using Raven's Progressive Matrices, and the Cattell Culture Fair Test.

Engle *et al.* used both exploratory and confirmatory factor analysis in order to check their putative categorization of tests into separate groups. They went on to use latent variable analysis to extract the common variance from these clusters, and structural equation modelling to study the relation between them. The results of their analysis are shown in Fig. 11.1. This showed common variance between the short-term and working memory clusters, both of which were associated with intelligence. However, when they controlled for working memory, the STM factor ceased to correlate with intelligence, whereas the correlation with working memory remained at a substantial $r = 0.50$, despite controlling for short-term verbal memory. They found no evidence that the recency effect in free recall correlated with short-term memory, consistent with the suggestion that it does not constitute a standard phonological loop task, as indeed was suggested by Baddeley and Hitch (1974), as discussed in Chapter 6. Random generation did not appear to be closely related to any of the other measures. We will return to this point later.

Engle *et al.* interpret their results in terms of a hierarchical model, proposing a system comprising a limited pool of attentional capacity, supplemented by a temporary verbal storage system; they note this has features in common with the original Baddeley and Hitch model.

A broadly equivalent latent variable analysis emphasizing visuospatial rather than verbal measures was carried out by Miyake *et al.* (2001). They tested subjects on a set of tasks selected to measure executive performance; they also included tasks which they predicted would reflect short-term visuospatial storage, and others aimed at measuring visuospatial manipulation. Their executive tasks comprised the Tower of Hanoi, in which subjects must solve a spatial problem that involves planning and foresight, while a second executive task involved random generation. Spatial manipulation was measured using a task involving the comparison of rotated letters, together with a dot matrix spatial manipulation task. One visuospatial STM task was Corsi

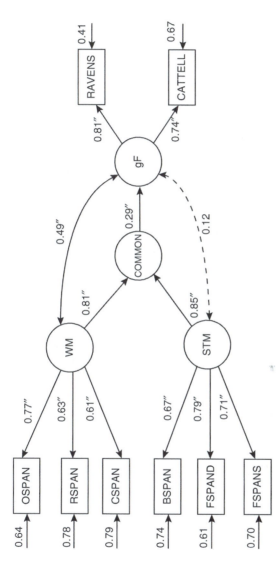

Fig.11.1 A path model relating working memory, STM and fluid intelligence. Variance common to STM and WM has been removed. The curved lines represent correlations between gF (fluid intelligence) and the residual for STM and WM. Note however that the STM tasks were all verbal in nature. Data from Engle et al. *Models of Working Memory*, 1999 p. 109.

block-tapping, whereby the experimenter taps a path through an array of blocks, which the subjects must then imitate. A second required the subject to retain and reproduce an array of dots within a matrix.

Latent variable analysis suggested that the short-term visual memory and visuospatial working memory tasks were much more closely related to executive processing than Engle *et al.* found was the case with verbal STM. A simple two-factor model fitted their data, with short-term and working memory being associated, and separable from executive processing without the need for memory storage. Logie (1995) has also observed that visuospatial STM appears to be more attentionally demanding than verbal STM.

Both the Engle *et al.* and Miyake *et al.* studies are broadly consistent with the Baddeley and Hitch proposal of a multimodal executive system aided by separate verbal and visuospatial subsystems that provide temporary storage. However, differences did occur between these two sources of evidence, with Miyake *et al.* (2001) producing clear evidence for a separable visuospatial and Engle *et al.* (1999), a separate verbal STM. This presumably reflects the particular tasks included in the two studies: it would however clearly be desirable to have both STM components reflected in the same study.

Bayliss *et al.* (2003) attempted to achieve this using a series of novel tasks that explicitly aimed at using carefully matched visuospatial and verbal tasks that provided separate measures of processing efficiency, storage and of their combination as reflected in visuospatial and verbal complex span tasks. Two studies were performed, one with eight-year-old children and the other with university students. Both gave clear evidence of a domain-general component reflecting processing efficiency, together with two domain-specific storage components, one verbal and the other visuospatial. There was, in addition, a residual component which they tentatively suggest may reflect the capacity to coordinate two simultaneous tasks. Bayliss *et al.* (2003) conclude that their results are inconsistent with an interpretation of complex working memory span in terms of a single resource pool that is shared between storage and processing. The data are, however, entirely consistent with a multicomponent model that distinguishes between domain-specific visuospatial and verbal short-term storage systems, and a domain-general attentionally limited executive processing system.

There thus appears to be growing agreement that separable components do exist and are coordinated by some kind of overall attentionally limited system. In summing up the views of some ten working memory theorists, following several days of intense and interactive discussion, Miyake and Shah wrote:

> We hereby declare the bankruptcy of a completely unitary view of working memory.
> . . . Rather than debating whether working memory is unitary or not, the key issue

may be to specify the source(s) of domain-specific effects found in both experimental (e.g. dual task) studies and correlational studies.

(Miyake and Shah 1999, p. 449)

11.4.3 Implication for theories of working memory

Have the sophisticated latent variable analyses revealed anything that was not already known? If they prove replicable and generalizable, they certainly have. For example, the suggestion that verbal short-term memory is much more readily separable from executive processes than visuospatial makes sense of a range of existing data, and demands explanation. One possibility is that rehearsal in verbal memory is less attention-demanding than its visuospatial equivalent. Baddeley (2000) suggested that, whereas rehearsal within the episodic buffer and the visuospatial system involves paying continued attention to the material being rehearsed, maintaining material using the phonological loop is much less attention-demanding. The reason is that familiar verbal material such as digits or words can be literally regenerated by the process of speech, either overt or covert. Furthermore, if the material retained involves a limited set of over-learned items such as digits, long-term knowledge may be used to 'clean up' the memory trace during repeated rehearsals, or at final retrieval. Visuospatial STM is more likely to involve unfamiliar material such as novel matrix patterns, which do not allow either of these strategies.

An exciting potential use of latent variable analysis is that of providing a more detailed account of the subprocesses involved in working memory. As discussed earlier, the analysis of the concept of inhibition by Friedman and Miyake (2004) has already begun to fractionate this complex concept into separate components, identifying which tasks are relevant and showing what cognitive skills are influenced by such components. A good example of the potential of this method is provided by Miyake *et al.* (2000), who tackle the complex but crucial issue of the extent to which executive processes may be fractionated.

11.5 Fractionating the central executive

As we saw earlier, research using simpler correlational methods, testing with either neuropsychological patients or normal subjects and using clinically developed 'frontal lobe' tasks, has typically produced rather disappointing results with many positive correlations between tasks, but of a magnitude that rarely exceeds 0.3 (Duncan *et al.* 1996; Shallice and Burgess 1996). This probably reflects a number of problems, including:

1 That the executive is multicomponent;

2 That it depends largely, but almost certainly not exclusively, on the frontal lobes;

3 That this is a large and complex area of the brain that is almost certainly also responsible for other processes; and finally;

4 That executive processes are typically recruited in order to tackle non-routine situations that may call for different strategies at different times., hence providing unreliable test scores (Rabbitt 1997).

Latent variable analysis, with its capacity to extract common variance even from tasks where the reliability is somewhat low, is therefore ideally suited to this problem.

Miyake *et al.* (2000) began by proposing a range of plausible executive subprocesses and selecting several measures of each, then confirming that they each cluster around what can reasonably be assumed to reflect a relevant latent variable. They then applied their findings to study a range of established candidate measures of executive processing. These included dual task performance, the Wisconsin Card Sorting Task, the Tower of Hanoi, random generation and Turner and Engle's operation span.

Candidates for underlying executive processes that might account for performance on these standard measures included the following: *prepotent inhibition*, as described previously, which they measured using the anti-saccade task, the Stroop test, and a task requiring the response to an occasional stop signal that intervened within a series of highly practiced, speeded responses. A capacity for *updating working memory* was measured using the classic task in which subjects have to remember the latest state of a range of variables that are constantly changing (Yntema and Trask 1963). Other updating tasks involved keeping track of changing tones, and continuing to remember the last four letters of a continuous stream, and reporting them whenever the stream was unpredictably interrupted. A third cluster of three tasks measured *set switching capacity* using the tasks developed by Jersild (1927) and Rodgers and Monsell (1995). One task involved switching between addition and subtraction, a second involved letter-number pairs, and required alternation between processing the number and the letter, while the third utilized the local-global perceptual distinction. A series of local items, such as digits, were spatially arranged so as to form a constellation or pattern that was itself a digit. Subjects were required to alternate between responding at the local and at the global level.

The analysis indicated that different subtypes of proposed executive measures did indeed give rise to a range of identifiable latent factors. As expected, when these were applied to the study of clinically used target tasks, none proved to be process-pure, although the tasks did differ in the extent to which they drew upon the various proposed underlying executive processes. Hence the Wisconsin Card Sorting Test loaded particularly heavily on set shifting, reassuringly since it does indeed involve switching from one category to another. The Tower of Hanoi appeared to be particularly sensitive to level of inhibition, as did random generation, while the operation span task was most closely related to updating. Dual task performance was not strongly related to any of these measures. That does not, of course, mean that it is not an executive task, simply that no relevant process has yet been identified using the present array of measures.

At this stage therefore, latent variable analysis does appear to be a very promising technique. However, experience of the use of psychometric measures in fields such as ageing, and indeed in the study of intelligence itself, suggests a degree of caution at this point. However if these results prove robust, and other laboratories using somewhat different versions of similar tasks produce broadly comparable results, then picking apart the complex threads that make up the central executive may prove to be a more tractable task than it first appeared.

11.6 **Working memory and education**

One way of testing the robustness of a theory is to take it out into the world, and attempt to use it to tackle important practical problems. Susan Gathercole and colleagues have carried out an extensive programme of research that began by developing a working memory test battery suitable for schoolchildren of a wide range of ages. The battery provides measures of central executive, phonological loop and visuospatial sketchpad performance and was applied by Gathercole and Pickering (2000b) to children who were having difficulty at school with English and/or mathematics. They found that poor performance was associated with low scores on the central executive measures, and to a lesser extent on those reflecting the phonological loop. A similar pattern was found when studying a separate group of children categorized as having special educational needs (Gathercole and Pickering 2001).

A subsequent correlational study related performance on their battery to grades obtained on standardized national examinations, with performance on their WM battery using a larger sample of seven- and eight-year-olds. At age seven, performance on mathematics and English was associated with working memory score, with the more complex span tests being particularly sensitive. Another sample tested at age 14 showed a similar association with WM scores for mathematics and science, but not in the case of English. They point out that, whereas at seven years old the English tests relied principally on basic literacy skills, at age 14, a child is expected to respond in essay form to questions concerning books and plays they have studied. This is an important reminder that, despite the importance of working memory, scholastic performance is also likely to depend on many other factors.

11.6.1 **An automated working memory battery, the AWMA**

While the initial test battery was clearly successful in its broad aims, Gathercole *et al.* were concerned that their selection of tasks may have tended to emphasize verbal processing, and to give inadequate weight to complex visual working memory tasks. The test was also somewhat lengthy, and required a trained tester. They attempted to remedy both these shortcomings by developing an automated version of the test, with a somewhat modified set of component tasks. The Automated Working Memory Assessment (AWMA) comprised three tests of verbal STM, three of visuospatial STM, three of verbal complex span and three testing visuospatial complex span (Alloway *et al.* In press).

The battery was administered to 709 children aged between four and eleven years, and the results were analysed using structural equation modelling, attempting to fit the data with two-, three- or four-component models. They found a three-component model provided the best fit, with clusters that were compatible with the division of working memory into a central executive and associated visuospatial and verbal STM systems (see Fig. 11.2). The three factors were, however, quite strongly intercorrelated, with the link between the central executive and visuospatial processing being the strongest, a pattern we have noted earlier. This visuospatial link was most marked in the younger, four- to six-year-old children, with the pattern becoming more balanced as children got older.

11.6.2 **Children with specific deficits**

Gathercole and colleagues have gone on to study subgroups of children with specific patterns of cognitive deficits. Archibald and Gathercole (2006) studied a group of children with Specific Language Impairment (SLI), a pattern of deficit that certainly includes language, but is often rather less specific than its name would imply. They found that their SLI group were impaired on verbal complex memory span and nonword repetition, implying both a central executive and phonological loop deficit, whereas their visuospatial STM and working memory was comparatively spared (Archibald and Gathercole, 2006). A subsequent study examined the performance of 14 children diagnosed as suffering from SLI and 14 age-matched controls using a battery developed by Bayliss *et al.* (2003) to separate out storage and processing for both visuospatial and verbal materials. They found that the SLI group was significantly slower on both visuospatial and verbal processing, but that accuracy was only significantly impaired in the complex working memory tasks that involve verbal storage, regardless of whether this was combined with verbal or visuospatial processing. Once again this suggested a combined central executive and phonological loop deficit.

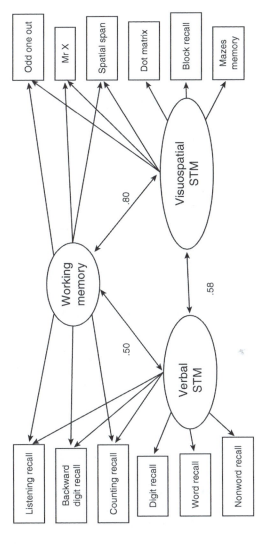

Fig. 11.2 The three-component model that provided the best fit for performance on the Automated Working Memory Assessment battery. Data from Alloway et al. (2006) In: Verbal and visuospatial short-term and working memory in children: are they separable? *Child Development*, **77**, 1698–1716.

It appears therefore that a relatively pure phonological loop deficit does not of itself have a major long-term effect on intellectual development, but does produce a relatively subtle deficit in the acquisition of new names or phonological forms. This result has clear implications for the nature of the link between the phonological loop and vocabulary acquisition discussed in Chapter 2. While a pure phonological loop deficit will hinder vocabulary development, it is a combination of this with weak executive capacity that is particularly harmful. Even in children with poor executive skills the role of the phonological loop reduces as vocabulary develops. This was shown clearly in a study of language development in learning–disabled children by Jarrold *et al.* (2004). We found a link between the phonological loop-based measures and vocabulary acquisition which disappeared in later years, presumably as a result of the growing dominance of other factors such as general intelligence and degree of language exposure.

11.6.3 Working memory in the classroom

By this point it should be clear that a wide range of versions of complex memory span tasks are capable of predicting everyday cognitive performance rather well. While this is gratifying, I would be disappointed if the concept of working memory simply produced a new set of intelligence tests. Indeed Gathercole's work suggests that children may have poor working memory without being low in intelligence. She and her colleagues decided to carry out an observational classroom study to see if they could gain insight into the nature of the problems such children encounter.

It rapidly became clear that there were many such problems (Gathercole *et al.* 2006). Children with low WM span have difficulty following instructions. This is unsurprising in the case of some instructions that were observed, such as 'Put your sheets on the green table, put your arrow cards in the packet, put your pencil away and come and sit on the carpet.' Problems occur even with shorter instructions. One child, Nathan, was handed his computer login cards and told to work on computer 13. He failed to do so as he had immediately forgotten which computer to use.

Other situations occur when the child must cope with simultaneous processing and storage, for example generating a sentence, remembering how to spell the words and then writing them without forgetting the sentence. Unfortunately aids to academic performance such as the use of number lines in arithmetic often require simultaneous processing and are particularly hard for such children to use.

Gathercole and colleagues are building on these initial observations to develop methods whereby teachers are able to identify such children, who the teachers typically describe as inattentive and unmotivated. They do not identify these children as having memory problems, although the children themselves complain that they forget what to do. Teachers do, however, appear receptive to the idea of a working memory deficit, and keen to know how to detect and help such children. Booklets for teachers have now been developed and are currently being used in an intervention study to test the effectiveness of instructing teachers in how to identify and then help children with working memory problems.

11.7 **Conclusion**

In conclusion, the study of individual differences in working memory has now advanced beyond the initial stage of demonstrating the predictive power of complex working memory span measures. As a result, the basic concept of working memory has been used to develop measures that are proving applicable to the analysis of a range of educational problems, that are beginning to suggest possible solutions.

Chapter 12

Neuroimaging working memory

Throughout its relatively short life, cognitive psychology has from time to time encountered new ideas, methods or techniques that on their arrival seemed likely to transform the field. Some did, as in the case of the information-processing metaphor, based on the computer, while others, such as transformational grammar in psycholinguistics, mathematical modelling in the field of memory, or signal detection theory in perception, have been absorbed as part of standard practice: methods that are useful without dramatically changing the underlying theoretical landscape. In the field of human memory, there is no doubt about the technique that is currently generating the most excitement, namely neuroimaging. Furthermore, the study of working memory appears to feature particularly strongly in this development. Imaging data are used throughout the present book, combined with other evidence relevant to the particular issues discussed. This approach is sufficiently important for current developments in working memory to merit a separate chapter, one that does not attempt to review the huge and growing array of experimental findings in any detail, but rather concentrates on a limited number of topics for which enough data have been accumulated to allow some estimate to be made as to both the strengths and weaknesses of such an approach.

This is not an area in which I myself have been heavily involved, although I have collaborated in a few neuroimaging studies. Fortunately, a number of review papers are beginning to emerge that attempt to draw some broad and coherent conclusions from the complex and varied patterns of data produced by imaging studies of working memory (see Owen 1997, Smith and Jonides 1997; Henson 2001). I will begin by giving a brief account of the major neuroimaging methods that have so far been used to study working memory, for the benefit of readers not already familiar with this rapidly expanding area.

12.1 Positron emission tomography (PET)

This is the method that initially gave rise to the excitement about imaging. It involves the use of a cyclotron to produce radioactive water or glucose that is then injected into the subject. It is transported by the blood, and can then be detected as gamma radiation, with an array of detectors used to locate points of maximum activity. These correspond to points at which blood flow is greatest. When a particular part of the brain is used heavily, it is assumed to absorb and emit more radiation than when it is in a resting state. Hence a visual stimulus will, for example, result in increased emission from an area that is crucial for the early stages of vision (see Frith and Friston [1997] for a review).

The brain is, of course, in constant activity. For that reason, if one wishes to identify the activity resulting from a given cognitive process, such as memory storage, it is necessary to compare a condition involving storage with one for which all other factors are held constant, but storage is absent, using the so-called subtraction technique. This is, of course, exactly the logic underlying the use of dual task methodology in purely behavioural studies of working memory, where for example a comparison is made between a baseline short-term memory condition and the same task performed under articulatory suppression, with the difference reflecting the contribution made by subvocal rehearsal. The fact that the method works in the behavioural context suggests that it may be a good candidate for the use of imaging, which, as we shall see, proves to be the case.

Although most of the PET studies we shall describe are based on the measurement of blood flow, it is possible to study the distribution and activity of a number of important neurotransmitters by selecting ligands that bind to the relevant receptor site for that specific neurotransmitter and labelling them radioactively. In due course, I suspect that this approach to the role and operation of neurotransmitters will prove enormously fruitful in studying processes that have proved very hard to tackle using current experimental and neuropsychological techniques. However, the area is still at an early stage of development, and has not so far contributed greatly to our understanding of working memory.

PET studies based on blood flow have been very effective at identifying broad areas of sustained activation, but because of the time taken for the radioactive material to be circulated, absorbed and detected, this method is not suitable for identifying processes that change rapidly. It is also very expensive, since the short half-life of the nucleotides used means that each laboratory must have a fully staffed cyclotron on site. There is also an obvious limit to the amount of radioactivity to which an individual subject can be allowed to be exposed. This not only prevents repeated experimental testing of subjects, but also creates problems for serial studies of development or disease progression. With PET, there is also a need for medical supervision in addition to the requirement for physiochemical, engineering, and statistical support, making this a very expensive tool.

12.2 **Functional magnetic resonance imagery (fMRI)**

This method capitalizes on the fact that when the brain is placed in a strong magnetic field, different atomic nuclei align themselves in different orientations. This allows the identification of areas that are used by the brain when performing a given activity by providing a measure of the activation of any given region of the brain. Identification relies upon brain oxygen level differences (the BOLD response) between different tasks. This method has the advantage that no radioactivity is involved. Furthermore, it is capable of detecting changes as they occur in real time. The degree of spatial resolution depends upon the strength of the magnet, with early studies typically having magnets of 1.5 tesla, whereas currently strengths of up to 7 tesla are increasingly used. Although such magnets are expensive, the system as a whole is less expensive to run than PET, and given its temporal and spatial resolution is used increasingly widely for studies of cognitive function. Furthermore, its apparent safety means that fMRI can be used repeatedly on the same subject.

The method does, however, have some practical constraints. The presence of a powerful magnet places substantial limits the type of equipment that can be used in its vicinity. The technique involves imaging 'slices' of the brain, and this in turn involves changing the magnetic field, an extremely noisy procedure that sounds to the subject like being in an iron tube that is being struck from time to time with a sledgehammer. Finally, the use of spoken responses is problematic, as speech causes movement which interferes with the resolution of the image. Despite these technical problems, the field is advancing rapidly, with a particularly welcome development being that of event-related imaging whereby the scan may be yoked to individual stages of an experimental procedure. This allows such factors as encoding, storage and retrieval to be imaged separately.

12.3 **Electroencephalography (EEG)**

This method involves recording the electrical activity of the brain from scalp electrodes, and is the oldest of the three methods described. It has been used clinically for identifying epileptic abnormalities for many years, with an array of electrodes used, for example to identify epileptic foci. Methods were refined using the *evoked response potential* (ERP) technique, whereby the processing of a single stimulus such as a click can be traced through the electrophysiological wave form it produces (see Kutas and Dale [1997] for a review). For many years this seemed to represent a sophisticated but rather arcane backwater of cognitive psychology, with little link to more mainstream cognitive theory. This has changed dramatically in recent years, and its methods have been used with great success in the study of attention (see Posner and Petersen [1990] for a review), and memory (see Rugg [1995] for a review). This method has the advantage of allowing considerable temporal precision, although its spatial resolution is inevitably limited by the need to pick up signals that have passed through the skull, and that are the aggregate of many different processes. This method has been used rather less in the study of working memory than have PET and fMRI, but it seems likely that it will in future play an increasingly large role, since it is considerably less expensive than the other methods, and is totally non-invasive.

12.4 **Other techniques**

The challenge of observing the activities of the living brain continues to attract technical attention. There are, for example, procedures such as MEG, in which the magnetic activity of the brain is sensed, although this currently requires equipment that is only now becoming more widely available. At the time of writing this review, it had had little impact on the study of working memory. I am sure this will change as MEG offers a more direct non-invasive method allowing precise temporal resolution, which can usefully be combined with fMRI.

Another method this is likely to increase in importance is tractography, whereby MRI is used to trace the myelinated tracks that form the white matter of the brain. These form a network of links between brain areas that were described by nineteenth-century neuroanatomists but have since been largely neglected. Recent work has reactivated interest in what could be important systems that allow areas of the brain that are not anatomically close to communicate with speed and efficiency, rather in the way that major intercity highways facilitate trade. Fig. 12.1 shows one example of a system of white matter tracts that might plausibly be assumed to be involved in the operation of the phonological loop. At the time of writing, tractography is limited to generating structural images, but I understand that it should be possible to develop functional tractography in the near future.

Finally, mention should be made of methods of interfering with the activity of specific areas of the brain. One such technique is that of magnetic stimulation, whereby a powerful magnetic field temporarily interrupts processing in the area of the cortex within its field. In my own case, plans to use this technique to study the phonological loop were discouraged by the discovery that when applied to the necessary area for interfering with rehearsal, it was liable to cause toothache in the unfortunate subject! It seems likely that such problems will be resolved, providing a useful tool for making focused temporary

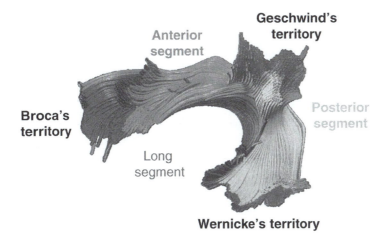

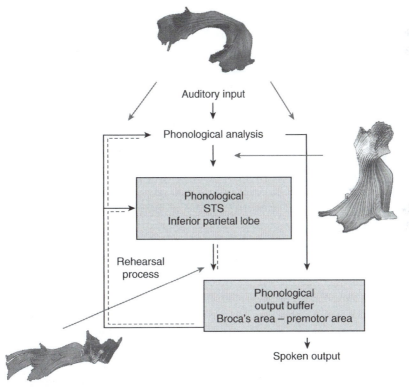

Fig. 12.1 The upper figure represents a reconstruction of the arcuate tract which connects Broca's and Werinicke's centres. (Data from Catani et al. 2004). The lower panel represents a possible mapping onto the phonological loop model (Catani et al. 2005 modified). In: Perisylvian language networks of the human brain. *Annals of Neurology*, **57**, 8–16. Reproduced with permission from John Wiley & Sons, Inc.. Please see Colour Plate 1 for a colour version of this figure.

'reversible lesions' in specified brain areas, although it does have the limitation that it can only be applied to superficial cortical areas.

An established though comparatively rarely used method involves stimulation by the neurosurgeon of the brain of a conscious patient during surgery. The brain does not have pain receptors, and the method is useful in checking out the function of a particular area of the brain during surgery to relieve epilepsy, a surgical procedure that can be very helpful, provided that one is sure that the area of brain removed is not crucial for the cognitive or other functioning of the patient. Penfield (1958) reported the evocation of what he somewhat controversially suggested were autobiographical memories, while Ojemann (1978; 1994) has used the method to explore regions involved in language and short-term memory.

12.5 **The naming of parts**

Much of what follows concerns the association between particular cognitive functions and specific brain regions. These can be identified in a number of different ways. One may refer to the activation of a general area of the brain, such as the temporal or occipital lobe. It is, of course, necessary to specify whether activation is in the right or left side of the brain, or is bilateral. As these are relatively large areas, it is common to further specify the location as the anterior (frontal) or posterior (rear) area of the lobe, or possibly around the boundary of two lobes, as in the case of the temporo-parietal location of the storage component of the phonological loop, which tends to overlap the temporal and parietal lobes. To complicate matters further, it is possible to use other brain features as an identifying mark, such as the Sylvian fissure that separates the temporal lobes from the parietal and frontal areas. Hence, the phonological storage area could be, and is sometimes, referred to as peri-Sylvian, around the area of the Sylvian fissure. A potentially more precise account of localization was provided by Brodman (1909) on the basis of the brain's underlying cytoarchitecture and cellular structure, with each area assigned a number. The implication is that the cellular differences that occur across different brain regions have significance for the function performed by these different areas of the brain, although to the best of my knowledge, it is still far from clear how cellular structure and cognitive function are linked.

An example of these various terminological possibilities is provided by the area responsible for subvocal rehearsal, which may be referred to as left prefrontal, Broca's Area, or Brodman's Area 44 (typically shortened to BA 44), while the area responsible for phonological storage can be described as peri-Sylvian, at the junction of the parietal/temporal lobes, or as BA 40. In all of these cases, the reference is to the left hemisphere. Just to further complicate matters, activity of the phonological loop may sometimes result in activation of the analogous areas of the right hemisphere, although typically not nearly so extensively (Awh *et al.* 1996). Such right hemisphere activity tends to occur under conditions of heavy load, suggesting that it may represent either a simple overflow of activity, or possibly the recruitment of other processes to cope with the potential overload. Further complication is provided by the fact that a given activation tends not to occur exclusively in a single Brodman area, but to overlap. Hence, Broca's area and the control of rehearsal will often overlap area 6, referred to as activation in area 44/6.

12.6 What have we learned from imaging working memory?

As someone outside the imaging field, how is one to evaluate the work that appears? In my own case, I begin by attempting to understand the question asked by a given study, and then hope to find a reasonably simple and coherent answer. Of course the pattern of activation across the brain is extremely complex, resembling a range of mountains of which only the major peaks, and possibly troughs, are identified. In the case of PET, the peaks are averages of processes extending over many seconds, and possibly changing dramatically within that time. What constitutes a peak is, of course, dependent upon the statistical analysis of a huge mass of data, using methods which are likely to be much less familiar than is the case for the standard analytic procedures used in more standard experimental papers. By changing the statistical detection threshold, peaks may appear or disappear. Furthermore, in the case of many fMRI studies, the results are often displayed in a binary way, as if a part of the brain was either active or inactive. Furthermore, imaging studies are expensive, and particularly in early papers, containing relatively few subjects, with different scans within the same subject being treated as statistically independent events in a way that would not be acceptable in a standard experimental cognitive study. These problems are gradually being addressed, but still create difficulties in evaluating and comparing data from different studies and across laboratories.

12.6.1 Imaging the working memory subsystems

So what would I hope to see? First of all, as a non-expert, it would be an advantage if results were simple and coherent enough to understand without extensive further training. Secondly, I would hope that such results would replicate both within and between laboratories. Thirdly, it would be reassuring if the results fitted plausibly into our existing knowledge from studies using normal and neuropsychological subjects, and, in the case of neuropsychological studies, if the areas of activation observed were broadly consistent with the evidence based on earlier data from anatomical lesions. If these criteria are broadly met by a range of studies applying imaging to working memory, the question then arises as to whether imaging can tell us things about working memory that we did not already know. I am optimistic on all these points, but the picture is still far from clear.

The study of working memory has gained enormously in popularity and justifiably or not, in credibility from studies that have attempted to use the multicomponent model as a basis for investigations using neuroimaging. In an important early PET study of the phonological loop, Paulesu *et al.* (1993) contrasted the activation produced by a task involving memory for letters, with a second task in which subjects made rhyme judgements, something that is known to depend on subvocalization. They identified one area, the boundary between the left parietal and temporal lobes that appeared to be associated with memory storage, Brodman Area (BA) 40, and a second in the left frontal region that appeared to linked to subvocal rehearsal, BA 44. The first of these areas coincided with the location of damage typically associated with patients having a very specific phonological STM deficit (Vallar and Shallice 1990), while the frontal activation coincided with Broca's Area, classically associated with the capacity for speech production.

At about the same time as the Paulesu *et al.* study, an equivalent experiment on the imaging of visuospatial short-term memory was published by Jonides *et al.* (1993). They also used the subtraction technique, requiring subjects to remember the location of each of three dots. After a delay of three seconds, a circle appeared on the screen, and the subject was required to say whether or not it coincided with one of the dots. This condition was contrasted with one in which the circle and dots appeared simultaneously, hence removing the need for retention. In contrast to the Paulesu *et al.* phonological study, they found activation to be principally in the right hemisphere with particular activity in the right temporo-parietal area (Brodman Area 40), the occipital lobe (BA 19), the pre-motor area (BA 6) and the inferior prefrontal region (BA 47). Subsequent replications have confirmed this pattern of activity, with some indication of bilaterality, and a suggestion that two parietal areas may be involved (BA 40 and 7). This literature is reviewed by Smith and Jonides (1997).

Although Paulesu *et al.* were the first to image the phonological loop system, the most extensive investigation of working memory using neuroimaging has been carried out by Edward Smith and Jon Jonides at the University of Michigan. Such systematic, careful and well-designed work is still rather rare in imaging, where the excitement of the new technique all too often tends to encourage a 'gold rush' approach, with groups staking their claim to a phenomenon and an area before immediately moving on to find another claim to stake. The consequence is that a number of apparently important and exciting effects may not have been replicated by other groups, or if they have, may have given somewhat different results, which may or may not be attributable to differences in procedure. For that reason I will concentrate initially on a relatively small number of studies of working memory, mainly from the Michigan group, before discussing the question of consistency across paradigms and laboratories.

12.6.2 Distinguishing visual and verbal working memory

Smith *et al.* (1996) carried out the first direct comparison of verbal and visuospatial working memory, within the same study. Subjects were shown either four letters, or an array of three dots. This was followed by a delay and then by a probe item, comprising either a letter or a circle. If a letter, the subject was required to remember whether it had occurred in the prior set, or if a circle, whether it coincided spatially with the location of one of the dots. In both cases, the control condition involved presenting the stimuli and the probe simultaneously, hence removing the need for memory. The results are shown in Fig. 12.2. As in the case of Paulesu *et al.* (1993), they observed activation from the verbal task in the left hemisphere, Brodman Areas 40 and 44. Consistent with their own earlier work, the dot task activated principally the right hemisphere, and in particular, areas 40 and 6.

A second experiment presented the four letters in specific locations, subsequently testing for retention of either the name or the position. Once again, letter name recall led predominantly to left hemisphere activation and location memory principally right. Their third experiment involved a more active running memory span procedure, known as the N-back technique, whereby the subject monitors a stream of letters, responding when, in the Smith *et al.* case, a presented letter corresponded to the letter shown two back in the sequence. This, of course, requires the subject to constantly update, store and discard items, involving considerably more manipulation and a greater executive load than is typical with the normal memory span task. Level of load can be varied from one-back, which simply involves detecting repetitions, up to three-, or even four-back, requiring the subject to hold and manipulate simultaneously four different letters. Smith *et al.* found that this task activated the same left hemisphere region as the simple four letter probe task, suggesting that it is performed using the phonological loop. However, frontal activation was also found, presumably reflecting the additional executive load. This task is particularly convenient for fMRI studies, as it is a verbal task where detection of a repetition can be signalled by a simple button press, and does not require an overt verbal response, which has the disadvantage of causing head vibration and interference with the scan.

A PET study by Awh *et al.* (1996) used a verbal letter recall task, again finding activation in left hemisphere areas 44 and 6, with further activation on the boundary of areas 40 and 7, in the anterior cingulate, and in the right cerebellum, which links with the left hemisphere. A replication of the two-back continuous verbal memory task also activated areas 40, 7, 44, and 6 in the left hemisphere, this time also showing some left cerebellar and Supplementary Motor Area (SMA) activation. On this occasion rather more right hemisphere activity was detected in areas 6 and 7 and SMA, and once again the right cerebellum and anterior cingulate were involved. A third experiment attempted to use subtraction methods to isolate the rehearsal component. Unlike Paulesu *et al.* who inferred rehearsal from a rhyme judgement task, Awh *et al.* used subvocal repetition of an over-learned counting sequence. Subtracting this pattern of activation from that resulting from the memory task indicated that areas 40, 7 and SMA in the left hemisphere were all involved in the memory component, together with some right hemisphere activation in BA 7 and the SMA, and the usual right hemisphere cerebellar activity.

So far all the imaging studies of visual and verbal working memory described have used visual presentation. In the case of the subsystems of working memory, however, it is clear that these are not dependent on modality of presentation. Hence, phonological similarity effects occur with both visual and auditory presentation, as do visuospatial imagery effects (Baddeley 1986). In a further replication of their earlier findings, Schumacher *et al.* (1996) presented letters either visually or auditorally. The same areas were activated as in previous studies, regardless of input modality. Finally, in an extension of the study involving the N-back technique, Cohen *et al.* (1997) varied the load between zero, where subjects simply detected a prespecified letter, to three-back. Once again, BA 44 was highly active, suggesting the use of subvocal rehearsal, as was the region in the temporo-parietal region (BA 40) that tends to be associated with phonological storage, as evidenced by both scanning and lesion studies. Both brain areas showed some effect of storage load, but the effect was particularly clear in BA 40, the region typically associated with phonological storage.

The consistency across this series of studies is impressive. It should, however, be mentioned that at least two studies failed to replicate the role played by area 40. One of these, a study by Grasby *et al.* (1993), could be attributable to a less sensitive design in which the crucial comparison was made across subjects, rather than across conditions within the same subject. This was not, however, the case with a study by Fiez *et al.* (1996). They required their subjects to retain either five words that were semantically related, five unrelated words, or five nonwords. They found a very different pattern of activation from that reported by the Michigan group, with extensive dorsolateral activation of the prefrontal cortex, the superior motor cortex and the left, rather than the right, cerebellum. They found no significant increase in activity within the left parietal lobe, Broca's area or the right cerebellum, all areas repeatedly activated in the Smith and Jonides studies.

Jonides *et al.* (1998) suggest that the difference stems from the material used by Feiz *et al.* two-thirds of which involves semantically relatable meaningful words, which are likely to encourage the use of quite different strategies from those available in recalling letters or digits. Jonides *et al*'s follow-up study discouraged the use of semantic coding, resulting in a pattern of results that was much closer to their own earlier work than to that of Feiz *et al.* One interesting divergence is, however, in finding somewhat stronger activation in area 40 in the right rather than in the left hemisphere, suggesting that even their nonwords may offer somewhat different coding options from those used with letters or digits.

In conclusion, while the work of Feiz does not, in my view, negate the substantial and well-replicated findings from Paulesu *et al.* and from the Smith and Jonides group, they do point to the question of replication across laboratories. We will return to this issue. This in turn raises the potentially crucial importance of the strategy adopted by the subject, an issue that is, of course, also crucial in more behavioural studies of working memory, where there is evidence that subjects tend to abandon phonological coding when errors become frequent (Hall *et al.* 1983; Baddeley 2000; Hanley and Bakopoulou 2003). This is likely with sequences of five nonwords, or when semantic coding becomes easier, as with the semantically related condition used by Feiz *et al.* The strategy adopted by the subject remains an important but neglected variable in imaging studies.

12.6.3 **Rehearsal**

The nature of rehearsal in the sketchpad is much less clear than in the phonological loop. One possibility is that rehearsal involves continued attention to stimulus location or possibly to the representation of the stimulus. This was tested in a behavioural study by Awh *et al.* (1998). They performed a dual task experiment in which the subject was required to remember a spatial location and, at the same time, respond to an occasional visual discrimination task. When the task coincided with the location being retained, the discrimination was more rapid, suggesting that active retention, and by implication rehearsal, was accompanied by sustained attention to that location, as predicted. Further support is provided by an fMRI study by Awh *et al.* (1997), who presented an array of three dots to either the left or right visual field. From time to time, a grid was presented to one or other visual field, and its evoked response recorded. When the grid was presented to the same hemisphere as was being used to retain the dot array, it evoked a stronger response than when it was presented to the other visual field, suggesting once again that retaining a spatial array involves activating the part of the brain responsible for that visual area. The suggestion of an attentional rehearsal procedure is consistent with earlier work arguing for an association between visual attentional control and Brodman Area 7 in the right parietal cortex (e.g. Corbetta *et al.* 1993). More specifically, Henson (2001) suggests a possible rehearsal loop linking occipital storage through a visual attentional rehearsal link operating between the right parietal area (BA 7), a pre-motor area (BA 6) and the right inferior frontal lobe (BA 47). How these findings relate to the possible role of eye movements in spatial rehearsal as described in Chapter 4 remains an interesting question.

12.6.4 **The visuospatial distinction**

Most of the visual memory studies so far described have involved retention of spatial location. However, other studies have required memory for the shapes of objects. In one study, Smith *et al.* (1995) used abstract shapes, finding more left hemisphere activity than was typically obtained using a spatial array. However, Courtney *et al.* (1997), using faces, found a more right hemisphere distribution of activity. There are a number of possible reasons for this discrepancy. First of all, it seems likely that faces are not typical of other visual objects, and appear to activate a specific anatomical region, the fusiform face area. A second possibility is that the subjects in the study by Smith *et al.* may have been using verbal coding to help them retain the abstract shapes. It is difficult to prevent subjects using some kind of verbal coding, even when it is counter-productive (Brandimonte *et al.* 1992).

Smith and Jonides (1999) interpret the visual–spatial distinction (see Chapter 4), in terms of studies on non-human primates which also provide evidence for two separate contributions to visuospatial memory, comprising a ventral stream concerned with coding object information, and a dorsal stream concerned with spatial information (Mishkin *et al.* 1983; Wilson *et al.* 1993). Reviewing a series of studies on visuospatial working memory, Smith and Jonides (1999) report a similar tendency for memory for the location of an object to activate more dorsal regions than does memory for the object itself. They then go on to perform a meta-analysis of studies on visual working memory. The combined results are shown in Fig. 12.2, which illustrates a statistically significant tendency for object memory to activate more ventral, and spatial memory more dorsal, areas. On the other hand, however, to the untutored eye, one of the most striking features of Fig. 12.2 is the degree of variability within this significant overall trend. We will return later to this point.

The phonological loop would seem to be more readily amenable to experimental control, and hence likely to offer a better estimate of the inherent variability of results from scanning studies of working memory. Smith and Jonides present a similar meta-analysis for verbal working memory (see Fig. 12.3). Here, the pattern is somewhat clearer, with left hemisphere activation clearly greater than the right, and studies in which storage is maximized leading to activation in the more parietal regions, while those that emphasize executive processing are more frontal. It is, nevertheless, still salutary to note the degree of variability.

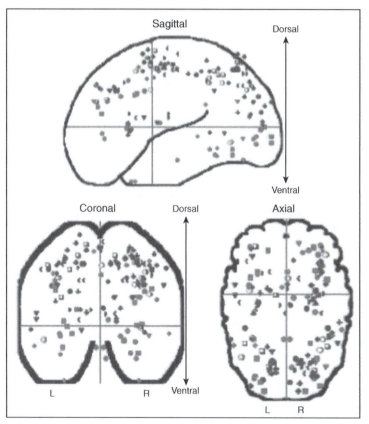

Fig. 12.2 Combined data for studies involving STM for visual objects (pink) or spatial location (blue). The distinction is principally between ventral locations for objects, and dorsal for locations. Data from Smith and Jonides 1999. Figure 4. In: Storage and executive processes in the frontal lobes. *Science*, **283**, 1657–1661. Reproduced with permission from AAAS. See Plate 3 for a colour version of this figure.

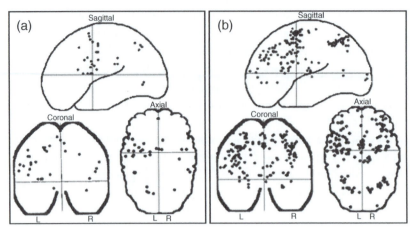

Fig. 12.3 Combined data for studies involving STM for verbal material (a), or storage plus executive processing (b). In each case the three figures represent activation foci as if seen through a 'glass brain' viewed from the side (sagittal), the front (coronal) of from the top (axial). In: Smith E.E. & Jonides, J. (1999). Storage and executive processes in the frontal lobes. *Science*, **283**, 1657–1661. Reproduced with permission from AAAS.

12.7 **Imaging the central executive**

Perhaps the most influential programme of research based on neuroimaging was that associated with the pioneering studies carried out by Posner and Raichle (1994), whose work on visual attention was seminal in convincing the field that this was a viable and profitable methodology for advancing cognitive neuroscience. Studying visual attention using PET methodology, they concluded that switching attention from one object to another involves three separable processes, each associated with a different anatomical location. The first of these, disengagement from the initial stimulus, involves right parietal activity. Moving the eyes then requires activation of the superior colliculus, a large midbrain area. This is followed by activity in the pulvinar, a nucleus in the thalamus which enhances frontal activity (Posner and Fan 2004).

Posner's coherent and consistent programme of research appears to produce a convincing picture of an attentional control system that may be fractionated into subcomponents, which in turn are associated with specific brain regions. The work was, however, focused very specifically on visual attention rather than executive control in general. The possibility of using neuroimaging to tease apart the processes underlying executive control has subsequently attracted the attention of many laboratories, producing a large range of findings. As in the case of lesion studies, the evidence strongly points to the importance of the frontal lobes in the operation of the central executive, but again like the lesion studies, as the questions become more precise, the degree of agreement diminishes.

12.7.1 **The N-back task**

One of the most popular tasks for studying executive function is the N-back task, which, as described earlier, has the advantage of requiring the active maintenance of material in immediate memory, under conditions in which the memory load can be systematically varied while the surface features of the task remain constant. It also has the advantage that it can be used for both verbal and non-verbal materials. Using this method, Braver *et al.* (1997) observed activation bilaterally in the dorsolateral prefrontal, inferior frontal and parietal areas, with activation level increasing linearly with load. It may be recalled that this was also found by Jonides *et al.* (1997) and Smith *et al.* (1996), using both verbal and non-verbal material, and finding the expected lateralizations whereby the verbal task particularly impacts on the left, and the non-verbal on the right hemispheres.

The fact that the N-back task has been used so frequently has enabled Owen *et al.* (2005) to conduct a meta analysis, which is shown is Fig. 12.4. The top panel shows the activation when verbal, object and spatial N-back tasks are combined, in each case using the control for that individual study as an individual baseline, before combining the results. Overall, there is clear bilateral involvement of both the frontal lobes and parietal areas, consistent with the assumption that both central executive and visuospatial and phonological subsystems are involved. The next panel shows the results for verbal tasks, in which there is again clear bilateral frontal involvement and an emphasis on left hemisphere activation, as one would expect if the phonological store is involved. The data are less clear in the case of the two visual–spatial components, which again involve frontal activation, together with greater evidence of right hemisphere involvement. The number of areas with significant activation is rather less than for the verbal tasks. However this may simply reflect the smaller number of studies contributing to these analyses, hence making statically significant activation less likely. In general, however, this pattern is consistent with the assumption that the N-back task is demanding, and that is has a different pattern for verbal and visuospatial tasks. The breadth of activation is consistent with the assumption that the task is an effective one for loading working memory, but is less suitable for more analytic purposes.

12.7.2 **Random generation**

Another task that demands executive control is that of random generation. Frith *et al.* (1991) studied performance when subjects were required to press keys at random, comparing it to a condition in which they pressed in response to particular stimuli. They found bilateral activation of the dorsal-frontal areas. In a verbal equivalent involving the comparison between random number generation and counting, Jahanshahi *et al.* (2000) also found

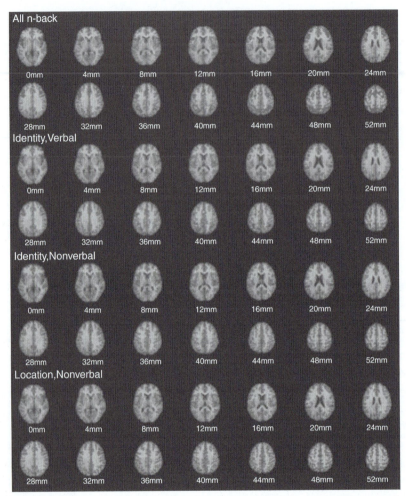

Fig. 12.4 Meta-analytic activation maps for all n-back studies combined (top panel), tasks involving verbal memory (second panel), those involving non verbal retention of identity (third panel), and those involving retention of location (bottom panel). (From Owen *et al.* 2005 Figure 1). In: N-Back working memory paradigm: a meta-analysis of normative functional neuroimaging studies. *Human Brain Mapping*, **25**, 46–59. Reproduced with permission from John Wiley & Sons, Inc.. Please see Colour Plate 4 for a colour version of this figure.

bilateral dorsolateral activation, but whereas left hemisphere activation correlated negatively with degree of randomness achieved, no such relationship occurred for the right hemisphere.

Another form of generation task is provided by self-ordering, in which subjects must make a series of choices. On each test an array of items is presented, with the subject required to point to a different item every trial, avoiding repetition.

This task, like random generation, tends to be impaired in frontal lobe patients (Petrides and Milner 1982). When the task involves pointing at abstract designs, activation is principally in the right dorsolateral prefrontal area (Petrides *et al.* 1993), whereas self-ordered digit pointing resulted in bilateral activation of the dorsolateral prefrontal areas, as did a task involving monitoring digits sequences for a specific target.

12.7.3 Dual-task performance

As discussed earlier, one function of the central executive is assumed to involve the capacity to perform two tasks at the same time (Baddeley *et al.* 1991). D'Esposito *et al.* (1995) studied tasks involving spatial rotation and semantic judgement, both independently and combined. Under combined conditions they reported that dorsolateral prefrontal areas were activated, suggesting that this area is responsible for the capacity to combine two tasks. Unfortunately, this has not proved easy to replicate. Klingberg (1998) required subjects to perform luminance judgement and pitch perception tasks independently and together, but found no area that specifically responded to task combination. Goldberg *et al.* (1998) studied the Wisconsin Card Sorting Task and auditory shadowing, observing that degree of dorsolateral activity was actually *reduced* when the two were combined. Fletcher *et al.* (1995) also observed a reduction in dorsolateral activation when an elaborative verbal coding task was combined with a visuomotor task. It perhaps worth noting that both the Goldberg *et al.* card sorting and Fletcher *et al*'s verbal elaboration task involved executive processing and frontal activation when performed alone. Reduction of such activation may plausibly reflect the abandonment of an attentionally demanding strategy used in single task conditions, as a result of the need to perform a second attentionally demanding task (Rosen and Engle 1994).

The question of subject strategy is, of course, crucial in cognitive studies, whether using behavioural or neuroimaging methods. However, whereas purely behavioural studies would typically tackle the issue by using a range of converging experiments that explicitly investigate such issues (see for example the study by Klauer and Zhao [2004] described in Chapter 4), this is rarely the case in imaging research, where issues of cost and availability have often tended to lead to conclusions based on a single experiment using a small group of subjects. Fortunately this is changing as the field develops.

12.7.4 Planning

A similar lack of unanimity appears across studies of planning, using variants of the Tower of Hanoi task. For example, Baker *et al.* (1996) observed right dorsolateral prefrontal activation together with bilateral activation in the pre-motor and parietal areas, none of which were found by Owen *et al.* (1999), who observed principally *left* dorsolateral prefrontal activation. It seems likely that subtle differences in the nature of the two tasks may have led to the discrepancy. This does, however, lead one to question the degree of replicability and coherence found across studies in this area.

12.8 Meta-analyses of executive processing

Duncan and Owen (2000) addressed this issue using a meta analysis in which they combined data from a wide range of studies, in the hope that they would reveal a clear mapping of specific executive subprocesses onto particular anatomical locations. They began by categorizing the tasks used across studies into five separate clusters, each plausibly separable from the other four at a behavioural and cognitive level. They comprised (1) auditory discrimination, (2) self-paced response production, (3) task switching, (4) spatial problem-solving, and (5) semantic word processing. Despite the wide range of tasks, all appeared to show maximum activation within a relatively narrow area, comprising the mid dorsolateral, mid ventrolateral and dorsal anterior cingulate regions.

Analysis of the combined data therefore did indeed prove to yield a surprising degree of regularity, although not as expected, linked to the executive process involved. Hence, all five measures seem to depend heavily on three frontal regions, the dorsal and anterior cingulate, the mid dorsolateral, and mid ventrolateral areas. Somewhat surprised by this pattern, Duncan and Owen used a more extensive selection of studies, this time categorizing studies in terms of the apparent underlying task demands. Once again they selected five subgroups, comprising (1) response conflict tasks such as the Stroop test, (2) tasks involving the processing of novel material or procedures, (3) tasks with high working memory load, (4) tasks requiring retention over a long working memory delay, and (5) tasks involving perceptual difficulty. As Fig. 12.5 shows, exactly the same three regions emerged, namely the anterior cingulate, mid dorsolateral and mid ventrolateral areas of the frontal lobes, regardless of the nature of the executive demand.

Duncan and Owen interpret their results with some degree of caution, pointing out that the failure of the array of current data to distinguish between the whole range of executive tasks anatomically does not mean that in principle they are not differentiable. It may simply be that there is insufficient resolution within current methods to allow fine distinctions to be made across studies in which subtle differences in both behavioural and neuroimaging methodology are likely to occur. Furthermore, tasks never provide pure measures of underlying cognitive processes, hence many apparently diverse

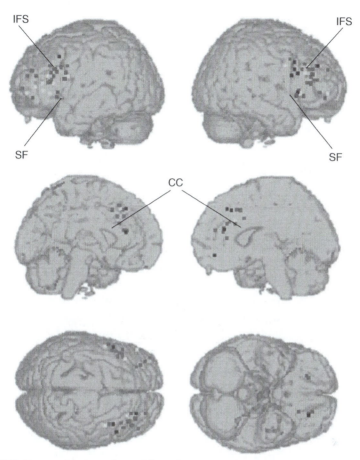

Fig. 12.5 Systematic comparison of frontal activations associated with five cognitive demands. Activations are from studies of response conflict (green) task novelty (pink) number of elements in working memory (yellow) working memory delay (red) and perceptual difficulty (blue). Shown are lateral (top row) and medial (middle row) views of each hemisphere, along with the whole brain views from above, (bottom left) and below (bottom right). (CC: Corpus collosum; IFS: Inferior frontal sulcus; SF: Silvian fissure). (Figure 2 from Duncan and Owen 2000). In: Common regions of the human frontal lobe recruited by diverse cognitive demands. *Trends in Neurosciences*, **23**, 475–483. Reproduced with permission from Elsevier. Please see Colour Plate 2 for a colour version of this figure.

executive tasks are likely to have at least some processes in common. Duncan and Owen also point out that some differences do appear to be present. For example, studies concerned with retrieval from episodic memory produce activations that are consistently anterior to those derived from the array of executive measures sampled.

As Duncan and Owen point out, many small areas, which may not be detectable by fMRI, within the frontal lobes appear to be connected to multiple other regions distributed more widely (Pucak *et al.* 1996). Further reason for caution is raised by single-unit recording studies which have identified some frontal neurons, widely distributed in both the ventral and dorsal regions, that appear to switch from coding object to coding spatial information, depending on which is crucial on a given test trial (Rao 1997). If there is this degree of flexibility at the level of the individual neuron, might there not be a similar amount of variability at the broad regional level of analysis provided by PET and fMRI studies? Finally, even if individual units are stable in their function, stimulation studies by Ojemann (1994) suggest that function may change dramatically within a few millimetres, a level of analysis beyond the discriminative capacity of fMRI. His studies involved patients who were undergoing neurosurgery to relieve epilepsy. One way of avoiding the surgical removal of tissue that is cognitively crucial is to explore the function of the area in question by means of electrical stimulation. Using this method, Ojemann found that stimulation may disrupt naming at one point, changing to disruption of counting a few millimetres beyond. Such results do not, of course, mean that a given type of processing is limited to such a micro region, but it does suggest that the architecture may vary on a scale that would be hard to detect using current imaging procedures.

12.9 Imaging retrieval processes

A common criticism of much imaging work is that although confirming earlier conclusions based on behavioural studies and work with neuropsychological patients, it is essentially confirmatory, and has told us very little that is new. Probably the first counter example to this claim was offered by the use of imaging to study retrieval processes. Here, the Hemispheric Encoding Retrieval Asymmetry (HERA) hypothesis certainly goes beyond conclusions that had been drawn from behavioural studies. Originally proposed by Tulving *et al.* (1994), it argues on the basis of a series of PET studies that whereas the encoding of memories and retrieval from semantic memory depend principally upon left frontal areas, retrieval from episodic memory is principally dependent on the right frontal lobe.

This was a somewhat counter-intuitive claim, given that there appears to be little evidence from neuropsychological lesion studies of a crucial role for the right frontal region in episodic retrieval. It has generated a considerable number of further studies from a range of laboratories. These are reviewed by Nyberg *et al.* (1996), who report 16 PET studies that have specifically examined memory encoding, of which 13 identified the left prefrontal area as crucial.

Of 33 studies concerned with episodic retrieval, they report 29 that involve right prefrontal activation. Other studies using fMRI report broadly similar results (e.g. Buckner *et al.* 1998).

The HERA hypothesis has not, however, gone without its critics. Objections include the use of a non-memory baseline, which may exaggerate the influence of more general cognitive processes, which frequently involve right frontal activation (Nolde *et al.* 1998a). Nolde *et al.* (1998b) demonstrate that when a more difficult episodic recognition task is used, wherein source memory must be evaluated, left frontal activity predominates, while a study by Ranganath and Paller (2000) using ERP measures reached a similar conclusion. They presented their subjects with a sequence of pictured objects or animals, which were represented in either a large or small format. When subjects were simply required to recognize whether that object has been shown earlier, activation was predominantly right frontal, but changed to bilateral when the subjects were also required to recall whether it was presented in a large or small format.

Interpretation of the asymmetries that frequently do occur remains controversial. Tulving *et al.* (1994) regard the right frontal activation as being the signature of a specific 'retrieval mode' that is essential for efficient episodic retrieval. Shallice *et al.* (1994), on the other hand, argue for an interpretation in terms of the monitoring and verification of candidate responses, rather than retrieval per se. There is thus no doubt that the HERA hypothesis has stimulated interesting novel ideas in the area of retrieval. However, it remains controversial, and it is probably too soon to see it as a clear example of the way in which neuroimaging is capable of further extending our understanding.

12.10 **Some conclusions**

12.10.1 **Hopes fulfilled?**

What should I conclude from my brief foray into the neuroimaging literature? The answer to this question seems to depend upon how much emphasis is placed on the various meta-analyses of the large and growing number of studies. Let us consider my initial criteria. The first is that of simplicity and coherence. Considering the meta-analyses as a whole, where the conclusions are simple, they appear not to be coherent. For example the visual-verbal hemispheric difference does not always come through clearly. The object versus spatial distinction does not appear to apply consistently within the frontal regions, despite the earlier evidence from both animal and human studies. Data on executive processes are also far from clear. Are there many different frontal areas reflecting separable executive processes as Shallice (2002) proposes, or, as Duncan and Owen suggest, do many different tasks place demands on the same broad area?

My second hope was that results would replicate across different laboratories. This is certainly sometimes the case as with the Paulesu *et al.* (1993) and the Michigan studies (Smith *et al.* 1996). Such consistency does not, however, characterize the field more generally, as reflected in the meta-analyses.

My third hope was that results would be broadly consistent with existing data from lesion studies and with existing behavioural findings in experimental cognitive psychology. In the absence of clear conclusions from the meta-analyses, it is hard to argue strongly for coherence. It is of course almost invariably the case that the results of individual studies are related by their authors to prior evidence and existing theory, and are typically found to be consistent. However, this could reflect the post hoc justification of results that are sufficiently complex as to allow multiple interpretations.

12.10.1 **Some problems**

A less gloomy assessment of the situation would be to suggest that this field is not yet sufficiently coherent and well-controlled to be suitable for meta-analysis. Problems are likely to be encountered at least three levels. The first of these concerns the experimental paradigms used. These are often complex, and tend to be designed principally so as to be useable within an imaging context, rather than on the basis of their capacity to provide a relatively pure measure of the hypothetical concept or process that forms the focus of the study. Even in relatively simple tasks such as phonological memory, crucial differences occur. Cognitive studies tend to use immediate serial verbal recall in which subvocal rehearsal is likely and retention of order required. Scanning studies on the other hand typically involve recognition of an individual item from a set, with order information often not being involved. Order is required in the N-back task, which is regarded as measuring executive processes. This task certainly does demand executive manipulation, but also requires maintaining order information, which may well not be executive in nature. The situation becomes yet more complex when one attempts to separate out further hypothetical executive processes. Task analysis here is likely to be even more complex, reflecting our comparative ignorance of the functioning of the central executive at a behavioural level.

A further problem concerns the strategy adopted by the subject. Two subjects given the same task and the same instructions may well perform that task in quite different ways. In a typical purely behavioural cognitive study, this problem would be tackled by replication using a range of different procedures in order to check the possibility of such strategic factors (cf. Klauer and Zhao 2004). Given the financial and temporal constraints on imaging studies this is not currently possible, resulting, I suspect, in an important source of potential inconsistency both within and between studies.

A third and major potential source of 'noise' is likely to come from the practicalities of how conclusions are drawn from each study, what baseline is used, what criteria are set, and precisely how peaks of activation are mapped onto anatomical location. The use of Brodman areas is helpful for communication, but to the best of my knowledge, it is not clear what the functional significance might be of the neuronatomical differences between locations on which Brodman based his classification.

These potential problems are not sufficient to argue against an attempt at meta-analysis, which does have the potential advantage of both combining data from many sources and allowing individual differences to be minimized. They do, however, caution against drawing too gloomy a conclusion from such attempts.

12.10.2 **What next?**

What is the alternative? My own inclination is to take most seriously data from studies carried out in the laboratories which appear to combine three things. The first is good cognitive psychologists who understand both the underlying theory and methodology required for studies of working memory. The second is that it should be backed by first rate imaging expertise and facilities. Thirdly, the work should be part of a coherent programme, rather that a series of one-off studies. That is not to claim that all other studies should be discounted, but is merely a means by which I myself can attempt to form a view on this important but complex area.

To summarize, neuroimaging clearly provides a potentially important additional way of investigating the brain's cognitive function. In the case of working memory, it seems to provide evidence for a broad distinction between left hemisphere verbal and largely right hemisphere visuospatial processing, with the further distinction between more ventral coding of object information, in contrast to more dorsal processing of spatial information. The evidence also supports the view that the temporary storage components of working memory tend to be associated with parietal areas, while more anterior regions within the frontal lobes are more likely to be involved in the manipulation of information. Methods are constantly being developed and refined, so the future will offer a much more fine-grained dissociation of regional specialization.

A critic could argue, however, that compared to the hopes initially raised, the results obtained so far have tended to reinforce existing theory, rather than develop new insights. This is not for lack of theoretical speculation but rather reflects a lack of agreement across studies concerning both data and interpretation. The data are highly complex and noisy, and the mapping of paradigms onto theory consequently tends to be equivocal. It is, however, important to bear in mind that data we have been discussing simply concerns anatomical localization, what is sometimes disparagingly referred to as 'the new phrenology'. My own view is that the real power of the techniques will emerge with the current rapid development of new measures that have two substantial advantages. The first concerns the ability to identify processing systems on the basis of associations between areas that are active, using dynamic causal modelling (Friston *et al.* 2003) a powerful statistical method of establishing the functional connectivity between brain areas. The second stems from the greater temporal resolution of MEG, providing the capacity to identify the temporal order in which different activations occur and to relate this to well-developed cognitive models.

Chapter 13

Working memory and social behaviour

The previous chapters have varied considerably in content and methodology, but all have in common a direct concern with the concept of working memory. This chapter, and indeed the remainder of the book, depart from this pattern in being concerned with the task of placing the concept of multicomponent working memory in a broader context. Very little of what follows describes research that directly addresses working memory. I hope to convince you however that the areas to be discussed, namely social psychology, cognition and emotion, consciousness and action control have important links with working memory. Such links can, I believe, provide a potentially fruitful way of viewing the fields in question, while enriching the concept of working memory by placing it within a broader context. At the same time, however, it is important to bear in mind that I am by no means expert in any of these fields. If, as I hope, readers are stimulated to explore such links further, they would do well to do so in consultation with colleagues better qualified than myself.

13.1 What controls behaviour?

Norman and Shallice (1986) proposed that behaviour is controlled by two processes. The first involves control by automatic schemata, allowing well-established and habitual patterns of behaviour to control routine activities. Habitual activities thus rely on environmental control rather than on executive processes, and hence place little demand on attentional processes. When automatic control proved inadequate, a second more attentionally demanding component, the Supervisory Attentional System (SAS), is capable of intervening and potentially resolving the ongoing problem. Such problems might arise either because of a close conflict between competing schemata, or because of lack of sufficient information. It is this latter component, the SAS, that I proposed as a possible mechanism for the central executive component of working memory (Baddeley 1986).

However, an adequate theory of working memory needs to address both of these components: while cognitive psychology has, in recent years, tended to focus on executive control rather than the influence of habit, the opposite has been the case in social psychology, where there has been extensive work on the automatic influence on behaviour of attitudes and prejudice. Clear discrepancies may occur between *stated* socially desirable conscious attitudes and *actual* behaviour reflecting implicit prejudice. This has led social psychologists to the development of implicit measures of habitual patterns of thought and values. The power of such implicit processes has encouraged the development of an approach to theory that emphasizes the control of behaviour by the environment, or in terms of the Norman and Shallice model, by habits and schemata rather than by the SAS.

Such a view is presented by Bargh and Ferguson (2000). Indeed, they go further, proposing that all behaviour whether controlled automatically, through existing schemata, or apparently by effortful and deliberative processes, is essentially equivalent, except that we have discovered the mechanisms for one form, but not the other. They propose that 'The distinction between automatic and controlled processes ... breaks down entirely because these controlled processes are themselves being controlled by determined, automatic goal structures' (Bargh and Ferguson 2000, p. 939). Whether or not one accepts this as a reasonable interpretation of the available evidence, there is no doubt that an adequate theory of executive control must at least take into account the more automatic and schema-driven aspects of the system.

13.2 Habits, schemata and deterministic control

13.2.1 Control without awareness?

The possibility that non-conscious processing might influence behaviour has been a major focus of controversy among cognitive psychologists in recent years. In the 1970s and 80s this principally concerned the issue of perception without awareness (e.g. Marcel 1983; Weiscrantz 1986), extending in the 1980s and 90s to the extensive study of implicit memory and learning (e.g. Schacter 1994; Shanks and St John 1994). In a classic series of studies of unconscious visual word processing, Marcel (1983) developed a paradigm whereby the subject was required to process a briefly presented word, either pronouncing it, deciding whether it was a word or nonword, or judging its meaning. It was shown that performance on these tasks could be influenced by priming involving the presentation of a prior word. Priming may occur even though the prior priming word has been presented very briefly, and immediately followed by a random pattern mask, conditions under which subjects typically deny perceiving the first word. For example, presenting and masking the word *money* will result in the subject interpreting the ambiguous word *bank* in terms of a financial institution, rather than the edge of a river. In another study, presenting and masking the word *doctor* facilitated the subsequent reading of the associated word *nurse* (Marcel 1983). There is no doubt that obtaining such effects requires a good deal of experimental skill, so as to avoid awareness while insuring that some processing is possible, but in general the presence of implicit perceptual processing now appears to be well-established, not only for words but also for a wide range of other stimuli (Cheesman and Merikle 1984).

In the area of long-term memory, the importance of implicit factors is also well established. In the case of densely amnesic patients, for example, prior presentation of a word or a line drawing facilitates its subsequent processing just as much for amnesic as control subjects, despite the fact that amnesic patients deny ever having experienced the prior presentation (Warrington and Weiskrantz 1968). For example, prior presentation of a word such as *AMBULANCE* will help both amnesic and normal subjects to provide the letters needed to provide the missing letters in the sequence _M_U_A_C_, although the patients will have no memory of having just seen the word (see Baddeley 1998, Chapter 19) for further discussion. Such priming effects have been extensively studied, and shown to be dependent on quite different variables from those that influence the capacity to consciously remember having recently experienced those items (Roediger 1990; Schacter 1994; Squire 1992).

Implicit priming methods have been used extensively in social psychology where they have the advantage over more explicit techniques of disguising the purpose of the study, and hence minimizing the possibility that subjects may be behaving in a particular way in order to fulfil, or possibly refute, the expectations of the experimenter. Such studies typically go beyond the simple demonstration of implicit influences on perception or memory, using such influences to study complex topics such as attitudes, goals and social behaviours. Such studies in social psychology offer an important source of evidence concerning the more implicit influences on executive control. I will describe a sample of these studies before going on to discuss their possible interpretation.

One of the earliest of such phenomena to be studied was behavioural mimicry. This is seen most obviously in flocks of birds or shoals of fish, where all members of the group appear to change direction at the same time. In the case of humans, such imitation is slightly less obvious, but nonetheless well established. One of the most prevalent forms of such apparently imitative behaviour occurs in the posture adopted during conversation where surprisingly frequently one notices that both members of the conversation have assumed the same stance, arms folded for example, or hand in pocket. In one experimental study of this effect, Chartrand and Bargh (1999) required a subject and a confederate to jointly examine and evaluate a series of photographs. The confederate was required either to touch her face frequently, or else to swing her foot. Videotapes of the subject were then independently judged and the number of face touchings and foot swingings counted. Clear evidence of imitation was found. When the confederate touched her face frequently, so did the subject. When, instead, she swung her foot, this increased the subject's foot swinging.

It is suggested that such behaviour implicitly aims to establish positive rapport between the two people who are interacting. This was tested in a second study; this time it was the confederate who actively imitated the actions of the subject, or refrained from this. Subjects subsequently rated the imitating confederates as more likeable. Clearly such imitation needs to be subtle: consciously and obviously imitating someone, 'aping their behaviour', tends to be regarded as ironic and insulting.

The tendency to imitate unconsciously was noted by William James (1890), who refers to it as 'ideomotor action', whereby thought leads to action by 'the free flow of stream of consciousness'. A more recent interpretation is offered by the discovery in single cell recording studies of so-called mirror neurons, whereby certain cells are activated by both the performance of an action, and perceiving that action performed by another (Rizzolati and Arbib 1998). Mirror neurons appear to be particularly associated with the pre-motor area of the brain.

13.2.2 Implicit perception

The work of investigators like Marcel has been extended within the social domain, with a demonstration that emotional attitudes can implicitly be primed. Hence, subjects who are required to perform a lexical decision task in which they must categorize a string of letters as a word or a nonword respond more rapidly when the word has been preceded by a prime with a similar emotional tone. Hence, briefly presenting and masking the word 'nice' will speed the decision that 'cheerful' is a real word, while slowing down a similar judgment on 'mournful' (Bargh and Ferguson 2000). Subliminal verbal priming can also influence self-rated mood (Chartrand and Bargh 1999), as indeed can the prevailing weather. In one study, people were telephoned on either a grey miserable day, or a bright sunny one and asked their opinion on a range of issues. Their ratings were more negative in bad weather. However, when they were first asked about the weather, the effect disappeared as if they were able to allow for it in their subsequent judgements (Schwarz and Clore 1983). We will return to this point in our discussion of what is implied by the claim that behaviour is 'determined' or 'controlled'.

Finally, it has been known for many years that stimulus-response compatibility can be influenced by emotional tone. Solarz (1960) showed that when subjects were required to classify stimuli as 'good' or 'bad' by pushing or pulling a lever, they responded more rapidly when required to push the lever away for 'bad' and pull toward them for 'good'. Chen and Bargh (1999) showed that this effect also occurs when the emotional words are used as primes, presented below the threshold of awareness. It appears to be the case, therefore, as Bargh claims, that emotional stimuli of which the subject is unaware are capable of influencing perception, mood, decision and motor behaviour.

13.2.3 Emotions and attitudes

There is considerable evidence to suggest that incoming stimuli are automatically evaluated as positive or negative (see Chapters 14 and 15), capable of acting as emotional primes, influencing the evaluation of an item that immediately follows, even when the emotional prime is masked, and hence below the subjects threshold of awareness. For example, Krosnick et al. (1992) presented slides of people going about their everyday activities: each slide was preceded by an emotionally related slide, either positive, such as a basket of kittens, or negative, a bucket full of snakes. Attitudes to the people shown performing the neutral tasks were then tested. People preceded by subliminally presented pleasant slides were rated more positively than those following negative images.

Similar priming effects have been found for words (Fazio 1986), and even for nonwords and meaningless shapes, with those rated negative facilitating avoidance and those with positive ratings priming approach responses (Duckworth et al. 2002).

13.2.4 Motives and goals

The examples that we have discussed so far all refer to levels of influence that could potentially be operating only over relatively brief intervals. There is, however, evidence for more long-lasting effects. In a highly influential study, Milgram (1963) noted that his student subjects could be induced to deliver what they believed to be electric shocks of almost lethal intensity to fellow participants in an experimental study, given appropriate social pressures. In this case, it was sufficient simply to require his Stanford student subjects to play the role of prison warders, in control of fellow students assigned the role of prisoners.

In a somewhat gentler version of this paradigm, Bargh et al. (1996, Experiment 1) first required their subjects to unscramble words to form sentences. One group was given sentences comprising many polite words, whereas rudeness featured more prominently in the sentences unscrambled by the other group. Having completed this task, subjects were required to leave the room and contact the experimenter, who was conversing in the hall outside. The experimenter ensured that the conversation continued for a full ten minutes, or until the subject interrupted. While 63per cent of people primed with impolite words interrupted, only 17 per cent of those with polite words broke in. A third neutral word control group interrupted on 37 per cent of occasions.

Not only is it possible to influence what people do by priming attitudes, it is also possible to influence the way in which they subsequently evaluate their behaviour, which in turn can influence subsequent tasks. Bargh and Chartrand (1999) primed subjects with achievement-related or neutral words before giving them an anagram-solving task, which was described to them as an activity simply designed to fill the subsequent interval. The anagrams could be easy or hard, and were followed by a mood-rating task. Only those subjects who had been primed with achievement words were influenced by the anagram-solving task, with those given easier items rating themselves as subsequently happier. In a subsequent experiment, instead of the mood scale, subjects were required to perform the verbal tests of the Graduate Record Examination. Those who had experienced the achievement words followed by the easy anagrams scored more highly.

13.2.5 **Cultural control?**

As a cognitive psychologist, my initial response to the findings reported by Bargh and Ferguson was one of scepticism. Surely one *knows* that much of our behaviour is consciously controlled? Not so, say Bargh and Ferguson, citing substantial evidence to indicate that the sense of agency, the extent to which behaviour can be attributed to individual, rather than to situational factors, is heavily dependent on culture. Consider for example a study by Latané and Darley (1968) who chose to study theology students who were assigned to speak on the topic of the Good Samaritan. Unbeknown to the students, rather than being part of the theology course, this requirement formed part of a social psychological experiment, where the first component involved performing a separate and apparently independent task, which was arranged to run late. As the students hurried to their assignment, they encountered someone who appeared to be sick and needed their help. Despite the obvious relevance to the issue they were about to address, most, like the Pharisee, ignored the appeal for help, and passed by on the other side. The social pressure of not being late was apparently stronger than acting on theological or ethical grounds.

While this may reveal a rather shocking degree of hypocrisy to Western eyes, Choi *et al.* (1999) suggest that it would be less likely to surprise observers from an East Asian culture such as Korea. 'Westerners' (in most studies, that means US college students), typically appear to attribute cause to the action of a person, which in turn is attributed to their personal qualities, good or bad, helpful or selfish, whereas Eastern and South Asian students are much more likely to take the circumstances surrounding the action into account in interpreting it.

Even when simply asked to describe an acquaintance, Shweder and Bourne (1982) found that US students described acquaintances in terms of more abstract personality traits, whereas Indians were more likely to mention such contextual factors as their role in the family and their occupation. Subsequent work by Miller (1987) showed that the tendency to rely on personal trait descriptions increased in US subjects between the ages of eight and fifteen, but did not change for Indians. When Miller (1984) asked subjects ranging from eight-year-olds to adults to select a piece of behaviour by acquaintances that had good, and one that had bad outcomes, Indian Hindu subjects were twice as likely to interpret the situation selected in terms of context than US subjects, who were twice as likely to use character traits as explanatory concepts. This was particularly the case with bad behaviour. Once again, the US tendency to use character traits increased with age.

The East-West difference even occurs in interpreting the behaviour of fish within cartoons. When asked to account for the behaviour of an individual fish that joins or leaves a shoal of other cartoon fishes, US students give an account in terms of the character of the fish, whereas Chinese students were more likely to attribute the behaviour to contextual factors. The effect is not limited to carefully designed experiments: Morris and Peng (1994) analysed US English-speaking and Chinese newspaper accounts of two tragedies, in both of which an individual (a student and a postal worker) killed his supervisor and fellow workers. While the English account emphasized dispositional factors with statements like 'the man was mentally unstable' and 'disturbed', the Chinese newspaper emphasized context, his failure to get along with the supervisor, the lack of religion in Chinese culture, and the possible effects of recently reported mass slayings in Texas.

The difference between cultures remains, even when the context is emphasized. Jones and Harris (1967) required their student subjects to prepare and deliver a speech in favour of or against Castro, to other students who were then required to judge the speaker's beliefs. Despite being informed of the specific instructions given to the speaker, American students were likely to disregard this crucial contextual information, judging positive speakers to be pro-Castro to a much greater degree than did Korean students, given the same information. Nisbett et al. (2001) attribute these and other related differences between US and Asian cultures as stemming from an analytic Aristotelian view of the world by Westerners, in contrast to a more holistic Confucian view of the world by Asian people. They suggest that the one stresses the individual person and the importance of debate, while the other emphasizes social obligation and harmony.

While this is an interesting speculation that offers one interpretation of the pervasive and intriguing differences observed, I am a little uncertain as to whether the contemporary attitudes of US students should be taken as representative of the last two millennia of Western culture. It would be interesting to see if a similar pattern emerges in other Western cultures that are less individualistic than the US. Would Scandinavian students behave in the same way, for example? What would be the case for people from a different age group or religious persuasion? However, regardless of the specific interpretation of these intriguing findings, they do support Bargh's claim that the assumption within our culture of the individual's total control of his or her actions is by no means universal, and may be greatly exaggerated. Within a working memory context, they provide a reminder of the potential importance of habitual processes that we may easily neglect in favour of an emphasis on the processes of executive control.

13.3 The sense of agency

13.3.1 Physiological evidence and the 'user illusion'

At first sight, one of the strongest arguments against the deterministic position proposed by Bargh and Ferguson is the simple feeling of agency, that we decide when we act and what we do. Dr Johnson is said to have responded to the idea of determinism by kicking a stone and declaring 'I refute you!' But is it the case that this apparently unpredictable act is in fact a refutation? Norretranders (1999) has argued that this is not the case and that our sense of agency is simply a trick played on the mind by the brain, what he terms 'the user illusion'. Norretranders cites as support for this view a much-discussed study by Libet (Libet *et al.* 1983; Libet 1985) in which subjects were asked to press a lever from time to time, reporting when they 'decided' to make the response. Their report was in terms of the position on a clock that they continually observed. At the same time, the electrophysiological activity of their motor cortex was observed. A somewhat surprising finding was that the cortical activity began up to half a second *before* subjects reported the decision, as if the motor activity caused the decision, rather than vice versa. This conclusion proved highly controversial (see comments following the paper by Libet [1985]), but the phenomenon has been broadly replicated, as we shall see below. Bargh and Ferguson, using this evidence in support of their argument for determinism, suggest that Libet's result demonstrates the way in which a subject's behaviour is controlled by the experimental instructions.

This issue is addressed in a study by Haggard and Eimer (1999) which followed up the Libet effect. The paradigm was essentially that used by Libet, with the exception that subjects were given two keys, one for the right and one for the left index finger. They were asked to choose for themselves, on any given trial, which finger to use. Haggard and Eimer recorded two different electrophysiological potentials, a General Readiness Potential that typically precedes *all* movement, and a Lateralized Readiness Potential, that is associated with the activity of the supplementary motor area (SMA), and with the selection of *specific* movements. Again subjects observed a clock, and were asked to note when they 'first began to prepare' a movement, and when they actually moved, using either the left or the right finger. The first response to occur was the General Readiness Potential, associated with movement in general. This was followed by the lateralized readiness potential for the left or right finger with an earlier component of the potential being associated with reported preparation, and only then followed by a verbal report of the decision to move. Their results thus confirmed Libet's observation that the earliest electrophysiological movement sign of awareness does indeed appear to occur earlier than the intention to move, but occurs earlier than the *actual* movement.

In another study, Haggard and Magno (1999) again required subjects to note the time at which they made a movement. On some occasions, their response would be associated with transcortical magnetic stimulation (TMS) whereby a magnetic field is used to produce highly localized neural interruption that can prevent the functioning of the area in question during stimulation. This was applied to either the primary motor cortex or to the SMA. On this occasion, subjects were asked to respond as rapidly as possible to a stimulus. When TMS was delivered to the primary motor cortex, known to be involved in movement control, it produced a long delay in overtly responding, but had only a small effect on the time to *report* the making of the response. In contrast, stimulation of the SMA, which is associated with response selection, had little effect on reaction time but markedly slowed the awareness report, suggesting that conscious awareness is associated with the SMA, rather than with the later processes of controlling the muscles making the response.

The Libet effect thus appears to be replicable, with the initiation of move-ment being mostly associated with the primary motor cortex while the sense of awareness appears to depend upon the SMA. The suggestion by Bargh and Ferguson that behaviour is simply being controlled by the experimenter does not seem to give an adequate explanation. The subject is not told which of the two responses is required, nor is the precise time specified. So what determines the response and when it is made? The Libet effect is clearly inconsistent with a naive realist view of the control of action, whereby a conscious decision is first made and then enacted as a chain of motor responses. Awareness is present, but does not appear to be primary.

13.3.2 The role of working memory

Does this therefore mean that the conscious decision is irrelevant? Surely not. Consider, for example, diving into a cold swimming pool. You may have committed yourself to plunging in but still vacillate on the brink, until suddenly you find yourself in the water, with no recollection of having taken that final decision as to when to plunge. Conscious awareness may be relevant, but not crucial to the timing of the act.

Of course, the fact that some of our behaviour is under the control of environmental stimuli does not imply that this is the whole story. A somewhat more even-handed assessment of the recent line of research in social psychology is that proposed by Gilbert (2002), who suggests that judgements are generally the products of non-conscious systems that operate quickly, on the basis of scant evidence and in a routine manner, and that then pass their rapid approximations to consciousness, which slowly and deliberately adjusts them. In short, while many of our judgements are rapid and automatic, they are open to reflection and revision, a process likely to depend heavily on working memory.

Gilbert illustrates his point by citing a hypothetical situation in which a child, Willy, breaks his aunt's priceless Ming vase. As he points out, the attitude of young Willy's aunt to his action would be different if she thought he was trying to help by dusting it, as opposed to using it as a convenient target to practice his catapult aim. In short, one of the functions of consciousness is to allow what he terms 'inferential correction', whereby an initial judgement may be modified on the basis of additional contextual information. As we saw in the discussion of cultural differences in belief in agency, different societies place different amounts of emphasis on contextual variables, but even individuals from a culture that is low in sensitivity to social context would be likely to make at least some differentiation between the two vase-breaking scenarios. It is this later process of reflection that is likely to depend most heavily on the storage and executive capacity of working memory.

A number of experiments by Gilbert and colleagues investigate the extent to which correction of an immediate impression may depend upon cognitive resources, one of the assumed hallmarks of the central executive. Gilbert *et al.* (1988) exposed their subjects to a video of a young woman being interviewed, but with the sound turned off. Their task was to judge her personality, deciding in particular whether she was characteristically an anxious person. On the video, she certainly seemed to betray a relatively high level of anxiety. Subjects were given one further source of help, namely a subtitle indicating either that she was being interviewed about the potentially embarrassing and stressful topic of sexual fantasies, or was being asked about a more neutral subject, world travel. A series of such topics were announced to the subjects: for one group these were all anxiety-provoking, and for the other, all neutral. Under standard baseline conditions, subjects modified their judgement on the basis of the subtitles, judging the speaker to be a generally less anxious person when they assumed she was being interviewed on embarrassing topics. However, in a second condition subjects were given the additional task of keeping track of and remembering the various topics. This group successfully recalled more of the topics in a later test, but were less likely to take them into account in evaluating the interviewees' personality. They clearly possessed the extenuating information, but were less likely to use it, presumably because they were directing attention to the memory task rather than to using the supplementary information to interpret the video.

In another study, Gilbert *et al.* (1992) showed that degrading the visual quality of the videotape, hence making the task more difficult, also diminished the extent to which subjects took into account the extenuating information. However, if instead of making their judgement immediately they were given a few moments of reflection, then the extenuating information was brought into account, leading to a more contextually sensitive judgement of the young interviewee. This suggested that the failure to take extenuating circumstances into account stemmed from lack of capacity to combine the relevant information, rather than to inadequate initial processing. In a later study, Gilbert and Gill (2000) showed that subjects' self-assessment of their own personality could be influenced by background music, provided that they have to make responses under time pressure, an effect that dissipates when the subjects were given time to reflect, again suggesting that although we may be influenced automatically by environmental cues when the central executive is overloaded this does not preclude an important role for working memory under less demanding conditions.

Gilbert (2002) showed similar effects of the limited-capacity executive system on whether a subject will categorize a new statement as true or false. As he points out, this is related to the classical philosophical disagreement between Descartes and Spinoza concerning the nature of understanding and its relationship to belief. Descartes proposes a sequential process whereby a person first of all understands a statement, and only then decides on the basis of evidence whether it is true or false. In contrast, Spinoza suggests that once we understand something we implicitly believe it, only subsequently correcting our belief if the evidence suggests error. If Spinoza was correct, then reducing attentional resources should hamper this later correction processes, leading a bias towards accepting statements as true when under time pressure. This is what Gilbert (2002) observed.

As Gilbert points out, we tend to have a positive bias in judging the world, and as Wason and Johnson Laird (1972) observed, when seeking information about the world or testing hypotheses as a scientist, we tend to look for confirmation of our assumptions, rather than pursue a more efficient strategy of testing for disconfirmatory evidence. On average, this is probably a sensible strategy in a world where our assumptions about how it works are usually correct. It does, however, make us potentially very vulnerable to manipulation by advertisers and self-seeking politicians, unless we are prepared to use our attentionally demanding executive processes to evaluate such messages. Suppose, then, that we assume some form of executive control over our views of the world and our actions upon it; how might such a system work?

13.4 Working memory and self-control

The section that follows reflects my assumption that self-control is an important function of working memory, and in particular of the central executive. While cognitive psychologists are beginning to study control mechanisms, for example through the analysis of inhibitory effects as discussed in the previous chapter, this is a relatively recent development. In contrast the issue of self-control has been investigated by social psychologists for over 20 years. The following section describes some of this research.

13.4.1 A feedback loop model of self-control

Carver and Scheier (1981) proposed a model of self-control that resembles the TOTE (Test-Operate-Test-Exit) model proposed by Miller *et al.* (1960). It assumes a series of standards that are to be achieved, comprising goals, ideals and a series of operations or processes through which such goals might be achieved. The results of such operations are monitored to see to what extent they approximate to the relevant standards. Failure of self-control may result from deficits at any of these various stages. The first stage may fail because the person might have incompatible goals, or possibly inappropriately ambitious aims. As we saw, the process of monitoring involved in the second stage requires attention, and may be disrupted by distraction, or by some other factor such as the influence of alcohol. Thirdly, control may break down at the operational level. The hungry dieter may be unable to resist the offer of the fragrant, sizzling cheeseburger on the grill in front of him. Failure at this level implies some kind of strength concept, not unlike the concept of strength of will.

Baumeister and Heatherton (1996) use this model as a basis for their analysis of the practically very important issue of failure of self-control. As they point out, a huge number of social problems can be regarded as following from loss of self-control. Obvious examples include alcoholism, drug addiction, obesity, smoking and addiction to gambling. An understanding of the processes involved in self-control and its breakdown is therefore is of enormous practical significance. Baumeister and Heatherton divide their review into cases whereby behaviour is *under-regulated*, and those where it is *misregulated*.

13.4.2 Control failure due to under-regulation

One category of regulation failure comes from simple *inertia*, where an existing habit is allowed to continue. Within the Norman and Shallice (1986) model, this is equivalent to a situation in which an existing schema or habit overcomes the longer term intention operating through the SAS, as when a habitual route to the office causes a wrong turning when going shopping on a Saturday morning. Simple inertia is probably one of the most common sources of lapses in control. Many smokers, for example, although being fully aware of the potential long-term physical risk, not to mention the short-term financial cost, nevertheless persist in their habit. The other side of this particular coin is what Baumeister and Heatherton refer to as '*transcendence*', a happy state whereby the attraction of the short-term goals, such as the pleasure of the first cigarette in the morning, is overridden or transcended by a long-term goal of staying alive and healthy. This is assumed to reflect the successful operation of the SAS, or in working memory terms, the central executive. Within the Norman and Shallice model, the third member of this trinity, which they term *acquiescence*, occurs when the forces of transcendence, as reflected in the operation of the central executive, momentarily lose their power to control behaviour. This situation is discussed in more detail in the section on craving discussed in Chapter 14.

As they point out, there are two ways of conceptualizing this fall from grace: as an irresistible impulse or a momentary lapse. Considered more closely, they suggest, the irresistible impulse theory seems a less than wholly convincing explanation. Even something as simple as smoking a cigarette requires one to find the right time and place, not always easy these days. It is not, as they point out, just a matter of 'simply going limp, becoming passive and letting it happen'. Marlatt and Gordon (1985) cites the case of a compulsive gambler, who quarrelled with his wife just before a business trip from San Francisco to Seattle. Instead of driving due north to Seattle, he decided on the 'scenic route' via the casino city of Reno (due east), where he stopped and parked. Needing money for the parking meter, he went into the nearest building which just happened to be a casino. Having decided on just a single bet to test his luck, he emerged some three days later. This episode clearly represents more than a single brief lapse, and can perhaps best be seen as a series of lapses under sustained pressure from a powerful impulse. He probably did not make a deliberate explicit choice to gamble at any one point, but he could not be regarded as the passive victim either. There appears to be a cost to self-control under such circumstances, and very often, it seems that once the initial lapse has occurred, there may be a tendency to abandon all further constraint, resulting in this case in a three-day gambling binge.

Personal violence seems often to follow a similar pattern, with frustration and anger building up to a point at which violence ensues, a situation that is often exacerbated by the capacity of alcohol to reduce the degree of self-control. This might appear to be the most convincing evidence for the irresistible impulse interpretation; it is certainly frequently used within the courts as a mitigating plea. Even here, however, what is regarded as irresistible appears to depend upon social norms. Bing (1991) reports that certain insults between teenage urban gangs are generally accepted as justifying violence while others are not. Homicide rates are higher in the American South than elsewhere, but only in response to arguments (Nisbett 1993), a useful piece of information for the traveller! The crime of 'running amok', whereby a man loses his self-control and attacks and kills innocent bystanders, was traditionally accepted in Malaysia as an understandable result of an irresistible impulse resulting from stress, but when British rule took a less lenient view and imposed heavy penalties, despite its irresistibility, its incidence rapidly declined (Carr and Tan 1976).

A similar conclusion about the resistibility of irresistible impulses is reached by Berkowitz (1978) from his study of violent British criminals. He describes, for example, a case of a husband beating his wife's lover with his fists, breaking off a bottle, realizing that use of this might well kill the man, putting it aside and continuing to beat the lover unconscious. In general, therefore, it seems likely that although powerful motives may lead to lapses of control which then escalate, the case for irresistibility is, despite its popularity with defence counsels, less than irresistible.

13.4.3 Individual differences in self-control

There are many reports of positive associations between rated self-control and social adjustment. For example, Maszk et al. (1999) found that children rated as having good self-control had higher social status and were more popular with their classmates. Longitudinal studies have shown that low ratings of self-control are associated with subsequent tendencies to delinquency (Pulkkinen and Hamalainen 1995). Gottfredson and Hirschi (1990) argue that poor self-control lies at the root of much antisocial behaviour and aggression in adults, a conclusion supported by Avakame (1998).

13.4.4 **Self-ratings of control**

Many self-rating questionnaires contain subscales aiming to measure self-control. A questionnaire study by Gramzow *et al.* (2000) studied factors associated most strongly with emotional distress. They found that measures of self-control, ego strength and 'hardiness' were strongly negatively associated with emotional distress. Other aspects of the self such as self-consistency, or self-esteem as measured by the discrepancy between the real and the ideal self, were less closely linked to emotional well-being.

Encouraged by this, Tangney *et al.* (2004) have developed a questionnaire comprising 36, or in its shortened form, 13 items. Subjects simply have to mark as true or false a series of simple statements about themselves, such as:

> I am lazy.
> I refuse things that are bad for me.
> I often act without thinking.
> I am not easily discouraged.

In their initial study they collected data from 350 students, who also completed a range of other measures, including that of social desirability, a measure of the extent to which the responder likes to please others. Correlations between social desirability and their measure of self-control ranged between 0.54 and 0.60. While it is not intrinsically implausible that people who have good self-control might also tend on the whole to prefer to be liked by others, this clearly presents a problem of interpretation, since social desirability might simply reflect a tendency for people to give answers to questions of self-control that they think will be approved by the tester. For that reason, Tangney *et al.* used analysis of covariance to control for social desirability before drawing the conclusions described below regarding other correlates.

In general, the scale has good qualities of reliability, even when reduced to 13 items. Its validity was assessed by association with a range of other measures. These indicated that individuals who rated themselves high in self-control were less likely to report eating disorders or alcohol problems such as binge drinking. The participants had also taken a standard personality test which assessed the so-called 'big five' personality factors. After covarying social desirability, self-control was associated with reported conscientiousness, emotional stability, positive interpersonal relations and with supportive rather than conflicting family relations. Finally, high scorers tended to report higher grade point averages than low scorers.

While the findings of Tangney *et al.* are clearly encouraging, suggesting that this line of research is worth pursuing, the fact that all the measures are based on self-report limits the weight one would want to place on the test at this point. Fortunately it is a very short and convenient measure on which further data are already beginning to accumulate from other laboratories.

Supervisors who score high on the self-control measure are judged as more trustworthy by their subordinates (Cox 2000). Engels *et al.* (2000) observed that high scorers tend to be lower on juvenile delinquency and adolescent alcohol abuse, while Finkel and Campbell (2001) report that they also find that high scorers have better interpersonal relations. A final issue addressed by Tangney *et al.* is the question of whether the relationship between self-control and adjustment is linear, or whether excessive self-control may lead to maladjustment, the control freak problem. They find no evidence of this in their own study, although clearly this issue needs to be explored more extensively.

In conclusion, although much of the evidence is based on self-report or ratings, there does appear to be a reasonably convincing case for a common sense notion that people differ in their degree of self-control. Currently available evidence suggests that self-control is a very positive social trait, and that it may well reflect the operation of a cognitive control process of substantial theoretical and practical importance.

13.4.5 Self-control: the muscle analogy

Suppose we accept that people differ in their capacity for self-control: what might be the mechanism underlying such individual variation? Muraven and Baumeister (2000) suggest that the capacity for self-control has a good deal in common with the way in which a muscle operates, hence implicitly emphasizing the energetic rather than the control aspects of the way in which action is governed. They suggest that this capacity reflects the 'operate' phase of a control system, rather than other components such as goal setting or monitoring. They make three assumptions: first that self-control is resource-limited, second that there is a limit to the number of behaviours that can be controlled at any one time. Both of these could apply equally well to a system that was information-limited, depending for example on attentional capacity. This is not the case, they suggest, for their third assumption, namely that the system has after-effects leading to depletion, analogous to the fatiguing of a muscle. They further assume that this is specific to tasks that involve the need to maintain action despite short-term temptations. Such temptations are assumed to reflect desirability. Hence it is the hedonic character of a situation that is crucial rather than the overall difficulty of the tasks involved. Finally, they observe that it is possible to build up the capacity for self-control, just as it is to strengthen a muscle. Muraven and Baumeister present evidence for each of these assumptions.

13.4.6 Strength depletion

Muraven *et al.* (1998) describe studies in which subjects performed two consecutive tasks. When both involved self-control, the second was performed less well than would otherwise be the case. For example, subjects watched an arousing video during which they were instructed to suppress any visible or audible responses. They then moved on to an apparently separate study in which they were required to squeeze a handgrip as hard and as long as possible. Subjects who had been required to suppress any emotional response to the video were less persistent in maintaining their handgrip – the hand became fatigued – than were control subjects. This effect did not appear to be a simple effect of mood; whether the video was sad and distressing, or light-hearted and funny, prior suppressors were less able to maintain a grip. In another study, subjects were instructed to *avoid* thinking about a specified topic, such as a white bear, something that Wegner (1994) has shown is difficult to achieve. This again led to reduced persistence on a subsequent unrelated task, attempting to solve puzzles that were in fact insoluble.

The negative after effects of environmental stressors may also deplete the capacity for self-control. Subjects exposed to unpredictable bursts of noise subsequently performed less well on a proof-reading task carried out under quiet conditions. Noise-exposed subjects also proved to be less frustration-tolerant. However, giving subjects a button which would allow them to switch off the noise if necessary reduced this effect, even when subjects did not in fact choose to press the button (Glass *et al.* 1969). Lack of control tends to induce what Seligman has termed 'learned helplessness', whereby a subject becomes passive as if abdicating control (Seligman 1975; Hiroto and Seligman 1975). Other stressors have similar effects: for example Sherrod (1974) studied over-crowding effects in female high school students. Groups of eight students were made to wait in either a small room or a spacious one, before going on to attempt a series of unsolvable puzzles. Crowding reduced persistence on the puzzle task. A similar effect on subsequent performance from exposure to a foul stench has been demonstrated by Rotton (1983).

However, while such after effects of stress clearly occur, and are consistent with the depleted muscle analogy, it seems equally plausible to assume that exposure to Glass *et al*'s unpredictable noise, and Rotton's bad smells may simply have dissipated any goodwill involved in serving in psychological experiments, rather than depleting the participant's willpower in general. Even though studies typically go to some lengths to imply that the two components of the experiment are separate, with tests carried out by different people, both are likely to be seen as reflecting on the general character of psychologists, and their willingness to make unreasonable demands of their volunteer subjects. Subjects may thus simply be opting out of the implicit contract between experimenter and participant.

This withdrawal of goodwill hypothesis is difficult to test, but is tackled by Schmeichel *et al.* (2003). They suggest that ego depletion, the fatiguing of the processes underpinning self-control, should only influence cognitive tasks that make reasonably heavy executive demands on the subject. They describe two experiments in which they contrast tasks that are assumed to be executively demanding, and those that are assumed to be less so. In one study, subjects were shown an emotional film and are either left free to respond, or required to suppress any emotion. Following this, they performed two tasks, both of an intellectual nature. One, the Cognitive Estimates Test, was developed to measure executive processes in patients, and requires the subject to use a combination of general knowledge and problem-solving skills to come up with approximate answers to novel questions such as 'How long does it take to iron a shirt?', or 'How many seeds would you find in water melon?'. The second test involved a test of crystallized knowledge such as needed to perform a vocabulary test, or to answer questions such as 'Which city is known as the Windy City?'. Although both are likely to correlate with intelligence, only the first demands the active application of executive processes. They found a significant difference between the two groups only on the estimates test, with those who had suppressed emotion performing more poorly. Measures of self-reported emotion at the time of the second test showed no difference between the groups.

Schmeichel *et al.* interpret their results in terms of ego depletion, which they argue reduces the capacity or willingness of the subject to engage in active cognitive processing, while having much less effect on more automatic processes, concluding:

> When the self is depleted by previous regulatory exertions, one set of mental processes is impaired, but another set is unaffected. In the terms of Baddeley's (1986, 1996) WM model, ego depletion hinders the control functioning of the central executive.
>
> (Schmeichel *et al.* 2003, p. 43).

They go on to point out that although task complexity and executive demand is one factor that influences sensitivity to ego depletion, such demands are not necessary primarily cognitive. Clear effects of ego depletion have been detected on tasks as simple as the continued squeezing of a hand dynamometer (Baumeister *et al.* 1998). Such a task may not be cognitively demanding, but it does involve control over behaviour which must be sustained in competition with other more attractive actions, such as releasing the grip as fatigue builds up.

Schmeichel *et al.* argue, I think convincingly, that their results are not attributable to changes in emotion, and suggest that a motivational interpretation is inconsistent with the difference between the two types of task, and with the lack of any effect of the order in which two contrasted tasks were performed by subjects. I am less convinced that Baumeister has yet ruled out interpretations based on changes in motivation rather than ego depletion per se. Hence, although I think this study begins to address the important but difficult question of motivation, further research is likely to be needed before the issue is settled.

There does, however, seem to be supporting evidence from a range of field studies, where resentment against an unsympathetic and demanding experimenter does not provide a convincing explanation. In many real-world situations, a period of stress results in an impaired capacity to maintain self-control, whether it is measured by relapse in people who are trying to quit undesirable habits such as smoking, (Cohen and Lichtenstein 1990), heroin addiction (Marlatt and Gordon 1980) or drinking in alcoholics (Hodgins *et al.* 1995), while even social drinkers, tended to drink more after a period of being required to suppress thoughts (Muraven, Collins and Nienhaus, 1999a).

13.4.7 Mood regulation

Muraven and Baumeister suggest that attempting to maintain a positive mood may also place heavy demands on self-control, particularly when external events make this difficult. Breaking a diet regime is more likely, for example, following a bad mood (Greeno and Wing 1994). In an eating study by Baucon and Aiken (1981), dieting and non-dieting subjects took part in an experiment which began with a puzzle. Failure on the puzzle resulted in dieters eating more food when subsequently given the opportunity, whereas the effect was exactly opposite for non-dieters. This interaction rules out a simple interpretation based on a link between frustration and appetite.

13.4.8 Vigilance decrement

Muraven and Baumeister relate their concept to the decline of performance that is reported in the classic vigilance tasks in which subjects must sustain attention over a period of time. Consistent with this view is the observation that, given the appropriate initial levels of expectancy (Colquhoun and Baddeley 1964) simple perceptual detection tasks do not show the classic performance decrement overtime. Decrement does however occur when the subject needs to hold each stimulus in working memory and compare it with the next item, for example deciding whether two successive visual stimuli are of equal length (Davies and Parasuranam 1982; Parasuranam 1984). This effect is particularly marked in patients suffering from Alzheimer's disease, who show executive deficits, but who tend otherwise to show relatively good sustained attention (Baddeley *et al.* 1999; Perry *et al.* 2000), and in children diagnosed as suffering from attention deficit hyperactivity disorder (ADHD), which is assumed to reflect poor self-control (Barkley 1977a; b).

13.4.9 **Training effects**

Muraven *et al.* (1999b) placed volunteer subjects on a two-week regimen of practicing self-control. One group attempted to improve posture, a second practiced mood regulation, while a third group was assigned the tedious chore of maintaining an eating diary. At the end of two weeks, training and control subjects were tested on persistence using a handgrip task. Subjects who had participated in any of the training programmes, on average maintained their handgrip longer than the control subjects. While consistent with the muscular analogy of self-control, as Muraven *et al.* concede, other interpretations are possible. These include enhanced self-confidence, or possibly a stronger feeling of commitment to their academic environment, possibly related to avoidance of cognitive dissonance: 'I've put all this effort into doing what I'm asked, so it must be a good thing to do' (Festinger 1957).

There is, however, broadly supporting evidence in studies of attentional training in neuropsychological patients, where practice on tasks that involve self-control does appear to increase the patient's capacity to perform other demanding tasks which are unrelated to those practiced (Ball *et al.* 2002; Klingberg *et al.* 2005). This contrasts with practice on other cognitive deficits, such as memory, where there is little evidence that mnemonic exercise improves memory performance (Cicerone *et al.* 2005).

13.4.10 **Alternative explanations**

The muscle analogy does appear to have been useful in generating experiments that investigate the nature of self-control. However, alternative hypotheses do seem possible in many of these studies. Muraven and Baumeister consider some of these, for example the possibility that tasks that demand self-control impact on the subject's mood, which in turn influences subsequent performance. They point out that a number of studies have included mood ratings (Glass and Singer 1972; Green and Rogers 1995; Muraven *et al.* 1998), and found no difference between high-and low-demand groups, while at least one study has also attempted to use both self-rating and physiological measures, neither of which detected any effect (Spacapan and Cohen 1983).

To a cognitive psychologist, more used to concepts of information and control than to those involving energy and effort, the most obvious interpretation would seem to be in terms of reduced attention rather than depleted self-control. Since self-control may often have its effect through a greater capacity or will-ingness to sustain attention, separating these interpretations will not be easy. Indeed, the very concept of sustained attention against distraction seems to demand some form of further explanation. All our discussions of the central executive so far have been concerned with the way in which behaviour is controlled, why we choose one action rather than another, and how that action is subsequently modulated. What has been left out, however, is the crucial question of why we behave at all. What is it that is controlled? We clearly need to supplement accounts of control that rely purely on specifying the flow of information within a system, bringing in energy-based concepts to fulfil the role played in earlier theoretical systems by ideas such as mental energy (Freud 1904), drive (Hull 1943) and arousal (Broadbent 1958; Kahneman 1973). One important approach to this problem is through the study of emotion and its impact on cognition. This forms the topic of the next two chapters.

13.5 Conclusions

I have tried in this chapter to illustrate three areas in which the study of working memory might benefit from research in social psychology. The first concerns the extent to which thought and action may be implicitly controlled, where the work of Bargh and colleagues is particularly relevant to the role played by schemata and habit in the Norman and Shallice (1986) model of executive control. The second concerns the way in which social behaviour reflects the attentionally limited supervisory attentional system within this model, with the work of Gilbert and Baumeister being particularly relevant. The third issue concerns the clear need for a concept of energy or drive within cognitive psychology, a need that will be further discussed in subsequent chapters.

The reader will have noted, however, that this chapter contains virtually no research directly related to working memory. Why should that be, if the link is so important? In my own view, the answer is cultural. The applied experimental approach to working memory has been strongest in Britain, where the social psychology tradition has focused on the group level, tending to reject the North American experimental approach that relates most closely to cognitive psychology. If this chapter can do anything to encourage the bridging of this gap, it will have served its purpose.

Chapter 14

Working memory and emotion I
Fear and craving

During the early years of the last century, psychology was assumed to comprise three related but separate areas – cognitive, orectic and conative psychology. Orectic was the term used to denote the study of emotion, and conative, the study of will. The second half of the century saw the dominance within human experimental psychology of cognitive psychology, based on the development of the information-processing metaphor, with its emphasis on control overshadowing the equally important topic of motivation, of why we do one thing rather than another. Indeed, why do we do anything at all?

I suspect this neglect stemmed largely from the difficulty of studying emotion and the will within the laboratory. There has, for example, been a lack of research on the neurobiological basis of emotion, which until recently relied largely on animal studies, and which continues to be extremely productive (see, for example LeDoux [1996] and Panksepp [1998]). However, this work is beyond my already over-extended remit, and competence. Instead, I propose to concentrate on work that appears to be clearly relevant to the multicomponent WM model, focusing on two emotions of obvious clinical relevance, namely anxiety and depression, and limiting my coverage to work on humans. This still leaves a very large and diverse literature. For that reason, as in the first part of this book, my review will be guided (or misguided?) by my own experience and interests. This reflects an early concern with performance in dangerous environments stemming from an involvement in open-sea diving research, together with a much more extended interest in linking cognition and emotion through the study of patients with emotional problems. My involvement here was indirect through the setting up within my Cambridge Unit of a group of research-orientated clinical psychologists. Their success in bridging clinical and cognitive psychology is illustrated through the journal they founded, *Cognition and Emotion*, and in the two editions of what I understand has been a highly influential book, *Cognitive Psychology and Emotional Disorders* (Williams *et al.* 1988; Williams *et al.* 1997). As will become clear, my own views have been strongly influenced by those of my ex colleagues, and although

I have tried in writing the next two chapters to take a balanced view, giving full weight to subsequent work and to other theorists, I suspect it would be unwise to assume that I have fully succeeded.

I should begin with a definition. While I accept the distinction between emotion as a physiological state and its psychological counterpart, unlike LeDoux (1996), I do not propose to use his term 'feelings' for the psychological state. Instead, I also use the term emotion for psychological states, on the grounds of common usage. On the few occasions when I discuss the physiological aspects of emotion, I will try to ensure that there is no ambiguity. In line with the development of my own interests I will begin by discussing the effect on cognition of relatively extreme emotions.

14.1 Cognition in extreme emotion

It is a truism that it is difficult to think calmly, persistently and coherently while experiencing an extreme emotion, hence expressions like 'he was beside himself with rage', or she was 'out of her mind with grief'. A very good account of the impact on thought of extreme emotion is given by Philip Roth in describing his response to the discovery that his 86-year-old father had a brainstem tumour that was in an advanced state of development. Surgery was possible, but was likely to create further pain and distress, while doing nothing meant simply waiting for his father's condition to gradually deteriorate even further. 'I can't read. God knows, I can't write either – I can't even watch a stupid baseball game. I absolutely cannot think. I cannot do a thing' (Roth in *Patrimony* 1991, p. 129).

To the best of my knowledge, there is little empirical work on this state. This is hardly surprising, as I doubt if volunteering to take part in a psychological experiment would have been high on Roth's list of chosen activities at that time. However, there have been studies of the effects of another powerful emotion, namely fear. Such effects are clearly of considerable importance to the wartime activities of a soldier, or to performance in equally dangerous but less aggressive occupations such as bomb disposal, or the work of firemen fighting a blaze. Although collecting experimental data in the middle of a battle, or a fire, presents practical problems, there have been a number of studies using either simulated danger, or danger that accompanied a voluntary but hazardous sporting activity.

Perhaps the most extreme of these studies was a series of experiments carried out by the US army before ethics committees became a standard feature of research. Berkun *et al.* (1962) designed a piece of equipment that was allegedly a radio transmitter. It was arranged that during a military exercise the equipment would fail, but would be accompanied by instructions for its reactivation.

The instructions were complex, and in fact involved a number of separate stages, each comprising a scorable subtest. A series of field experiments were run in which the equipment 'broke down', either under non-stressful or stressful circumstances. The stressors included in one case a simulated radiation accident, in another, an incident in which the unfortunate subject was led to believe that he had just blown up one of his fellow soldiers, and needed to radio urgently for help! One unfortunate subject in this latter condition panicked and attempted to leave the scene, only to be ordered to return by the experimenter lurking in the bushes, an event the soldier subsequently reported as the prompting of his conscience. In a third incredible experiment, troops on a plane were informed that it was due to crash, and that to obtain adequate insurance they would need to complete a form, which would then be placed in a crash-proof container. Once again, the form in fact, comprised a series of cognitive tests. It will come as no surprise that the unfortunate subjects in each of the experiments performed much more poorly when they were under a life-threatening stress than equivalent groups under control conditions.

What about cognitive effects of extreme positive emotions? These appear to be even less studied than extreme fear. However, there is evidence to suggest that the elation following the successful landing of novice parachutists may be at least as disruptive as their pre-jump anxiety (Macdonald and Labuc 1982), while data from manic depressive patients suggest that cognition is at least as severely disrupted during mania as it is when in the depressive phase (Bulbena and Berrios 1993; Murphy *et al.* 1999).

14.1.1 **The nature of the cognitive deficit**

The studies by Berkun *et al.* (1962) are concerned with extreme levels of fear. Would other, perhaps even positive emotions have a qualitatively similar effect, and is that effect always to impair performance? This is probably not the case. The Murphy *et al.* (1999) study, for example, found that manic patients were impaired on tests of memory and planning while depression led to difficulties in switching attention.

It seems likely, in the case of fear, that the Yerkes-Dodson law will apply. This proposes an inverted U-shaped relationship between performance and level of arousal. Depending on the task there is an optimum level of arousal, with arousal levels below and above this point leading to poorer performance (Yerkes and Dodson 1908). Hence running fast is likely to peak at a higher level of fear than threading a needle. It has also been suggested (Broadbent 1971; Baddeley 1972) that the optimal level of arousal will depend upon task complexity, with high arousal being best for simple motor tasks such as running or operating a simple control system such as steering a car, whereas lower levels are optimum for finer or less-practiced skills such as threading a needle or operating a tracking system with delayed non-linear feedback. Evidence for this view comes from a study by Walker and Burkhardt (1965) of missile control performance under operational conditions. They collected operational field data for three types of control system, the simplest being a lagged velocity control, the next being control based on acceleration, and the hardest involving acceleration combined with a lag. All three led to good performance in low risk conditions. However, as risk increased in general severity from a 2 per cent aircraft loss, through 5 per cent up to 10 per cent, the maximum risk regarded as operationally acceptable, control error rate increased, steadily for the simple control system and dramatically for the most complex.

14.1.2 The attentional narrowing hypothesis

It has been suggested that high arousal causes a narrowing of the field of attention. This is supported by a study on divers tested under stressful under-water conditions, and on an equivalent surface task (Weltman *et al.* 1970; Weltman *et al.* 1971). Divers were required to perform a central task, and also at the same time to detect occasional peripheral light signals. Under stress, performance on the central task was maintained, but peripheral signals were less well detected. The narrowing of attention under stress features promi-nently in literature on eyewitness testimony, with the so-called 'gun focus' effect. Subjects viewing an emotionally threatening situation such as a hold-up, or a person escaping a crime with a bloodstained implement, tend to focus their attention on the source of threat, and to be less able to report details of the assailant than are subjects under less threatening conditions (Loftus 1979; Christianson and Loftus 1991).

Implicit in the attentional narrowing hypothesis is the assumption that attentional capacity is limited, hence, if more attention is focused on one object, less will remain for others. Thus, the unfortunate soldiers studied by Berkun *et al.* (1962) were presumably devoting a substantial amount of their attention to wondering if and how they might escape their terrible situation. This type of explanation has been applied to the frequent observations of generally poor memory performance in patients with emotional disorders (Dalgleish and Cox 2002) and was proposed by Ellis as the Resource Allocation Model (Ellis and Ashbrook 1988; Ellis and Moore 1999).

It follows from this model that anything that uses up attentional capacity is likely to exacerbate the effects of emotion. This was tested directly by MacLeod and Donnellan (1993) who used two groups of normal subjects, selected as being either high or low on trait anxiety, the self-rated tendency to be an anxious person. Subjects were required to perform a verbal reasoning task in combination with either an easy concurrent verbal task (repeatedly uttering zero), or the more demanding task of repeating a sequence of six digits, with the sequence changing after each repetition. As predicted, anxious subjects performed more poorly, showing an increased effect of the demanding secondary task. Presumably, the hard secondary task induced anxiety, which further diminished attentional capacity.

A study of my own (Baddeley 1966d) was concerned with the effect on deep-sea divers of nitrogen narcosis, the drunkenness that occurs when breathing air at depths of one hundred feet or more. We tested divers using a simple motor task in which they were required to move screws from one end of a brass plate to the other as rapidly as possible. They were tested both on land and underwater, at depths of both 10 feet, when free of narcosis, and at 100 feet. A second group was tested entirely under dry conditions, with the equivalent pressures of 10 and 100 feet being obtained within a diving chamber. We found that performing the task underwater slowed subjects down, as did performing under the influence of narcosis. However, when these stresses were combined, by testing divers in the open sea at 100 feet, performance was impaired to a much greater extent than would be expected by simply adding the effects of water and depth.

What was causing this interaction? We discovered the answer inadvertently in a later experiment. Our first study had been carried out from a boat out on the open sea. The subjects were a mixture of amateur divers, members of the Cambridge University Diving Club, and soldiers, Royal Engineers who had been trained for shallow diving but were not experienced at open sea diving, where it is necessary to dive straight down 'into the blue'. Our later replication also used student and army divers. However, on this occasion the divers entered the water at a shallow point and gradually followed the bottom down to the test site at 100 feet, a much less threatening experience (Baddeley *et al.* 1968). Under these conditions, we observed the expected decrement from performing under water, together with a narcosis effect that was no greater than that observed in the dry pressure chamber. It seemed likely that the crucial factor that produced the interaction between open-sea narcosis and depth was degree of anxiety.

We tested this directly in a later study under much more stressful conditions off the Scottish coast (Davis *et al.* 1972). We used student divers and measured anxiety level both electrophysiologically and in terms of subjective rating scales. Under these conditions, our divers were indeed anxious at depth, and again showed a much greater effect of depth when tested under water. We assume that the interaction therefore came from a combination of the well-established cognitive decrement from nitrogen narcosis, coupled with the challenge of performing under more stressful conditions. When 100 feet beneath the waves, it is not unreasonable to devote at least some of your attention to ensuring that nothing is going wrong.

14.1.3 Attentional focus and intrusive thoughts

It is, however, important to note that even under these stressful conditions, not all tasks show such a clear interaction. A later study compared open-sea performance of amateur divers breathing either air, or less narcotic oxyhelium, this time studying performance at 200 feet, which was regarded at that time as the maximum accepted depth for air diving. Performance on the screw plate task again showed the predicted interaction with depth, but this was not found in the case of a demanding verbal reasoning task (Baddeley and Flemming 1967).

A possible explanation of this unexpected result is provided by a series of studies by Lavie (Lavie 1995; 2000) in which she demonstrates that the capacity of irrelevant peripheral stimuli to disrupt a visual processing may *decrease* as the level of difficulty of the central task becomes greater. With a demanding perceptual task, attention is focused firmly on the relevant stimuli. With an easier task, however, there may be sufficient spare attentional capacity to take in more peripheral and potentially distracting stimuli. Lavie (1995; 2000) has concentrated on visual attention, but it seems probable that the effect is more general, when attention is focused on a demanding central task, there will be less likelihood of scanning either the mental or physical environment for other sources of information. Presumably, in the case of our divers, the reasoning task was sufficiently absorbing to reduce attention to potentially worrying environmental cues. Indeed, in the case of one diver, it caused him to discount the fact that his air was running out due to a leak, leading to a rapid and potentially highly dangerous subsequent ascent.

The capacity for a demanding cognitive task to focus attention on the task in hand has interesting implications for studies of stress, since the very tools that have been devised to measure decrement may have had the effect of reducing it by helping the subject to avoid disruptive intrusive thoughts. This possibility has implications for helping people avoid such disruptive thoughts, as we shall see later.

How then might anxious and intrusive thoughts be avoided? One way would be to focus attention on a non-threatening task which, if sufficiently demanding, will shut out irrelevant thoughts. Evidence for this was produced by Teasdale *et al.* (1995) in a study in which we periodically questioned subjects about their thoughts during the repeated performance of a range of tasks. The more practice subjects had on each task, the more automatic it became, and the greater the likelihood of irrelevant thoughts. Such thoughts could however be reduced by adding a further task. This did not need to be demanding provided it involved the occasional requirement to make a simple decision. Teasdale *et al.* concluded that the development of a sustained and potentially disruptive stream of thought depended on the continued availability of the central executive. It appears that such intrusive and irrelevant thought sequences can be disrupted in normal subjects at least, relatively easily, encouraging Levey *et al.* (1991) to base a proposed treatment of insomnia on this approach, requiring their subjects to disrupt the stream of sleep-disruptive thoughts by subvocally uttering a single word at random intervals, the requirement for randomness preventing the suppression becoming automatized and hence ineffective, as occurs in the more traditional method of getting to sleep by counting imaginary sheep.

14.1.4 **Working memory and the worry hypothesis**

What precisely is the mechanism whereby emotion interfere with cognition? One explanation is in terms of Michael Eysenck's *processing efficiency theory* (Eysenck 1992). This assumes a limited capacity working memory system, that under conditions of threat may become unduly preoccupied with thoughts of what might go wrong, leaving less capacity for the task in hand. Efficiency may be maintained, however, provided more effort is invested. When this is insufficient to maintain performance a new strategy may be adopted. If this in turn fails cognitive decrement results (Eysenck and Calvo 1992). Subjects who are highly anxious are likely to be more challenged by distraction from potential threats, and under stress to begin to show cognitive deficits, sometimes referred to as the *worry hypothesis*. This has been explored in a series of studies that have required subjects to process passages of text which they are subsequently required to recall. Comparison is then made between student subjects who are high, and those who are low in self-rated trait anxiety. Calvo *et al.* (1994) found that anxious subjects were able to maintain their level of comprehension, but did so by making more regressive eye movements while reading. When this strategy was not possible because the words were presented one at a time, anxious subjects still maintained their performance on comprehension but responded more slowly and showed more overt articulation, especially in a condition in which they were trying to ignore irrelevant speech (Calvo *et al.* 1993). However, when both regressive eye movements and subvocal rehearsal were prevented by combining single word presentation, irrelevant speech and articulatory suppression, then a clear difference emerges, with high anxiety subjects showing poorer comprehension (Calvo and Eysenck 1996).

14.1.5 **The role of repression**

In the experiments just described, subjects developed coping strategies to compensate for the disruptive effect of anxiety. Another means of coping, however, is to attempt to suppress the anxiety. This way of dealing with anxiety appears to reflect a relatively stable personality trait that can be detected reliably using questionnaire measures. Such subjects are termed *repressors* and when tested in a potentially stressful situation, for example before giving a public talk, tend to *report* relatively low levels of anxiety, while at the same time showing clear objective signs of anxiety, as indexed by physiological measures (Newton and Contrada 1992; Weinberger 1990). This raises the obvious question as to whether such subjects are simply lying about their experience, or are genuinely able to suppress anxious thoughts and feelings. This was investigated by Derakshan and Eysenck (1998) in a study in which carefully selected samples of subjects performed a reasoning task under both a light and a heavy concurrent cognitive load.

The primary task was one that is known to rely heavily on working memory, in which subjects had to verify sentences purporting to describe the order of two letters, for example, *A is not preceded by B – AB* (Baddeley 1968; Baddeley and Hitch 1974). The heavy load required subjects to hear and repeat back sequences of six random numbers at the same time as responding to the reasoning task, while the light load condition involved simply hearing and repeating six zeros. They selected subjects who were either high or low in self-rated anxiety, with each group being divided into those with a high, and those with a low tendency to suppress anxiety, resulting in four groups. All groups performed the reasoning task under high and low concurrent memory load conditions.

As expected, the groups did not differ in their level of performance under low load, whereas the imposition of a demanding secondary task clearly impaired the performance of the group of subjects who were anxious both in terms of their self-rating and physiological response. The crucial comparison, however, concerned the fourth group, the physiologically anxious repressors. In this case, their performance was consistent with their subjective report; despite showing clear physiological signs of anxiety, their performance resembled that of the non-anxious group. It appears to be the case that the repressors were indeed suppressing their anxiety successfully, and not simply lying about their feelings. That in turn raises the interesting question of whether anxious people can be trained to repress their anxiety. One could perhaps argue that some forms of cognitive therapy for anxiety states might be regarded as training in thought control, and indeed in repression.

Further evidence on this issue comes from studies of anxiety in people who voluntarily engage in dangerous sports such as parachuting. Epstein (1962; Fenz and Epstein 1962) studied novice and experienced parachutists, recording their GSR and self-rated enthusiasm for the jump at various stages before and after the jump. Novices become gradually more aroused and less enthusiastic as the jump approaches, with the pattern reversing post-jump. The experienced jumpers do show anxiety, but it is displaced from the time of the jump, a process Epstein attributes to a process of learning, whereby training results in anxiety being inhibited around the jump. From an evolutionary viewpoint, the capacity to learn to 'keep a cool head' would seem to be advantageous. Following the discrimination model developed for animal learning by Spence (1937), Epstein suggests that the distribution of inhibition is narrower and more peaked than that of anxiety, leading to a displacement of the point of maximum anxiety away from the jump time, a phenomenon known as peak shift. The results obtained by Epstein are intriguing, but could represent either the effects of training, or possibly reflect selective drop out, if only the repressors persevere. A longitudinal study would be one way of deciding between these possibilities.

The evidence so far is consistent with the view that negative thoughts, and perhaps also strongly positive thoughts, may occupy working memory. They are likely to influence the operation of both the central executive and the episodic buffer, and hence disrupt the performance of other cognitive tasks. Furthermore, it appears to be possible to learn to inhibit anxiety, both in connection with specific situations such as parachuting, and as a more general personality trait. There are, however, many people and many situations in which anxiety is not controlled, potentially leading to considerable suffering, and exacerbated by the associated impairment in cognitive capacity and disruption of social activity.

14.2 Clinical studies of anxiety and cognition

Williams *et al.* (1997) describe two patients, both of whom suffered seriously from anxiety. Patient M.M. had a specific phobia concerning birds. Her job involved working in a small aircraft hangar; occasionally birds would fly in and become trapped, causing her to become upset and tearful. She was afraid of both live and dead birds, and avoided walking past markets or butcher's shops where there might be poultry hanging. Her fear extended to remote stimuli in her environment that could potentially be interpreted as birds, for example, a flapping shape on the road, which might in fact turn out to be a piece of plastic sheeting.

A second patient, T.S., suffered from a general anxiety disorder (GAD). Such patients not only have a high level of worry, but their worries are less controllable, less realistic and less easy to correct than worries in the normal population

(Craske *et al.* 1989). T.S. worked in a shipyard as a welder, but had been unable to work for some time because of a chronic state of anxiety. This resulted in trembling and sweating whenever he was in the company of co-workers, a state of affairs that not only interfered with his social relations, but also began to have an impact on the quality of his work, which in turn increased his anxiety. Outside the work situation, he found that he was abnormally sensitive to bad news in the newspaper, spotting even the most remote example almost immediately, which then set up thoughts of the terrible things that might happen to his wife and himself. This became a strain on his wife, which further increased his anxiety.

14.2.1 **Attentional bias in anxious patients**

Williams *et al.* (1997) focus on such patients as an important component of their project of applying the techniques and concepts of cognitive psychology to the study of emotion in general, and more specifically, to the problems of patients with emotional disorders. They suggest that an important component of anxiety states such as those just described comes from the tendency of patients to bias their attention *toward* the object or situation of fear. They propose that such a bias can operate across any of a range of modalities, visual, auditory or tactile, and that it is involuntary, although potentially subject to voluntary control, given the appropriate therapeutic techniques. They further suggest that anxiety is liable to be triggered environmentally, either externally through the patient's surroundings, or internally as a result of thoughts and memories. They suggest that this is an exaggeration of a normal response whereby it is protective to be aware of potential dangers, and for extra vigilance to be employed when the threat seems greatest. Furthermore, they accept that emotionally based bias is not limited to negative feelings. For example, when one is about to buy a house, there is a tendency to notice 'for sale' signs everywhere, even when travelling in a part of the country where one has no intention of living. Similarly, having bought a new car, one tends to notice the equivalent model wherever one drives.

Evidence of this type of attentional bias has been available for many years. For example, Parkinson and Rachman (1981) studied mothers whose children were about to undergo tonsillectomy. They studied two groups, one whose children had just been admitted for the operation, and another for whom the operation was less imminent. The mothers were asked to try to detect words that were embedded in music, and which comprised three different types; directly relevant (e.g. *bleeding, injection, operation*), a second type that was acoustically similar but not relevant (e.g. *breeding, inflection, operatic*), and a third control set (e.g. *newspaper, bird, uniform*). Mothers whose children had been admitted showed higher detection of the directly relevant words, and intermediate detection of acoustically similar words, but were not different from the non-admitted group, on control words.

Other studies have used the dichotic listening procedure, whereby subjects repeat words fed into one ear and attempt to ignore those fed into the other. Under these conditions, bulimic subjects were more likely to hear the word 'fat' presented on the unattended channel than were control subjects who did not have an eating disorder (Schotte *et al.* 1990). Both the hospital anxiety and the eating disorder studies could, however, simply reflect a general response bias, rather than an effect of anxiety. The critical words may, for example, have a lower detection threshold, possibly because they feature more frequently in the experience of the experimental group.

14.2.1 The problems of response bias

In an attempt to avoid the response bias problem, Mathews and MacLeod (1986) moved to a design in which the crucial words were not required as a response at any point. Subjects were required to respond manually to a series of neutral visual stimuli. At the same time they were required to repeat words presented to one ear, while ignoring the opposite ear. The unattended words could be either neutral or threatening, and both anxious and non-anxious subjects were tested. Neither group was able to report the unattended words, but when these were threatening, they led to a slowing down of reaction time to the visually presented neutral target pictures in the anxious group, suggesting that shutting the emotional words out was attentionally demanding for anxious subjects. As there was no requirement to utter the emotional words, a response bias seems a less plausible explanation than one based on differential perceptual sensitivity.

An ingenious method of avoiding the problem of response bias in studies using visual presentation is provided by the dot probe technique used extensively by Mathews and colleagues. MacLeod *et al.* (1986) presented their subjects with two words, one above the other. The subject's task was to name the upper word. Shortly after the disappearance of the word, a dot would sometimes appear, to which the subject should respond by pressing a button as rapidly as possible. High-and low-anxiety patients were tested with material that included threat words that could occur in either the upper or lower position. The crucial question was how long it took to respond to the dot. All subjects responded more rapidly if the dot was in the upper location, the one they had just named. When a threat word had appeared in the upper position, anxious subjects responded more rapidly than controls. However, if a threat word had appeared in the lower position, they, but not the control subject, responded to the upper dot more slowly. It appears therefore that their attention had been attracted towards the threatening word, an effect that occurred despite the fact that both the dot stimulus and the manual response were themselves neutral.

Further evidence against a simple response bias interpretation comes from a study by MacLeod and Mathews (1988), who tested high-and low-anxiety medical students, using the dot probe task and a mixture of neutral and exam-related words. When tested during an exam-free period, neither group showed any effect of word class. However, when tested a week before the exam, the anxious students showed a faster response to a dot that immediately followed an exam word in that location, as if their attention had been drawn to the source of their anxiety while the control students showed the opposite effect, being somewhat slower following an exam word, as if avoiding it. Mogg *et al.* (1990) demonstrated that even a very brief stress, produced by the need to attempt anagrams which, in fact, were insolvable, led to bias in the direction of threat words using the dot probe task.

14.2.2 **The emotional Stroop task**

Ingenious though the dot probe task is, it is important not to rely too much on a single paradigm. Fortunately an alternative approach to the same problem has been developed, using a modification of the Stroop test. In the classical Stroop, subjects are required to name the colour in which a range of words is printed, and in the critical condition, the words themselves are colour names, with the print colour inconsistent with the name, for example, the word *red* printed in green ink. Under this conflict condition, naming the print takes longer than it would take to name the ink colour of a non-colour word, which in turn takes longer than naming the print colour of a row of x's. The *emotional Stroop* task is a variant in which the words are not colour names, but are selected for their potential emotional significance.

For example, Watts *et al.* (1986) showed that people with an exaggerated fear of spiders took longer to name the print colour of spider-related words, such as 'web' and 'hairy', than more general anxiety words such as 'failure' and 'pain'. Mathews and MacLeod (1985) were interested in how specific the effects could be. They tested anxious people whose principal anxiety was either social, or related to potential physical threat. They found a different pattern of responses, with each group being particularly sensitive to words related to their own source of anxiety. A similar association has been found for drug over-dose versus general anxiety words in people who had attempted self-poisoning (Williams and Broadbent 1986), while similar dissociation between words selected for their relevance to social phobias words and panic attack-related words were found in the two differing patient groups by Hope *et al.* (1990).

It is, however, important to note that conscious awareness of the stressful or neutral word in not necessary for the emotional Stroop effect to occur. For example, a mere 20 msec exposure of anxiety-related words followed by the colour-naming component of the task is sufficient to slow the colour naming response of anxious patients (MacLeod and Rutherford 1992; Mathews and MacLeod 1994). No such effect occurred in patients who were depressed but not anxious (Mogg *et al.* 1993).

One final point should be made. We have interpreted the available data as evidence that emotional stimuli differentially attract attention. However it is also possible to account for these results by assuming that emotion makes it harder to break off attention, possibly by impairment of inhibitory processes (Fox 1994; Fox *et al.* 2001). The implications for a general distraction by worry hypothesis are broadly equivalent for these two interpretations, although they have different implications at the level of more detailed models. These will be discussed next.

14.3 Modelling the impact of anxiety and cognition

One aspect of the relationship between fear, anxiety and attention appears to enjoy quite broad agreement, namely its evolutionary function as an early warning device for detecting potential danger (Oatley and Johnson-Laird 1987). Ohmän (1993; 1996) makes a convincing case for the evolutionary nature of a rapid pre-attentional orientation towards threat, demonstrating that certain potentially harmful stimuli such as snakes and toadstools are detected more readily than less harmful natural stimuli such as flowers, and are furthermore more readily conditionable to an avoidance response. LeDoux (1996) has elegantly teased out the neural pathways associated with responses to sources of fear, demonstrating two separate pathways, both leading to the amygdala, which deals with emotional responses. One is direct and extremely rapid, while the other takes an indirect route via the cortex. It seems likely that these correspond to preconscious and conscious processing respectively.

Because of its clinical importance for understanding and treating anxiety disorders, there has been a growing interest in attempting to explain the relationship between anxiety and cognitive function. One of the earliest, and certainly most clinically influential interpretations was that proposed by Beck (1976), which gave rise to the development of cognitive therapy for both anxiety and depression. It has been particularly influential in the treatment of depression, and will be discussed in the next chapter.

14.3.1 Cognitive models of anxiety and performance

Williams *et al.* (1988; 1997) propose an account of the interaction between emotion and cognition that it is directly influenced by recent developments in cognitive psychology. They propose a preconscious detection system, followed by an evaluation system. Depending on the degree of threat signalled by the evaluation system, the stimulus is either paid attention, or inhibited. Individual differences occur in the evaluation process, with subjects who are high on the trait of anxiety tending to focus on the potential threat, while those who are low on this trait ignore the threat. It has however been suggested that this latter assumption is implausible from a evolutionary viewpoint, since it appears to predict that such patients will consistently continue to ignore a threat, however great it is (Mathews and Mackintosh 1998; Mogg and Bradley 1998). This approach also appears to assume that patients who have both depression and anxiety will show the same tendency for the pre-attentive detection of threat stimuli as are shown by anxious but non-depressed patients, which does not appear to be the case (Bradley *et al.* 1995; Mogg and Bradley 1998).

In order to avoid these problems, Mogg and Bradley (1998) propose a modification of the Williams *et al.* model, their cognitive-motivational hypothesis. This assumes that stimuli have both a valence, positive or negative, and a motivational component. Anxiety is assumed to be motivationally aversive, leading to a heightened level of attention, a rapid response to threat and increased autonomic activation. Like Williams *et al.* they assume two stages, one involving the detection and evaluation of the potentially threatening stimulus, and the other being concerned with developing and mobilizing subsequent cognitive processing. Unlike Williams *et al.* they interpret the influence of trait or state anxiety as operating via a bias in the evaluative process. Anxious subjects will tend to have a lower threshold beyond which a potential threat will attract attention (see Fig. 14.1). They make a further assumption regarding the function relating degree of threat to a likelihood of attracting attention, with slightly negative stimuli tending to inhibit attention that is to be actively ignored. They suggest that the apparently paradoxical tendency for a low degree of threat to lead to inhibition of attention has two positive functions. The first of these is to aid the focus of attention, and discourage a tendency for every mildly negative stimulus to demand processing. The second they suggest may be a resulting tendency for cognition to be slightly positively biased, which given the tendency of negative feelings to reduce activity, provides an evolutionary advantage. In connection with this assumption, they propose that anxiety is an aversive emotional state that encourages action, whereas depression is amotivational. We will return to the Mogg and Bradley model in the next chapter.

14.3.2 Anxiety and long-term memory

Given that anxious subjects are attentionally biased towards anxiety-provoking stimuli, one might expect a similar bias in subsequent recall. There is, however,

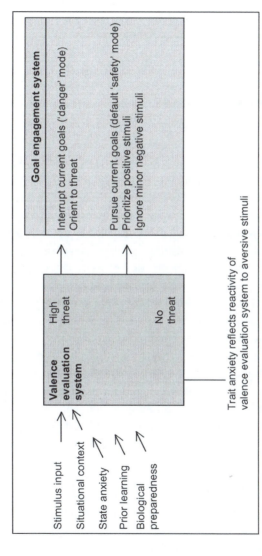

Fig. 14.1 Model proposed by Mogg and Bradley (2005) to account for the influence of anxiety on cognitive function. From Mogg and Bradley (2005). In: A cognitive-motivational analysis of anxiety. *Behav Res Ther*, **36**(9), 80. Reproduced with permission from Elsevier.

little robust evidence for such a bias based on either recall of autobiographical memories (Levy and Mineka 1998; Wenzel *et al.* 2002) or of experimentally presented material (Mogg *et al.* 1987; Sanz 1996). Although there is some evidence for enhanced recall of threat-related words in panic disorder patients (e.g. McNally *et al.* 1989), a recent review of the extensive literature on anxiety and memory by MacLeod and Mathews (2004), concludes that 'most experimental studies have failed to demonstrate that anxious individuals ... consistently display enhanced recall or recognition memory for emotionally threatening material' (Macleod and Mathews 2004, p. 180).

14.4 Addiction and craving

In discussing the effects of extreme emotion on cognition, we suggested that a similar pattern might operate for both positive emotions, such as the exhilaration felt by a novice parachutist having successfully completed a jump, and negative emotions such as the anxiety preceding the jump. Virtually all the more detailed analysis we have covered so far, however, has been limited to the study of fear and anxiety. While this certainly constitutes the most extensive area of analysis, an alternate source of evidence is provided by a studies of craving, the extreme form of desire that tends to be associated with addiction, another problem of enormous and growing practical concern.

For present purposes we will use the term addiction to refer to a physiological dependency, and craving to refer to the psychological state that is associated with it. As in the case of fear, the two are correlated but separable. Physiological appetitive signs such as salivation and increase in heart rate show a rather low correlation with subjectively rated desire for food, alcohol or drugs (Monti *et al.* 1993; Maude-Griffin and Tiffany, 1996). Furthermore, the physiological cues are not always very specific (Marshall and Zimbardo 1979; Schachter and Singer 1962), suggesting a possible common component. Garavan *et al.* (2000) used fMRI to study the brain activity of cocaine-addicted subjects either viewing a film involving cocaine, or a sex film. They found a similar pattern of activation for the two films.

14.4.1 Craving and cognition

Craving could be regarded as the mirror image of anxiety, the one biasing attention towards a source of threat and the other resulting in excessive attention to stimuli that evoke the object of desire. Craving can be induced by simply instructing the subject to form an image of the desired object or substance (Cepeda-Benito and Tiffany 1996; Zwaan and Truitt 1998), with the rated vividness of the image being correlated with the subsequent reported level of urge (Drobes and Tiffany 1997; Tiffany and Hakenewerth 1991).

As in the case of anxiety, craving can induce an attentional bias. Using the previously described dot probe technique, Mogg *et al.* (2003) showed that nicotine-deprived smokers were more likely to detect a stimulus located near a smoking-related picture that had just been removed, than to a neutral image, an effect that has shown to be related to the reported strength of craving (Walters *et al.* 2003). As is the case for anxiety, such biasing effects appear to be pre-attentive, since they can be obtained under conditions whereby the relevant pictures are followed by a pattern mask that prevents conscious awareness that any pictures have been presented.

A number of studies have shown that cognitive performance may be disrupted by craving. For example, impaired cognitive performance has been found in people on slimming diets. Although it was initially thought that these might reflect low blood sugar, (Benton and Sargent 1992), this was later discounted (Green and Rogers 1995; Green *et al.* 1997). Green and colleagues proposed instead that the preoccupying thoughts of food and body shape that accompany dieting (Rogers and Green 1993; Warren and Cooper 1988) may have disrupted performance by occupying the subject's limited WM capacity.

Green and Rogers (1998) used the Baddeley and Hitch model as a basis for comparison between dieting and control subjects, finding impairment on immediate serial recall of letters and on the Tower of London reasoning task, while finding normal strategic use of the phonological loop and visuo-sketchpad systems. A subsequent study by Vreugdenburg *et al.* (2003) measured both cognitive performance and level of preoccupying thoughts in carefully matched groups differing only in whether they were currently dieting. Dieters showed an impairment on a dual task paradigm in which arithmetic was combined with articulatory suppression or random generation, and on phonological loop tasks. Bivariate correlational analysis indicated that between 53 per cent and 96 per cent of the variance due to dieting status could be attributed to the extent of preoccupying thoughts reported by the dieters. The suggestion by Green and colleagues that the Baddeley and Hitch model might provide a useful basis for the study of craving has been further elaborated by Kavanagh *et al.* (In press) into a general theory of desire and craving which they term the *Elaborated Intrusion* theory (Kavanagh *et al.* 2005).

14.4.2 The elaborated intrusion theory of craving

The theory originated in a speculative interpretation of a puzzling clinical claim, namely that the disturbing flashbacks that accompany post-traumatic stress disorder may be reduced by a procedure whereby the patient watches the therapist's moving finger. We suggested that this might be related to the effect of eye movements on the visuospatial sketchpad (Baddeley 1986; Postle *et al.* 2006), which could, perhaps reduce the vividness of the patients disturb-ing images (Baddeley and Andrade 2000). Andrade *et al.* (1997), using evoked images in normal subjects, confirmed that this was indeed the case, a result subsequently replicated by van den Hout *et al.* (2001).

My own involvement with the project ceased at this point, but Andrade and Kavanagh continued to collaborate, extending it to Kavanagh's interest in addiction and craving, first though a series of empirical studies, leading to a theory of desire and its capacity to disrupt cognitive function. The crucial aspect of this disruption is assumed to be the presence of elaborated intrusions within working memory. The model resembles Eysenck's worry hypothesis, except that it is focused on appetitive urges rather than anxiety, and is spelled out in rather more detail.

The theory is based on the assumption that desires – whether for food, alcohol, cigarettes or a loved one – will result in appetitive targets automatically triggering intrusive thoughts. This occurs either though physiological cues as in the case of hunger pangs, by external cues such as the smell of food, or by cognitive association, such as the rattle of plates in a dining room. This is assumed to have two effects, one automatic and associated with pleasure or relief, and the second cognitively mediated, and involving elaboration on the cue, for example thinking about the meal ahead, a process which typically involves imagery, often but not exclusively visual. Such elaborations then interfere with the operation of working memory by displacing more constructive thoughts, as in the case of disruption by worry. The sensory images simulate the characteristics of the target, leading to further stimulation which is temporarily emotionally rewarding. However it amplifies the awareness of the somatic or emotional deficit leading to longer term frustration.

Kavanagh *et al.* (2005) support their theory on the basis of a range of studies. A self-report study by May *et al.* (2004) of feelings associated with craving finds the two most common reports to be physiologically cued 'I felt hungry/thirsty' or else appeared unannounced 'I suddenly thought about it', suggesting that the subject was either unaware of the stimulus or had forgotten it, a conclusion supported by a study on alcohol misusers who, when asked to report the source of thoughts of drinking over the last 24 hours claimed in 92 per cent of the cases that the idea ' just popped up'.

In contrast, the elaborative stage typically appears to depend on imagery (May *et al.* 2004; Salkovskis and Reynolds 1994). Kemps *et al.* (2004) asked dieting women or control subjects to generate food-related images and rate their vividness. The images increased the degree of reported craving, while a concurrent visual working memory task reduced both vividness and level of craving. Further evidence of the interaction between craving and imagery came from a study by Panabokke *et al.* (2004) who found that the requirement to form an irrelevant visual image such as a game of tennis reduced craving in smoking-deprived subjects. As in the case of anxiety and worry, such elaborative intrusions potentially disrupt working memory, as measured either by extended reaction times in a probe decision task (Franken *et al.* 2000), or in the processing of complex sentences (Zwaan and Truitt 1998), an effect that was particularly clear for low working memory span subjects.

Despite the initial positive effect of imaging the desired substance, the absence of fulfilment soon leads to negative emotional effects of anxiety, frustration and anger, typically involving the amygdala and anterior cingulate areas of the brain (Kilts *et al.* 2001), with a similar pattern occurring across a range of cravings including tobacco (Zinser *et al.* 1992) and cocaine (Powell *et al.* 1992). The negative mood in turn makes the deprivation cues more available, leading to an increase in sensitivity to cues related to the craved substance when the patients are required to perform a stressful test.

14.5 **Conclusion**

Our review of the effects of danger and elation, of anxiety and craving, suggest that they all appear to be able to disrupt working memory. While the mechanism is likely to differ in detail, in each case, the effect seems to be attentionally based. Cues that may on occasion be pre-attentively detected lead to elaborated thought patterns, and hence reduce the processing capacity of working memory that is available for the task in hand. Such an interpretation can readily be accommodated by the multicomponent model whereby potentially threatening stimuli are able to gain access and disrupt the central executive. In the case of craving, the intrusive thoughts are positive in nature, resulting in their further elaboration within the episodic buffer. This may appear to offer the hope of a single overall interpretation of the relationship between working memory and emotion. Before reaching this conclusion, we should consider a further emotional disturbance of great practical importance, namely depression. I will discuss depression in the next chapter, before returning to the question of how to accommodate emotion within the mulitcomponent model of working memory.

Chapter 15

Working memory and emotion II

Depression and the wellsprings of action

As we saw in the previous chapter, there appears to be a good deal of agreement as to how working memory is disrupted by anxiety. An evolutionary-based warning system is able to detect potential sources of threat, often pre-attentively, leading to the interruption of ongoing thought processes. While it is clearly valuable to have such a monitoring system, when the threshold is set too low, as in general anxiety disorder (GAD), or when inappropriate learning endows a previously neutral stimulus with anxiety-provoking characteristics, as in phobias, the system can malfunction, creating major problems for everyday cognition. As we saw, attention can also be disrupted, and cognitive processing pre-empted by appetitive stimuli, provided these are strong enough, as in the craving for food of a strict dieter or for drugs in an addict. While these findings do not differentially support a multicomponent model of working memory, they fit neatly into such a system, and in the case of Kavanagh *et al*'s (2005) analysis of desire and craving, were directly influenced by the model. My initial hope was that the cognitive disruption shown in depression might also fit the same pattern. It is certainly the case that anxiety and depression frequently co-occur (Mogg and Bradley 2005). That does not, of course, necessarily mean that they have a common mechanism or that they are causally linked.

15.1 **Comparing the effects of anxiety and depression**

The effects of anxiety as reflected in GAD can be summarized as follows: anxiety has a major impact on attention, at both a preconscious and conscious level (Öhman and Soares 1994). It tends to be externally focused on potential sources of threat. It energizes, presumably preparing the organism for fight or flight. As such its evolutionary value is clear. Finally, it has relatively little impact on long-term memory except under extreme conditions such as post-traumatic stress disorder, when it can lead to vivid and intrusive memories. To what extent does depression share these characteristics?

Depression appears to have less of an effect on attention then anxiety, with little evidence for a pre-attentive effect. Unlike anxiety, depression tends to be internally focused, with rumination on negative thoughts being a prominent feature, and is de-energizing, tending to lead to apathy rather than action (Nolen-Hoeksema *et al.* 1993; Pyszynski and Greenberg 1987). Depression does, however, influence long-term memory to a greater extent than does anxiety. Finally, its evolutionary value is far from obvious, although a wide range of evolutionary explanations have been proposed. These differences, which are summarized in Table 15.1, will be discussed in turn.

15.1.1 Attention and depression

As we saw in the previous chapter, much of the influence of anxiety on cognition comes from its impact on attentional and pre-attentional processes which lead to the interruption of executive control. While there is certainly some evidence of attentional disruption in depression, its effects appear to be less marked, leading Williams *et al.* (1997) to suggest that in contrast to the pattern of findings from studies of anxiety, depression does not have a major and robust effect on attention.

A slightly different view is taken by Gotlib and colleagues, who have obtained evidence for attentional bias in depressed patients from a number of studies. In one experiment, Gotlib *et al.* (2004a) presented sad, angry or neutral faces for 1000 msec to control subjects and to patients suffering from either depression or GAD. The depressed patients directed more attention to the sad faces, in contrast to an earlier study by Mogg *et al.* (2000) which used a shorter 500 msec exposure and found no effect. A subsequent study (Gotlib *et al.* 2004b) found no effect of depression on attention as measured by emotional Stroop performance, but did observe an attentional bias towards sad faces in depressed patients, together with a negative memory bias. However, the memory and attentional effects were uncorrelated, a result that they interpret as supporting

Table 15.1 Summary of the major differences between anxiety and depression.

Fear and anxiety	Depression
Major pre-attentional and attentional disruption of cognition	Weaker purely post-attentional effects
Effect on learning principally due to distraction	Disruption of learning attributable to lack of initiative
Little evidence of mood-congruent disruption of retrieval	Major mood-congruency
Evolutionary context clear	Evolutionary context controversial

the distinction between the effects of attention on anxiety and depression proposed by Williams *et al.* (1997), rather than the unitary view of Beck (1976) and Bower (1981). Gotlib *et al.* propose a distinction between the *pre-attentive* effect of anxiety on attention that is detectable even when threatening stimuli are presented subliminally, and *post-attentional* bias towards emotion-relevant stimuli that may also occur for depression. This requires longer stimulus exposure and may be found in both GAD and depressed patients.

A broadly similar conclusion is reached by Mogg and Bradley (2005) in a recent review of studies of depression and GAD, concentrating on two frequently used attentional tasks – emotional Stroop and visual probe – as described in the previous chapter. They identify ten studies of unmasked emotional Stroop performance in GAD, all of which showed the predicted bias. Of nine equivalent studies in depression, only four showed an effect. Three of these involved self-related negative material. They report only two masked emotional Stroop experiments comparing GAD and depressed patients. Both showed bias in the anxiety patients but not the depressed. A broadly similar pattern emerged for the visual probe task, with 10 out of the 12 anxiety studies showing an effect as compared to 2 out of 11 for depression.

Such a clear distribution is particularly striking, given that GAD and depression have a very high rate of clinical comorbidity. In one clinical study, two-thirds of patients with a diagnosis of major depression were also diagnosed with anxiety, and a third of patients with GAD were also diagnosed as suffering from depression (Brown *et al.* 2001). Indeed patients in Mogg *et al.*'s own studies comparing depression and GAD had equivalent levels of anxiety, differing only in whether they were also depressed (Bradley *et al.* 1995; Mogg *et al.* 1993; 2000). So why did the depressed patients not show a bias effect, if they were as anxious as the GAD patients who did? Mogg and Bradley (2005) consider and reject a number of possible explanations, opting instead for a depression-related motivational deficit, proposing that depressed and anxious patients are indeed both biased towards negative stimuli, but that the subsequent 'goal engagement responses' are relatively unresponsive in depression.

They note that the Williams *et al.* (1997) view could be sustained by assuming a difference between an external focus on possible sources of threat in GAD patients, versus an internal focus in depression. However, they reject this on the grounds that this should lead to both internally and externally focused biases. I am not entirely convinced by this argument. If the principal source of threat to depressed patients is internally represented, for example a challenge to their already low feeling of self-worth, then this may well generate anxiety that is strongly associated with the patient's internal world rather than the external cues employed by the experimenter. Consistent with this interpretation is the fact that self-descriptive negative stimuli, presumably reflecting an internal focus, featured in three of the six studies showing bias effects in depression, compared to only one of the 20 demonstrations of bias in GAD.

In conclusion, although the details remain controversial, there appears to be agreement between Williams *et al.* (1996), Gotlib *et al.* (2004a, b) and Mogg and Bradley (2005) on the need to maintain a distinction between the robust and pre-attentional effects of GAD on attention, and the much weaker post-attentional bias effects sometimes seen in depressed patients.

15.1.2 Disruption of memory by depression

Patients who are depressed frequently complain of problems in day to day remembering (Blaney 1986; Watts 1993). There is also objective evidence for poorer learning in such patients. In a classic study, Cronholm and Ottosson (1961) studied the capacity of depressed patients and control subjects to learn and recall prose passages and pairs of words and shapes; they found a clear deficit in the patients. Rude *et al.* (1999) used an experimental analogue of prospective memory in which they required the patient to remember to perform some act in the future; they also found performance to be impaired by depression. Depressed patients frequently complain of memory problems, with the incidence of complaint being correlated with level of depression (Scogin, *et al.* 1985). However, a study by Kahn *et al.* (1975) found that although the frequency of memory *complaints* in patients correlated with level of depression, complaint level did not correlate with *objective* measures of memory performance.

Why should depression interfere with learning and memory? Ellis and Ashbrook (1988) offer an interpretation which they term the Resource Allocation Model (RAM), that is somewhat similar to the worry hypothesis proposed to account for the disruption of performance by anxiety. They propose that intrusive depressive thoughts absorb some of the patient's limited processing capacity, hence disrupting learning. An alternative view is proposed by Hertel and Hardin (1990), who suggest that depressed patients simply lack initiative, and hence tend not to use active strategies to enhance their performance. Evidence consistent with this interpretation comes from a number of studies that have shown an interaction between the effects of depression and the nature of the material to be learned. For example Weingartner *et al.* (1981) found a depressive deficit for unstructured word lists, which disappeared when structure was provided; presumably, lack of structure demands initiative in imposing the active organization that is necessary for learning (Tulving 1962; Mandler 1967). Similarly, Potts *et al.* (1989) found that providing material with the potential for active elaborations benefited control subjects more than depressed patients, and Hertel and Rude (1991) found that providing a clear structure within the material removed the disadvantage previously shown by depressed subjects.

Hertel's initiative hypothesis seems to demand some form of dynamic concept such as mental energy, a concept that regrettably appears to have vanished from cognitive psychology, despite the efforts of Broadbent (1971) and Kahneman (1973) to emphasize its importance. This account of the general impairment in learning and memory as resulting from a depletion of energy contrasts with Ellis's resource allocation model, which resembles the worry hypothesis in postulating what is effectively a cognitive distraction effect. These competing interpretations are presumably open to testing by some of the previously described techniques used to investigate the worry hypothesis (Calvo and Eysenck 1996; Derakshan and Eysenck 1998), where Ellis's model would presumably make different predications from Hertel's lack of initiative hypothesis. To the best of my knowledge, these lines of investigation have not yet been explored.

15.1.3 Memory for emotional material

Perhaps the most intensively studied feature of memory and depression is the mood congruency effect, whereby a depressive mood facilitates the retrieval of negative memories. The mood congruency effect is clinically important because it also applies to the accessibility of autobiographical memories. By biasing the retrieval to those memories that are negatively toned, it exacerbates depression, setting up a downward spiral. Teasdale *et al.* (1980) manipulated the mood of their student subjects using the Velten (1968) technique which encourages the subject to feel a mood consistent with each of a series of statements which they are required to read in an empathetic manner. They range from the mild 'Things are not quite what I would like them to be' to the very depressing 'Looking back on my life I wonder if I have accomplished anything really worthwhile.' Statements aimed at inducing positive mood include 'All in all I am pretty pleased with the way things are going' up to 'Life is so full and interesting it's great to be alive!' The technique appears to work, as measured by subjective self-report and also as reflected in objective measures such as writing speed and speech rate (Clark 1983a).

When asked to recall pleasant or unpleasant experiences, and produce the first memory that comes to mind, happy mood facilitates happy recollections and vice versa, a result that has been replicated by a number of investigators (Bower 1981; Madigan and Bollenbach 1982; Snyder and White 1982). Similar effects are also found using patients who have diurnal fluctuation in mood, with unhappy memories being more likely to be recalled under high levels of depression (Clark and Teasdale 1982), a result that was replicated using more typical depressed patients (Clark and Teasdale 1985). This pattern contrasts with that of normal subjects who tend to have a positive recollective bias under baseline conditions (Blaney 1986).

It is important to note that robust mood *congruency* effects depend on the material recalled being emotionally toned, in contrast to mood *dependency* effects, in which the recall of *neutral* words is enhanced when the emotional state during learning is reinstated at recall, a much less robust phenomenon (Bower *et al.* 1981; Schare *et al.* 1984). Mood dependency does sometimes occur, however, when the neutral words are self-referent (Gotlib and Hammen 1992; Williams and Scott 1988). It is interesting to note that the few demonstrations of attentional bias in depression were chiefly achieved using self-referential materials.

15.1.4 Depression and self-evaluation

A further feature of depression is its negative impact on evaluation of oneself and of the world, and the resultant impact on choice and action. A number of studies have examined this experimentally by inducing unhappy, neutral or happy moods in normal subjects. Low mood results in reduced satisfaction with life in general (Schwarz and Clore 1983; Schwarz *et al.* 1987), and with one's own level of social skill (Forgas *et al.* 1984). Depressed mood results in future enterprises being regarded as more risky (Johnson and Tversky 1983), and on the attribution of past failures to one's own inadequacy (Forgas *et al.* 1990). Schwarz and Clore (1983) investigated the effect of the weather on estimates of life satisfaction. Subjects were telephoned during sunny or rainy weather and asked about their general satisfaction with life. Sunny days led to consistently higher ratings, an effect that disappeared if they were first asked about the weather. It thus appears that such implicit sources of mood can be avoided if made explicit. In another experiment Schwarz and Clore (1983) induced mood by requiring the recall of a positive or negative life event. Again this influenced subsequent ratings by their subjects of life satisfaction. This effect was, however, absent in a group explicitly asked how the recall had made them feel, before making their life satisfaction ratings. It appears that mood affects can be avoided, provided we are aware of them.

The negative effects of mood are not specific to the context in which the gloom is induced. Johnson and Tversky (1983) found that the estimated risk of subsequently dying of cancer was increased by a story of death by fire just as much as a death by cancer story. Similarly Kavanagh and Bower (1985) found that imagining a romantic failure reduced subjects' estimate of successfully dealing with a snake, just as much as that of enjoying their next ten dates.

Mood also influences interpretation of events that have happened. Forgas *et al.* (1990) used video films to induce a happy, sad or neutral mood and then questioned the subject about previous end-of-term examinations, asking them to attribute their result to either ability, effort, luck or situational factors, and then to make equivalent judgements about a typical student. Under neutral mood the characteristic pattern emerged of taking more credit for their successes than blame for their failures, a tendency that subjects did not apply to the imaginary typical student. In the happy mood they assumed that both they and the typical student were more responsible for successes than failures. When a bad mood was induced, however, subjects tended to blame themselves for failures, but not to apply this harsh judgement to failures of the typical student, consistent with the previously discussed tendency for depression to direct attention inwards to one's self and one's limitations.

15.1.5 Negative thoughts and rumination

As one might expect from the evidence of mood dependency, patients who ruminate tend to have more prolonged depression (Nolen-Hoeksema 1991). In a study of students responding to a natural disaster, namely an earthquake, Nolan-Hoeksema and Morrow (1991) found that those students with a more ruminative style were significantly more likely to be depressed ten days and seven weeks after the event, regardless of their initial level of depression. Fennell *et al.* (1987) studied the tendency of depressed and control subjects to generate spontaneous depressive thoughts. Subjects were required either to describe a series of pictures shown on slides, or simply to look at a patch of light. From time to time they were asked about their thoughts and their level of depression, which was also measured by speed of movement. When staring at the patch of light, depressive thoughts occurred on 56 per cent of the probe tests and were typically independent of the stimulus or the surroundings. When given a potentially distracting task, describing the pictures, such thoughts reduced to 10 per cent. This activity also reduced levels of depression as measured by both self-rating and motor speed, suggesting that the state of depression may need to be maintained, and hence can be broken by activities. This is consistent with our investigations of stimulus-independent thoughts in non-depressed subjects, described in the previous chapter, which implicated the central executive component of working memory as crucial to both the prevention and disruption of such ruminations (Teasdale *et al.* 1993; 1995).

To summarize, depression has less effect than anxiety on attention but is often associated with complaints of poor memory. This appears to reflect lack of initiative during learning rather than a direct memory deficit. Retrieval from long-term memory is influenced by mood congruency, which tends to prolong rumination, further depressing mood, and having a negative influence on evaluation of the present situation and future plans.

15.2 Psychological theories of depression

Psychological interpretations of depression tend to fall into four broad categories, each emphasizing a different facet of the problem, namely psycho-analytic, behavioural, control-based and cognitive. Psychoanalytic approaches stem from Freud's (1917/1986) suggestion that depression results when anger, prompted by loss or bereavement, is turned inward by the patient. Behavioural theories tend to attribute depression to low rates of social reinforcement leading to withdrawal and inactivity, with the depressive reaction potentially then being rewarded by sympathy from friends and family (Coyne 1976; Lewinsohn 1975). The control theory approach is also concerned with becoming locked into an appropriate feedback loop, an influential example being the concept of *learned helplessness*. When an animal or person is confronted with negative consequences that occur unpredictably, regardless of what action is taken, they will adopt a passive and helpless response to the apparently insoluble problem, a response that is manifest as depression (Seligman 1975). While the original version has been questioned as an adequate model for human depression, other forms of control theory have been developed (Abrahamson *et al.* 1978; Pyszcynski and Greenberg 1987). The most influential theoretical approach in recent years' however, has been Beck's (1976) cognitive theory of depression.

Beck's theory was principally based on clinical observation, and proposed that depression comprises three components. The first of these is the presence of automatic thoughts, thoughts that seem to occur to the patient unprompted by events and that are often accepted without question. Note the similarity to the occurrence of such unprompted thoughts in craving, as discussed in the last chapter. The negative nature of the unprompted thoughts tends to disrupt mood, leading to a downward spiral of elaborated thoughts. This downward spiral comprises the second stage of the model, and involves negative views of the self (e.g. 'I am a failure'), the world around ('This place is going to the dogs') and the future ('Things are just getting worse'). This is accompanied by systemic logical errors, (e.g. interpreting a friend's failure to telephone as evidence of a quarrel), over-generalization ('I've lost this friend, I always lose my friends'), black/white thinking ('If I lose this friend I might as well be dead') and many others. A third and crucial component is the presence of depressogenic schemata, persisting assumptions about the world and the way in which it is structured and related to the self. These are destructively negative, and are assumed by Beck typically to be acquired during childhood. The crux of his theory is the causal status that he assigns to such long-standing negative schemata.

Beck's views have been extremely influential through his subsequent development of cognitive therapy for depression, whereby patients are encouraged to identify their negative assumptions, test them, and in due course to develop ways of avoiding the downward spiral of depression, and to build a less negative representation of themselves (Beck 1976). However, while there is no doubt that Beck's work has led to a major improvement in the treatment of depression, the underlying theory encounters a number of difficulties, including:

1 There is evidence to suggest that the dysfunctional negative beliefs may be a consequence rather than a cause of depression, as they tend to change when patients recover (Simons *et al.* 1984) even when treatment focuses on behaviour rather than cognition (Imber *et al.* 1990; Rehm *et al.* 1987).

2 Attitudes, which presumably continue to be based on the dysfunctional underlying schemata, appear to return to normal when depressed patients recover (Teasdale 1988).

3 The theory says little about the importance of social and environmental factors in causing depression (Brown and Harris 1978; Coyne and Gotlib 1983).

4 The theory also ignores the importance of genetic and biological factors, as reflected for example in diurnal or seasonal fluctuations in level of depression, or in the effects of pharmacological treatments.

5 The theory neglects the distinction between 'cold' and 'hot' cognition. Patients may *know* that their views are irrational, and that they are not really hopelessly inadequate, but nevertheless do not *feel* as though this is the case.

A distinction between two levels of cognitive processing lies at the heart of Barnard's (1999) Interactive Cognitive Subsystems (ICS) model of cognitive processing. The model was originally developed to give an account of language processing (Barnard 1985), was then applied to human-computer interaction, and subsequently in collaboration with Teasdale, developed to provide an account of depression (Teasdale and Barnard, 1993). The ICS model is somewhat complex, and could be seen as containing within itself a form of multicomponent working memory, specified in some detail, which can indeed be mapped onto my own model. The central or executive component is split into two, the propositional and implicational systems. The *propositional* system, is open to conscious awareness and responsible for explicit, relatively emotion-free 'cold' cognition. It is linked to the second component, the *implicational* system, which is responsible for 'hot' cognition, and is linked among other things to cues from the body associated with emotion. I would regard this distinction as being necessary, and its absence from the current multicomponent model of working memory as reflecting a clear limitation to the scope of the model.

I do however have some reservations about the ICS model. The first is that it assumes an equivalent architecture for all its peripheral sensory-based subsystems. I can appreciate that this might offer an elegant computational solution, but it is not one that appears to map in any detail on to the empirical evidence distinguishing for example the phonological loop and the sketchpad, and does not seem to have led to any further understanding of the operation of these subsystems. A second problem stems from the model's complexity. Given so many components, each operating at several levels, and all interacting with each other, it is difficult to have a clear understanding of exactly how the model works. Indeed it is probably only valid to make predictions by running the model, which in turn will require many assumptions about the parameters, and considerably more computational expertise than I, or I suspect, many potential users of the model possess.

I propose instead to suggest a model that is perhaps similar in spirit to ICS, but is very much simpler. The model is consistent with the spirit of Beck's observations, but does not accept his assumption of the primacy of negative schemata. It is a model that is compatible with the influence of neurobiological and pharmacological factors, and is associated with a plausible account of the evolutionary significance of depression. Finally, although I think it does represent a new formulation, I should emphasize that most of its components already form part of other approaches to cognition and emotion.

15.3 The wellsprings of action

One crucial difference between fear and depression is that fear energizes whereas depression leads to apathy. If we are to understand this difference, we need a theory of motivation, and its capacity to drive and control behaviour. As noted earlier, this has been a neglected area in cognitive psychology since the concept of arousal became unfashionable in the 1970s, at least in part because of the difficulty in progressing far beyond what could be seen as a simple measure of the overall alertness of the system. Fear, lust and the excitement of watching a good sporting contest are all likely to be associated with high levels of arousal, but also to differ in important ways. Furthermore, given a moderate level of arousal, the theory does not tell us why we choose to do one thing rather than another – in short it is not a theory of motivation. If cognitive psychology is to offer a broad account of action, then it needs to combine theories of information processing and control with a theory of motivation and volition.

15.3.1 The valenced world hypothesis

The problem of volition was very clearly set out over 250 years ago by the great empiricist philosopher, David Hume. His views provide a good starting point, presenting a lucid account of what still seems to be the most probable solution, what I shall term the *valenced world* hypothesis. This assumes that the world we perceive and recall is not emotionally neutral, but that its features are positively or negatively toned. Hume asserts that 'Reason is and ought to be the slave of the passions, and can never pretend to any other office than to serve and obey them' (Hume 1739/1978, p. 415). He proposes that the mechanism of control stems from the capacity of the emotions to reflect the 'prospect of pain or pleasure from any object ...'(ibid., p. 414). The resulting impulse arises 'not from reason but it is only directed by it'.

Hume goes on to explain that by emotion he does not only refer to the extreme emotions such as anger, fear and lust, suggesting that 'again there are certain calm desires and tendencies which tho they be real passions, produce little emotion in the mind, and are more known by their effects than by their immediate feeling or sensation' (ibid., p. 407). He cites as examples benevolence and resentment, a love of life and kindness to children, which he describes as emotions that may readily be mistaken for reasoning. He contrasts these 'quiet passions' with more violent passions such as the desire to punish someone who has harmed you, going on to attribute strength of mind to 'the prevalence of the calm passions above the violent' (ibid., p. 418). Finally, he notes that the complexity of this array of passions may make it difficult to choose the correct way ahead, concluding 'from these variations of temper, proceeds the great difficulty of deciding concerning the actions and resolutions of men where there is a contrariety of emotions and passions' (ibid., p. 418).

In short, Hume proposes that our actions are determined by our desires both positive and negative, as these are reflected in the world around us. He notes that these may not be felt as strong emotions, and that strength of mind or self-control reflects the capacity to allow the positive but weak emotions to avoid being swamped by the more unruly passions. As an eighteenth-century philosopher, Hume was forced to rely on his own reason and introspection. The amount of empirical evidence that has accumulated on this topic in the last two centuries is not impressive, but it would, I think, tend to support Hume's views.

Despite its importance, the issue of what drives behaviour has, for many years, been substantially neglected by cognitive psychology and cognitive neuropsychology, a neglect that is fortunately now beginning to be remedied. This revival of interest has been strongly influenced by the work of Anthony Damasio (1994), who addresses the issue in his book *Descartes' Error*. The book begins by considering the classic case of Phineas Gage, a nineteenth-century railroad foreman who had the misfortune to be involved in an accident whereby an explosion caused a sharp spike to be driven through his eye socket and the frontal lobe of his brain. He recovered from this terrible event remarkably well, with little apparent intellectual damage, but with a profound change in character. An account by the physician who treated him (Harlow, 1868) describes his transformation from someone with 'a well-balanced mind ... a shrewd smart businessman, very energetic and persistent' to someone who was now 'fitful, irreverent ... impatient of restraint or advice when it conflicts with his desires, at times pertinaciously obstinate, yet capricious and vacillating' in short 'Gage was no longer Gage' (Harlow 1868 quoted in Damasio 1994, p. 8).

Although Gage is the best-known example of such a case, he is by no means unique. Damasio describes one of his own patients, Elliot, a very successful business man who, following the removal of a frontal lobe brain tumour, presented a pattern of behaviour that was very like that shown by Gage. He was intellectually still highly able, passing a whole range of neuropsychological tests with apparent ease. He retained all his social and language skills and had returned to his job, but with disastrous results. He appeared to have lost all his earlier good sense and judgement, going on to fail in a succession of subsequent jobs and personal relationships. Why? To understand this question, Damasio proposed his *somatic marker hypothesis* which has much in common with Hume's earlier view, although backed up by evidence from Damasio's extensive neuropsychological experience, and by a proposed neuroanatomical mechanism. For present purposes, however, we will concentrate on the implications of the hypothesis at the psychological level.

Damasio begins, like Hume, by emphasizing the importance of the emotions in driving and guiding behaviour. He also stresses the importance of what Hume terms 'the calm passions'. Damasio makes a distinction between *emotions*, defined in terms of their somatic or bodily character, and *feelings*, which are their consciously detectable counterparts. The somatic marker hypothesis proposes that it is these feelings that guide action, serving as negative 'alarm bells' or positive 'beacons of incentive'. He proposes that 'somatic markers are a special instance of feelings generated from secondary emotions ... connected by learning to predicted future outcomes of certain scenarios' (Damasio 1994, p. 174).

Like Hume, Damasio stresses the importance of learning, furthermore suggesting that 'a somatic state, negative or positive, caused by a given representation, operates not only as a marker of a value of what is represented, but also as a booster for continued working memory and attention' (ibid., pp. 197–198). Damasio thus emphasizes the importance of maintaining behaviour. He goes on to amplify this point, asserting that 'there are thus three supporting players in the process of reasoning over a vast landscape of scenarios generated from factual knowledge; *automated somatic states*, with their biasing mechanisms; *working memory*; *and attention*' (ibid., p. 198, author's emphasis).

Damasio thus places a good deal of weight on the importance of both the storage capacity of working memory and on its attentional control.

Damasio thus interprets volition in terms of navigating through a world comprising an array of objects and options, all of which are suffused with positive or negative feeling or valence. What is the evidence for such a view? That cited by Damasio (1994) is largely neuropsychological. He suggests that the lack of an adequate somatic marker system will result in an inability to use emotion to make judgements, emphasizing the importance of such somatically–based intuitive hunches in a wide range of tasks, from minor issues such as choosing the date for a meeting, to crucial decisions such as who to marry. He describes the action of a patient with frontal lobe damage resulting in loss of this capacity, who was given two possible dates for his next appointment. When the patient opened his diary he began to list the possible pros and cons for each date, combining and weighing each one in turn for a full half hour, at which point Damasio proposed one of the dates, evoking the response 'that's fine!'

Rationally weighing and combining all the possibilities is, of course, an important activity, and the inability to make even a simple choice between dates suggests a major potential handicap. What processes might underpin such a capacity? There are two obvious necessities. One involves the capacity to maintain and manipulate information in working memory. The other is a hedonic judgement process that allows the positive and negative features of the various options to be evaluated. I suggest that depression reflects the malfunctioning of this hedonic detection and evaluation system.

15.4 **Working memory and depression**

The hedonic detector hypothesis assumes a system that is capable of picking up positive or negative associations from an object or representation within the episodic buffer component of working memory. It is assumed to be capable of averaging across a complex array of stimuli to produce a rapid summation, in a manner analogous to a Geiger counter being pointed at an object or array. Unlike the Geiger counter, however, I assume that it is capable of detecting both positive and negative valences. It can therefore evaluate complex situations that comprise a mix of good and bad features. I assume the system to be attentionally controlled, so that either a single selected object or the whole array may be evaluated. In deciding whether to buy a house, for example, we may have an initial overall positive impression, but accompanied by some negative feelings. By considering aspects of the house separately we may then be able to decide how important these are; for example is it the decorations that can easily be changed that are the focus of the negative component, or an unpleasant outlook, which can not.

The object evaluated may be in the external environmental or internally generated, in both cases being held in working memory. This allows comparing the house being viewed with one seen earlier. When decisions are complex, it is likely to be necessary to focus on specific components, or to call into working memory other evidence from long-term memory.

Such executive processing is likely to be demanding, requiring exactly the kind of multitasking that is impaired in patients such as those discussed by Damasio (Shallice and Burgess 1991; Burgess *et al.* 2000). While many everyday choices are likely to be rapid, and possibly automatic, complex decisions such as which of two houses one should buy are clearly likely to be heavily dependent on both working and long-term memory. Such decisions are likely to be difficult because they place heavy reliance on working memory to process complex arrays of stimuli which must be evaluated, and the result maintained while other complex arrays are set up and the results compared.

The proposed hedonic evaluation system has five crucial features, namely:

1 The neutral point of the valence scale.

2 Its sensitivity, that is its capacity to detect change from that level.

3 Its capacity to store such judgements.

4 Its capacity to discriminate between such stored options.

5 Its stability.

Individuals may differ on any or all of these. If the neutral point at which readings become positive is set genetically at a chronically high level what used to be termed a melancholic temperament will result, as in the case of an old friend who, on being given the apparently positive news that he had achieved tenure, responded 'Oh dear, I'll never leave now!' The opposite setting would lead to someone who is unfailingly cheerful and optimistic. Insensitivity is likely to lead to a failure to discriminate between hedonic levels, and consequently to problems of social adjustment such as those exhibited by Damasio's patients, a deficit that could result from a hedonic evaluation problem, but which might also in principle stem from an executive, storage or processing deficit. Finally, the stability of the system may vary across individuals, resulting in fluctuation of mood over short or long intervals.

Application of this complex hedonic guidance system is likely to be particularly difficult when it is used to evaluate plans for future action. Such plans will inevitably be lacking in accurate, hedonically reliable detail, making comparative evaluation difficult. It is thus hardly surprising that patients with frontal lobe problems find this problematic, since they tend to have major problems in both strategy generation and multitasking (Shallice 1988; Shallice and Burgess 1991). This effect is illustrated in a study by Alderman (1996) concerned with a programme for rehabilitating brain-injured patients with behavioural problems by means of a token economy system. This involved rewarding socially appropriate behaviour with tokens that could later be cashed as privileges. Most patients benefited from this regime, but a subsample did not. The most prominent cognitive deficit in such patents was an incapacity for dual task performance of the type found by Baddeley *et al.* (1997) to be impaired a subgroup of patients with frontal lobe damage who showed dysexecutive behaviour in their everyday life. It is tempting to suggest that maintaining appropriate social behaviour is itself a dual task activity, in which it is important to maintain your own goals while bearing in mind the aims and needs of others. Our results, however, may simply mean that dual tasking and appropriate social behaviour depend on parts of the brain that are anatomically close to each other, and hence likely to be lesion-damaged at the same time, while being functionally separate.

Even healthy normal people however, are poor at estimating the hedonic impact of possible future developments. This was studied by Gilbert *et al.* (1998), using both laboratory experiments and a field study in which academics approaching a decision on their job tenure were asked to estimate how they would feel one year after the decision, if it were positive or negative. Happily, those who failed to obtain tenure were considerably more cheerful a year later than they had anticipated, whereas those given tenure were somewhat less elated than they expected. Gilbert *et al.* interpret the results in terms of a failure to include in the future decision a wide array of variables that influence and mediate one's satisfaction with life, over and above the decision that forms the focus of the assessment.

It is perhaps also worth noting that we appear to be equipped with a formidable array of techniques for defending our self-esteem against such blows of fortune. These include taking credit for success when it occurs, but denying responsibility for failure (Zuckerman 1979) leading to the successive selective forgetting of failure and remembering of success and praise (Crary 1966; Mischel *et al.* 1976). We readily accept praise, but tend to be sceptical of criticism (Kunda 1990; Wyer and Frey 1983), often attributing such criticism to prejudice on the part of the critic (Crocker and Major 1989).

Given this formidable array of strategies for bolstering our self-esteem, it is perhaps unsurprising that our self-perception tends not to correlate very highly with the view of us reported by our friends and colleagues. Could this be because we are aware of inner virtues that we would not expect them to notice? Probably not, since we wrongly predict that their views are likely to resemble our own (Shrauger and Schoeneman 1979).

Taylor and Brown (1988) argue that the tendency to have an unduly rosy view of ourselves is a healthy one.

> The individual who responds to negative, ambiguous or unsupported feedback with a positive sense of self, a belief in personal efficacy, and an optimistic sense of the future will, we maintain, be happier, more caring and more productive than the individual who receives the same information accurately and integrates it into his or her view of the self, the world and the future.
>
> (Taylor and Brown 1999, p. 60)

While a Micawber-like conviction that all will be well is unlikely to be a recipe for success in coping in a complex and not entirely benevolent world, a slight tendency to look on the bright side probably is more energizing than the opposite bias, which in depression leads to rumination and inaction (Pyszynski and Greenberg 1987). In short, a degree of positive bias in the hedonic detection system is probably advantageous.

15.4.1 The hedonic detector and depression

I suggest that depression reflects an inappropriate setting of the neutral point of the hedonic detection system. This is likely to have two effects. The first involves rumination and the search for the cause of negative affect. This will result in a second consequence, the pernicious effect of mood congruency, whereby low mood results in a bias towards negative memories, hence deepening the depression.

The hedonic threshold is assumed to be set biologically, but to be influenced by outside events. Endogenously depressive patients are assumed to have a chronically high threshold for detecting positively valenced cues, hence the world in general is evaluated in a more negative way. This is assumed to be mediated neuropharmacologically, and thus can be influenced by drug therapy. Degree of stability may also vary across individuals leaving the hedonic neutral point liable to fluctuation, either diurnally (Clark and Teasdale 1982), or a seasonal basis, as in Seasonal Affective Disorder, while its range may also fluctuate over the moderate to high threshold range as in unipolar depression, or from very high to very low as in manic depression (Bulbena and Berrios 1993; Murphy *et al.* 1999).

The function of the hedonic system is to evaluate the environment, including past experiences and future plans. When these are negative, the signal will of course tend to negative, leading to rumination and a search for a solution to the problem. If there is no solution, with all options being negative, then a state of *learned helplessness* may occur, resulting in depressive passivity (Seligman 1975). If there is no obvious outside cause, then the system will look for an internal explanation, potentially leading to self-blame, and the retrieval of negative rather than positive self-schemata leading, as Beck (1976) observed, to further depression.

Can the hedonic detector hypothesis account for the degree of apathy that appears to accompany depression, other than through learned helplessness hypothesis? I suggest that it can. The hedonic valence hypothesis proposes that positive action depends on what Damasio terms 'beacons of incentive'. If these are perceived to burn less brightly, positive incentives will progressively decline and with them the urge to act constructively.

Pharmacological treatment of depression presumably operates by endogenously resetting the neutral point, whereas cognitive therapy operates by attempting to break into the downward spiral of rumination, helping the patient to retrieve positive rather than negative memories, and to test and reject inappropriately negative interpretations of the world (Williams 1984). This is likely to take longer than drug treatment, but has the advantage of equipping the patient with strategies for coping in future, hence reducing relapse rate (Teasdale *et al.* 2000). Combining pharmacological and psychological therapy appears to offer the most effective treatment for severe depression.

15.5 **Emotion and the multicomponent model**

Given that emotion does appear to influence the operation of multicomponent working memory, how can it be fitted into the model? Given that the effects of anxiety can operate pre-attentionally, then we have to assume a threat detection system that is able to bypass working memory. However, since working memory is likely to be an important tool in evaluating the options and responding appropriately, there is clearly a need to have a second route which operates through the working memory, a two-component solution that is of course entirely consistent with the elegant neurobiological work of LeDoux (1996) and others.

We have suggested that depression depends crucially on a hedonic detection and evaluation system, and that this, together with the capacity to maintain and manipulate hedonically valenced information plays a central role in conscious, and possibly also implicit decision-making. Within the current model, the central executive is assumed to be an attentional system, with no intrinsic storage capacity, while neither the loop nor the sketchpad would appear to be well equipped for handling and manipulating valenced information. Given that the valence of the stimulus or situation is likely to be dependent at least in large part on prior experience, combined with the capacity for maintenance during decision-making, the obvious component to locate this would be in the episodic buffer. The modified working memory model is shown in Fig. 15.1 with information regarding threat shown by red arrows, positive information by yellow, and negatively valenced information by blue.

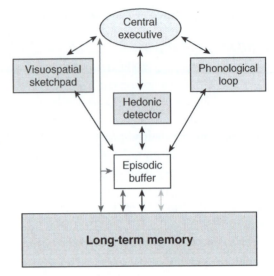

Fig. 15.1 Adaptation of the Baddeley (2000) working memory model to include the impact of emotional factors on working memory. The red arrows indicate threat detection, the blue negative valance and the yellow positive.

15.5.1 **Developing the model**

If the simple hedonic detector hypothesis is to prove theoretically fruitful, it is important to devise a method of studying its operation, preferably one that is simple and robust. What options are available?

One method that has dominated the field in recent years is the Iowa Gambling Task (IGT), devised by Bechara *et al.* (1994; 1997) to test Damasio's somatic marker hypothesis. This will be discussed in more detail later in the chapter, but we should note that for present purposes the task has two disadvantages. First, it is relatively complex, and secondly it is concerned with acquiring and using new valences, whereas our initial need is for a method of measuring the system that evaluates existing valences.

We have come up with a tentative first step in the process of measuring the operation of the detector, which we are beginning to test. The task involves presenting the subject with a series of stimuli, and simply requiring a valency judgement. Our hypothesis is that variables that change the neutral point of the hedonic detector will be reflected in the proportion of positive and negative judgements. If the method is successful, then we hope to treat the hedonic detector in the same way as we would a sensory system.

We might, for example, ask whether the operation of the detector may be influenced by mood when judging either internal or external stimuli, or both. If so, does this mood effect apply across the whole range of valences, for example does low mood make the whole scale shift such that negative stimuli become very negative and positive less positive, and is this process progressive, as appears to be the case for the influence of negative mood on autobiographical memory? Does our model require a separate form of STM system for storing emotion, or is emotional valency conveyed indirectly through links to LTM, as I suspect? A related question is whether the persistence of mood over time requires active storage, and if so does this depend on working memory? Again I suspect that both activation in LTM and the continued maintenance of emotion at an implicit neurobiological level would seem to be strong candidates for this role. Even without these aspects of emotion, however, there are plenty of potentially fruitful lines of research to be pursued if we are to develop an adequate theory of the way in which working memory is influenced by emotion.

15.5.2 **An evolutionary perspective**

One attractive feature of the generally agreed interpretation of the influence on cognition of anxiety and fear is its plausibility within an evolutionary context. It makes sense to assume that a system that detects potential threat should have both pre-attentive and attentive immediate access to working memory. While this will have obvious survival value, when operating inappropriately, it is likely to interfere with normal functioning. But what is the advantage conveyed by depression to the survival of the species?

A large range of evolutionary hypothesis have been proposed. These include seeing depression as a plea for help (Lewis 1934), as a means whereby the organism can conserve effort and resources (Thiery *et al.* 1984), as a response to loss or bereavement (Freud 1986; Oatley and Johnson-Laird 1987), or as yielding in social conflict (Price *et al.* 1994). A review of this literature is provided by Messe (2000), who adds a further interpretation of depression, proposing that it is a mechanism that facilitates disengagement from unreachable goals.

However, while all of these describe situations that may well be associated with depression, there is little clear evidence for the primacy of any one interpretation. Furthermore, they typically focus on environmental influences and tend not to be closely linked to biological mechanisms, or to give an account of endogenous depression and its tendency, in some cases, to fluctuate over time, on a daily or seasonal basis.

I suggest that the hedonic detector hypothesis is at least as plausible as its competitors within an evolutionary context. A mechanism that is central to the motivational control of choice and action is of obvious evolutionary value, making it worth the very substantial cost of its potential for malfunction in depression.

15.6 **Emotion: a broader view**

This chapter has been one of the most difficult to write. It started as an attempt to extend what seemed like a relatively clear link between working memory and emotion, as reflected in the impact of anxiety on cognition. When applied to depression, this simple model did not seem to work, and in an attempt to make it work I came up with the hedonic detector hypothesis. I went on to discuss this with colleagues much more knowledgeable that I myself, and found them encouraging, suggesting that the idea was broadly plausible, relatively novel and worth developing. They were also helpful in suggesting other things that I should read. It rapidly became clear that the range of relevant literature was large, diverse and developing rapidly. The prospect of basing this chapter on a thorough and scholarly review began to recede rapidly, and with the rest of the book complete, I decided to stay relatively closely to my initial version, but to add a brief postscript referring to two areas that should be included in a more substantial treatment.

15.6.1 Psychological theories of emotion

First, in lamenting the lack of interaction between studies of emotion and studies of cognition, I have been somewhat ethnocentric, concentrating on the information-processing approach to cognitive psychology within which the multicomponent model was developed. There has continued to be a very healthy concern for emotion within other traditions, both European (e.g. Scherer 1984; Frijda 2004), and in North America (e.g. Leventhal 1980; Lazarus 1982; Zajonc 1984). Unlike my own efforts, many of these approaches have attempted to capture the fact that emotions are not simply positive or negative, but rather, comprise an array of complex and subtle differences, emotions which as Hume proposed may be just as important in guiding behaviour as the more dramatic emotions such as fear and anger. I would like to briefly describe just one framework that captures this diversity while being consistent with my own rather simplistic proposals.

Leventhal and Scherer (1987) propose a model in which emotions range from relatively simple reflex-like behaviour through to elaborate cognitive-emotional patterns that may involve relatively complex interactions within and between implicit and explicit levels of processing. They attempt to combine theories of emotion and cognition, observing that 'regardless of the degree of independence of emotion and cognitive mechanisms, theories of emotion will remain primitive unless they address the nature of the process and the type of cognitive contents that give rise to particular emotions' (Leventhal and Scherer 1987, p. 13). Their model assumes five stages of evaluation comprising (1) A novelty check, (2) A check of intrinsic pleasantness, (3) A goal/need significance check, (4) A coping potential check and finally (5) A norm/self compatibility check. The simple hedonic evaluation process suggested earlier would appear to fit reasonably well with the second of these, which determines whether the stimulus event is pleasant and should be approached, or unpleasant leading to avoidance, a process based on both innate feature detection and learned associations.

These five decision stages are then applied at each of three processing levels, the sensory-motor, the schematic and the conceptual. Rather than describe all 15 cells of this framework, I will illustrate its application when applied to the second state, the check of intrinsic pleasantness that approximates most closely to my concept of a hedonic detector. At the sensory motor level, innate preferences and diversions will operate, for example avoidance of pain or sudden loud noises, or the attraction of food to the hungry organism. Higher schematic level evaluation will be based on learned preferences and aversions, the attractiveness of a location associated with food and safety, or avoidance of one associated with an enemy, for instance. At the conceptual level, evaluation will be based on the recall of anticipated or indirectly derived positive and negative information, for example choosing to travel to a location that has abundant ripe fruit at that time, via a route that is free of enemies. At this point, I will simply note that my own simplistic speculations are broadly consistent with this much richer framework, and observe that if my own views are to develop, they are likely to gain from closer contact with this literature.

15.6.2 Neurobiological approaches to emotion

As noted earlier, much of the work on emotion in the past has relied on animal studies, a situation that is now changing with a rapid increase of research on emotion in humans. One obvious reason for this is the development of neuroimaging, which allows a much more sophisticated analysis of the effects of emotion than proved possible using purely behavioural methods. A second reason, in my own judgement, stems from the interest in emotion prompted by Damasio's work, which emphasizes the importance of emotion for everyday cognition, proposing that it is linked to somatic stimuli, and that it operates through clearly specified brain regions. Finally, the development of the Iowa Gambling Task (IGT) has provided an experimental method for testing the predictions of the somatic marker hypothesis. However, Damasio's hypothesis has not escaped criticism, and since it forms the basis of the hedonic processor hypothesis just described, these criticisms will be discussed briefly, together with their implications for my own view.

15.6.2.1 Are somatic markers really somatic?

This is not an easy question to answer. Öhman and Soares (1994) and Parra *et al.* (1998) found no correlation between magnitude of automatic arousal and capacity of the subjects to predict shock in a masked conditioning paradigm.

However, a later study by Katkin *et al.* (2001) found that a subgroup who were able to judge their own heart beat did show a positive correlation with success in using the masked cues to 'guess' whether a shock will occur, in line with the proposal that 'gut feel' decisions may be viscerally based.

Others have studied patients for whom somatic feedback has been compromised, and measure their capacity for emotional judgements, including IGT performance. Results have not, so far, provided strong support for the hypothesis (North and O'Carroll 2001; Heims *et al.* 2004). However, autonomic feedback is based on a range of different physiological routes, and it is difficult to be sure that all have been eliminated in any given study (Craig 2002). Furthermore, such patients have typically grown up with normal autonomic feedback, allowing hedonic valences to be learned, and presumably used as a substitute for more direct visceral cues.

Other sources of evidence include the presence of autonomic responses, such as the electrodermal response that suggests an autonomic component in the IGT in normal subjects, and its abnormality in patients who fail the IGT (Bechara *et al.* 1997; Blair and Cipolotti 2000). Broadly supportive evidence is also accumulating from neuroimaging studies associated with Damasio's proposals that the orbitofrontal area of the frontal lobes is crucial both for emotion and for decision-making.

15.6.3 **Is the orbitofrontal cortex crucial?**

Damasio's proposal that the orbitofrontal cortex is central to the operation of the somatic marker system came from observing the area of brain damage in his classic patients. These were of course rather small in number, suggesting a clear need for replication. While there have been a number of demonstrations of impaired decision making associated with damage to the orbitofrontal (OBF) cortex, many such patients also have damage to other areas including anterior dorsal lateral cortex and cingulate gyrus (Bechara *et al.* 1994; 1997; 1998). Manes *et al.* (2002) attempted to avoid this problem by comparing patients with discreet OBF lesions with dorsolateral and dorsomedial patients and patients with large frontal lesions. The OBF patients performed at control levels on three decision-making tasks, although they were slower, whereas the dorsolateral and dorsomedial patients were impaired on the IGT, as were the group with large frontal lesions. Manes *et al.* conclude that both ventral and dorsal aspects of the prefrontal cortex are probably involved in IGT performance.

Other evidence for the importance of the prefrontal cortex has come from neuroimaging studies. For example Coricelli *et al.* (2005) using fMRI studied the 'regret' following the subject's discovery that they had chosen the wrong gamble, finding enhanced activity in the medial orbitofrontal region and the amygdala.

Activation in this area is also sensitive to affectively based decision-making in patients with mania (Elliott *et al.* 2004), and has been shown to be one of a number of frontal areas involved in mood-congruent processing biases in depressed patients (Elliott *et al.* 2002). In general, therefore, the evidence appears to be accumulating for a probable role for orbitofrontal cortex in hedonically based decision-making, probably in conjunction with a number of other regions, one of these being the amygdala. This structure has long been known to be associated with the acquisition of fear responses (LeDoux 1996) and more recently has also been shown to be associated with the response of depressed patients to emotional faces (Sheline *et al.* 2001).

However, there is also evidence from animal studies for the importance of the amygdala in a wider range of emotions, including positive reward. Wutz and Olds (1963) showed that animals would learn to press a bar for a reinforcement that involved the electrical stimulation of the amygdala. Subsequent lesion studies have also implicated the amygdala in both positive and negative reinforcement (Everitt *et al.* 2003; Kelly 2004). This is confirmed by a recent study by Knapska *et al.* (2006) using an immunolabelling technique and finding separate regions of the amygdala responding selectively to appetitive and aversive learning. While much of the evidence is so far based on animal studies, it is plausible to assume a role for the amygdala both in positive and negative hedonic learning and in hedonic evaluation in humans. In conclusion, while we are still far from a detailed understanding of the role of specific anatomical regions in emotion and decision, Damasio's proposals appear to be receiving broad support.

15.6.4 The Iowa Gambling Task

While the IGT has played an important role in extending the range of the somatic marker hypothesis (Bechara *et al.* 1994; 1997; 1998) the task is somewhat complex, suggesting that under certain circumstances it might depend on working memory, rather than providing a simple measure of somatic marker acquisition. Bechara *et al.* (1998) reject this interpretation on the grounds that patients showing impairment on the IGT did not fail an executive working memory task. Unfortunately, however, the only working memory task they used was a delayed matching procedure. Although this is regarded as a test of working memory in the animal literature, it has not to the best of my knowledge been shown to be a suitable neuropsychological measure of executive functioning in humans. Even if it did prove appropriate for detecting frontal lobe damage in humans, as Chapters 7 and 8 indicate, it is unwise to regard any single task as an adequate measure of executive capacity. Furthermore, the group sizes in their study were small, and patients with frontal lesions are notoriously variable in their performance deficits (Rabbitt 1997).

Positive evidence for an involvement of working memory in the IGT is presented by Hinson *et al.* (2002; 2003) while Maia and McClelland (2004) also criticise the assumptions on which the IGT is based. Hence, while the IGT has been valuable in stimulating research in this area, it is open to criticism. It would of course be unreasonable to assume that any single experimental task could provide an adequate test of a theory that is as potentially important as the somatic marker hypothesis. No doubt other, and preferably simpler, methods will be developed in due course.

How serious is the controversy surrounding the IGT for my own version of the somatic marker hypothesis? In my view, not at all: the hedonic valence hypothesis that forms the basis of my proposal does not depend on the validity of any single experimental measure. It does however reinforce my view that we need to develop other preferably simpler measures. These should include direct measures of hedonic judgement, and of the storage and manipulation of hedonic features in working memory. These can then in due course be combined with measures which, like the IGT, are designed to study the capacity for new hedonic learning.

15.7 **Conclusions**

Fear, craving and depression all disrupt working memory in ways that support the claim by Damasio and LeDoux that the transformation of physiological emotional stimuli into psychological feelings is mediated by working memory. In the case of fear and craving, the disruption occurs because implicit emotional cues lead to explicit elaboration, a process that involves both the storage and the executive components of working memory. In the case of depression, the effects are assumed to operate principally through a hedonic detector and comparator mechanism that underpins the control of action by motivation. An inappropriate setting of the neutral point of the comparator leads to a self-perpetuating feedback loop whereby both situational evaluation and autobiographical memory become progressively more negative. This process is exacerbated by the tendency for rumination to lead to inactivity as the 'beacons of incentive' are dimmed.

The hedonic detector hypothesis has the advantage of linking biological and psychological approaches to depression within a broad and plausible evolutionary context. It remains to be seen whether a more detailed model can be developed, and if so whether it could eventually contribute to the further development of methods of treatment.

Chapter 16

Consciousness

Perhaps the greatest change over the last 20 years within cognitive psychology and cognitive science more generally has been the acceptance of consciousness as a legitimate and tractable scientific problem. During much of the twentieth century the field was enmeshed in the philosophical tangles of the body-mind problem, and stifled by the empirical limitations of introspectionism. More recently, it has gradually become clear that neither of these represent the sort of fundamental obstacle that was originally feared. Furthermore, the need to account for phenomena such as blindsight and implicit memory, in which perception and recall were clearly proceeding in ways that were at variance with the conscious experience of the perceiver or the rememberer, argued strongly for the need to bring back the study of conscious awareness into the empirical psychological fold.

There were of course still those who took a quasi-mystical approach to the topic (Eccles 1976; Penrose 1994), while others proposed that some totally new type of science will be necessary if we are to understand why we have the particular conscious experiences or qualia that we do. A good example of the latter view is the argument from the hypothetical case of a colour-blind vision scientist. It is suggested that this investigator might well learn everything there is to know about colour vision, but would still not understand the underlying system in the same way as his colleagues with normal colour vision. It is unclear to me, however, that this situation is any different from the case of someone studying the flight of butterflies. However adequate his understanding, he would be unlikely to ever be able to flit from flower to flower. His knowledge would be explicit, and totally different from the presumably implicit knowledge still necessary to allow the butterfly to fly. My own view is that the task of science is to understand the world explicitly, and that an explicit understanding of consciousness is simply part of that task.

16.1 A pragmatic approach to consciousness

I assume that consciousness is a particular natural solution to one or perhaps a range of biological problems that has resulted from the processes of evolution.

I suggest that this pragmatic and empirical approach to the understanding of consciousness is both viable and fruitful, given the technical and experimental methods now available to cognitive psychology and neuroscience.

A detailed discussion of consciousness is beyond the scope of the present review of working memory. Discussion of the more philosophical aspects is provided by Marcel and Bisiach (1988), Dennett (2001) and Gray (2004), while a more general overview of the field is given by Baars (1997). However, as has become increasingly obvious over the years, conscious awareness appears to be closely related to executive control, and hence to the operation of working memory. The multicomponent model of working memory originally finessed the issue of conscious awareness by postulating a homunculus-like central executive. More recently, however, conscious awareness has featured directly within a working memory framework, initially as a phenomenon to be studied (Baddeley 1993; Baddeley and Andrade 1998), and subsequently through its central role in the concept of an episodic buffer. The outline that follows reflects my own current views on the topic of consciousness which, as will become clear, have similarities to what Baars (2002a) has described as the *global workspace hypothesis*. This assumes that working memory has evolved to serve a range of functions, notably including that of providing a workspace where information from many disparate sources can be combined and used both to understand our current situation, and to plan future action.

Baars cites at least a dozen sources that have independently advocated such a view, including Dennett (2001), who proposes that consciousness represents 'a distributed society of specialists that is equipped with a working memory called global workspace, whose contents can be distributed to the system as a whole' (Dennett 2001, p. 42). In discussing consciousness, however, it is useful to distinguish between two aspects of the concept: one concerned with its energizing and arousal aspects, while the other is concerned with its direction and control. These will be discussed separately.

16.2 **Core consciousness**

The term core consciousness was proposed by Damasio (2000), and can best be considered by contrasting the state of consciousness with that of being unconscious. Consciousness in this sense is absent in deep sleep, deep coma and under deep anaesthesia. The fact that depth has to be specified clearly implies that core consciousness is not an all-or-none state. The basic difference between sleep, coma and wakefulness appears to reflect the operation of the upper brainstem, the hypothalamus and thalamus. Under deep sleep, we appear to lack any awareness. In other levels of sleep, such as rapid eye movement

(REM) sleep, the presence of dreams which can sometimes be subsequently recalled, clearly implies some form of consciousness, a state that is also reflected in the electrical activities of the brain.

Depth of coma is a medically important variable which, in the case of head injury for example, correlates with the likelihood of recovery (Brooks *et al.* 1987; Teasdale and Jennett, 1974). Careful monitoring of depth of unconsciousness can also be an important indicator of whether the patient is recovering or declining. Both processes, however, tend to be very gradual and not easily observed. In order to facilitate this, Wilson *et al.* (2001) have developed a scale, the Wessex Head Injury Monitor (WHIM), based on the fact that despite some variability, functions tend to recover broadly in the same order.

A patient may recover from coma but yet appear to be quite unaware of his or her surroundings. The state known as *persistent vegetative state* typically reflecting damage to the upper brainstem and hypothalamus, may involve a normal sleep/wake cycle, but show no evidence of the patients being aware of their surroundings. It is important to differentiate this from the *locked in syndrome* in which the unfortunate patient may be entirely aware of what is going on, but be unable to respond due to paralysis, other than minimally, typically by moving the eyes. This minimal response can be used to develop a laborious but effective means of communication.

In persistent vegetative syndrome, patients are neither conscious nor able to control their actions. This contrasts with the form of unconsciousness known as *epileptic automatism* which may follow periods of mental absence in patients. During an absence, the patient's eyes will glaze over and he or she will remain motionless. This state may be followed by quite complex and organized behaviour which appears to occur in the absence of conscious awareness. Hence a patient might stand up, cross the room, open a door and go out, subsequently recovering consciousness and having no memory of the last few moments. This is typically associated with epileptic activity influencing the cingulate cortex and/or thalamus.

Just as one can have action without consciousness, so one may have consciousness without action, a state which tends to reflect damage to the cingulate cortex. An example is that of 'akinetic mutism' in which a patient may be entirely conscious, but unable to initiate activity. On recovery patients may well be able to report their experience, which is typically not due to motor paralysis but to a deficit in the capacity to initiate action. Baddeley and Wilson (1986) tried to study the autobiographical memory of one such patient. Our procedure involved presenting a series of verbal cues and asking the patient for personal recollections prompted by the cues. Of the 12 cues we gave him, only one evoked a response. To the cue *dog*, he responded 'sealyham', a breed of dog. A week later we obtained exactly the same single response to our set of cues. On questioning his wife, she confirmed that he had previously been bitten by a sealyham dog, the one incident that appeared to have been vivid enough to spur him into verbal response.

16.3 **Consciousness under anaesthesia**

One way in which conscious awareness may be manipulated in normal subjects is through anaesthesia. This became an area of considerable practical importance following a number of reports by patients undergoing surgical operations, that they had remained conscious, despite appearance to the contrary. While highly undesirable, this is possible since patients are given a 'cocktail' of drugs which aims not only to suppress conscious awareness and reduce pain, but also to serve as a muscle relaxant, which could thus have the effect of leaving a patient still conscious, but incapable of action, and hence of communicating this fact. Most anaesthetics also contain a third tranquillizing compound which typically leads to amnesia regarding anything experienced under the anaesthetic. Hence the relatively small number of reports of consciousness under anaesthesia may well be an underestimate (John *et al.* 2001).

A number of studies have attempted to detect memory for events occurring during surgical operations, using either explicit or implicit memory paradigms (see Andrade 1995; 2005). An early study used anaesthesia during dentistry. During the treatment the experimenter made a point of uttering the phrase 'Stop – I don't like his colour – his lips are too blue'. None of the ten patients exposed to this alarming message subsequently recalled it spontaneously, but four produced a verbatim recall under hypnosis and another four showed fragmentary recall. Subsequent studies typically using less dramatic material have produced more mixed results; Andrade (1995) cites eight studies in which pairs of words were presented, and subsequently tested for recall, of which only two studies showed positive results. Other studies have used implicit methods to test for retention, as these are less likely to suffer from the amnesic effects of anaesthetic. In one case, for example, subjects were instructed under anaesthetic that on recovery they should demonstrate recall by tugging their ear lobe. Of nine such studies carried out, three obtained positive results. Slightly stronger evidence comes from studies in which the patient was given encouraging suggestions under surgery, such as 'You will feel well', or 'You will want to get up soon after surgery'. Here 12 out of 17 studies found evidence of slightly better recovery in patients with positive suggestions.

One problem with virtually all of these studies is that of degree of anaesthesia. Clearly the anaesthetist will not wish to give the patient a heavier dose than necessary, and it is entirely plausible to assume level of sedation will fluctuate during the operation, possibly being quite light at some point. Later studies have therefore tried to monitor level of anaesthesia continuously. Andrade *et al.* (1994) systematically varied the dose of isoflourane in a study using normal volunteer subjects, who were not undergoing treatment, and hence did not have the additional muscle relaxant and tranquillizing drugs. Their task was to listen to a sequence of spoken words, and respond manually when a word was repeated. Such responding is of course not possible under normal conditions of surgical anaesthesia which include muscle relaxants. When a word was repeated immediately, subjects on the lowest level of isoflourane detected it every time, in contrast to a 40 per cent detection rate at double the dose. After a lag of sixteen intervening words, subjects in the drug-free condition detected the repetition 60 per cent of the time, as opposed to 30 per cent for the low dose, while the high dose subjects never detected the delayed repetition.

Depth of anaesthesia can to some extent be reduced by stimuli that would be expected to increase arousal level, such as shouting or using the subjects' given name. In an attempt to simulate the possible effect of making a surgical cut, Andrade *et al.* delivered a mild electric shock when the subject had stopped responding. This typically evoked a definite, but slight, recovery of response.

The principal function of this study was to attempt to validate electrophysiological measures of level of awareness. In general, the results were encouraging, suggesting that awareness can be monitored by behavioural measures, and that such measures are closely associated with electrophysiological activity of the brain. In recent years there has been a general acceptance of the need to monitor depth of anaesthesia before concluding that any apparent subsequent memory can not be attributed to processing the material during a periodic fluctuation in depth of consciousness. When these precautions are taken, there seems to be good evidence for perceptual priming during anaesthesia as measured, for example by stem completion. A list of words is presented under anaesthetic, and the subject later asked to 'guess' a word beginning with a given stem. Prior presentation biases the subsequent 'guess', even in amnesic patients. For example having been presented with the word 'taste', the previously anaesthetised patient is more likely to complete the stem TA— with that word than with 'table', a more likely response in the absence of priming. However, there does not appear to be evidence of the capacity to associate two previously presented but unrelated words (Andrade 2005; Deeprose and Andrade 2006).

It is clearly the case that our state of conscious awareness tends to fluctuate even under conditions of normal everyday life. When we first wake up we tend to be drowsy, with a level of alertness increasing through the forenoon, and declining at some point when we become fatigued (Folkard 1996). Similarly, external circumstances can influence our level of arousal, from low, when we are perhaps half-listening to a boring lecture, through to extremely high when we are threatened, for example, by a fierce dog. Level of arousal also differs dramatically in certain psychiatric patients. Within the normal population, it is clear that some people appear to have great mental and physical energy, while others are habitually lethargic. Insofar as I am aware, however, this obviously important phenomenon appears to have been relatively little studied by cognitive psychologists since the 1960s when arousal was still a popular topic within cognitive psychology (Broadbent 1971; Kahneman 1973). It is high time for the topic to be revisited.

16.4 Conscious control and the global workspace hypothesis

Virtually all studies of working memory have operated using subjects who are fully conscious, and have been concerned with the control and utilization of consciousness, rather than its overall level. This is certainly the case with what I would regard as the dominant approach, the previously mentioned global workspace hypothesis, which will be described, drawing particularly on a recent review of this approach by Baars (2002a), who distinguishes several subhypotheses, which we will consider in turn.

1 *Explicit processing demands global workspace.* Baars cites a study by Dehaene *et al.* (2001) which uses fMRI to study the processing of words presented visually under normal and backward masked conditions, under which subjects can no longer report the stimulus word. Normal perception results in widespread activation in visual, parietal and frontal areas that are not activated when the mask disrupts conscious awareness of the word. Such results are consistent with the second of Baars' points, namely:

2 *Conscious perception allows wide access to information throughout the brain.* Executive processes tend to make consciously processed information available from a range of different encodings, whereas implicit coding, such as occurs in masked perceptual priming, tends to be specific to the modality concerned.

3 *Working memory depends on consciousness.* This is also a major assumption of my own current approach to working memory. In addition to referring to the role of consciousness in the episodic buffer, Baars refers to recent work by John *et al.* (2001) who studied EEG during six working memory tasks. Interpretation does, of course, depend on the assumption that the given electrophysiological responses are indeed markers of conscious awareness.

4 *Consciousness allows the novel combination of material.* This of course is one of the principal functions attributed to the episodic buffer. It is striking that

although individual words can be primed subliminally, multiple word combinations seem not to be primable, when they are masked or are presented on the unattended channel of a dichotic listening study (Greenwald and Liu 1985), or, as mentioned earlier, under anaesthesia (Deeprose and Andrade 2006). The essence of conscious language comprehension is, of course, the derivation of meaning from the combination of words within the utterance; this suggests that language comprehension demands at least a minimal degree of conscious awareness, although as Chapter 9 suggests may make only minimal demands on the central executive.

5 *Consciousness is essential for explicit learning and episodic memory.* Good mnemonic strategies depend on their capacity to integrate previous unassociated material by conscious manipulation, for example by means of interacting visual imagery. This issue of the binding together of previously unrelated stimuli is likely to play a central role in attempts to analyse the episodic buffer into its subcomponents and subprocesses.

The question of whether learning may ever occur unconsciously remains unresolved. Evidence for learning during sleep or during deep anaesthetic typically depends upon studies in which the depth of consciousness was not monitored (Andrade 1995). There is, of course, abundant evidence for implicit learning in which the learner is not consciously aware of the detailed nature of what is being learned. For example, the acquisition of the grammar of one's native language involves the apparent mastery of rules without necessarily knowing what those rules are (Reber 1993). Note, however, that in all such cases, it is not the material itself that is unconscious, but the relations operating within it. Both appear to depend upon capacity of the basic material to reach conscious awareness (see Shanks and St John 1994; and Baddeley 1998 Chapter 19, for reviews).

6 *Consciousness allows the monitoring and adjustment of motor control.* A great deal of our behaviour depends upon feedback loops that are too rapid for direct conscious access, as in the case of many complex motor skills. However, when behaviour breaks down, conscious control can often intervene to provide an alternative solution. Hence, a subject who is required to aim at an underwater target will initially perform badly because of the refracting effect of the water, but can then improve performance by consciously allowing for the refraction (Judd 1908). A good sports coach will be able to identify problems in skilled motor behaviour, such as swinging a golf club, and can then utilize conscious control to correct them, subsequently relying on practice to make the changed action increasingly automatic, eventually allowing it to operate with minimal attention. Haier *et al.* (1992) demonstrated this process experimentally in subjects

who were practiced extensively on the computer game Tetris, while concurrently monitoring brain activity. Initially, wide areas of the brain were highly active when the game was played: after two weeks' practice the level of activation was much lower, a result that is consistent with the hypothesis of reduced attentional demand.

16.4.1 The theatre of consciousness

Baars (1997 p. 43) suggests that 'all unified theories of cognition today involve theatre metaphors'. A version proposed by Baars himself places at its centre working memory, which Baars likens to the stage on which the various cognitive actors may perform, illuminated by the spotlight of attention. The less well-illuminated portion of the stage represents aspects of immediate memory that are not currently in focal attention. The 'actors' constitute information from three types of input, namely: (1) The overt senses of hearing, feeling, touching and so forth; (2) Quasi-sensory information that is self-generated, such as internal speech and visual imagery, and finally (3) Ideas that are essentially non-sensory in nature, although they may have visual or verbal associations. The actions of these various informational components are controlled behind the scenes by a number of executive processes which include a 'director' (the self), and a 'spotlight controller'; both are influenced by a range of local contexts. Finally, the working memory stage and its performers are viewed by an unconscious audience comprising a somewhat mixed bag of memory systems, interpreters, automatic processes and motivational systems.

Although this analogy may seem somewhat strained, Baars (1997) does make good use of it as a basis for a broad overview for the general reader of current knowledge of research on consciousness. Any metaphor will inevitably have its limitations, but the Baars' theatre does have two major advantages. The first of these is its capacity to reflect the sheer complexity of those factors that interact with consciousness, together with the central importance of attentional control. Secondly, it does so using a metaphor that is readily understood, as reflected in Patrick Rabbitt's succinct definition of extreme old age as the time when 'the theatre of the mind is the only show in town'.

To what extent does this theatre metaphor provide a useful basis for developing a scientific theory? The answer will surely depend upon the scientific user. In my own case, there are a number of features of the concept that I would want to change, or at least elaborate. Treating the all-important actors as simply reflecting different sources of information neglects the progress that we have made in dividing up such sources into visuospatial and auditory-verbal, for example. Of course, the metaphor of an actor is sufficiently flexible to allow a huge range of interpretations, but then the lack of any real constraint is likely to reduce its explanatory value. Finally, I am unhappy about the very passive role assigned to the 'unconscious audience'.

So, how would I reorganize the theatre? Who would I keep in and who would I sack? First, I would not wish to sack any of the participants, as I think that Baars makes a good case for the importance of all of the components. I would, however, change the metaphor from the theatrical analogy of active display and a relatively passive audience to a much more interactive one. I see working memory as lying at the heart of a system that is built to *do* things. Furthermore, I suggest that all the participant components are interdependent, with the importance of each depending on the particular circumstances. I would therefore choose the metaphor of *government*.

If we use as our example a modern state, then the working memory might be equivalent to those aspects of government that are obvious to the world; the making and enforcing of laws, decisions on how to interact with other governments, changes in financial policy and so forth. All of these, of course, are likely to be based upon a huge amount of less visible underlying activity. Thus although the laws are enacted by a government, their implementation will depend on the Civil Service, and local government, which will themselves depend on communications and transport systems, medical support systems, and, of course, on the voters or, in the case of a totalitarian system, the army. Like the government, conscious working memory appears at first sight to be uniquely important, but like government, it crucially depends on its interaction with a huge range of implicit activities that underpin its operation. So, is there a clear mapping of cognitive functions onto state functions such as the army, transport, medicine and industry? I doubt it, other than to observe that both consciousness control and government involve many different subcomponents, varying in size and method of control, and being influenced to a greater or lesser degree by an explicit source of executive control, and in turn influencing each other and the central controller. Their complexity does not, of course, mean that they are impossible to study, simply that we should not expect any easy answers.

But what constitutes the government? Here, I am inclined to agree with Baars in assuming that there is someone, or something, a committee perhaps, in charge of activities. Like Baars, I am happy, for the present at least, to assign this role to a traditional but constitutionally constrained senior minister, popularly known as the self.

16.5 **A neural basis for cognitive workspace**

As Baars emphasized, the idea that consciousness forms part of a system that operates as a global workspace is one that has attracted growing support in recent years. As a result, it is now becoming possible to develop increasingly specific hypotheses as to how the brain might achieve consciousness, and what function this might serve. An excellent example of this is provided by Dehaene and Naccache (2001) in their introduction to a special issue of the journal *Cognition*, concerned with consciousness.

Dahaene and Naccache begin with a number of basic assumptions. First, they propose that considerable information processing is possible *without* the intervention of consciousness, but that when consciousness is involved, it demands attention. Attentional resources then allow consciousness to perform its three basic functions, namely: (1) Prolonging the duration of information maintenance, (2) Allowing information from different sources to be combined in novel ways, and (3) The generation of spontaneous behaviour. It is perhaps worth noting that these three overlap very closely with the functions attributed to the coordinated operation of the central executive and episodic buffer components of working memory.

Dahaene and Naccache go on to review the evidence for their basic assumptions. Although we present evidence for all of these elsewhere, given the importance of the assumptions, some redundancy is perhaps justified. Furthermore, as befits their more neurobiological emphasis, most of the evidence cited by Dehaene and Naccache comes from neuropsychological, neuroimaging, or electrophysiological studies and as such, complements the evidence based on cognitive and social psychology presented elsewhere.

16.5.1 Cognitive processing is possible without consciousness

For this assumption, Dehaene and Naccache rely heavily on the neuropsychological evidence, particularly that of blindsight in which patients with cortical blindness appear to be able to respond appropriately to stimuli in their blind field, while denying awareness (Weiskrantz 1997). Comparable phenomena have now been demonstrated in a wide range of fields, including object recognition, colour vision, language, perception, reading and amnesia (see Köhler and Moscovitch 1997). A specific example comes from the area of prosopagnosia, in which a brain-damaged patient found photographs of his relatives no more familiar than those of complete strangers, but nevertheless showed a differential electrodermal response (Bauer 1984). Further evidence of processing without awareness comes from the study of patients with hemineglect, who following damage to the right hemisphere, appear to be unaware of objects presented in their left visual field. For instance, a word (e.g. *doctor*) presented in the neglected field could not be reported by the patient. It was however sufficient to speed up the processing of a related item (e.g. *nurse*), presented to the intact visual field (McGlinchey-Beroth *et al.* (1993), a result that extends earlier evidence of the semantic processing of unmasked words that are not consciously reportable (Marcel 1983).

16.5.2 Attention is necessary for consciousness

It has been known for many years that when visually presented objects fall outside the attended part of the visual field, they are not reported (Triesman and Gelade 1980). This point is emphasized by Mack and Rock (1998), who required their subjects to perform a demanding visual discrimination task at a specified visual location. Under these circumstances, subjects fail to notice stimuli that would be readily detected under less demanding conditions, for example, a large black circle in the fovea, leading Mack and Rock (1998 p. ix) to conclude that 'there seems to be no conscious perception without attention'.

A related phenomenon is the *attentional blink*, whereby subjects are exposed to a sequence of rapidly presented visual stimuli, with the instruction to report one specific type of item, for example, animals. Subjects are able to do this even at very rapid rates, and can identity more than one target item provided they are well separated. However, if the second item comes shortly after the first, detection is much less likely (Raymond *et al.* 1992). It is as if the subject's attention is briefly captured by the first target, leading to the immediately subsequent targets being missed. An even more dramatic illustration of the importance of attention comes from the phenomenon of *change blindness*. In this paradigm, the subject while walking in the street might be stopped and engaged in conversation by a stranger (the experimenter). Two people (accomplices) carrying a screen then appear and walk between the subject and his interlocutor, the experimenter. While he is made invisible by the screen, a dramatic physical change is made, for instance the experimenter puts on a large hat. Subjects almost invariably fail to notice this, and when told about the change, are incredulous (see O'Regan *et al.* 1999). However large the hat, if the subject did not attend to the state of the experimenter's head, its changed appearance will not be noticed.

16.5.3 Some cognitive operations do require consciousness

1 *Maintaining information.* As Sperling (1960) showed in his classic studies of iconic memory, although we may have an *initial* access to an array of twelve letters, only about four are capable of being maintained, through a process of focused attention followed by rehearsal. Fuster (1954) Fuster and Alexander (1971) and Goldman-Rakic (1957) have shown that the capacity to remember the location of a visual stimulus, in order to make an

eye movement to it some seconds later, depends upon the continued activity of cells within the frontal cortex, an area that is heavily involved in the control of working memory in humans (see Chapter 12).

2 *Novel combination requires consciousness.* This capacity, which we have attributed to the operation of the episodic buffer and central executive system, was studied in an ingenious experiment by Merikle *et al.* (1995). They performed a variant of the Stroop task in which subjects were required to name colour patches as rapidly as possible. Each patch was preceded by a colour word. When the word was congruent, it speeded the colour naming task, and when incongruent, slowed it. Two colours were used, red and green. In one condition, 75 per cent of the cues were incongruent; and under these circumstances, subjects became aware of the bias and appeared to be able to use it to speed up the more frequent incongruent responses. Hence, if the word red was usually followed by a green patch, subjects made the correct response 'green' more rapidly than they would if such mismatches occurred less frequently.

In a further condition, the colour word primes were masked by being immediately followed by a pattern, with the result that subjects were unable to report what word was presented. Despite masking the classic Stroop effect continued to occur with an incongruent word slowing down colour naming, suggesting that the word had been processed, despite lack of awareness. Under these circumstances, however, subjects were incapable of taking strategic advantage of the condition in which incongruent cues occur 75 per cent of the time. In a subsequent study Merikle and Joordens (1997) demonstrate a similar failure to take strategic advantage of bias when the primes were not masked, but were presented outside the focus of attention.

Finally, it is noteworthy that blindsight patients never initiate behaviour in response to stimuli within their blind field. Despite evidence that they are able at some level to access information about such stimuli, they cannot use such information strategically. Similarly, amnesic patients are well able to demonstrate normal implicit learning, but are unaware of what they have learned, and hence cannot use it intentionally. This has a major effect on their capacity to live a normal life, emphasizing the importance of explicit knowledge for the efficient operation of mental workspace.

16.5.4 A theoretical framework

Dehaene and Naccache base their interpretative framework on three basic assumptions: (1) The mind is modular (2) Consciousness is non-modular, and (3) Attention can be used to mobilize and amplify neural processes. These will be discussed in turn.

16.5.4.1 Modularity of the mind

Dehaene and Naccache propose that 'a given process, involving several mental operations can proceed unconsciously only if a set of adequately interconnected modular systems is available to perform each of the required operations' (Dehaene and Naccache 2001, p. 12). They suggest, for example, that it is possible for a masked fearful face to result in unconscious priming, because there are dedicated neural systems in the superior coliculus, pulvinar, and right amygdala that subserve the attribution of emotional priming to faces (Morris *et al.* 1999). They further assume that many such systems may operate in parallel, and that they may exist at a range of different levels, from such basic functions as emotional priming and postural control up to the operation of learned skills such as reading which are based on complex high-level cognitive processing.

16.5.4.2 Non-modular consciousness

In contrast to this wide range of modular implicit processes, they propose that the conscious mind is non-modular, comprising a distributed neural system or 'workspace' with long-distance connectivity that can potentially interconnect multiple specialized brain areas in a coordinated, though variable manner', (Dehaene and Naccache 2001, p. 13). Although this system is not itself modular, it does serve to make connections between many of the systems that are themselves modular. They suggest that at least five types of system must be interconnected in order for the global workspace to operate adequately. These include:

1 Higher level perceptual systems;
2 Motor systems;
3 Long-term memory;
4 Evaluative processes, and finally,
5 Attentional control.

  Suppose we take the example of reading a letter from an old friend saying that he is about to visit. Visual perception is needed to identify the words on the page and motor control to move your eyes appropriately. Access to various types of long-term memory is required, including lexical and semantic for the interpretation of the sentence, and probably autobiographical and episodic memory will be needed to take in the meaning of the letter. This in turn is likely to have an evaluative component, hopefully, a pleasant anticipation of meeting your friend again. Finally, the whole of this process will depend on attentional control, allowing you to focus on the task of reading the letter and interpreting its significance, rather than simply sinking into a reverie about old times.

16.5.4.3 Attentional control of neural processes

This leads on to the third major assumption made by Dehaene and Naccache, which concerns the capacity of attention to mobilize and amplify neural processes. They propose that 'top-down attentional amplification is the mechanism by which modular processes can be temporarily mobilized and made available to the global workspace, and therefore to consciousness' (Dehaene and Naccache 2001, p. 14). They propose that processing will only become conscious if it is amplified, and maintained over some minimal period of time. Within the current working memory model, this could be regarded as utilizing the central executive to ensure storage in the episodic buffer. Because this process may occur across many different modular systems, they suggest that it argues for 'the absence of a sharp anatomical delineation of the workspace system' (ibid., p. 14), a view that is also similar to the assumptions underpinning the episodic buffer (Baddeley 2000).

16.5.5 **The sense of self**

Dehaene and Naccache also incorporate the sense of self within their framework. They propose that each brain has multiple representations of itself at different levels, extending from the basic subcortical homeostatic mechanisms through the representation of the body at a somatic, kinesthetic and motor level, up to personal representation of a concept of our bodies and faces, and such long-term memory representations as autobiographical and episodic memories. Each of these is regarded as a separable modular system, but one which can be made accessible through the global workspace of consciousness, and within that workspace allowed to interact with other modules. Such representations can be operated on by reasoning and by verbal manipulation, and hence used to plan future action. To take a trivial example, the decisions of whether to have that second helping of pudding is likely to be influenced by body state, 'I'm full, but it was delicious!'; social factors, 'would I look greedy? No, it would simply show how much I appreciate our hostess's food!'; future planning, 'I ought to eat less, but why start right now?'; and action, 'yes, please!' These multiple layers of representations of the self, each of which can be activated, maintained and manipulated, provide a possible basis for our capacity for reflexive or higher-order consciousness.

16.6 **Consciousness and working memory**

The chapter so far has concentrated on a particular approach to tackling the enormously challenging question of how to explain consciousness. The approach is based on the assumption that consciousness serves as a mental workspace, and that the phenomenological experience accompanying consciousness provides an important component of its function, allowing different levels of representation, which allow multiple stimuli to be simultaneously registered. The availability of multiple levels is combined with the capacity for reflexivity, the ability to represent and manipulate the contents of one level, at another. This provides a very powerful mechanism for registering the environment and relating it to past experience, which can in turn be used to model the present, using that model to simulate and hence to predict the future and plan further action. At the heart of such a system lies the capacity for the temporary storage and manipulation of information which is the hallmark of working memory.

The multicomponent model of working memory evolved from the attempt to answer a much less ambitious question than the nature of consciousness. We began with the question of whether it was necessary to have separate long- and short-term storage systems, and if so to ask what function they served. We made no mention of phenomenology, although I must admit that I thought of the visuospatial sketchpad as the seat of the phenomenological experience of visual imagery, and the central executive as the attentional controller of some form of mental workspace. Implicitly therefore, we were making assumptions about two of the basic questions associated with consciousness, namely the nature of qualia, the philosophical term for conscious experience such as the particular redness of a rose, while at the same time serving as the system involved in explicit control of action.

Our somewhat tentative attempt to tackle the role of working memory in conscious awareness began with a series of experiments that investigated the role of the subsidiary visuospatial and phonological subsystems of working memory in visual and auditory imagery, as described in Chapter 5 (Baddeley and Andrade 2000). We were pleased to discover that we were able to obtain coherent and meaningful data from subjective judgements of vividness, and to give some provisional answers to our initial questions. We were somewhat surprised to discover that the relevant phonological and visuospatial subsystems played a relatively small part in visual imagery, except when they were needed to maintain temporary information. Our concept of an executive at that time lacked explicit storage capacity, and hence was not well suited to filling the theoretical gap. This was one of the number of results that prompted us to postulate a new component of working memory, the episodic buffer.

The buffer differs from our earlier concept of a central executive in being principally a multidimensional storage device, actively controlled by the executive. As described in Chapter 9, we are currently investigating the importance of executive control in the operation of our hypothetical buffer system, and currently finding a greater degree of automatic control than we had initially anticipated. It seems likely that the buffer is a limited capacity system for holding representations, with its capacity potentially being increased by multidimensional chunking. We are currently investigating the conditions under which creation of such chunks is automatic, as apposed to demanding of attentionally limited executive resources. Regardless of the answer, or more likely a series of answers, to this question, we expect the concept of a multidimensional storage system to continue to be a necessary component of the working memory model.

The second major feature of consciousness, its capacity to serve as a limited capacity workspace, was more explicitly part of the original multicomponent model of working memory. Indeed the term 'working memory' was chosen to emphasize its functional character. Our model differs from the previously described models of consciousness, however, in containing a number of components that are almost certainly not explicitly conscious. For example the phonological loop depends on rehearsal which in turn reflects existing language habits and articulatory processes, some but by no means all of which may become explicitly available to conscious reflection. One of the advantages of the loop is that rehearsal seems to proceed with minimal conscious control, allowing awareness to be utilized to maximize other aspects of processing. Hence, while I would be inclined to identify the episodic buffer with the representation of events that are currently in conscious awareness, much of the machinery that feeds the buffer is probably not typically itself open to conscious manipulation. In making this point I am not criticizing previously described approaches to consciousness, but rather pointing to our different emphases. The work I described earlier is focused on the fascinating and important topic of understanding conscious awareness and control. In my own case, I am focusing on a system for storing and manipulating information which incidentally, but importantly, contains a component that is assumed to underpin our capacity for conscious awareness. The capacity for reflective awareness is central to our ability to cope flexibly and creatively with a complex and changing world. It is, however, just one component of a complex system; an organism that remained locked in thought would not have survived for very long. To be effective, thought must lead to action; but not always. Sometimes it is better to inhibit action, while many of our actions appear to proceed without conscious monitoring. The complex and subtle relationship between thought and action forms the topic of the next chapter.

Chapter 17

The multilevel control of action

In this chapter we move from the higher realms of consciousness to the apparently more mundane question of how movement is controlled. I say *apparently* mundane because I hope to convince you first, that the control of active movement is a rich and intriguing research area, and secondly that it contains within itself some of the central questions of how thought relates to action.

The study of movement control has been a highly active area in recent years, although much of the work appears to have been concentrated at a biomechanical level, or to be driven by a neo-Gibsonian approach, with little regard for the relevance of internal representations such as schemata, or of cognitive concepts such as Shallice's SAS (Kelso 1995; Shaw 2003; Turvey 2004). That is not to say that a detailed analysis at the perceptual-muscular level is unimportant, but merely to suggest that a higher level of analysis may be necessary even to account for the performance of a task as apparently simple as picking up a glass and drinking.

Disorders of action have formed a rich and intriguing area of neuropsychological study in recent years. A range of the available evidence will be reviewed first, followed by an interpretation offered by Frith *et al.* (2000), which relies heavily on the distinction between automatic and non-automatic sources of control. They propose a theory that explicitly aims to go beyond motor control and to cover the control of action more generally, including social behaviour as a form of action. I will begin by discussing sources of evidence that are broadly consistent with Bargh's theme of the importance of implicit control, going on to consider evidence for which this interpretation appears to be insufficient, leading on to an outline of the Frith *et al.* (2000) model.

17.1 Implicit control of action

We tend to think of our actions as intentional and explicit, controlled by our needs, desires and intentions, in contrast to Bargh and Ferguson's (2000) emphasis on the external cueing of automatic responses. There is a good deal of evidence to suggest that implicit cues of the type discussed by Bargh may indeed be important in the control of movement. Frith *et al.* argue that the neuropsychological evidence, based on patients for whom the control of action is disturbed, provide important insights into how our actions are normally controlled. Consider the following examples.

17.1.1 Brain stimulation and movement

As Bargh and Ferguson noted, it is possible to produce an action by stimulating the appropriate area of the cortex (Penfield 1958). Stimulation of the central thalamic nucleus of a conscious patient results in his clenching his fist (the patient had no idea why he had performed this act). This, of course, simply means that it is possible to intervene within the overall system, and to influence the movement without the requirement for active initiation. As we shall see, the same effect can be produced at an even more peripheral level by vibrating the extensor or flexor arm muscles.

17.1.2 Utilization behaviour

Patients with bilateral damage to the frontal lobes sometimes show behaviour that appears to be excessively driven by the immediate stimulus situation. Seeing a matchbox on the table, such a patient may spontaneously take out a match and strike it. If the clinician's cup of coffee is on the desk, they will quite happily drink from it. When asked whose coffee it is, they answer correctly, and when asked why they drank, without embarrassment, reply that it was because they were thirsty.

Utilization behaviour was first studied in detail by L'Hermite (1983). He describes some striking examples of this type of socially anomalous behaviour. On one occasion, a number of pieces of medical equipment were left on the desk when he saw a 52-year-old lady. She picked up a syringe, whereupon the intrepid doctor L'Hermite removed his jacket and shirt and she injected him! On another occasion, a patient visiting the doctor's apartment was shown the bedroom, where the sheets were turned back. He promptly undressed, removed his wig, and got into bed.

A subsequent systematic investigation of utilization behaviour is described by Shallice *et al.* (1989), who established that it is one of a range of symptoms of the dysexecutive syndrome that may accompany frontal lobe damage. It is characteristic of utilization behaviour that the patient does not deny the action, or claim that it is something that could not be avoided, but justifies it as a reasonable thing to do. The actions are typically part of a well-learned pattern that is strongly linked to some aspect of the stimulus situation. The link may be at a relatively low level, such as striking a match, when the patient is simply reflecting what Gibson would term the *affordance* of the object, its potential for use. Such affordance may include quite complex behaviour, as in the case of the syringe. It is, of course, importantly the case that objects also have affordances for normal subjects. Such affordances play an important role in the capacity to function efficiently in a rich and complex environment. Presumably however, in the normal case, socially inappropriate triggering of the afforded behaviour is inhibited by a social convention, or by the domination of action by some other more high level plan or script, the 'looking around someone-else's house' script, for example, rather than the 'going to bed' one.

17.1.3 Tourette's syndrome

In this condition, behaviour is emitted as if impelled by some powerful stimulus outside the patient's control. Patients may be unable to control the urge to make sporadic, apparently meaningless movements, tics, or to utter irrelevant words, which may often be obscenities, causing the patient considerable embarrassment. Behaviour can be suppressed by considerable effort, but tends to emerge as the pressure to respond apparently builds up. The patient is typically fully aware that their behaviour is unreasonable, but finds it impossible to avoid.

17.1.4 Slips of action

Cueing of an inappropriate action by the environment is not, of course, limited to patients with frontal lobe damage. Reason and Mycielska (1982) studied such mental lapses in some detail, principally using diaries and self-report. Typical examples include setting off to drive to the supermarket on a Saturday morning, and finding yourself driving to work. William James (1890) describes an example not unlike that of L'Hermite's patient, although less bizarre. The person in question went upstairs to dress for dinner, and having removed his day clothes, absent-mindedly put on his night clothes and went to bed.

The Norman and Shallice SAS model of executive control was, of course, explicitly developed to account for such behaviour, as well as that of patients with frontal lobe damage. They suggest that such slips of action reflect the control of behaviour by external environmental stimuli, an interpretation that is entirely consistent with the Bargh and Ferguson thesis. Such examples of absent-mindedness, however, differ from the patient's utilization behaviour, in that the perpetrators of the error are likely to show embarrassment at this departure from what they regard as the normal explicit attentional control of their actions, whereas the patients appear to regard their behaviour as perfectly normal.

17.1.5 Blindsight

In all the examples cited so far, the subject has been aware of the stimulus that cued their behaviour, with the problem stemming from a failure to inhibit an associated but inappropriate response. Some intriguing work by Marcel (1998) indicates that overt awareness is not necessary for this cueing function to occur. Marcel describes a series of experiments with patient G.Y., who suffers from *blindsight*. This condition may occur when patients suffer blindness in part of their visual field as a result of damage to the occipital lobes of the cortex (Weiscrantz 1986). Such patients will deny the capacity to see anything in the blinded area, but if asked to guess, can detect the presence of a stimulus substantially above chance levels.

Marcel studied the capacity of G.Y to reach out and touch an object within his blind field. Not only was the patient able to do this, but when the object varied in shape, G.Y. was able to configure his hand appropriately, shaping his grasp differently for a horizontal and a vertical rod. Despite this, the patient was unable to consciously report the shape or orientation of the object. It was as if the hand 'knew' enough to be able to make appropriate adjustments, but that this knowledge was not accessible to conscious awareness. A further study (Marcel 1993) asks the question of whether the patient can use the shape his hand has adopted immediately before contact as a cue to the shape of the object. However, although G.Y. can report the shape of the object that has been grasped, presumably using tactile and haptic cues, if the process is interrupted after the hand has taken up the correct shape, but before contact has been made, the patient cannot use the orientation of the hand as a cue to predict the shape of the object that is about to be grasped. This observation is consistent with other evidence to be discussed later, in suggesting that we do not have good conscious access to the detailed information we are using to perform familiar but complex action sequences.

17.1.6 Anosognosia

Whereas blindsight offers an example of the utilization of information apparently unconsciously, the opposite may occur in anosognosia, where patients may claim to have made a movement even though they have not done so, and indeed are incapable of moving the limb in question. Brain-damaged patients with cognitive deficits are often aware of their problems, but can on occasion remain apparently completely unaware of their incapacity. This does not appear to reflect Freudian denial, and is typically associated with damage to the right hemisphere of the brain. Hence, it almost always affects the left, but not the right limb, suggesting an organic rather than a psychodynamic origin. Bisiach and Geminiani (1991) describe patients who have lost the capacity to move an arm as a result of brain damage, while retaining the capacity to detect the fact that it has been moved passively when blindfolded. When asked to move their arm they claim, wrongly, to have done so. An anosognosic patient with a plegic leg, completely unable to walk, might declare himself about to walk upstairs or to be able to run for a bus.

Anosognosia is by no means limited to motor behaviour: it is not uncommon in amnesia, where one densely amnesic patient I studied kept interrupting the experiment to remark that she prided herself on her memory, forgetting that she had already said this multiple times. Indeed, patients may even deny conditions as apparently obvious as blindness (Anton 1899). Hence, although anosognosia for deficits of movements exists, it is by no means limited to defective control of action, and hence will probably require a more extensive explanation than offered here.

Many of the examples given reflect behaviour that is anomalous to the observer, but not to the subject. Hence, while these cases offer an intriguing explanatory challenge, they could be seen as broadly supportive of Bargh and Ferguson's suggestion that behaviour reflects a subject's response to environmental or internal cues. This view is less easy to sustain in the face of the phenomena that will be described next. Instances will be described in which the actions performed are anomalous to both the observer and the patient or subject, implying two or more levels of control that appear to be in conflict, one being explicit and the other implicit, and often 'unwanted' by the patient. We will begin with the strange phenomenon of the phantom limb.

17.1.7 **Phantom limbs**

A patient who has had a limb amputated may continue to experience it, even though it is visually obvious that the limb is no longer present, and hence that this is some form of illusion. The illusion can be a very disturbing one since the limb can continue to feel painful or to itch, without, of course, the possibility of scratching it (Ramachandran and Hirstein 1998). Patients may initially have the capacity to 'move' the phantom limb, but often lose this apparent capacity over time. It is also the case that stimulation of some other part of the body, such as the face, may be felt as a touch to the phantom. Ramachandran attributes the anomalous mapping of sensation onto other parts of the body to neural regeneration, whereby areas of the cortex that were previously linked to the now absent arm or finger, are taken over by neural systems that subserve other parts of the body, controlled by cortical areas adjacent to those that previously served the missing limb.

Another anomalous perceptual experience is that of supernumerary limbs. Hari *et al.* (1998) describe a patient with a defective left arm, who experienced two left arms whenever he was instructed to move his defective arm while looking away. One arm appeared to be in the initial arm location, and one in the new position. Looking at the arm or having it touched caused the 'old' arm to disappear. This patient, who appeared unable to update the position of the arm when moved, had damage to the supplementary motor area (SMA) and right frontal damage together with some evidence of congenital abnormality of the corpus collosum, the structure that facilitates the communication between the two hemispheres of the brain.

Yet a third perceptual disorder is that of the *alien hand* (Banks *et al.* 1989). This may occur in stroke cases where one hand and arm may be paralyzed. On occasion, patients will deny ownership of the arm and hand in question, attempting to push it away, sometimes even accusing the doctor of sewing on some other person's arm or hand. As in the case of anosognosia, this is typically associated with right hemisphere damage.

The cases we have discussed so far all involve anomalous perception, experiences that appear to the patient to be as strange as they do to the observer who hears about them. Even stranger is the anarchic hand sign, in which the anomaly extends beyond perception to action, with the patient's hand behaving as if it had a will of its own.

17.1.8 **The anarchic hand**

Della Sala *et al.* (1994) review evidence from some 39 cases from the literature and from their own files. They describe a characteristic case, G.P., who was participating in a meal with her family and the neurologist concerned with her case. Part way through, her left hand suddenly reached over to pick a pile of fish bones from the plate of her neighbour; the hand then proceeded to thrust them into the patient's own mouth, much to her embarrassment. Later in the meal, the mischievous hand reached over to take her brother's ice cream; the patient then attempted to assert control with her other hand, resulting in the ice cream falling to the floor. Other instances include a patient described by Parkin (1996) who regularly experienced conflict between the two hands. Hence on one occasion, the right hand was attempting to button her dress while the left hand was busy unbuttoning it; when the right hand attempted to choose a television channel, the left would interfere and change it. An even more extreme case is described by Banks *et al.* (1989): a patient's anarchic hand would attempt to strangle her, on occasion even in her sleep, resulting in the need to tie it down when she went to bed.

While these bizarre actions might seem to suggest some psychogenic or Freudian interpretation, they appear to result from a specific lesion to the medial wall of the frontal lobe contralateral to the alien hand. As in many disorders of action control, the SMA is implicated, often together with evidence of more general cortical damage.

In almost all the cases discussed so far, the anomalous perception or behaviour has been associated with some kind of brain damage. The final examples will involve illusions affecting motor control in normal people.

17.1.9 When hand and eye disagree

Goodale *et al.* (1986; 1991) utilized the Titchener illusion to explore a potential conflict between control by hand and by eye. The illusion relies on the fact that the apparent size of an object such as a circle is influenced by its context. Hence given two central circles of equal size, one surrounded by smaller circles and the other by larger circles, the latter will appear smaller. Goodale *et al.* modified the illusion by presenting it as an array of discs, with the subject being asked to pick up the central disc. Under these circumstances, the extent to which the hand opens in anticipation of the grasp adapts to the *correct* size of the discs, not the perceived size. Hence, the hand appears to have a source of evidence that is more reliable than that provided by conscious perception. As the fingers have not yet touched the disc, the information is presumably visual, but implicit. This is, of course, reminiscent of the previously described blindsight patient, who is capable of adjusting his hand to the shape appropriate for grasping an object which he is unable to consciously report (Marcel 1998).

17.2 A model of motor control

Within the tradition initiated by Kenneth Craik during the Second World War (Craik 1947), Frith *et al.* (2000) have used concepts from servo engineering to create a model of the control of action. They use as their basis a model of motor control proposed by Wolpert *et al.* (1995) which involves two basic concepts, that of *prediction*, whereby the state that is to be achieved is represented, and *control*, whereby the motor commands are provided that are necessary for reaching the desired outcome. They also propose the existence of at least three states of the system.

17.2.1 Predictive processes and motor control

Predictors, or forward models, are needed to anticipate movement and compensate for sensory change that will inevitably occur during the movement. When we move our eyes, the pattern of excitation on the retina changes. An efferent copy of the movement command is then used to correct our perception of the world. If we did not have this capacity to allow for movement, the world would appear unstable, moving as our eyes move. It is easy to demonstrate of this by moving one's eye by pressing the eyelid gently.

Under these conditions, the world appears to move at the same time. Movement of the eye is involuntary, and hence no efferent copy of the movement has been delivered to the system. Voluntary movement feeds such efferent information into the system, allowing us to filter out the effects of movement and maintain accuracy in a task such as reaching for a glass while moving our gaze.

Wolpert *et al.* assumed that action continues to be *monitored* by checking that the sensory information flowing into the system is indeed that predicted. If a mismatch between predicted and observed feedback occurs, then it may be necessary to modify the action so as to compensate. Hence if the glass were on a slight slope and had begun to slide, then the arm could extend further to allow for this. Such modifications demand a further type of process component, namely *controllers*.

Controllers involve inverse rather than forward models. They provide motor commands, receive information as to the desired end point of the movement, and work out the joint and muscle commands necessary to achieve it. Wolpert proposes that they do so using what he describes as a 'divide and conquer strategy'. (Ghahramani and Wolpert 1997; Wolpert and Kawato 1998). He assumes that multiple controllers exist, each being carefully tuned to a specific sensorimotor context. They are assumed to work together probably, on a hierarchically organized basis, with conflict-resolution processes to be used when more than one subprogramme might potentially be appropriate.

Two distinct processes are proposed. First of all, what Gibson (1979) referred to as the 'affordances' of objects are used to shape an action. Affordance is the capacity of an object to be used in a particular way. Hence, a chair would offer the affordance of sitting, but it might also afford its use as a table, or something to stand on to reach a high shelf. Affordances therefore are considerably richer and more complex than simple stimulus characteristics, or indeed objects, reflecting as they do the potentially creative use of the past experience of the organism. Consider for example the task of picking up an egg. Its shape will determine the nature of the grip, probably with the fingers surrounding the egg so as not to allow its smooth surface to lead to dropping it. Knowledge of the fragility of eggs is also likely to determine how hard the grip is, a fact that will also, of course, be determined by how heavy the subject expects the egg to be. Any discrepancies between the predicted and expected outcome of the movement will then used to modify the action. Hence, if the egg turned out to be made of some extremely heavy metal, then the grip would tighten.

The control of movement is assumed to depend upon no fewer than five separate representations. First of all, the *desired state* may be represented. Secondly, the *predicted state* will allow this to be monitored. In order to reach this state, the necessary *motor commands* must be registered within the system, and the appropriate *motor feedback* registered. Finally, the actual state of the system at any given time can be provided by *checking* the match between the motor commands and the resulting sensory feedback.

17.2.2 The role of awareness

Not all of this information is necessarily accessible to subjective awareness. The affordances offered by stimuli within the environment may well be inaccessible to conscious reflection, as may be the motor commands. Goodale *et al.* (1986; 1991) studied a pointing task in which the target occasionally jumped as the subject was responding. Subjects adapted their pointing, but appeared not to notice the adjustment they had made.

There is, of course, ample evidence that we *can* be aware of our movements, not only of movements that actually occur, but also when movement is imagined. In the case of mental practice, imagining repeatedly performing a skill such as basketball shooting can lead to an improvement in performance (Feltz and Landers 1983). Such mental practice can lead to physical changes, as when imagined leg exercises increase heart rate and respiration (Decety *et al.* 1991). Imagining the movement of a lever activates the same area of the brain as does the actual movement (Stephan *et al.* 1995). Similarly, preparing a movement and holding it in readiness involves similar areas of the brain to those involved in imaging the movement (Jeannerod 1994), with the SMA being principally involved (Stephan *et al.* 1995).

Knowledge of the current state of the motor control system is, however, often implicit. When feedback is as predicted, the subject may be oblivious of it; however, people are much more likely to note a mismatch between the desired and expected state. An intriguing instance of this occurs in the case of tickling, where a person tickled by another becomes acutely aware of a barrage of unpredictable tactile stimulation. The stimulation ceases to be unpredictable when you try to tickle yourself, when the tickling effect becomes dramatically less (Weiskrantz *et al.* 1971). Blakemore *et al.* (1998) extended Weiskrantz's work by showing that introducing a brief unpredictable delay between the movements of the self-tickler and the delivery of a tactile sensation, resulted in the return of the sense of being tickled.

Fig. 17.1 shows the motor control system proposed by Frith *et al.* Let us suppose that you are making an omelette and want to pick up an egg. Your goal would be that of cracking the egg. Let us assume therefore that the desired state of the action would lead to you clutching the egg and preparing to break it on the edge of the basin. The movement controllers would set up a chain of subactions which integrate your perception of the egg and its location with

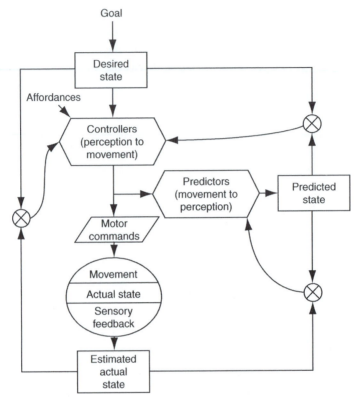

Fig. 17.1 The basic components of a motor control system based upon engineering principles that form the basis of the interpretation of the control of action proposed by Frith *et al.* (2000). Based on Frith *et al.*, Abnormalities in the awareness and control of action. In: *Philosophical Transactions of the Royal Society in London B* **355**, 1773 Figure 1. Reproduced with permission from the Royal Society.

reaching and grasping movements. These in turn would involve motor commands leading to movement that would take into account the actual state and position of your arm and hand, and that would be accompanied by ongoing sensory feedback. This in turn would be used to estimate the expected state, given performance of that action. The controllers would be influenced by an array of affordances, including the shape of the egg and its likely weight and fragility. The successful achievement of the goal would be monitored at three points, each marked on Fig. 17.1 by a cross. One of these performs a match between the desired state and the estimated actual state, which in turn is derived indirectly from the stream of motor commands combined with the sensory feedback. As the arm extends and the hand shapes to pick up the egg, the discrepancy between the actual and desired states will reduce to a point at which the goal is achieved.

Let us assume that the egg is on a slight slope and begins to roll away from you. The predicted location of your hand will no longer coincide with the desired state, with the mismatch leading you to adjust the controllers by extending the arm further, which in turn will modify the predictors to a point at which the mismatch between the desired and predicted states disappears.

A third point of comparison is included by Frith *et al.* explicitly to account for the way in which mental practice may improve performance. Suppose you are practicing basketball shots. Your imagined location and the desired state, putting the ball in the hoop, would be linked by implicitly activating the necessary motor commands, and then checking the prediction from this outflow against what would be expected on the basis of prior experience of sensory feedback. While this may not be the most rapid way to improve a skill, since adequate prediction does of course depend on extensive prior experience, there is clear evidence that it does in fact work (Feltz and Landers 1983). Given the dependence on prior experience within the model, Frith *et al.* would presumably predict no mental practice effect for novel skills.

17.2.3 Disorders of perception and action

17.2.3.1 Apraxia

Frith *et al.* illustrate the functioning of the model in terms of a range of abnormalities of perception and action control. The term *optic ataxia*, sometimes known as Balint's syndromes refers to a group of patients who have difficulty grasping objects, although they can see them perfectly clearly. The patients make a broadly appropriate movement, but execute it very clumsily. For example, the hand may fail to open in time to grasp the object, or may be placed at an inappropriate orientation or location (Jeannerod *et al.* 1994). Frith *et al.* attribute this to a failure to utilize the context to fine-tune the detailed movement, a failure at the level of affordances within their model. Interestingly, patients can sometimes use prior knowledge of an object to substitute for immediate perceptual information. For example one patient could pick up a lipstick, but not a cylinder of the same dimensions (Jeannerod *et al.* 1994). Temporary storage can also be useful in this connection. A study by Milner *et al.* (1999), contrasts two cases. Patient D.F. can grasp objects, but not recognize them. A brief delay, however, forcing reliance on memory, completely disrupts her grasping ability. Exactly the opposite pattern occurred with an optic ataxic patient, whose reaching behaviour improved after a brief delay. Presumably information in memory was more accurate than the faulty sensory information.

There are in fact many forms of apraxia in which the capacity to initiate and/or control voluntary movement is impaired. These range from difficulties in vocal articulation in which aphasic patients are unable to produce speech sounds in the correct order, to dressing apraxia where a patient seems not be able to 'remember' how to put on a pair of trousers or a shirt. They may also depend on the nature of the cue, hence some patients can obey an instruction such as 'comb your hair', but cannot imitate the action (De Renzi 1982; Shallice 1988).

Frith *et al.* contrast the case of optic ataxia, in which the affordances offered by the environment are not adequately utilized, with the case of the anarchic hand, whereby the delinquent limb performs acts that are inconsistent with the patient goals, but which are precise and appropriately attuned to the affordances of the stimulus situation. Both hands remain sensitive to input from the environment, and are able to respond to the relevant affordances, but optic ataxia patients fail because they can not use the visual information to guide action properly, while the anarchic hand patient feels disconnected from the activity of the hand because of a lack of top-down control.

17.2.3.2 The role of the Supplementary Motor Area

As Della Sala *et al.* (1994) noted, patients showing the anarchic hand sign typically have unilateral damage to the SMA, a higher order motor control area concerned with co-ordination between different movements. In contrast, the damage in apraxic cases is typically to the parietal lobe, an area involved in the ability to make accurate individual reaching and grasping movements (Passingham 1998). Mushiake *et al.* (1991) trained monkeys either to press a sequence of buttons in response to lights, or to perform the same sequence of movements from memory. The externally cued response predominantly activated primary motor cortex, whereas the remembered movement was more strongly associated with activation of SMA.

17.2.3.3 Anarchic hands and phantom limbs

It may be recalled that the anarchic hand is often associated with damage to the SMA. This symptom could be interpreted as reflecting a failure of the desired goal state to control movement of the hand and arm governed by the lesioned side of the SMA, while still being able to control the other arm. Utilization behaviour is assumed to result from a broader lack of inhibitory control, which allows the system to be driven by affordances to a much greater extent than would normally be the case. An analogous case for a normal person is provided by the slips of action that tend to occur when distracted, and hence not applying strong goal-directed inhibitory control over the system. Under these circumstances, strongly based habitual affordances may override the current goal plan to produce an unwanted action slip.

Frith *et al.* interpret the phantom limb phenomenon by assuming that neural plasticity results in a reorganization of the cortex, such that the area that previously served the absent limb is taken over by somatosensory feedback from another part of the body. Patients sometimes feel that they can move their limb because they are still sensitive to the efference of motor commands that then feed into the predicted state. If the limb is repeatedly observed not to move, then eventually this association may extinguish, resulting in the gradual disappearance of the illusory capacity to move the phantom limb.

17.2.3.4 Anosognosia

The case of patients who experience supernumerary limbs can also be explained in terms of failure to integrate information from motor commands with that from sensory feedback, resulting in two inconsistent messages regarding the location of the limb. When the limb is touched it provides further information which allows one of perceived state of affairs to dominate.

In cases of anosognosia the patient may claim to be performing some act which is impossible because of the paralysis of one of the limbs. For example, a patient with a paralyzed left arm might claim to be able to clap hands, making one-handed clapping movements and claiming that they are performing this act normally (Ramachandran 1996). This often occurs in association with unilateral neglect for the left side of space, whereby patients fail to attend to items and objects in their left visual and/or motor field. This is usually associated with right hemisphere damage. An important feature of anosognosia is the patient's belief that they can perform some act such as clapping their hands or walking up stairs, despite clear evidence of disability: the failure to either realize, or learn to recognize the disability, would seem to implicate processes beyond motor control. The fact that anosognosia may occur for other deficits such as amnesia or even blindness would also seem to implicate a more general system involved in evaluation of available evidence. Such a function is often attributed to the right frontal region (Owen 1997).

The model of action control proposed by Frith *et al.* was, of course, tied very clearly to the study of motor control. They did, however, suggest that it might be applied much more widely. A good example of this is the attempt by Frith (1989) to explain some of the strange beliefs, attributions and sometimes actions that comprise what are known as the positive symptoms of schizophrenia.

17.2.4 Hallucinations and delusions

Virtually all the perceptual and motor illusions of agency and control described so far have resulted from physical brain damage or from the manipulation of perceptual feedback in normal subjects. However, it is important not to neglect one other source of evidence of disorders of perception of agency, those found in the hallucinations and delusions which form some of the more striking positive symptoms associated with schizophrenia.

The symptoms of schizophrenia are commonly divided into two categories: positive and negative. Positive symptoms involve distortions of behaviour and experience such as delusions of persecution and feelings of grandeur, hallucinations of a visual or an auditory nature, feelings of depersonalization and delusions of agency, whereby the patient feels that he or she is being controlled by outside powers. Negative symptoms include depressed affect and impaired cognitive processing which may extend to attention and frequently also includes impaired episodic memory (Frith 1992; McKenna *et al.* 2002).

17.2.4.1 Auditory hallucinations

Schizophrenic patients often appear to experience voices 'in the head'. The voices often make critical remarks about the patient, and may form part of a more extended delusion. One patient discussed by Baddeley *et al.* (1996), for example, believed that his brain and various internal organs were being removed by 'angels.' When asked why he thought this, he referred to pains in his head and body, and when pressed further and asked why he did not attribute the pain to a normal headache, claimed that it was because of what the angels said. He also had a good angel who spoke with a somewhat different accent (BBC English).

There is evidence to suggest that auditory hallucinations are increased by presenting unstructured fluctuating noise, and reduced by the presentation of more structured stimuli such as speech or music, or by requiring the patient to read aloud (Margo *et al.* 1981). Evidence is accumulating to suggest that patients in fact generate the voices themselves, subvocally, in short via the phonological loop. Random noise provides input that can be interpreted as language, whereas structurally coherent music, speech and articulatory suppression appear to disrupt the cycle of subvocal generation, and prevent auditory hallucination (McGuire *et al.* 1993).

17.2.4.2 Thought broadcasting

Thought broadcasting, whereby a patient believes that he is being controlled by the wishes of others, interferes with immediate verbal recall, as would be expected if implicit activation of the phonological loop was involved (David and Lucas 1994). Neuroimaging studies implicate Broca's area in auditory hallucinations, again consistent with the view that they are being actively generated by the patient (McGuire *et al.* 1993). To summarize, auditory hallucinations involve an auditory quasi-verbal experience which appears to be self-generated but is perceived as external, and often interpreted as reflecting an outside agent attempting to control the patient. Frith (1992) regards them as part of a more general category of delusions of control which reflect a disorder of self-monitoring.

17.2.4.3 **Delusions of control**

These are of two kinds. In the first the patient falsely believes that he is influencing outside events. One example occurred in a patient who lived in Yorkshire, England, who was convinced that his thoughts influenced the behaviour of crowds of people in Australia. More common is the second type where the patient feels that they are being controlled by others. This may be associated with a general feeling of passivity, as with the patient who commented, 'my fingers pick up the pen, but I don't control them. What they do has nothing to do with me' (Frith 1992). The source of external control may be identified with a particular individual. 'The thoughts of Eamon Andrews (a T.V. personality) come into my mind. He treats my mind like a screen and flashes his thoughts onto it' (Frith 1992). On occasion, such thought insertion can be much more serious as when potentially harmful suggestions appear to be made by a powerful figure such as God or the Devil.

Frith (1992; Frith *et al.* 2000;) gives an account of both auditory hallucinations and delusions of agency as part of his general theory of the control of action. He suggests that they represent a failure of self-monitoring, with auditory hallucinations representing the patients' own, often disordered thought processes. These lead to subvocal verbalization, which is not recognised as self-generated because the appropriate feedback process is defective. Patients may create a delusional world in an attempt to make sense of these strange experiences. In the case of auditory hallucinations, they are typically attributed either to supernatural beings such as evil angels, or the Devil, or to powerful government agencies. Patients commonly believe their mind is controlled by advanced technological means, where the controller is often thought to be either the police or the state. In contrast to the confabulations of patients with frontal lobe damage (Baddeley and Wilson 1986), delusions appear on the whole to be stable and consistent, with deluded patients no more likely to show evidence of general executive deficit than are the non-deluded (Baddeley *et al.* 1996).

Frith suggests that the personal and social content of hallucinations and of delusions of control reflects the operation of a common neural component, which he also associates with a capacity to intuit what other people are thinking, sometimes referred to as depending on a 'theory of mind' (U. Frith 1989) This underlies the capacity to put oneself in another person's position, taking account for example of what they do and do not know, in order to predict their behaviour. It is a capacity that is particularly impaired in autism, and may be compromised even when the level of intellectual functioning is otherwise high (U. Frith 1989).

Frith proposes that the theory of mind mechanism allows a forward modelling strategy whereby we can anticipate the behaviour of others.

Neuroimaging studies suggest that reading passages that place a heavy demand on the need to put oneself in the place of others in order to comprehend them involve activation in the medial-frontal areas, areas that are also actively involved in hallucinatory and delusional activity in schizophrenia patients (Frith 1992; Silberzweig *et al.* 1995).

17.3 Implications of motor control for working memory

Granted that hallucinations, delusions and demonstrations of illusions of motor control are intrinsically interesting, and that the modification of Wolpert's model by Frith *et al.* makes a promising start on attempting to understand this puzzling array of strange phenomena, why is it of relevance to working memory? In order to answer this, we should return to Bargh and Ferguson's (2000) review of the extent to which social behaviour is largely controlled by automatic processes, and their suggestion that there is no reason to assume that consciously mediated actions are controlled in any different way.

Having demonstrated that goals can be induced implicitly, Bargh and Ferguson reject the distinction between automatic and controlled processes on the grounds that 'these control processes are themselves being controlled by determined, automatically operating goal structures' (Bargh and Ferguson 2000, p. 939). They further suggest that in a standard psychological experiment, 'the experimental situation requires the participants to delegate to the experimenter, control over what they do' (Bargh and Ferguson 2000, p. 393), concluding that the control here is still external. Even when subjects perform concrete actions and create plans for future action, it is suggested that their behaviour can be defined as 'delegation of control to the environment', with the novel and non-habitual behaviours being enacted automatically and non-consciously when the designated environmental event cue occurs (Gollwitzer 1993, p. 174). Bargh and Ferguson do not deny the potential complexity of the underlying mechanisms, but by emphasizing implicit processes and external stimulus control as representing the whole of behaviour, their review encourages a simplistic stimulus-bound view of action control, a view that is emphasized by their stressing of automaticity and their frequent use of the terms control and determinism.

I would suggest that the richness and complexity of concepts and mechanisms needed to give an account of simple reaching and grasping behaviour emphasizes the importance of resisting the temptation to place too much emphasis on purely automatic processes. So what lessons might we learn from motor behaviour that might usefully be applied to the more general executive control of behaviour?

1 *Complexity.* The range of deficits and delusions described make it clear that the system involved is highly complex and capable of breaking down at

many points, ranging from the fine-tuning of movement in optic ataxia, through to failure to acknowledge gross motor deficit in anosognosia.

2 *Control is Multilevel.* Performance can break down at any of a range of different levels, from a failure to adequately tune receptors in ataxia, through perceptual disorders, where patients may believe they have an additional limb, to blindsight where, despite sufficient information for the hand to adopt an appropriate shape, this information cannot be used to plan behaviour because it is not available to conscious awareness.

3 *Interaction Between Components.* Under normal conditions, the various components work together so efficiently that the need for coordination is rarely obvious. It becomes obvious in the many cases of agnosia, where, depending on the location of the lesion, problems may occur in identifying an object but not in reaching for it or the opposite, adequate reaching and failure to identify. In other cases patients may be capable of imitating an action but not making it in response to a request, while others can respond to environmental stimuli, but not imitate.

4 *The Importance of Awareness.* This is the point at which the data are perhaps most strongly at odds with the proposals of Bargh and Ferguson. As Frith *et al.* observe, it seems impossible to give a reasonable account of the data without considering not only the presence or absence of awareness, but also its characteristics. A patient with the anarchic hand sign may be only too aware of the antics of the hand that cannot be controlled, leading to huge embarrassment. It is not easy to give an account of the control of both the normal and anarchic hand without assuming different levels of control with differential access to conscious awareness.

5 *The Sense of Agency is not Unitary.* Patients with the anarchic hand sign are aware of the action of both hands, but their sense of agency, of being able to control what is happening, is present for one but not the other, although both may simultaneously be performing coherent actions, which may indeed be in direct conflict.

The Frith *et al.* model is at an early state of development, but as they suggest, provides a possible interpretation of executive control more generally. It captures a number of important features of the data, including its complexity and the need for control at a number of different levels. The fact that the authors found it necessary to make strong assumptions about the role of awareness is an important corrective to the emphasis on automaticity in much of the social psychology literature. The willingness to assume that awareness itself need not be simple and unitary is also a potentially important aspect of the model. Its recognition of the importance of habits and automatic processes, and its stress on the importance of inhibitory processes for action control are, of course, consistent with the Norman and Shallice (1986) SAS model of action control that has featured in our own attempts to model the central executive component of working memory.

17.4 **Conclusions**

It is clear that the control of action is complex and operates at a range of different levels. Does that present a problem for Bargh and Ferguson's determinist position? They would surely accept the complexity of control, that evolution has shaped our control processes effectively, and that brain damage or illness might interfere with their smooth running. In my view, the crucial problem for their unitary implicit control view is encapsulated in the case of the Della Sala's anarchic hand patient. Both her 'good' right hand and her 'mischievous' fishbone-stealing left hand are well controlled, in that both can use environmental cues to accurately grasp food and bring it to her mouth. However, only the right hand appears to be governed by integrated high-level goals that are accessible to reflection, in short to be under conscious control.

Chapter 18

Working memory in context

Life, the universe and everything

I began this book about five years ago. I knew there was no chance of doing a thorough review of the huge literature that has accumulated since my 1986 book, but planned to produce an extended essay that summarized and justified my own current views on working memory, and placed them in a broader context. As the book progressed, it became clear that I needed to go back to the literature and check the half-remembered evidence, which in turn demanded wider reading, prompting further thoughts on the issues, and soon making it clear that considerably more than an extended essay was involved.

In order to place the concept of working memory in a broader context, I began to read more widely, to see new links with fields such as social psychology and clinical psychology, and to realize that many of the ideas that were developing had powerful echoes of classic questions within the philosophy of mind. I began my career with a strong interest in philosophy; indeed I considered pursuing a degree in philosophy, later opting for psychology on the grounds that it might be hard to earn a living as a philosopher. Furthermore, philosophy in Britain was becoming increasingly dominated by linguistic analysis under the influence of Wittgenstein in Cambridge and Austin in Oxford, an approach that I found increasingly sterile. Consequently, I came to regard philosophy, or at least the philosophy of mind, as little more than a game of armchair psychology played under rather sterile linguistic rules.

In recent years, it has become increasingly clear to me that my work, and that of others within cognitive science, is implicitly based on a range of philosophical assumptions that are nonetheless influential for being unconscious. In my own case, the issue surfaced most clearly with the question of the extent to which conscious awareness plays a role in visuospatial imagery (Baddeley 1993; Baddeley and Andrade 1998). As part of my attempt to re-educate myself, I decided to reread a book by Magee (1987), based on a series of television interviews in which distinguished contemporary philosophers were invited to explain and discuss the work of a classic philosopher or school. This rekindled my enthusiasm and surprised me with the number of contemporary issues of cognitive neuroscience that are prefigured in the work of our philosophical forefathers. I was also intrigued to discover how sympathetic I found certain views, perhaps unsurprisingly British Associationists, notably Locke and Hume, and how unsympathetic I found other approaches such as those of Hegel and Sartre. There were also a few surprises, including a very nice argument for the importance of implicit knowledge presented by Heidegger.

On reflection, I should probably not have been so surprised, given that the classic philosophy of mind was presumably based on reasoning about evidence based on observation and self-observation, a major source of my own ideas, and I assume of those of many of my colleagues. The difference, of course, is that we now have a much wider range of objective techniques that allow our intuitions to be tested empirically, together with a richer and more complex set of conceptual tools for their theoretical development. In this final chapter therefore I would like to indulge my old interest in philosophy, speculating about the place of working memory from an evolutionary viewpoint and briefly discussing some of the points at which the philosophy of mind and the empirical study of working memory intersect each other.

18.1 **An evolutionary perspective**

Evolutionary approaches to psychology are currently both fashionable and controversial. Fashionable because they place psychology within a broader biological context, and, by suggesting the potential evolutionary advantage or disadvantage of a particular function or behaviour, can give clues as to new ways of tackling old problems. In my own case, for example, a question from an old friend about the possible evolutionary value of the phonological loop led directly to the very productive line of research on the loop as a language acquisition device (see Chapter 2). I continue to find an evolutionary framework fruitful, as the chapter on depression indicates, although it is of course too soon to know whether my own evolutionary speculation will in fact prove to be any more productive than other attempts to explain depression.

Evolutionary explanations, though, tend to be controversial, often derided as 'Just so stories' because they resemble the charming children's tales by Rudyard Kipling about how the elephant got its trunk, and the leopard its spots. In short, such explanations are criticized as pure speculation given a spurious air of respectability by being linked to evolutionary theory. One problem with such explanations is that they tend to be very hard to test. Hence, although I am intrigued by the suggestion from the paleoanthropologists Coolridge and Wynn (2001; 2004) that the possession of working memory was the crucial advantage held by *Homo sapiens* over Neanderthal man, I find it very hard to see how this could be adequately tested.

There is, however, a third possible use for evolutionary explanations, which is to provide a useful framework for integrating and summarizing a field. This is the purpose of the next section, which attempts to place working memory in its cognitive context by asking what biological function it serves within a broad evolutionary framework. As a rhetorical device, I propose the following question. If you were to design an organism such as *Homo sapiens*, able to operate within a complex changing physical environment, which cognitive capacities would you require and why? My purpose here is not to advocate intelligent creation, but rather to indulge in some very general reverse engineering, to simply consider the mind in the context of the problems it would presumably need to solve in the process of evolution.

One way of designing our new organism would be to choose an ecological niche and carefully engineer it to cope within those circumstances. This clearly has been a very successful evolutionary strategy in the case of sharks, jellyfish and many insects that have flourished far longer than we have. Provided the niche remains, then the organism is likely to continue to flourish. The opposite strategy seems to have evolved in the case of *Homo sapiens*, who appears to be built for flexibility, able to adapt to a wide range of rapidly changing environments by using non-evolutionary solutions, such as those offered by the development of language and the capacity to create tools and elaborate them into complex machines. Our task is to consider, in the broadest terms, what kind of system might be able to achieve this.

If our organism is able to adapt flexibly to a changing world, then it would need to perceive that world. We clearly do that through a series of sensory channels such as vision, touch and hearing. Each comprises other sub-channels: in the case of vision, for example, separate streams of information regarding shape colour, movement and location.

As a naive realist, I assume that such sensory channels are stimulated by objects, and that it is helpful in coping with the world to be able to re-assemble data from the various channels into representations of coherent objects. As discussed in Chapter 8, I assume that the episodic buffer component of working memory provides the medium within which such complex stimuli are reassembled and integrated with knowledge from other sources, and made available to conscious awareness.

If our organism is to make full use of the information available, then some form of learning is needed. Probably the simplest way to achieve this is through the gradual accumulation of evidence, capitalizing on the fact the world is a broadly stable place, in terms of its basic perceptual characteristics. Implicit learning mechanisms provide an excellent and economical basis for such knowledge accumulation, typically with a minimal involvement of working memory (Baddeley 1998, Chapters 19 and 20; Schacter 1994; Squire 1992).

However, such a system is much less effective at dealing with an environmental change, as in the case of a travel route that has been safe for many years, but which was seen on the last trip to have been occupied by a fierce enemy. Simply averaging all the prior information available would result in disaster, whereas the capacity to remember this one occasion will not only lead to avoidance of an immediate threat, but would also allow the hypothesis to be formed that this may just have been a single, atypical event. This hypothesis could be carefully tested and the result used in future planning. This whole process, of course, requires episodic memory, the capacity to bind an experience to its temporal and physical context, to locate that experience in time and place (Baddeley *et al.* 2002b; Tulving 1989). Working memory is necessary for encoding such episodic memories, and while less clearly involved in retrieval, almost certainly plays a part in the subsequent evaluation of information retrieved (Baddeley *et al.* 1984; Craik *et al.* 1996; Naveh-Benjamin *et al.* 2000).

So far, our organism can perceive the world, and learn about it, and can remember particular incidents, but cannot act. This will obviously require a motor system and a method of control. Some of this control may be automatic, as when our eyes automatically follow a moving target or when our breathing responds to the level of carbon dioxide in our lungs. However, if we are to progress from simple reaction to planful action, then we need a device for planning and a system for holding and manipulating our plans. Planning essentially involves predicting what will happen. An obvious way to do this is to simulate an occasion that has occurred in the past. Such simulation requires a storage system with links to both perception and LTM – in short, a working memory. If we need a number of possible plans, then it is desirable to be able to step back and reflect on the alternatives, a process underpinned by the combined storage and reflective capacity of working memory, operating through the medium of consciousness.

Working memory therefore sits at the interface between perception and action, between learning and attention, substantially increasing the flexibility of the organism. Such an account might suggest, to use the stage metaphor proposed by Baars (1997), that working memory is not just the principal actor, but the whole show. As I hope the last few chapters have demonstrated, I believe this to be far from the case. Working memory storage capacity is small and consciously mediated action tends to be slow. Wherever possible, it is sensible to have our organism operating automatically, with our limited capacity working memory performing an overall watching brief and stepping in whenever this hugely varied and complex set of automatic processes appears to be failing, either through informational overload, through the demand for novel processes, or for future planning.

I suggest therefore that some form of working memory would provide an extremely useful piece of multipurpose equipment for our hypothetical biologically evolved organism. The multicomponent model represents one approach to conceptualizing such equipment.

18.2 Some philosophical implications

18.2.1 Consciousness

As the book developed, it became increasingly clear that my ideas were encroaching on three traditional areas of the philosophy of mind: the question of consciousness, the nature of the self and the problem of free will. The issue of consciousness has already been discussed in Chapter 16, based on my view that consciousness has evolved as a means of tackling certain problems, particularly: (1) binding information from the senses into integrated representations, (2) binding these in turn with information from long-term memory, and (3) serving as a global workspace. I was groping towards such a view when I began to read the work of Baars more extensively (Baars 1997; 2002a; b), and came across the excellent paper by Dehaene and Naccache (2001), work I have used extensively in Chapter 13. It is, however, perhaps worth returning to one point that appears to have troubled some cognitive scientists with an interest in the question of consciousness, including my late colleague at the Center for Advanced Studies at Stanford, Jeffrey Gray (Gray 2004). That is the question of *qualia*, the philosophical term for sensory phenomenological experience, for example the particular redness of a rose or tang of Stilton cheese.

I must confess that I differ from Gray and many others in that I see no reason for according qualia a special status. My own views are much closer to the suggestion by Dehaene and Naccache that

> the contents of perceptual awareness are complex, dynamic, multi-faceted neural states that cannot be memorized or transmitted to others in their entirety. These biological properties seem potentially capable of substantiating philosophers' intuitions about the 'qualia' of conscious experience, although considerable neuroscientific research will be needed before they are thoroughly understood.

> (Dehaene and Naccahe 2001, p. 30)

In short, qualia are simply one feature of a biological environment. Not everyone, of course, takes this view (Gray 2004).

The study of the phenomenological aspects of conscious awareness is a field in which neuroimaging is likely to be particularly productive. If one can identify a particular pattern of objectively observed activation that accompanies the subjective report of a particular percept, and show that this holds true across a range of subjects, then I would regard it as plausible to hypothesize that those subjects were encountering broadly equivalent experiences. One can then use that activation pattern as evidence of the presence or absence of such an experience in a new subject.

A good example of this occurs in the case of binocular rivalry in which one stimulus, for example a table, is presented to one eye, and another, perhaps a fish, to the other. Subjects typically report a fluctuation between seeing the table or the fish, but not both. When human subjects are tested in neuroimaging studies they show a very similar pattern of inferotemporal activation for a single percept and for the dominant percept in a rivalry situation (Tong *et al.* 1998). However, when subjects indicate a switch, extensive additional frontal activation occurs (Lumer *et al.* 1998). A similar paradigm can be used in recording from the brain of awake monkeys who are trained to make a different response to each of two rivalrous patterns. While lower level areas of visual processing (V_1–V_5) respond equivalently to either stimulus, inferotemporal cortex responds differentially with two patterns of activation, one associated with each of the two perceptual experiences that were behaviourally 'reported' (Leopold and Logothetis 1999).

Another example of the use of neurophysiological evidence to throw light on phenomenological concerns the phenomenologically based distinction made in studies of recognition between *remembering* something and *knowing* it. Remembering is associated with the subjective 're-experiencing' of the event, typically accompanied by the capacity to recollect associated detail, in contrast to knowing that an event has occurred, with an absence of this feeling of 'mental time travel' (Tulving 1989; Gardiner 2001). In studying Jon, a young man who has an atypical amnesia in which his recall is impaired but recognition relatively preserved, we noted that he appeared not to be able to use the 'remember' decision correctly (Baddeley *et al.* 2001c). He did not appear to have access to recollective experience, and seemed to be using the term simply to indicate his degree of confidence in the correctness of his response.

Subsequent research by Düzel *et al.* (2001), using an evoked response technique, supported this conclusion. Jon showed clear evidence of the pattern of activation typically associated with a 'know' response in normal subjects, with no evidence of the 'remember' pattern. Finally, a PET study by Maguire *et al.* (2001) managed to identify one or two autobiographical events that did evoke the associated recollections characteristic of the experience of 'remembering'. These, but no other memories, were associated with the characteristic 'remember' activation pattern. I suspect that, as we learn more about the patterns of activation associated with different memorial experiences, neuroimaging will provide an increasingly common tool for the analysis of the complex phenomenologically based processes underlying human memory.

A question that typically crops up whenever one discusses approaches to consciousness is that of whether animals are conscious, and if so could machines be conscious? I regard the case of animals as conceptually relatively straightforward. I do not regard consciousness as a simple unitary function, but rather as a multicomponent biological solution to a set of problems. It seems likely that some animals at least are likely to be conscious in the sense of having some kind of perceptual binding system, an episodic buffer in which sensory information can be integrated and represented. It may well be the case that the system also allows integration of information from a number of different senses; this would certainly be suggested by the growing evidence that animals may have episodic memory, in the sense of integrated memories concerning 'what', the 'where' and the 'when' of an episode which can be utilized to act in a constructive and purposeful way (see Clayton *et al.* 2002 for a discussion of this issue). I think that the capacity for reflexive consciousness is less likely to be prevalent in the animal kingdom, although I would accept the spot-on-the-face paradigm as prima facie evidence for some such capability in certain non-human primates. This task involves placing a small adhesive spot on the face of the subject, who is then allowed to look at a mirror. Most animals including primates appear not to 'realize' that it is on their own face, but some apes consistently appear to do so and immediately remove it (Gallup 1970).

What about machines? Here I suspect that certain defined aspects of consciousness such as the capacity to integrate information from a number of different sources, to function as a global workspace, and possibly to function reflexively may well be achievable by machines. I would have doubts, however, about claiming this is consciousness, since I suspect consciousness will also involve other functions. Even if these further tests were achieved, it would not necessarily mean that the machine would have a consciousness that was just like our own, since functions will vary according to the manner in which they are achieved. Kasparov and Big Blue may both be formidable chess players, but the way in which their results are achieved is very different. But could machines ever be conscious in the way that we normally understand the term? Given that I regard the human brain as a kind of machine, albeit a machine of enormous subtlety and complexity, it would seem arrogant and/or inconsistent to deny the possibility that the same biological problem might be solved in a similar way, but using hardware in place of the 'wetware' that nature has evolved. But it seems unlikely to happen in the near future.

18.2.2 The self

What is the link between consciousness and action? In Chapter 16, I agreed with Baars that the link was provided by the self. This complex and slippery concept was, like consciousness, barred from cognitive psychology for many years, before making a strong recovery in social psychology (Baumeister 1998) and a somewhat more tentative return to the study of cognition via theories of autobiographical memory (Conway 2002), and through the efforts of Ulrich Neisser, whose classic text (Neisser 1967) played a crucial role in what subsequently has become known as the cognitive revolution. Neisser organized a series of workshops on different aspects of the self including one on 'The remembering self' (Neisser and Fivush 1994). For present purposes, we will limit discussion to the role of the self in working memory, focusing particularly on the initiation and control of action.

For this purpose we accept the distinction proposed by Damasio (2000) between the *core self* and the *autobiographical self*. The core self is reflected in core consciousness, a multilevel stream of conscious input, both perceptually and self-generated, which in the multicomponent working memory framework would be identified with the episodic buffer. As is the case for the episodic buffer, Damasio assumes that core consciousness is crucially dependent on a number of separable sources. Some of these are physiologically based, and are referred to by Damasio as the *proto self*.

The core self is capable of acting and responding to its own actions. We may pinch ourselves to ensure that we are really experiencing a situation in which our actions and percepts are linked. As we saw in Chapter 17, when our actions and the feedback are dissociated we may become disorientated, as in the case of hemiplegic patients, who may deny ownership of a paralyzed arm, or deny the action of an hand that appears not to be under the conscious control of the patient as in the anarchic hand sign (see Chapter 17).

Within the working memory model, the capacity to act directly and reflexively would be likely to involve considerably more than the episodic buffer. It would certainly require the executive control capacities of the central executive, and on occasion probably also involve the phonological and visuospatial subsystems. The latter point is illustrated in the case of thought insertion in schizophrenia, where the patient believes that voices are commenting on him and possibly instructing him in certain actions, a process that appears to involve subvocalization and to implicate the phonological loop as well as executive processes (see Chapter 17).

Clearly, the self is much more than a simple action control system. Actions are likely to be based on the complex, historically based conglomerations of habits, beliefs and attitudes that comprises the autobiographical self. This system is stable but continuously developing and changing, and is heavily dependent on autobiographical memory. It is stored implicitly, but, as with semantic and episodic memory more generally, its contents and their products are available to conscious reflection.

The autobiographical self is not a simple unitary system, but can better be regarded as reflecting multiple selves, a view developed by Goffman (1959) in his concept of roles. For example, Mary may be both a mother and a daughter, a wife and a female friend, a business woman and a golfer, appearing somewhat differently in each of these roles. Such roles can of course conflict. Should she visit her mother's sick bed, or attend her daughter's school sports? When playing golf with her boss, how aggressive should she be? Life is of course easier if the various roles cohere, and we tend to value people who show 'integrity' (although possibly not elect them to high political office). In its extreme form, a lack of coherence can produce pathological states such as was fictionally illustrated by Robert Louis Stevenson's account of Dr Jekyll and Mr Hyde. This was based on the true story of Dean Brodie, an apparently eminently respectable inhabitant of Edinburgh who was simultaneously a manipulative psychopathic criminal. We shall return to the multiplicity of self in the next section, but before doing so should, I think, mention at least one other concept of the self, namely the *enacted self* (Baddeley 1994), the self as perceived by others.

We have previously discussed the self as a purely intrapersonal concept. However the theatrical analogy implied by Goffman's concept of roles potentially at least implies an audience, which may or may not perceive the role in the same way as the actor. Indeed in the case of politicians, I suspect that they may well regard appearance as more important than the reality. Furthermore, our own view of ourselves often does not coincide with that of others (see Chapter 13). Their views are inevitably based on evaluating our actions, including what we say, a less rich but perhaps a more reliable source of evidence than our self-interested introspections.

It would be a mistake however to over-emphasize the discrepancy between our self-perception and the view of others. Indeed, for some purposes we may well accept the judgement of others as more valid than our own. An expert's view of a golf swing for example may provide crucial information that is not directly available to the golfer. However, the perception of ourselves by others goes much deeper than this, as reflected in the case of R.J., a patient with bilateral frontal lobe damage who was left densely amnesic, inclined to confabulation but charming and amusing (Baddeley and Wilson 1988). When we retested him some months later he had suffered a small stroke. This additional trauma had tragically transformed him into a pathetic and incoherent figure, hardly able to put a together a single integrated sentence. When we spoke to his wife she pointed out that it was late in the day and he was tired and that sometimes, first thing in the morning, the old R.J. reappeared. It was as if the relatively small amount of additional brain damage had led to a condition in which he was no longer capable of holding together the multiple components that made up his self. In the brief periods when he had sufficient energy to hold together the components, then his enacted self resurfaced and was recognizable (Baddeley 1994).

Had R.J. simply lost his autobiographical memory? I suggest not; his initial head injury severely impaired his autobiographical memory, without apparently changing his personality as judged by his wife. Furthermore, one of the major problems following head injury is not the associated retrograde amnesia, but the feelings of a spouse that the patient has changed, and that 'this is not the person I married'. This is typically felt by the spouse, not the patient, suggesting a difference in the enacted self rather than the autobiographical self. The validity of self-report does of course lead directly on to the study of personality, a topic that lies beyond our present remit.

18.2.3 Action and free will

So, given consciousness and a multilevel self, how is this converted into action? The answer I propose is implicit in much that I have already written. In line with the distinction initially made by Norman and Shallice (1986), I suggest that an enormous amount of our activity is controlled automatically on the basis of environmental cues, existing habits and schemata, supplemented when necessary by automatic conflict resolution processes. However, while the presence of an environmental cue and a habit might explain why we do one thing rather than another, why should we do anything at all? Once again I suggest that we clearly need to reintroduce concepts of energy and motivation into cognitive psychology.

However, even if we do assume a rudimentary theory of motivation, that still leaves us with the question of how the non-habitual decision mechanism, the central executive or supervisory attentional system might operate. The fact that it does operate is amply illustrated by Chapter 17 in which it is clear that even the simple act of reaching and grasping may be controlled at a number of different and potentially incompatible levels, resulting in illusionary visual cues being overridden by the motor system, and in the case of the anarchic hand sign, the action of the consciously controlled hand being cancelled by the unconscious intervention of the other hand.

The fact that an apparently simple action may be controlled at several different levels is well illustrated by the act of breathing. Clearly breathing can operate at a non-conscious level, otherwise we would die of asphyxia when we went to sleep. One level of control is exercised automatically by the level of carbon dioxide in the lungs, but this can be overridden as when snorkelling, when it is important to resist the temptation to breath underwater, or indeed after surfacing, until the water has first been expelled from the snorkel. As the nineteenth-century neurologist Hughlings Jackson pointed out, there appears to be a hierarchy of control systems, with the more basic and automatic potentially being overruled by a higher system (Kennard and Swash 1989). There is of course a limit to this; we do not appear to be able to commit suicide by holding our breath since unconsciousness intervenes, and the automatic control of breathing will resume. Given the multilevel control of an action as apparently simple as breathing, we should not make the mistake of expecting choices that are sufficiently complex as to require the SAS to reflect the running off of a simple causal chain.

As described in Chapter 15, I am happy to pursue the line proposed initially by Hume (1978), further explored by Lewin (1951) and reintroduced by Damasio (1994), namely that the world is imbued with positive and negative valences, and that action involves steering a way through this array in a way that will maximize positive and minimize negative consequences. This of course raises the question of the timescale over which valences are averaged. Eating that chocolate now might give me immediate pleasure, but it might also produce longer-term guilt because I believe that I need to cut down the amount I am eating to preserve my long-term health. How do I decide whether to eat the piece of chocolate? Presumably I find some means of resolving the conflicting incentives, otherwise I would remain locked in stasis until like Buridan's ass, caught equidistant between two piles of hay, I would starve. I suspect in this situation a relatively basic conflict resolution algorithm would kick in, and I would find that while deep in contemplation, I had eaten the chocolate.

Suppose we consider instead the sadly topical case of a suicide bomber whose action, namely killing himself, might appear to be irrational. This is not so of course if he believes that his action will lead to paradise, and is prepared to tolerate the odium of killing large numbers of innocent people in order to gain this goal. Like many of our long-term goals, these are based on socially acquired beliefs, no doubt reinforced by being part of tightly knit group who share the same belief system.

An act based on the promise of paradise is, of course, hardly altruistic. There are however situations in which behaviour does appear to be altruistic, in the sense of not leading to the immediate or long-term benefit of the individual, and indeed perhaps leading to their annihilation. Parents will defend offspring to the death in a number of animal species, including I assume our own.

Furthermore, there is no reason to suspect that believing in an afterlife is a prerequisite for a soldier risking his life either in battle, or in a less aggressive area of danger such as bomb disposal or minefield clearance. These examples suggest that beliefs and social constructions, rightly or wrongly, can be an enormously powerful determinant of behaviour. In suggesting that people have free will, I am proposing that their actions are potentially determined by the balance of beliefs, needs, attitudes and habits that comprises their personal identity, the self. The fact that someone may have been induced to accept profoundly antisocial beliefs does not of course mean that they lack free will.

The concept of free will assumes the capacity to control one's actions. What of the case in which control is compromised in some way? Take the case that occurred recently of a driver towing a trailer along a motorway early one morning. Weather conditions were bad and he had had little sleep. His vehicle suddenly left the road just at a point where the road verged on a railway line. It plunged over the edge into the path of an ongoing passenger train, resulting in several deaths. Was he culpable? A court decided yes, given that he had been driving in an unfit state, and was alleged to have fallen asleep, and had done so under particularly dangerous conditions. His level of responsibility however is very different from what have been the case had he intentionally conducted such an act, a fact that was presumably reflected in the subsequent sentence.

What if the person is of 'unsound mind', a term used in Britain at a time when a conviction for first-degree murder would lead to hanging, provided the prisoner was regarded as 'responsible for his actions'. Does an insane assassin have free will? Let us suppose that he assumed his victim was the devil incarnate and that he was performing an honourable act in ridding the world of this fiend. In this case, I would argue that the murderer was still free to choose, but did so under the guidance of a set of highly dysfunctional and dangerous personal beliefs which certainly and obviously demand that society take action. What should happen next will reflect the beliefs that characterize the society passing judgement, its need to protect its citizens, together with society's propensity to categorize people as wicked or good, and to demand retribution.

What has all this to do with working memory? I suggest that implicit in our whole legal system is the issue of how and why actions occur, and that concepts such as 'irresistible impulse', and 'of sound mind' simply highlight this fact. A good theory that covers the role of working memory in thought and action will not solve our ethical problems, but it may help clarify our thinking.

18.2.4 Three wishes

As an experimental psychologist, a pragmatic empiricist, it feels strange to end on a note of amateur philosophical speculation. Having gone beyond just-so stories to contemplation of Life, the Universe and Everything (Adams1979), what next? How about the staple element of many traditional fairy stories, three wishes? What would my three wishes for the future of working memory be? Here they are: one is a rather modest plea, the second an unlikely equipment request, and the third, more grandiose, though perhaps more likely to be achieved.

18.2.5 Strategy

People are enormously flexible, and when confronted by tricky new problems, as in the typical psychology experiment, will seek out a range of solutions. Within cognitive psychology, this problem is confronted by systematically generating and testing a range of possible ways in which the subject might have produced the observed result without reliance on the system or processes assumed by the theory. In studies that use the exciting new techniques of neuroimaging to study cognition, it is currently simply too expensive to require a range of studies. So I wish we would try to rule out these alternative strategies before running the crucial studies, rather than simply relying on techniques that others have used and attributed to that function.

In the absence of the capacity to perform multiple neuroimaging experiments, it is essential that we develop better routine measures of what kind of strategy a subject is using. For example, it ought not to prove too difficult to decide whether the phonological loop is being used in a given task or not. So could we explore the basic question of how to use neuroimaging to detect strategies?

18.2.6 Cheap neuroimaging

Neuroimaging provides an invaluable tool for understanding human cognition, a tool that is continually being refined. Unfortunately however, it is an expensive tool, which leads to two problems. The first is that described above, namely that it is simply too expensive to produce watertight studies. Given the rapid rate of technological advance, I am sure that cheaper neuroimaging methods will appear. Unfortunately however, there are institutional pressures to obtain ever larger grants with the result that we are rewarded for making research ever more expensive, to become part of 'big science'. The pursuit of increasingly sophisticated and informative methods is clearly crucial to the development of neuroscience. Equally important, however, is the delivery of low-cost methods that can routinely be used to increase the reliability and validity of existing methodologies. So could I have a simple but robust inexpensive neuroimaging technique?

18.2.7 Motivation

As will become clear by now, I think the development of cognitive psychology as an information-processing discipline has been hugely productive. The other two domains of *orectic* and *conative* psychology, the study of emotions and the will, have, as discussed in Chapters 14 and 15, been comparatively neglected. If we are to continue to advance, it is clearly important to go beyond cognition and try to understand not only how behaviour is controlled, but why.

Why do we do anything? We need a theory of mental and physical energy, which should include an understanding of the individual differences that occur. Why do some people have so much more energy than others? Finally, we need to understand its pathology, including the physical and psychological determinants of its failure, and how these can be reversed.

18.3 Epilogue

What is the link between these rather airy speculations on life, the universe and everything, and our starting point, the rather more mundane study of the role of phonological similarity in recalling strings of consonants? The answer at one level is a year spent inhaling the heady vapours of Bay Area California where the Center for Advanced Study supplied both stimulating colleagues and time to think, though not to finish writing. At the end of my five-year journey, I do at least feel convinced that there is a link from the detailed experiments to the speculative conclusions. The insights and discoveries made during my year turned out to be considerably less original than they felt at the time. At least two colleagues at the Center for Advanced Study, for example, appeared to emerge with broadly similar ideas. I suspect we were all carried along by the same zeitgeist, concluding that a range of questions that had previously seemed limited to the domain of philosophy were in principle solvable and moreover were currently being tackled with some success by cognitive psychology and cognitive neuroscience.

I am happy to say that I remain convinced that the concept of working memory is playing a useful role in this development. Of course my particular multicomponent approach to working memory is by no means the only model available. It does, however, have a number of strengths. The basic model is simple, easy to understand and comes with a range of well-tried experimental techniques that have proved readily applicable across a wide range of fields, both basic and applied. It is a theory that has stayed close to the data. This has the disadvantage of making it less theoretically exciting than more daring speculations, but has allowed it to develop organically in a way that remains highly productive after over 30 years of empirical and theoretical development.

The multicomponent model has been criticized by a range of my younger colleagues for its lack of clear predictions (Andrade 2001), and by others for its reliance on simplistic reification of complex issues (Macken and Jones 2003: Parkin 1998). I am happy to accept these criticisms as an inevitable cost of the theoretical style I have adopted. The important feature of such homuncular concepts as the central executive and the episodic buffer is that they encapsulate important questions within a relatively simple conceptual framework. The success of such concepts ultimately depends on their capacity to stimulate empirical research and organize the resulting data.

Where the problems are as difficult as those facing the cognitive psychologist, I believe we must be prepared to accept steady if unspectacular progress, at the same time being alert to the possibility of the development of new techniques that may allow us to tackle the problems that were previously intractable. Cognitive psychology has benefited from a number of such developments during my own research career, the most important of which I regard as the adoption of the computer metaphor that underpins the so-called cognitive revolution (Broadbent 1958; Craik 1943; 1948; Neisser 1967). This was followed by a range of exciting conceptual breakthroughs, although the degree of excitement engendered does not always predict the magnitude of the contribution.

Transformational grammar (Chomsky 1957), mathematical modelling, Artificial Intelligence and the application of connectionism and parallel distributing processing models have all made, and continue to make, a real contribution to our understanding of the complexities of human cognition. In each case, novel ideas have excited the field and produced a quantum change. It seems likely that neuroimaging will add a powerful new tool to the neuroscientist's technical locker. Such a tool is only as good as its user however, making it important to have sound experimental methodology and a well-grounded theoretical framework that can guide the development of such techniques, and focus them on important and tractable questions. The multi-component theory of working memory has served this function in the past. I trust that it will continue to do so in the future.

References

Aaronson, D. (1968). Temporal course of perception in an immediate recall task. *Journal of Experimental Psychology*, **76**, 129–40.

Abrahamson, L. Y., Seligman, M. E. P. and Teasdale, J. D. (1978). Learned helplessness in humans: critique and reformulation. *Journal of Abnormal Psychology*, **87**, 49–74.

Adams, A. M. and Gathercole, S. E. (1996). Phonological working memory and spoken language development in young children. *Quarterly Journal of Experimental Psychology*, **49A**, 216–23.

Adams, A.-M. and Gathercole, S. E. (1995). Phonological working memory and speech production in preschool children. *Journal of Hearing and Speech Research*, **38**, 403–14.

Adams, D. (1979). *The hitchhikers guide to the galaxy*. London: Pan.

Alberoni, M., Baddeley, A. D., Della Sala, S., Logie, R. H. and Spinnler, H. (1992). Keeping track of conversation: impairments in Alzheimer's disease. *International Journal of Geriatric Psychiatry*, **7**, 639–46.

Alderman, N. (1996). Central executive deficit and response to operant conditioning methods. *Neuropsychological Rehabilitation*, **6**, 161–86.

Allen, R., Baddeley, A. D. and Hitch, G. J. (2006). Is the binding of visual features in working memory resource-demanding? *Journal of Experimental Psychology: General*, **135**, 298–313.

Alloway, T. P., Gathercole, S. E. and Pickering, S. J. (2006). Verbal and visuospatial short-term and working memory in children: Are they separable? *Child Development*, **77**, 1698–1716.

Allport, A., Styles, E. A. and Hsieh, S. (1994). Shifting attentional set: Exploring the dynamic control of tasks. In *Attention and Performance XV* (C. Umilta and M. Moscovitch eds), pp. 421–62). Cambridge, MA: MIT Press.

Allport, D. A. (1984). Auditory-verbal short-term memory and conduction aphasia. In *Attention and performance X: control of language processes* (H. B. D. G. Bouwhuis ed.), pp. 313–26). London: Lawrence Erlbaum.

Allport, D. A., Antonis, B. and Reynolds, P. (1972). On the division of attention: a disproof of the single channel hypothesis. *Quarterly Journal of Experimental Psychology*, **24**, 225–35.

Anderson, M. C. and Bjork, R. A. (1994). Mechanisms of inhibition in long-term memory: A new taxonomy. In *Inhibitory processes in attention, memory and language* (D. Dagenbach and T. H. Carr eds), pp. 265–325). San Diego, CA: Academic Press.

Anderson, M. C., Bjork, E. L. and Bjork, R. A. (2000). Retrieval-induced forgetting: evidence for a recall-specific mechanism. *Psychonomic Bulletin and Review*, **7(3)**, 522–30.

Andrade, J. (1995). Learning during anaesthesia: A review. *British Journal of Psychology*, **86(4)**, 479–506.

Andrade, J. (2001). *Working memory in perspective*. Hove: Psychology Press.

Andrade, J. (2005). Does memory priming during anaesthesia matter. *Anesthesiology*, **103**, 919–20.

Andrade, J., Kavanagh, D. and Baddeley, A. (1997). Eye-movements and visual imagery: A working memory approach to the treatment of post-traumatic stress disorder. *British Journal of Clinical Psychology*, **35**, 209–23.

Andrade, J. and Meudell, P. R. (1993). Is spatial information encoded automatically in memory? *Quarterly Journal of Experimental Psychology*, **46A(2)**, 365–75.

Andrade, J., E., K., Werniers, Y., May, J. and Szmalec, A. (2002). Insensitivity of visual short-term memory to irrelevant visual information. *Quarterly Journal of Experimental Psychology A*, **55**, 753–74.

Andrade, J., Munglani, R., Jones, J. G. and Baddeley, A. D. (1994). Cognitive performance during anaesthesia. *Consciousness and Cognition*, **3**, 148–65.

Anton, G. (1899). *Über die Selbstwahrnehmung der Herderkrankungen des Gehirns durch den Kranken bei Rindenblindheit und Rindentaubheit.* Archiv für Psychiatrie und Nervenkrankheiten, Berlin, **32**, 86–127

Archibald, L. M. and Gathercole, S. E. (in press b). Short-term and working memory in specific language impairment. In *Working memory in neurodevelopmental conditions* (T. P. G. Alloway, S. E. eds). Hove: Psychology Press.

Archibald, L. M. D. and Gathercole, S. E. (2006). Visuospatial immediate memory in Specific Language Impairment. *Journal of Speech Language and Hearing Research*, **49**, 265–77.

Atkinson, R. C. and Shiffrin, R. M. (1968). Human memory: A proposed system and its control processes. In *The psychology of learning and motivation: advances in research and theory* (K. W. Spence (ed.), vol. 2, pp. 89–195. New York: Academic Press.

Attneave, F. (1960). In defense of humunculi. In *Sensory communication* (W. Rosenblith ed.), pp. 777–82. Cambridge, MA: Holt, MIT Press.

Avakame, E. F. (1998). Intergenerational transmission of violence and psychological aggression against wives. *Canadian Journal of Behavioural Sciences*, **30**, 193–202.

Avons, S. E., Wright, K. L. and Pammer, K. (1994). The word-length effect in probed and serial recall. *Quarterly Journal of Experimental Psychology*, **47a**, 207–31.

Awh, E., Jonides, J. and Reuter-Lorenz, P. A. (1998). Rehearsal in spatial working memory. *Journal of Experimental Psychology: Human Perception and Performance*, **24**, 780–90.

Awh, E., Jonides, J., Smith, E. E., Schumacher, E. H., Koeppe, R. A. and Katz, S. (1996). Dissociation of storage and retrieval in verbal working memory: evidence from positron emission tomography. *Psychological Science*, **7**, 25–31.

Awh, E., Jonides, J., Smith, E., Hillyard, S., Anllo-Vento, L., Frank, L., Love, T., Buxton, R., Wong, E. and Swinney, D. (1997). Attention modulation of visual responses due to rehearsal in spatial working memory. *Society for Neuroscience Abstracts*, **23(2)**, 657–713.

Baars, B. J. (1997). *In the theater of consciousness.* New York: University Press.

Baars, B. J. (1999). Attention versus consciousness in the visual brain: differences in conception, phenomenology, behaviour, neuroanatomy and physiology. *Journal of General Psychology*, **126(3)**, 224–33.

Baars, B. J. (2002a). The conscious access hypothesis: origins and recent evidence. *Trends in Cognitive Sciences*, **6(1)**, 47–52.

Baars, B. J. (2002b). The illusion of conscious will. *Trends in Cognitive Sciences*, **6(6)**, 268–9.

Baddeley, A. D. (1963). A Zeigarnik-like effect in the recall of anagram solutions. *Quarterly Journal of Experimental Psychology*, **15**, 63–4.

Baddeley, A. D. (1966a). Short-term memory for word sequences as a function of acoustic, semantic and formal similarity. *Quarterly Journal of Experimental Psychology*, **18**, 362–5.

Baddeley, A. D. (1966b). The influence of acoustic and semantic similarity on long-term memory for word sequences. *Quarterly Journal of Experimental Psychology*, **18**, 302–9.

Baddeley, A. D. (1966c). The capacity for generating information by randomization. *Quarterly Journal of Experimental Psychology*, **18**, 119–29.

Baddeley, A. D. (1966d). Influence of depth on the manual dexterity of free divers: A comparison between open sea and pressure chamber testing. *Journal of Applied Psychology*, **50**, 81–85.

Baddeley, A. D. (1968). A 3-min reasoning test based on grammatical transformation. *Psychonomic Science*, **10**, 341–42.

Baddeley, A. D. (1968). How does acoustic similarity influence short-term memory? *Quarterly Journal of Psychology*, **20**, 249–64.

Baddeley, A. D. (1971). Language habits, acoustic confusability and immediate memory for redundant letter sequences. *Psychonomic Science*, **22**, 120–1.

Baddeley, A. D. (1972). Selective attention and performance in dangerous environments. *British Journal of Psychology*, **63**, 537–46.

Baddeley, A. D. (1976). *The psychology of memory*. New York.: Basic Books.

Baddeley, A. D. (1986). *Working memory*. Oxford: Oxford University Press.

Baddeley, A. D. (1990). The development of the concept of working memory: implications and contributions of neuropsychology. In *Neuropsychological impairments of short-term memory* (G. Vallar and T. Shallice eds), pp. 54–73. Cambridge: Cambridge University Press.

Baddeley, A. D. (1993). Working memory and conscious awareness. In *Theories of Memory* (A. F. Collins, S. E. Gathercole, M. A.Conway and P. E. Morris eds), pp. 11–28. Mahwah, NJ.: Erlbaum Associates.

Baddeley, A. D. (1994). The remembered self and the enacted self. In *The remembering self: construction and accuracy in the self-narrative* U. Neisser and R. Fivush (eds), pp. 236–42. Cambridge: Cambridge University Press.

Baddeley, A. D. (1996). Exploring the central executive. *Quarterly Journal of Experimental Psychology*, **49A(1)**, 5–28.

Baddeley, A. D. (1997).

Baddeley, A. D. (1998a). The central executive: a concept and some misconceptions. *Journal of the International Neuropsychological Society*, **4**, 523–6.

Baddeley, A. D. (1998b). *Human memory: theory and practice*. Hove, Sussex: Psychology Press.

Baddeley, A. D. (2000a). The episodic buffer: a new component of working memory? *Trends in Cognitive Sciences*, **4(11)**, 417–23.

Baddeley, A. D. (2000b). The phonological loop and the irrelevant speech effect: some comments on Neath. *Psychonomic Bulletin and Review*, **7(3)**, 544–9.

Baddeley, A. D. (2003). New data: old pitfalls. Comment on Ruchkin *et al. Behavioural and Brain Sciences*, **26**, 729–30.

Baddeley, A. D. (2003b). Working memory: looking back and looking forward. *Nature Reviews Neuroscience*, **4(10)**, 829–39.

Baddeley, A. D. and Andrade, J. (1994). Reversing the word-length effect: a comment on Kaplan, Rochon and Waters. *Quarterly Journal of Experimental Psychology*, **47A**, 1047–54.

Baddeley, A. D. and Andrade, J. (1998). Working memory and consciousness: an empirical approach. In *Theories of memory II* (M. Conway, S. E. Gathercole and C. Cornoldi eds), pp. 1–24. Hove, Sussex: Psychology Press.

Baddeley, A. D. and Andrade, J. (2000). Working memory and the vividness of imagery. *Journal of Experimental Psychology*, **129(1)**, 126–45.

Baddeley, A. D. and Fleming, N. C. (1967). The efficiency of divers breathing oxy-helium. *Ergonomics*, **10**, 311–19

Baddeley, A. D. and Gathercole, S. (1992). Learning to read: the role of the phonological loop. In *Analytic approaches to human cognition* (J. Alegria, D. Holender, J. Junca de Morais and M. Radeau eds), pp. 153–67. Amsterdam, North Holland: Elsevier Science Publishers B. V.

Baddeley, A. D. and Hitch, G. J. (1974). Working memory. In G. A. Bower (ed.), *Recent Advances in Learning and Motivation* (Vol. 8, pp. 47–89). New York: Academic Press.

Baddeley, A. D. and Hitch, G. (1977). Recency re-examined. In *Attention and performance*, vol. VI (S. Dornic ed.), pp. 647–67). Hillsdale, N.J: Lawrence Erlbaum Associates.

Baddeley, A. D. and Hitch, G. J. (1974). Working memory. In *Recent advances in learning and motivation*, vol. 8, (G. A. Bower ed.), pp. 47–89. New York: Academic Press.

Baddeley, A. D. and Hitch, G. J. (1993). The recency effect: implicit learning with explicit retrieval? *Memory and Cognition*, **21**, 146–55.

Baddeley, A. D. and Hull, A. J. (1979). Prefix and suffix effects: do they have a common basis? *Journal of Verbal Learning and Verbal Behavior*, **18**, 129–40.

Baddeley, A. D. and Larsen, J. (2003). The disruption of STM: a response to our commentators. *Quarterly Journal of Experimental Psychology A*, **56(8)**, 1301–6.

Baddeley, A. D. and Larsen, J. D. (in press a). The phonological loop unmasked? A comment on the evidence for a 'perceptual-gestural' alternative. *Quarterly Journal of Experimental Psychology*.

Baddeley, A. D. and Larsen, J. D. (in press b). Rejoinder: The phonological loop: some answers and some questions. *Quarterly Journal of Experimental Psychology*.

Baddeley, A. D. and Lieberman, K. (1980). Spatial working memory. In *Attention and performance VIII* (R. S. Nickerson ed.), pp. 521–39. Hillsdale: NJ: Lawrence Erlbaum Associates.

Baddeley, A. D. and Logie, R. H. (1992). Auditory imagery and working memory. In *Auditory imagery* (D. Reisberg ed.), pp. 171–97. Hillsdale, N J: Lawrence Erlbaum Associates.

Baddeley, A. D. and Logie, R. H. (1999). Working memory: the multiple component model. In *Models of working memory: mechanisms of active maintenance and executive control* (A. Miyake and P. Shah eds), pp. 28–61. Cambridge: Cambridge University Press.

Baddeley, A. D. and Scott, D. (1971). Short-term forgetting in the absence of proactive interference. *Quarterly Journal of Experimental Psychology*, **23**, 275–83.

Baddeley, A. D. and Warrington, E. K. (1970). Amnesia and the distinction between long- and short-term memory. *Journal of Verbal Learning and Verbal Behavior*, **9**, 176–89.

Baddeley, A. D. and Wilson, B. (1985). Phonological coding and short-term memory in patients without speech. *Journal of Memory and Language*, **24**, 490–502.

Baddeley, A. D. and Wilson, B. (1986). Amnesia, autobiographical memory and confabulation. In *Autobiographical memory* (D. Rubin ed.), pp. 225–52. New York: Cambridge University Press.

Baddeley, A. D. and Wilson, B. (1988). Frontal amnesia and the dysexecutive syndrome. *Brain and Cognition*, 7(2), 212–30.

Baddeley, A. D. and Wilson, B. A. (1993). A case of word deafness with preserved span: implications for the structure and function of short-term memory. *Cortex*, 29, 741–8.

Baddeley, A. D. and Wilson, B. A. (2002). Prose recall and amnesia: implications for the structure of working memory. *Neuropsychologia*, 40, 1737–43.

Baddeley, A. D., Baddeley, H., Bucks, R. and Wilcock, G. K. (2001a). Attentional control in Alzheimer's disease. *Brain*, 124, 1492–508.

Baddeley, A. D., Bressi, S., Della Sala, S., Logie, R. and Spinnler, H. (1991). The decline of working memory in Alzheimer's disease: a longitudinal study. *Brain*, 114, 2521–42.

Baddeley, A. D., Chincotta, D. and Adlam, A. (2001b). Working memory and the control of action: evidence from task switching. *Journal of Experimental Psychology: General*, 130, 641–57.

Baddeley, A. D., Chincotta, D., Stafford, L. and Turk, D. (2002). Is the word length effect in STM entirely attributable to output delay? Evidence from serial recognition. *Quarterly Journal of Experimental Psychology*, 55A, 353–9.

Baddeley, A. D., Cocchini, G., Della Sala, S., Logie, R. H. and Spinnler, H. (1999). Working memory and vigilance: Evidence from normal ageing and Alzheimer's Disease. *Brain and Cognition*, 41, 87–108.

Baddeley, A. D., Conway, M. A. and Aggleton, J. (2002). *Episodic memory*. Oxford: Oxford University Press.

Baddeley, A. D., de Figueredo, J. W., Hawkswell Curtis, J. W. and Williams, A. N. (1968). Nitrogen narcosis and performance underwater. *Ergonomics*, 11, 157–64.

Baddeley, A. D., Della Sala, S., Papagno, C. and Spinnler, H. (1997). Dual task performance in dysexecutive and non-dysexecutive patients with a frontal lesion. *Neuropsychology*, 11(2), 187–94.

Baddeley, A. D., Emslie, H., Kolodny, J. and Duncan, J. (1998a). Random generation and the executive control of working memory. *Quarterly Journal of Experimental Psychology*, 51A(4), 819–52.

Baddeley, A. D., Gathercole, S. E. and Papagno, C. (1998b). The phonological loop as a language learning device. *Psychological Review*, 105(1), 158–73.

Baddeley, A. D., Grant, S., Wight, E. and Thomson, N. (1973). Imagery and visual working memory. In *Attention and performance V* (P. M. A. Rabbitt and S. Dornic eds), pp. 205–17). London: Academic Press.

Baddeley, A. D., Lewis, V. J. and Vallar, G. (1984a). Exploring the articulatory loop. *Quarterly Journal of Experimental Psychology*, 36, 233–52.

Baddeley, A. D., Lewis, V., Eldridge, M. and Thomson, N. (1984b). Attention and retrieval from long-term memory. *Journal of Experimental Psychology: General*, 113, 518–40.

Baddeley, A. D., Logie, R., Bressi, S., Della Sala, S. and Spinnler, H. (1986). Dementia and working memory. *Quarterly Journal of Experimental Psychology*, 38A, 603–18.

Baddeley, A. D., Logie, R., Nimmo-Smith, I. and Brereton, N. (1985). Components of fluent reading. *Journal of Memory and Language*, 24, 119–31.

Baddeley, A. D., Papagno, C. and Vallar, G. (1988). When long-term learning depends on short-term storage. *Journal of Memory and Language*, 27, 586–95.

Baddeley, A. D., Thomson, N. and Buchanan, M. (1975). Word length and the structure of short-term memory. *Journal of Verbal Learning and Verbal Behaviour*, **14**, 575–89.

Baddeley, A. D., Thornton, A., Chua, S. E. and McKenna, P. (1996). Schizophrenic delusions and the construction of autobiological memory. In *Remembering our past: studies in autobiographical memory* (D. C. Rubin ed.), pp. 384–428. New York: Cambridge University Press.

Baddeley, A. D., Vallar, G. and Wilson, B. A. (1987). Sentence comprehension and phonological memory: some neuropsychological evidence. In *Attention and performance XII: the psychology of reading* (M. Coltheart ed.), pp. 509–29. London: Lawrence Erlbaum Associates.

Baddeley, A. D., Vargha-Khadem, F. and Mishkin, M. (2001c). Preserved recognition in a case of developmental amnesia: implications for the acquisition of semantic memory. *Journal of Cognitive Neuroscience*, **13(3)**, 357–69.

Baker, S. C., Rogers, R. D., Owen, A. M., Frith, C. D., Dolan, R. J., Frackowiak, R. S. and Robbins, T. W. (1996). Neural systems engaged by planning: a PET study of the Tower of London task. *Neuropsychologia*, **34**, 515–26.

Ball, K., Berch, D. B., Helmers, K. F., Jobe, J. B., Leveck, M. D., Marsiske, M., Morris, J. N., Rebok, G. W., Smith, D. M., Tennstedt, S. L., Unverzaat, F. W. and Willis, S. L. (2002). Effects of cognitive training intervention with older adults: a randomised control trial. *Journal of the American Medical Association*, **288**, 2271–81.

Baltes, P. B. and Lindenberger, U. (1997). Emergence of a powerful connection between the sensory and cognitive functions across the adult lifespan: A new window to the study of cognitive ageing? *Psychology and Ageing*, **12**, 12–21.

Banks, G., Short, P., Martinez, J., Latchaw, R., Ratcliff, G. and Boller, F. (1989). The alien hand syndrome: clinical and post mortem findings. *Archives of Neurology*, **46**, 456–9.

Bargh, J. A. and Chartrand, T. L. (1999). The unbearable automaticity of being. *American Psychologist*, **54**, 462–79.

Bargh, J. A. and Ferguson, M. J. (2000). Beyond behaviorism: on the automaticity of higher mental processes. *Psychological Bulletin*, **126(6)**, 925–45.

Bargh, J. A., Chen, M. and Burrows, L. (1996). The automaticity of social behaviour: direct effects of trait concept and stereotype activation on action. *Journal of Personality and Social Psychology*, **71**, 230–44.

Barkley, R. A. (1977a). *ADHD and the nature of self-control*. New York: Guilford Press.

Barkley, R. A. (1977b). Behavioral inhibition, sustained attention and executive functions: Constructing a unifying theory of ADHD. *Psychological Bulletin*, **121**, 65–94.

Barnard, P. J. (1985). Interactive cognitive subsystems: A psycholinguistic approach to short-term memory. In *Progress in the psychology of language*, vol. 2 (A. Ellis ed.), pp. 197–258. London: Erlbaum.

Barnard, P. J. (1999). Modelling working memory phenomena within a mulitprocessor architecture. In *Models of working memory: mechanisms of active maintenance and executive control* (A. Miyake and P. Shah eds), pp. 298–339. Cambridge: Cambridge University Press.

Bartlett, F. C. (1932). *Remembering: a study in experimental and social psychology*. New York: Cambridge University Press.

Basso, A. H., Spinnler, G., Vallar, G. and Zanobia, E. (1982). Left hemisphere damage and selective impairment of auditory verbal short-term memory: a case study. *Neuropsychologica*, **20**, 274.

Baucon, D. H. and Aiken, P. A. (1981). Effect of depressed mood on eating among obese and nonobese dieting persons. *Journal of Personality and Social Psychology*, **41**, 577–85.

Bauer, R. M. (1984). Autonomic recognition of names and faces in prosopagnosia: a neuropsychological application of the Guilty Knowledge Test. *Neuropsychologia*, **22**, 457–69.

Baumeister, R. F. (1998). The self. In *Handbook of social psychology*, 4th edn (D. T.Gilbert, S. T. Friske and G. Lindzey eds), pp. 680–740. New York: McGraw-Hill.

Baumeister, R. F. and Heatherton, T. F. (1996). Self-regulation failure: An overview. *Psychological Enquiry*, **7**, 1–15.

Baumeister, R. F., Bratslavsky, E., Muraven, M. and Tice, D. M. (1998). Ego-depletion: is the active self a limited resource? *Journal of Personality and Social Psychology*, **74**, 1252–65.

Bayliss, D. M., Jarrold, C., Baddeley, A. D., Gunn, D. M. and Leigh, E. (2005). Mapping the developmental constraints on working memory span performance. *Developmental Psychology*, **41**, 579–97.

Bayliss, D. M., Jarrold, C., Gunn, D. M. and Baddeley, A. D. (2003). The complexities of complex span: explaining individual differences in working memory in children and adults. *Journal of Experimental Psychology: General*, **132(1)**, 71–92.

Bechara, A., Damasio, A. R., Damasio, H. and Anderson, S. W. (1994). Insensitivity to future consequences following damage to human prefrontal cortex. *Cognition*, **50**, 7–15.

Bechara, A., Damasio, H., Tranel, D. and Damasio, A. R. (1997). Deciding advantageously before knowing the advantageous strategy. *Science*, **275**, 1293–5.

Bechara, A., Damasio, H., Tranel, D. and Anderson, S. W. (1998). Dissociation of working memory from decision making within human prefrontal cortex. *Journal of Neuroscience*, **18**, 428–37.

Beck, A. T. (1976). *Cognitive therapy and the emotional disorders*. New York: International Universities Press.

Bellugi, U., Wang, P. P. and Jernigan, T. L. (1994). Williams' syndrome: An unusual neuropsychological profile. In *Atypical cognitive deficits in developmental disorders: implications for brain function* (S. H. Broman and J. Grafman eds), pp. 23–56. Hillsdale, NJ: Erlbaum.

Benton, D. and Sargent, J. (1992). Breakfast, blood glucose and memory. *Biological Psychology*, **33(2–3)**, 207–10.

Benton, S. L., Kraft, R. G., Glover, J. A. and Plake, B. S. (1984). Cognitive capacity differences among writers. *Journal of Educational Psychology*, **76(5)**, 820–34.

Berkowitz, L. (1978). Is criminal violence normative behaviour? *Journal of Research in Crime and Delinquency*, **15**, 148–61.

Berkun, M. M., Bialek, H. M., Kern, R. P. and Yagi, K. (1962). Experimental Studies of Psychological Stress in Man. *Psychological Monographs: General and Applied*, **76**(15, Whole no. 534), 1–39.

Beschin, N., Basso, A. and Della Sala, S. (2000). Perceiving left and imagining right: dissociation in neglect. *Cortex*, **36(3)**, 401–14.

Beschin, N., Cocchini, G., DellaSala, S. and Logie, R. H. (1997). What the eyes perceive, the brain ignores: A case of pure unilateral representational neglect. *Cortex*, **33(1)**, 3–26.

Betts, G. H. (1909). *The distribution and functions of mental imagery*. New York: Teachers College, Columbia University.

Bing, L. (1991). *Do or die*. New York: Harper Collins.

Biran, I., Giovannetti, T., Buxbaum, L. and Chatterjee, A. (2006). The alien hand syndrome, what makes the alien hand alien? *Cognitive Neuropsychology*, **23**, 563–82.

Bireta, T. J., Neath, H. I. and Suprenant, A. M. (In press). The syllable-based word length effect and stimulus set specivity. *Psychonomic Bulletin and Review*.

Bireta *et al.* (2006) Psychonomic Bulletin and Review **13**. 434–8.

Bisiach, E. (1993). Mental representation in unilateral neglect and related disorders. *Quarterly Journal of Experimental Psychology*, **46A**, 435–61.

Bisiach, E. and Geminiani, G. (1991). Anosognosia related to hemiplegia and hemianopia. In *Awareness of deficit after brain injury* (G. P. Prigatano and D. L. Schacter eds), pp. 17–52. New York: Oxford University Press.

Bisiach, E. and Luzzatti, C. (1978). Unilateral neglect of representational space. *Cortex*, **14**, 129–33.

Bjork, E. L. and Healy, A. F. (1974). Short-term order and item retention. *Journal of Verbal Learning and Verbal Behavior*, **13**, 80–97.

Bjork, R. A. (2000). Learning versus performance: Current implications of an old distinction. *International Journal of Psychology*, **35(3–4 Special Issue)**, 1.

Bjork, R. A. and Whitten, W. B. (1974). Recency-sensitive retrieval processes. *Cognitive Psychology*, **6**, 173–89.

Blair, R. J. and Cipolotti, L. (2000). Impaired social response reversal. *Brain*, **123**, 1122–41.

Blake, J., Austin, W., Cannon, M., Lisus, A. and Vaughan, A. (1994). The relationship between memory span and measures of imitative and spontaneous language complexity in preschool children. *International Journal of Behavioral Development*, **17**, 91–107.

Blakemore, S. J., Wolpert, D. M. and Frith, C. D. (1998). Central cancellation of self-produced tickle sensation. *Nature Neuroscience*, **1**, 635–40.

Blaney, P. H. (1986). Affect and memory: a review. *Psychological Bulletin*, **99**, 229–46.

Bor, D., Duncan, J., Wiseman, R. and Owen, A. M. (2003). Encoding strategies dissociate prefrontal activity from working memory demand. *Neuron*, **37**, 361–7.

Boring, E. G. (1929). *A history of experimental psychology*. New York: Appleton-Century.

Bourke, P. A., Duncan, J. and Nimmo-Smith, I. (1996). A general factor involved in dual-task performance decrement. *Quarterly Journal of Experimental Psychology*, **49A**, 525–45.

Bower, G. H. (1981). Mood and memory. *American Psychologist*, **36**, 129–48.

Bower, G. H., Gilligan, S. G. and Monteiro, K. P. (1981). Remembering information about one's self. *Journal of Research in Personality*, **13**, 420–32.

Bradley, B. P., Mogg, K., Millar, N. and White, J. (1995). Selective processing of negative information: effects of clinical anxiety, concurrent depression and awareness. *Journal of Abnormal Psychology*, **104**, 532–6.

Brandimonte, M. A., Hitch, G. J. and Bishop, D. V. M. (1992). Verbal recoding of visual stimuli impairs mental image transformations. *Memory and Cognition*, **20**, 449–55.

Braver, T. S., Cohen, J. D., Nystrom, L. E., Jonides, J., Smith, E. E. and Noll, D. C. (1997). A parametric study of prefrontal cortex involvement in human working memory. *Neuroimage*, **5(1)**, 49–62.

Bregman, A. S. (1990). *Auditory scene analysis: the perceptual organization of sound.* Cambridge, MA: MIT Press.

Brener, R. (1940). An experimental investigation of memory span. *Journal of Experimental Psychology*, **26**, 467–83.

Broadbent, D. E. (1958). *Perception and communication.* London: Pergamon Press.

Broadbent, D. E. (1971). *Decision and stress.* London: Academic Press.

Broadbent, D. E. and Broadbent, M. H. P. (1981). Recency effects in visual memory. *Quarterly Journal of Experimental Psychology*, **33A**, 1–15.

Broadbent, D. E., Cooper, P. J., Fitzgerald, P. F. and Parkes, K. R. (1982). The cognitive failures questionnaire (CFQ) and its correlates. *British Journal of Clinical Psychology*, **21**, 1–16.

Brockner, J. (1984). Low self-esteem and behavioral plasticity: Some implications for personality and social psychology. In *Review of personality and social psychology*, vol. 4 (L. Wheeler ed.), pp. 237–71. : Sage.

Brodman, K. (1909). *Vergleichende Lokalisationslehre Der Grosshirnride In Ihren Prinzipien Dargestellt Aug Grund Des Zellenbaues.* Leipzig: Barth.

Brooks, L. R. (1967). The suppression of visualization by reading. *Quarterly Journal of Experimental Psychology*, **19**, 289–99.

Brooks, L. R. (1968). Spatial and verbal components in the act of recall. *Canadian Journal of Psychology*, **22**, 349–68.

Brooks, N., Campsie, L., Symington, C., Beattie, A. and McKinlay, W. (1987). The effects of severe head injury on patient and relative within several years of injury. *Journal of Head Trauma Rehabilitation*, **2**, 1–13.

Brown, G. D. A. and Hulme, C. (1995). Modelling item length effects in memory span: no rehearsal needed? *Journal of Memory and Language*, **34**, 594–621.

Brown, G. D. A. and Hulme, C. (1996). Non-word repetition, STM and word age of acquisition: a computational model. In *Models of short-term memory* (S. E. Gathercole ed.), pp. 129–48. Hove, Sussex: Psychology Press.

Brown, G. D. A., Neath, I. and Chater, N. (2002). A ratio model of scale-invariant memory and identification. *Unpublished manuscript.*

Brown, G. D. A., Neath, I. and Chater, N. (Unpublished). SIMPLE: A local distinctiveness model of scale – invariant memory and perceptual identification. *Unpublished manuscript.*

Brown, G. W. and Harris, T. (1978). *Social origins of depression.* London: Tavistock.

Brown, I. D., Tickner, A. H. and Simmonds, D. C. V. (1969). Interference between concurrent tasks of driving and telephoning. *Journal of Applied Psychology*, **33(3)**, 419–24.

Brown, J. (1958). Some tests of the decay theory of immediate memory. *Quarterly Journal of Experimental Psychology*, **10**, 12–21.

Brown, T. A., Campbell, L. A., Lehman, C. L., Grishman, J. R. and Mancill, R. B. (2001). Current and lifetime co-morbidity of DSM-IV anxiety and mood disorders in a large clinical sample. *Jounal of Abnormal Psychology*, **110**, 585–99.

Bruyer, R. and Scailquin, J. (1998). The visuospatial sketchpad for mental images: testing the multicomponent model of working memory. *Acta Psychologica*, **98**, 17–36.

Buckner, R. L., Koutstaal, W., Schacter, D. L., Dale, A. M., Rotte, M. and Rosen, V. (1998). Functional-anatomic study of episodic retrieval: II. Selective averaging of event-related fMRI trials to test the retrieval success hypothesis. *Neuroimage*, 7, 163–75.

Bulbena, A. and Berrios, G. E. (1993). Cognitive function in the affective disorders: a prospective study. *Psychopathology*, **26**, 6–12.

Burgess, N. and Hitch, G. J. (1992). Towards a network model of the articulatory loop. *Journal of Memory and Language*, **31**, 429–60.

Burgess, N. and Hitch, G. J. (1996). A connectionist model of STM for serial order. In *Models of short-term memory* (S. E. Gathercole ed.), pp. 51–72. Hove, Sussex: Psychology Press.

Burgess, N. and Hitch, G. J. (1999). Memory for serial order: a network model of the phonological loop and its timing. *Psychological Review*, **106**, 551–81.

Burgess, P. W. and Shallice, T. (1996). Response suppression, initiation and strategy use following frontal lobe lesions. *Neuropsychologia*, **34(4)**, 263–72.

Burgess, P. W., Veitch, E., Costello, A. and Shallice, T. (2000). The cognitive and neuroanatomical correlates of multitasking. *Neuropsychologia*, **38**, 848–63.

Calvo, M. G. and Eysenck, M. W. (1996). Phonological working memory and reading in test anxiety. *Memory*, **4(3)**, 289–305.

Calvo, M. G., Eysenck, M. W., Ramos, P. M. and Jimenez, A. (1994). Compensatory reading strategies in test anxiety. *Anxiety, Stress and Coping*. 7, 99–116.

Calvo, M. G., Ramos, P. and Eysenck, M. W. (1993). Test Anxiety and Reading: Efficiency vs effectiveness. *Cognitiva*, **5**, 77–93.

Campbell, J. D., Chew, B. and Scratchley, L. S. (1991). Cognitive and emotional reactions to daily events – the effects of self-esteem and self-complexity. *Journal of Personality*, **59(3)**, 473–505.

Cantor, J. and Engle, R. W. (1993). Working-memory capacity as long term memory activation: an individual-differences approach. *Journal of Experimental Psychology: Learning, Memory and Cognition*, **19**, 1101–14.

Caplan, D. and Waters, G. S. (1994). Articulatory length and phonological similarity in span tasks: a reply to Baddeley and Andrade. *Quarterly Journal of Experimental Psychology*, **47A**, 1055–62.

Caplan, D. and Waters, G. S. (1995). On the nature of the phonological output planning process involved in verbal rehearsal: Evidence from aphasia. *Brain and Language*, **48**, 191–220.

Caplan, D. and Waters, G. S. (1999). Verbal working memory in sentence comprehension. *Behavorial and Brain Sciences*, **22**, 77–126.

Caplan, D., Rochon, E. and Waters, G. S. (1992). Articulatory and phonological determinants of word-length effects in span tasks. *Quarterly Journal of Experimental Psychology*, **45A**, 177–92.

Carlesimo, G. A., Perri, R., Turriziani, P., Tomaiuolo, F. and Caltagirone, C. (2001). Remembering what but not where: independence of spatial and visual working memory in the human brain. *Cortex*, **37(4)**, 519–34.

Carlson, R. A. (1997). *Experienced cognition*. Mahwah, NJ: Erlbaum.

Carr, J. E. and Tan, E. K. (1976). In search of the true amok: amok as viewed within the Malay culture. *American Journal of Psychiatry*, **133**, 1295–9.

Carroll, J. B. (1993). *Human cognitive abilities*. New York: Cambridge University Press.

Carver, C. S. and Scheier, M. F. (1981). *Attention and self regulation: a control theory approach to human behavior*. New York: Springer-Verlag.

Case, R. D., Kurland, D. M. and Goldberg, J. (1982). Operational efficiency and the growth of short-term memory span. *Journal of Experimental Child Psychology*, **33**, 386–404.

Catani, M., Jones, D. K. and ffytche, D. H. (2005). Perisylvian language networks of the human brain. *Annals of Neurology*, **57**, 8–16.

Cepeda-Benito, A. and Tiffany, S. T. (1996). The use of a dual-task procedure for the assessment of cognitive effort associated with cigarette craving. *Psychopharmacology*, **127**, 155–63.

Cermak, L. S. and O'Connor, M. G. (1983). The anterograde and retrograde retrieval ability of a patient with amnesia due to encephalitis. *Neuropsychologia*, **21**, 213–34.

Chartrand, T. L. and Bargh, J. A. (1999). The chameleon effect: the perception-behavior link and social interaction. *Journal of Personality and Social Psychology*, **76**, 893–910.

Cheesman, J. and Merikle, P. M. (1984). Priming with and without awareness. *Perception and Psychophysics*, **36(4)**, 387–95.

Chen, M. and Bargh, J. A. (1999). Consequences of automatic evaluation: immediate behavioral predispositions to approach or avoid the stimulus. *Personality and Social Psychology Bulletin*, **25(2)**, 215–24.

Choi, I., Nisbett, R. E. and Noren Zayan, A. (1999). Casual attribution across cultures: variation and universality. *Psychological Bulletin*, **125**, 47–63.

Chomsky, N. (1957). *Syntactic structures.* : Moulton and Co.

Christianson, R. A. and Loftus, E. F. (1991). Remembering emotional events: The fate of detailed information. *Cognition* and *Emotion*, **5**, 81–108.

Cicerone, K., Dahlberg, C., Malec, J., Langenbah, N. D., Felicetti, T., Kneipp, S., Ellmo, W., Kalamar, A., Giacino, J., Harley, J., Laatsch, L., Morse, P. and Catanese, J. (2005). Evidence-based cognitive rehabilation: updated review of the literature from 1998 through 2002. *Archives of Physical and Medical Rehabilitation*, **86**, 1689–92.

Clark, D. M. (1983). On the induction of depressed mood in the laboratory: evaluation and comparison of the Velten and musical procedures. *Advances in Behavior Research and Therapy*, **5**, 27–49.

Clark, D. M. and Teasdale, J. D. (1982). Diurnal variation in clinical depression and accessibility of memories of positive and negative experiences. *Journal of Abnormal Psychology*, **91**, 87–95.

Clark, D. M. and Teasdale, J. D. (1985). Constraints on the effects of mood on memory. *Journal of Personality and Social Psychology*, **48**, 1595–608.

Clark, H. H. (1973). The language-as-a-fixed-effect-fallacy: a critique of language statistics in psychological research. *Journal of Verbal Learning and Verbal Behavior*, **12**, 335–59.

Clayton, N. S., Griffiths, D. P., Emery, N. J. and **Dickenson**, A. (2002). Elements of episodic-like memory in animals. In *Episodic memory* (A. D. Baddeley and M. Conway and J. Aggleton eds), pp. 232–48. Oxford: Oxford University Press.

Cocchini, G., **Logie**, R. H., **Della Sala**, S. and **Baddeley**, A. D. (2002). Concurrent performance of two memory tasks: evidence for domain-specific working memory systems. *Memory and Cognition*, **30(7)**, 1086–95.

Cohen, J. D., **Perlstein**, W. M., **Braver**, T. S., **Nystrom**, L. E., **Noll**, D. C., **Jonides**, J. and **Smith**, E. E. (1997). Temporal dynamics of brain activation during a working memory task. *Nature*, **386**, 604–8.

Cohen, S. and **Lichtenstein**, E. (1990). Perceived stress, quitting smoking and smoking relapse. *Health Psychology*, **9**, 466–78.

Colle, H. A. (1980). Auditory encoding in visual short-term recall: effects of noise intensity and spatial location. *Journal of Verbal Learning and Verbal Behaviour*, **19**, 722–35.

Colle, H. A. and **Welsh**, A. (1976). Acoustic masking in primary memory. *Journal of Verbal Learning and Verbal Behavior*, **15**, 17–32.

Collins, A. M. and **Loftus**, E. F. (1975). A spreading-activation theory of semantic processing. *Psychological Review*, **82**, 407–28.

Collins, A. M. and **Quillian**, M. R. (1969). Retrieval time from semantic memory. *Journal of Verbal Learning and Verbal Behavior*, **8**, 432–8.

Colquhoun, W. P. and **Baddeley**, A. D. (1964). Role of pre-test expectancy in vigilance decrement. *Journal of Experimental Psychology*, **68**, 156–60.

Coltheart, V. and **Langdon**, R. (1998). Recall of short word lists presented visually at fast rates: effects of phonological similarity and word length. *Memory and Cognition*, **26(2)**, 330–42.

Conrad, R. (1960). Serial order intrusions in immediate memory. *British Journal of Psychology*, **51**, 45–8.

Conrad, R. (1964). Acoustic confusion in immediate memory. *British Journal of Psychology*, **55**, 75–84.

Conrad, R. (1965). Order error in immediate recall of sequences. *Journal of Verbal Learning and Verbal Behavior*, **4**, 161–9.

Conrad, R. (1967). Interference or decay over short retention intervals? *Journal of Verbal Learning and Verbal Behavior*, **6**, 49–54.

Conrad, R. and **Hull**, A. J. (1964). Information, acoustic confusion and memory span. *British Journal of Psychology*, **55**, 429–32.

Conway, A. R. A. and **Engle**, R. W. (1994). Working memory and retrieval: a resource-dependent inhibition model. *Journal of Experimental Psychology: General*, **123**, 354–73.

Conway, A. R. A., **Cowan**, N. and **Bunting**, M. F. (2001). The cocktail party phenomenon revisited: the importance of working memory capacity. *Psychonomic Bulletin and Review*, **8(2)**, 331–5.

Conway, M. A. (2002). Sensory-perceptual episodic memory and its context: autobiographical memory. In *Episodic memory* (A. Baddeley and M. Conway and J. Aggleton eds), pp. 53–70. Oxford: Oxford University Press.

Conway, M. A., **Collins**, A. F., **Gathercole**, S. E. and **Anderson**, S. J. (1996). Recollection of true and false autobiographical memories. *Journal of Experimental Psychology: General*, **125**, 69–95.

Coolidge, F. L. and Wynn, T. (2001). Executive functions of the frontal lobes and the evolutionary ascendancy of Homo sapiens. *Cambridge Archaelogical Journal*, **11**, 255–60.

Coolidge, F. L. and Wynn, T. (2004). Working memory, its executive functions and the emergence of modern thinking. *Cambridge Archaelogical Journal*, **15**, 5–26.

Cooper, R. P., Shallice, T. and Farringdon, J. (1995). Symbolic and continuous processes in the automatic selection of actions. In *Hybrid solutions. Frontiers in artificial intelligence and application* (J. Hallam ed.), pp. 61–71. Amsterdam: IOS Press.

Corbetta, M., Miezin, F. M., Shulman, G. L. and Petersen, S. E. (1993). A PET study of visuospatial attention. *The Journal of Neuroscience*, **13**(3), 1202–26.

Coricelli, G., Critchley, H. D., Joffily, M., O'Doherty, J. P., Sirigu, A. and Dolan, R. J. (2005). Regret and its avoidance: a neuroimaging study of choice behaviour. *Nature Neuroscience*, **8**, 1255–62.

Coslett, H. B. (1997). Neglect in vision and visual imagery: A double dissociation. *Brain*, **120**, 1163–71.

Courtney, S. M., Ungerleider, L. G., Keil, K. and Haxby, J. V. (1997). Transient and sustained activity in a distributed neural system for human working memory. *Nature*, **386**, 608–11.

Cowan, N. (1992). Verbal memory span and the timing of spoken recall. *Journal of Memory and Language*, **31**, 668–84.

Cowan, N. (1999). An embedded-processes model of working memory. In *Models of working memory* (A. Miyake and P. Shah eds), pp. 62–101. Cambridge: Cambridge University Press.

Cowan, N. (2001). The magical number 4 in short-term memory: a reconsideration of mental storage capacity. *Behavioral and Brain Sciences*, **24**, 87–114.

Cowan, N. (2005). *Working memory capacity*. Hove: Psychology Press.

Cowan, N., Baddeley, A. D., Elliott, E. M. and Norris, J. (2003). List composition and the word length effect in immediate recall: a comparison of localist and globalist assumptions. *Psychological Bulletin and Review*, **10**(1), 74–9.

Cowan, N., Day, L., Saults, J. S., Keller, T. A., Johnson, T. and Flores, L. (1992). The role of verbal output time and the effects of word-length on immediate memory. *Journal of Memory and Language*, **31**, 1–17.

Cowan, N., Keller, T., Hulme, C., Roodenrys, S., McDougall, S. and Rack, J. (1994). Verbal memory span in children: speech timing clues to the mechanisms underlying age and word length effects. *Journal of Memory and Language*, **33**, 234–50.

Cowan, N., Nugent, L. D. and Elliott, E. M. (2000). Memory-search and rehearsal processes and the word length effect in immediate recal: A synthesis in reply to Service. *Quarterly Journal of Experimental Psychology*, **53A**, 666–70.

Cox, S. P. (2000). Leader character: a model of personality and moral development. *Doctoral Dissertation University of Tulsa*.

Coyne, J. C. (1976). Depression and the response of others. *Journal of Abnormal Psychology*, **85**, 186–93.

Coyne, J. C. and Gotlib, I. H. (1983). The role of cognition in depression: a critical appraisal. *Psychological Bulletin*, **94**, 29–34.

Craig, A. D. (2002). How do you feel? Interoceptors: the sense of the physiological condition of the body. *Nature Reviews*, **3**, 655–66.

Craik, F. I. M. and Lockhart, R. S. (1972). Levels of processing: A framework for memory research. *Journal of Verbal Learning and Verbal Behavior*, 11, 671–84.

Craik, F. I. M. and Watkins, M. J. (1973). The role of rehearsal in short-term memory. *Journal of Verbal Learning and Verbal Behavior*, 11, 671–84.

Craik, F. I. M., Govoni, R., Naveh Benjamin, M. and Anderson, N. D. (1996). The effects of divided attention on encoding and retrieval processes in human memory. *Journal of Experimental Psychology – General*, 125(2), 159–80.

Craik, K. J. W. (1943). *The nature of explanation*. London: Cambridge University Press.

Craik, K. J. W. (1947). Theory of the human operator in control systems: I. The operator as an engineering system. *British Journal of Psychology*, 38, 56–61.

Craik, K. J. W. (1948). Theory of the human operator in control systems: II. Man as an element in a control system. *British Journal of Psychology*, 38, 142–8.

Crary, W. G. (1966). Reactions to incongruent self-experiences. *Journal of Consulting Psychology*, 30, 246–52.

Craske, M. G., Rapee, R. M., Jackel, L. and Barlow, D. H. (1989). Qualitative dimensions of worry in DSM-III-R generalized anxiety disorder subjects and nonanxious controls. *Behaviour Research and Therapy*, 27(4), 397–402.

Crocker, J. and Major, B. (1989). Social stigma and self-esteem: the self-protective properties of stigma. *Psychological Review*, 96(4), 608–30.

Cronholm, B. and Ottosson, J. O. (1961). Memory functions in endogenous depression. Before and after electroconvulsive therapy. *Archives of General Psychiatry*, 5, 193–9.

Crowder, R. G. (1976). *Principles of learning and memory*. Hillsdale, NJ: Lawrence Erlbaum Associates.

Crowder, R. G. (1978a). Audition and speech coding in short-term memory: a tutorial review. In *Attention and performance VII* (J. Requin ed.), pp. 321–42. Hillsdale, NJ.: Erlbaum.

Crowder, R. G. (1978b). Mechanisms of auditory backward masking in the stimulus suffix effect. *Psychological Review*, 85, 502–24.

Crowder, R. G. and Morton, J. (1969). Precategorical acoustic storage (PAS). *Perception and Psychophysics*, 5, 365–73.

D'Esposito, M., Detre, J. A., Alsop, D. C., Shin, R. K., Atlas, S. and Grossman, M. (1995). The neural basis of the central executive system of working memory. *Nature*, 378, 279–81.

Dale, H. C. A. (1973). Short-term memory for visual information. *British Journal of Psychology*, 64, 1–8.

Dalgleish, T. and Cox, S. (2002). Mood and memory. In A. D. Baddeley and B. Wilson and M. Kopelman (eds), *Handbook of Memory Disorders*. Chichester, UK: Wiley. Page nos

Damasio, A. R. (1994). *Descartes error: emotion, reason and the human brain*. New York: Putnam.

Damasio, A. R. (2000). *The feeling of what happens*. London: William Heinemann.

Daneman, M. and Carpenter, P. A. (1980). Individual differences in working memory and reading. *Journal of Verbal Learning and Verbal Behaviour*, 19, 450–66.

Daneman, M. and Carpenter, P. A. (1983). Individual difference in integrating information between and within sentences. *Journal of Experimental Psychology: Learning, Memory and Cognition*, 9, 561–84.

Daneman, M. and Case, R. (1981). Syntactic form, semantic complexity and short-term memory: influences on children's acquistion of new linguistic structures. *Developmental Psychology*, 17, 367–78.

Daneman, M. and Green, I. (1986). Individual differences in comprehending and producing words in context. *Journal of Memory and Language*, **25**, 1–18.

Daneman, M. and Merikle, P. M. (1996). Working memory and language comprehension: a meta-analysis. *Psychonomic Bulletin and Review*, **3**, 422–33.

Daneman, M. and Tardif, T. (1987). Working memory and reading skill re-examined. In *Attention and performance*, vol. XII (M. Coltheart ed.), pp. 491–508. Hove: Lawrence Erlbaum Associates.

Darwin, C. J. and Baddeley, A. D. (1974). Acoustic memory and the perception of speech. *Cognitive Psychology*, **6**, 41–60.

David, (1994).

David, A. S. and Lucas, P. (1993). Auditory-verbal hallucinations and the phonological loop: A cognitive neuropsychological study. *British Journal of Clinical Psychology*, **32**, 431–41.

Davis, F. M., Osborne, J. P., Baddeley, A. D. and Graham, I. M. F. (1972). Diver performance: Nitrogen narcosis and anxiety. *Aerospace Medicine*, **43**, 1079–82.

Davies, D. R. and Parasuranam, R. (1982). *The psychology of vigilance*. London: Academic Press.

De Renzi, E. (1982). *Disorders of space exploration and cognition*. Chichester: Wiley.

De Renzi, E. and Nichelli, P. (1975). Verbal and non-verbal short-term memory impairment following hemishperic damage. *Cortex*, **11**, 341–53.

Deary, I. (2001). *Intelligence: a very short introduction*. Oxford: Oxford University Press.

Decety, J., Jeannerod, M., Germanin, M. and Pastene, J. (1991). Vegatative response during imagined movement is proportional to mental effort. *Behavioural Brain Research*, **42**, 1–5.

Deeprose, C. and Andrade, J. (2006). Is priming during anesthesia unconscious? *Consciousness and Cognition*, **15**, 1–23.

Dehaene, S. and Naccache, L. (2001). Towards a cognitive neuroscience of consciousness: basic evidence and a workspace framework. *Cognition*, **79**, 1–37.

Dehaene, S., Naccache, L., Cohen, L., Le Bilan, D., Mangin, J.-F., Poline, J.-B. and Rivire, D. (2001). Cerebral mechanisms of word masking and unconscious repetition priming. *Nature Neuroscience*, **4(678–680)**, 1–37.

Della Sala, S. and Logie, R. H. (2002). Neurospsychological impairments of visual and spatial working memory. In *Handbook of memory disorders*, 2nd edn (A. D. Baddeley, M. D. Kopelman and B. A. Wilson eds), pp. 271–92). Chichester: Wiley.

Della Sala, S., Gray, C., Baddeley, A. and Wilson, L. (1999). Pattern span: a tool for unwelding visuo-spatial memory. *Neuropsychologia*, **37**, 1189–99.

Della Sala, S., Marchetti, C. and Spinnler, H. (1994). The anarchic hand: a fronto-mesial sign. In *Handbook of neuropsychology*, vol. 9 (F. Boller and J. Grafman eds), pp. 233–55. Amsterdam: Elsevier.

Dennett, D. C. (2001). Are we explaining consciousness yet? *Cognition*, **79**, 221–37.

Derakshan, N. and Eysenck, M. W. (1998). Working memory capacity in high trait-anxious and repressor groups. *Cognition and Emotion*, **12**, 697–713.

DiVesta, E. J., Ingersoll, G. and Sunshine, P. (1971). A factor analysis of imagery tests. *Journal of Verbal Learning and Verbal Behavior*, **10**, 471–9.

Dosher, B. A. and Ma, J. J. (1998). Output loss or rehearsal loop? Output-time versus pronunciation-time limits in immediate recall for forgetting-matched materials. *Journal of Experimental Psychology: Learning*, **24(2)**, 316–35.

Downing, P. E. (2000). Interactions between visual working memory and selective attention. *Psychological Science*, **11**, 467–73.

Drewnowski, A. (1980). Attributes and priorities in short-term recall: a new model of memory span. *Journal of Experimental Psychology: General*, **109**, 208–50.

Drobes, D. J. and Tiffany, S. T. (1997). Induction of smoking urge through imaginal and in vivo procedures: Physiological and self-report manifestations. *Journal of Abnormal Psychology*, **106**, 15–25.

Dror, I. E. and Kosslyn, S. M. (1994). Mental imagery and aging. *Psychology and Aging*, **9(1)**, 90–102.

Duckworth, K. L., Bargh, J. A., Garcia, M. and Chaiken, S. (2002). The automatic evaluation of novel stimuli. *Psychological Science*, **13**, 513–19.

Duff, S. C. and Logie, R. H. (2001). Processing and storage in working memory span. *Quarterly Journal of Experimental Psychology*, **54A**, 31–48.

Dunbar, K. and Sussman, D. (1995). Toward a cognitive account of frontal-lobe function – simulating frontal-lobe deficits in normal subjects. *Annals of the New York Academy of Sciences*, **769**, 289–304.

Duncan, J. (1984). Selective attention and the organisation of visual information. *Journal of Experimental Psychology: General*, **113**, 501–17.

Duncan, J. and Humphreys, G. W. (1989). Visual search and stimulus similarity. *Psychological Review*, **96**, 433–58.

Duncan, J. and Owen, A. M. (2000). Common regions of the human frontal lobe recruited by diverse cognitive demands. *Trends in Neurosciences*, **23**, 475–83.

Duncan, J., Emslie, H., Williams, P., Johnson, R. and Freer, C. (1996). Intelligence and the frontal lobe: THE organisation of goal-directed behaviour. *Cognitive Psychology*, **30**, 257–303.

Düzel, E., Vargha-Khadem, F., Heinze, H. J. and Mishkin, M. (2001). Brain activity evidence for recognition without recollection after early hippocampal damage. *Proceedings, National Academy of Sciences of the United States of America*, **98(14)**, 8101–6.

Ebbinghaus, H. (1885). *Über das Gedächtnis*. Leipzig: Dunker.

Eccles, J. C. (1976). Brain and free will. In *Conciousness and the brain: a scientific and philosphical enquiry* (G. C. Globus and G. Maxwell and I. Savodnik eds), pp. 181–98. New York: Plenum Press.

Egly, R., Driver, J. and Rafal, R. D. (1994). Shifting visual attention between objects and locations. *Journal of Experimental Psychology*, **123**, 161–77.

Elliot, D. and Madalena, J. (1987). The influence of premovement visual information on manual aiming. *Quarterly Journal of Experimental Psychology*, **39A**, 542–59.

Elliott, R., Ogilvie, A., Rubinsztein, J. S., Calderon, G., Dolan, R. J. and Sahakian, B. J. (2004). Abnormal ventral frontal response during performance of an affective go/no go task in patients with mania. *Biological Psychiatry*, **55**, 1163–70.

Elliott, R., Rubinsztein, J. S., Sahakian, B. J. and Dolan, R. J. (2002). The neural basis of mood-congruent processing biases in depression. *Archives of General Psychiatry*, **59**, 597–604.

Ellis, A. W. (1980). Errors in speech and short-term memory: The effects of phonemic similarity and syllable position. *Journal of Verbal Learning and Verbal Behavior*, **19**, 624–34.

Ellis, H. C. and **Ashbrook, P. W.** (1988). Resource allocation model of the effects of depressed mood states on memory. In K. Fiedler and J. Forgas (eds), *Affect, Cognition and Social Behavior*. (pp. 25–43). Toronto: Hogrefe.

Ellis, H. C. and **Moore, B. A.** (1999). Mood and memory. In T. Dalgleish and M. Power (eds), *The handbook of cognition and emotion* (pp. 193–210). Chichester, UK: Wiley.

Ellis, N. C. and **Beaton, A.** (1993). Psycholinguistic determinants of foreign language vocabulary learning. *Language Learning*, **43(4)**, 559–617.

Ellis, N. C. and **Sinclair, S. G.** (1996). Working memory in the acquisition of vocabulary and syntax: putting language in good order. *Quarterly Journal of Experimental Psychology*, **49(A)**, 234–50.

Emerson, M. J. and **Miyake, A.** (2003). The role of inner speech in task switching: a dual-task investigation. *Journal of Memory and Language*, **48**, 148–68.

Engels, R., Finkenauer, C. and **den Exter Blokland, E.** (2000). *Parential influences on self-control and juvenile delinquency*. Netherlands: Utrecht University.

Engle, R. W. (1996). Working memory and retrieval: an inhibition-resource approach. In *Working memory and human cognition* (J. T. E. Richardson, R. W. Engle, L. Hasher, R. H. Logie, E. R. Stoltfus and R. T. Zacks eds), pp. 89–119. New York: Oxford University Press.

Engle, R. W., Cantor, J. and **Carullo, J. J.** (1992). Individual differences in working memory and comprehension: a test of four hypotheses. *Journal of Experimental Psychology: Learning, Memory and Cognition*, **18**, 972–92.

Engle, R. W., Carullo, J. W. and **Collins, K. W.** (1991). Individual differences in working memory for comprehension and following directions. *Journal of Educational Research*, **84**, 253–62.

Engle, R. W., Kane, M. J. and **Tuholski, S. W.** (1999a). Individual differences in working memory capacity and what they tell us about controlled attention, general fluid intelligence and functions of the prefrontal cortex. In *Models of working memory: mechanisms of active maintenance and executive control* (A. Miyake and P. Shah eds), pp. 102–34 Cambridge: Cambridge University Press.

Engle, R. W., Tuholski, S. W., Laughlin, J. E. and **Conway, A. R. A.** (1999b). Working memory, short-term memory and general fluid intelligence: a latent variable approach. *Journal of Experimental Psychology: General*, **128**, 309–31.

Englekamp, J. (1998). *Memory for actions*. Hove: Psychology Press.

Epstein, W. (1962). The measurement of drive and conflict in humans: Theory and experiment. *Nabraska Symposium on Motivation*.

Ericsson, K. A. and **Kintsch, W.** (1995). Long-term working memory. *Psychological Review*, **102(2)**, 211–45.

Eriksen, B. A. and **Eriksen, C. W.** (1974). Effects of noise letters upon the identification of a target letter in a nonsearch task. *Perception and Psychophysics*, **16**, 143–9.

Everitt, B. J., Cardinal, R. N., Parkinson, J. A. and **Robbins, T. W.** (2003). Appetitive behavior: impact of amygdala-dependent mechanisms of emotional learning. *Annals of the New York Academy of Sciences*, **985**, 233–50.

Eysenck, M. (1992). *Anxiety: the cognitive perspective*. Hove: Erlbaum.

Eysenck, M. W. and **Calvo, M. G.** (1992). Anxiety and performance - the processing efficiency theory. *Cognition and Emotion*, 6(6), 409–34.

Farah, M. J., Hammond, K. M., Levine, D. N. and Calvanio, R. (1988). Visual and spatial mental imagery: dissociable systems of representation. *Cognitive Psychology*, **20(4)**, 439–62.

Farmer, E. W., Berman, J. V. F. and Fletcher, Y. L. (1986). Evidence for a visuo-spatial scratch pad in working memory. *Quarterly Journal of Experimental Psychology*, **38A**, 675–88.

Farrand, P. and Jones, D. M. (1996). Direction of report in spatial and verbal short-term memory. *Quarterly Journal of Experimental Psychology*, **49A**, 140–58.

Fazio, R. H. (1986). How do attitudes guide behavior? In *Handbook of motivation and cognition*, vol. 1 (Sorrentino and Higgins eds), pp. 204–43.

Feltz, D. L. and Landers, D. M. (1983). The effects of mental practice on motor skill learning and performance – a meta-analysis. *Journal of Sports Psychology*, **5(1)**, 25–57.

Fennell, M. J. V., Teasdale, J. D., Jones, S. and Damlé, A. (1987). Distraction in neurotic and endogeneous depression: an investigation of negative thinking in major depressive disorder. *Psychological Medicine*, **17**, 441–52.

Fenz, W. D. and Epstein, S. (1962). Measurement of approach-avoidance conflict along a stimulus dimension in a test of thematic apperception. *Journal of Personality*, **30**, 613–32.

Festinger, L. (1957). *A theory of cognitive dissonance*. Stanford, CA: Stanford University Press.

Fiez, J. A., Raife, E. A., Balota, D. A., Schwartz, J. P., Raichle, M. E. and Petersen, S. E. (1996). A positron emission tomography study of the short-term maintenance of verbal information. *Journal of Neuroscience*, **16**, 808–22.

Finke, R. A. and Slayton, K. (1988). Explorations of creative visual synthesis in mental imagery. *Memory and Cognition*, **16**, 252–7.

Finkel, E. J. and Campbell, W. K. (2001). Self-control and accommodation in close relationships: an interdependence analysis. *Journal of Personality and Social Psychology*, **81**, 263–77.

Fitts, P. and Posner, M. (1967). *Human performance*. Belmont, CA: Brooks/Cole Publishing Company.

Fleishman, E.A. (1965). The description and prediction of perceptual-motor skill learning. In R, Glaser (ed.) *Training Research and Education* (pp. 137-175). New York: John Wiley and Sons.

Fleishman, E. A. and Parker, J. F. (1962). Factors in the retention and relearning of perceptual-motor skill. *Journal of Experimental Psychology*, **64**, 215–26.

Fletcher, T. C., Frith, C. D., Grasby, P. M., Shallice, T., Frackowiak, R. S. J. and Dolan, R. J. (1995). Brain systems for encoding and retrieval of auditory-verbal memory: an *in vivo* study in humans. *Brain*, **118**, 401–16.

Folkard, S. (1996). Body rhythms and shift work. In *Psychology at work*, 4th edn (Warr ed.), Harmondsworth: Penguin.

Forde, E. M. and Humphreys, G. W. (2002). The role of semantic knowledge in short-term memory. *Neurocase*, **8**, 13–27.

Forgas, J. P., Bower, G. H. and Krantz, S. (1984). The influence of mood on perceptions of social interactions. *Journal of Experimental Social Psychology*, **90**, 497–513.

Forgas, J. P., Bower, G. H. and Moylan, S. (1990). Praise or blame? Affective influences on attributes for achievement. *Journal of Personality and Social Psychology*, **59**, 809–19.

Fox, E. (1994). Attentional bias in anxiety: A defective inhibition hypothesis. *Cognition and Emotion*, **8**, 165–95.

Fox, E., Russo, R., Bowles, R. J. and Dutton, K. (2001). Do threatening stimuli draw or hold visual attention in subclinical anxiety? *Journal of Experimental Psychology: General*, **130**, 681-700.

Franken, I. H. A., Kroon, L. Y. and Hendriks, V. M. (2000). Influence of individual differences in craving and obsessive cocaine thoughts on attentional processes in cocaine abuse patients. *Addictive Behaviors*, **25**, 99–102.

Freud, S. (1904). Psychopathology of everyday life. In *The writings of Sigmund Freud* (A. A. Brill ed.). New York: Modern Library, 1938.

Freud, S. (1986). Mourning and melancholia. In *Essential papers on depression* (J. Coyne ed.), pp. 48–63. New York: New York University Press.

Friedman, N. P. and Miyake, A. (2004). The relations among inhibition and interference control functions: a latent variable analysis. *Journal of Experimental Psychology: General* **133**, 101–35.

Frijda, N. H. (2004). Emotions and action. In *Feelings and emotions: the Amsterdam symposium* (A. S. R. Manstead, N. Frijda and A. Fischer eds), pp. 158–73. Cambridge: Cambridge University Press.

Friston, K. J., Harrison, L. and Penny, W. (2003). Dynamic causal modeling. *Neuroimage*, **19**, 1273–302.

Frith, C. D. (1992). *The cognitive neuropsychology of schizophrenia*. Hove, Sussex: Erlbaum.

Frith, C. D. and Friston, K. J. (1997). Studying brain function with neuroimaging. In *Cognitive neuroscience* (M. D. Rugg ed.), pp. 169–96. Hove, Sussex: Psychology Press.

Frith, C. D., Blakemore, S. J. and Wolpert, D. M. (2000). Abnormalities in the awareness and control of action. *Philosophical Transactions of the Royal Society B*, **355(1404)**, 1771–88.

Frith, C. D., Friston, K. J., Liddle, P. F. and Frackowiak, R. S. J. (1991). A PET study of word finding. *Neuropsychologia*, **29**, 1137–48.

Frith, U. (1989). *Autism: explaining the enigma*. Oxford: Blackwell.

Fry, A. F. and Hale, S. (1996). Processing speed, working memory and fluid intelligence: evidence for a developmental cascade. *Psychological Science*, **7(4)**, 237–41.

Fry, A. F. and Hale, S. (2000). Relationships among processing speed, working memory and fluid intelligence in children. *Biol. Psychol*, **54**, 1–34.

Funahashi, S., Bruce, C. J. and Goldman-Rakic, P. S. (1989). Mnemonic coding of visual space in the monkey's dorsolateral prefrontal cortex. *Journal of Neurophysiology*, **61**, 331–49.

Fuster, J. M. (1954). *Memory in the cerebral cortex*. Cambridge, MA: MIT Press.

Fuster, J. M. (2002). Physiology of executive functions: the perception–action cycle. In *Principles of frontal lobe function* (D. T. Stuss and R. T. Knight eds). NY: Oxford Press.

Fuster, J. M. and Alexander, G. E. (1971). Neuron activity related to short-term memory. *Science*, **173**, 652–4.

Fuster, J. M. and Bauer, R. H. (1974). Visual short-term memory deficit from hypothermia of frontal cortex. *Brain Research*, **81**, 393–400.

Fuster, J. M. and Jervey, J. (1981). Inferotemporal neurons distinguish and retain behaviorally relevent features of visual stimuli. *Science*, **212**, 952–5.

Gallup, G. G., Jr (1970). Chimpanzees: self-recognition. *Science*, **167**, 86–7.

Galton, F. (1880). Statistics of mental imagery. *Mind*, **5**, 301–18.

Galton, F. (1883). *Inquiries into human faculty and its development*. London: Macmillan.

Garavan, H., Pankiewicz, J., Bloom, A., Cho, J. K., Sperry, L. and Ross, T. J. (2000). Cue-induced cocaine craving: neuroanatomical specificity for drug users and drug stimuli. *American Journal of Psychiatry*, **157**, 1789–98.

Garden, S., Cornoldi, C. and Logie, R. H. (2002). Visuo-spatial working memory in navigation. *Applied Cognitive Psychology*, **16(1)**, 35–50.

Gardiner, J. M. (2001). Episodic memory and autonoetic consciousness: a first-person approach. *Philosophical Transactions of the Royal Society of London, Series B*, **356(1413)**, 1351–61.

Gathercole, S. and Pickering, S. (2001). Working memory deficits in children with special educational needs. *British Journal of Special Education*, **28**, 89–97.

Gathercole, S. E. (1995). Is nonword repetition a test of phonological memory or long-term knowledge? It all depends on the nonwords. *Memory and Cognition*, **23**, 83–94.

Gathercole, S. E. (1996). *Models of short-term memory*. Hove, Sussex: Psychology Press.

Gathercole, S. E. and Baddeley, A. D. (1989). Evaluation of the role of phonological STM in the development of vocabulary in children: a longitudinal study. *Journal of Memory and Language*, **28**, 200–13.

Gathercole, S. E. and Baddeley, A. D. (1990). Phonological memory deficits in language-disordered children: is there a causal connection? *Journal of Memory and Language*, **29**, 336–60.

Gathercole, S. E. and Pickering, S. J. (2000b). Working memory deficits in children with low achievements in the national curriculum at 7 years of age. *British Journal of Educational Psychology*, **70**, 177–94.

Gathercole, S. E., Frankish, C. R., Pickering, S. J. and Peaker, S. (1999). Phonotactic influences on short-term memory. *J Exp Psychol Learn Mem Cogn*, **25(1)**, 84–95.

Gathercole, S. E., Lamont, E. and Alloway, T. P. (2006). Working memory in the classroom. In *Working memory and education* (S. Pickering ed.), pp. 220–41. London: Elsevier Press.

Gathercole, S. E., Pickering, S. J., Ambridge, B. and Wearing, H. (2004). The structure of working memory from 4 to 15 years of age. *Developmental Psychology*, **40**, 177–90.

Gathercole, S. E., Pickering, S., Hall, M. and Peaker, S. (2001). Dissociable lexical and phonological influences on serial recognition and serial recall. *Quarterly Journal of Experimental Psychology*, **54A**, 1–30.

Gathercole, S.E., Pickering, S.J., Knight, C. and Stegmann, Z. (2003). Working memory skills and educational attainment: Evidence from National Curriculum assessments at 7 and 14 years of age. *Applied Cognitive Psychology*, **17**, 1–16.

Gathercole, S. E., Willis, C. S. and Baddeley, A. D. (1991). Nonword repetition, phonological memory and vocabulary: A reply to Snowling, Chiat and Hulme. *Applied Psycholinguistics*, **12**, 375–9.

Ghahramani, Z. and Wolpert, D. M. (1997). Modular decomposition in visuomotor learning. *Nature*, **386**, 392–5.

Gibson, J. J. (1979). *An ecological approach to visual perception*. Boston, MA: Houghton Mifflin.

Gilbert, D. T. (2002). Inferential correction. In *Heuristics and biases: the psychology of intuitive judgement* (T. Gilovich and D. Griffin and D. Kahneman eds), pp. 167–84. Cambridge: Cambridge University Press.

Gilbert, D. T. and Gill, M. J. (2000a). The momentary realist. *Psychological Science*, 11, 394–8.

Gilbert, D. T., McNulty, S. E., Giuliano, T. A. and Benson, J. E. (1992). Blurry words and fuzzy deeds: the attribution of obsure behavior. *Journal of Personality and Social Psychology*, 62, 18–25.

Gilbert, D. T., Pelham, B. W. and Krull, D. S. (1988). On cognitive busyness: when person-perceivers meet persons perceived. *Journal of Personality and Social Psychology*, 54, 733–40.

Gilbert, D. T., Pinel, E. C., Wilson, T. D., Blumberg, S. J. and Wheatley, T. P. (1998). Immune neglect: a source of durablility bias in affective forecasting. *Journal of Personality and Social Psychology*, 75, 617–38.

Gisselgard, J., Petersson, K. M., Baddeley, A. D. and Ingvar, M. (2003). The irrelevent speech effect: a PET study. *Neuropsychologia*, 41(14), 1899–911.

Glanzer, M. (1972). Storage mechanisms in recall. In *The psychology of learning and motivation: advances in research and theory*, vol. 5 (G. H. Bower ed.). New York: Academic Press.

Glanzer, M. and Cunitz, A. R. (1966). Two storage mechanisms in free recall. *Journal of Verbal Learning and Verbal Behavior*, 5, 351–60.

Glass, D. C. and Singer, J. E. (1972). *Urban stress: experiments on noise and social stressors*. New York: Academic Press.

Glass, D. C., Singer, J. E. and Friedman, L. N. (1969). Psychic cost of adaptation to an evvironmental stressor. *Journal of Personality and Social Psychology*, 12, 200–10.

Glasspool, D. W. (1995). Competitive queuing and the articulatory loop. In *Connectionist models of memory and language* (J. Levy, D. Bairaktaris, J. Bullinaria and P. Cairns eds). London: UCL Press.

Glenberg, A. M., Bradley, M. M., Stevenson, J. A., Kraus, T. A., Tkachuk, M. J., Gretz, A. L., Fish, J. H. and Turpin, V. M. (1980). A two-process account of long-term serial position effects. *Journal of Experimental Psychology: Human Learning and Memory*, 6, 355–69.

Glucksberg, S. and Cowan, G. N. (1970). Memory for nonattended auditory material. *Cognitive Psychology*, 1, 149–56.

Gobet, F., Lane, P. C. R., Croker, S., Cheng, P. C.-H., Jones, G., Oliver, I. and Pine, J. M. (2001). Chunking mechanisms in human learning. *Trends in Cognitive Sciences*, 5, 236–43.

Goffman, E. (1959). *The presentation of the self in everyday life*. New York: Doubleday Anchor Books.

Goldberg, T. E., Berman, A. F., Fleming, K. and Ostrem, J. E. A. (1998). Uncoupling cognitive workload and prefrontal cortical physiology: a PET rCBF study. *Neuroimage*, 7, 296–303.

Goldman-Rakic, P. S. (1957). Circuitry of primate prefrontal cortex and regulation of behavior by representational knowledge. In *Handbook of physiology*, vol. 5 (F. Plum and V. Mountcastle eds), pp. 373–417. Bethesda: American Physiologial Society.

Goldman-Rakic, P. S. (1988). Topography of cognition: parallel distributed networks in primate association cortex. *Annual Review of Neuroscience*, 11, 137–56.

Goldman-Rakic, P. S. (1996). The prefrontal landscape: implications of functional architecture for understanding human mentation and the central executive. *Philosophical Transactions of the Royal Society (Biological Sciences)*, 351, 1445–53.

Goldman-Rakic, P. S. (1998). The prefrontal landscape: implications of functional architecture for understanding human mentation and the central executive. In *The prefrontal cortex: executive and cognitive funtions* (A. C. Roberts, T. W. Robbins and L. Weizkrantz eds), pp. 67–86. Oxford: Oxford University Press.

Gollwitzer, P. M. (1993). Goal achievement: the role of intentions. *European Review of Social Psychology*, 4, 141–85.

Goodale, M. A., Milner, A. D., Jakobson, L. S. and Carey, D. P. (1991). A neurological dissociation between perceiving objects and grasping them. *Nature*, 349, 154–6.

Goodale, M. A., Pelisson, D. and Prablanc, C. (1986). Large adjustments in visually guided reaching do not depend on vision of the hand or perception of target displacement. *Nature*, 320, 748–50.

Gooding, P. A., Isaac, C. L. and Mayes, A. R. (2005). Prose recall and amnesia: more implications for the episodic buffer. *Neuropsychologia*, 43, 583–7.

Gotlib, I. H. and Hammen, C. L. (1992). *Psychological aspects of depression: TOWARD a cognitive–interpersonal integration*. New York: Wiley.

Gotlib, I. H. and McCann, C. D. (1984). Construct accessibility and depression - An examination of cognitive and affective factors. *Journal of Personality and Social Psychology*, 47(2), 427–39.

Gotlib, I. H., Kasch, K. L., Traill, S., Joorman, J., Arnow, B. A. and Johnson, S. L. (2004). Coherence and specificity of information-processing biases in depression and social phobia. *Jounal of Abnormal Psychology*, 113, 386–98.

Gotlib, I. H., Krasnoperova, E., Yue, D. N. and Joorman, J. (2004). Attentional bias for negative interpersonal stimuli in clinical depression. *Journal of Abnormal Psychology*, 113, 127–33.

Gottfredson, M. R. and Hirschi, T. (1990). *A general theory of crime*. Stanford, CA: Stanford University Press.

Gramzow, R. H., Sedikides, C., Panter, A. T. and Insko, C. A. (2000). Aspects of self-regulation and self-structure as predictors of perceived emotional distress. *Personality and Social Psychology Bulletin*, 26, 206–19.

Grasby, P. M., Frith, C. D., Friston, K. J., Bench, C., Frackowiak, R. S. J. and Dolan, R. J. (1993). Fractional mapping of brain areas implicated in auditory verbal memory function. *Brain*, 116, 1–20.

Gray, C. M. and Singer, W. (1989). Stimulus-specific neuronal oscillations in orientation columns of cat visual cortex. *Proceedings of the National Academy of Sciences*, 86, 1698–702.

Gray, J. A. (1995). The contents of consciousness: a neuropsychological conjecture. *Behavioral and Brain Sciences*, 18(4), 659–722.

Gray, J. A. (2004). *Consciousness: creeping up on the hard problem*. Oxford: Oxford University Press.

Green, M. W. and Rogers, P. J. (1995). Impaired cognitive functioning during spontaneous dieting. *Psychological Medicine*, 25(5), 1003–10.

Green, M. W. and Rogers, P. J. (1998). Impairments in working memory associated with spontaneous dieting behaviour. *Psychological Medicine*, 28(5), 1063–70.

Greeno, C. G. and Wing, R. R. (1994). Stress-induced eating. *Psychological Bulletin*, 115, 444–64.

Green, M. W., Elliman, N. A. and Rogers, P. J. (1997). The effects of food deprivation and incentive motivation on blood glucose levels and cognitive function. *Psychopharmacology*, 134(1), 88–94.

Greenwald, A. G. and Liu, T. J. (1985). Limited unconscious prcessing of meaning. *Bulletin of the Psychonomic Society*, **23(4)**, 292.

Grossberg, S. (1978). Behavioral contrast in short-term memory: serial binary memory models or parallel continuous memory models? *Journal of Mathematical Psychology*, **3**, 199–219.

Grossberg, S. (1987). Competitive learning: from interactive activation to adaptive resonance. *Cognitive Science*, **11**, 23–63.

Grossi, D., Becker, J. T., Smith, C. and Trojano, L. (1993). Memory for visuospatial patterns in category fluency. *Journal of Clinical and Experimental Neuropsychology*, **17**, 82–9.

Guitton, D., Buchtel, H. A. and Douglas, R. M. (1985). Frontal lobe lesions in man cause difficulties in suppressing reflexive glances in generating goal-directed saccades. *Experimental Brain Research*, **58**, 455–72.

Haggard, P. and Eimer, M. (1999). On the relation between brain potentials and the awareness of voluntary movements. *Experimental Brain Research*, **126**, 128–33.

Haggard, P. and Magno, E. (1999). Localising awareness of action with transcranial magnetic stimulation. *Experimental Brain Research*, **127**, 102–7.

Haier, R. J., Siegel, B. V., MacLachlan, A., Soderling, E., Lottenberg, S. and Buchsbaum, M. S. (1992). Regional glucose metabolic changes after learning a complex visuospatial motor task: a positron emission tomographic study. *Brain Research*, **570(1–2)**, 134–43.

Hale, S., Myerson, J., Rhee, S. H., Weiss, C. S. and Abrams, R. A. (1966). Selective interference with the maintenance of location information in working memory. *Neuropsychology*, **10(2)**, 272–85.

Hall, J. W., Wilson, K. P., Humphreys, M. S., Tinzmann, M. B. and Bowyer, P. M. (1983). Phonemic similarity effects in good vs. poor readers. *Memory and Cognition*, **11**, 520–7.

Hallet, P. (1978). Primary and secondary saccades to goals defined by instructions. *Vision Research*, **18**, 1279–96.

Hambrick, D. Z. and Engle, R. W. (2002). Effects of domain knowledge, working memory capacity and age on cognitive performance: An investigation of the knowledge-is-power hypothesis. *Cognitive Psychology*, **44**, 339–87.

Hanley, J. R. (1997). Does articulatory suppression remove the irrelevant speech effect? *Memory*, **5**, 423–31.

Hanley, J. R. and Bakopoulou, E. (2003). Irrelevant speech, articulatory suppression and phonological similarity: a test of the phonological loop model and the feature model. *Psychonomic Bulletin and Review*, **10**, 435–44.

Hanley, J. R. and Broadbent, C. (1987). The effects of unattended speech on serial recall following auditory presentation. *Bristish Journal of Psychology*, **78**, 287–97.

Hanley, J. R. and Davies, A. D. (1995). Lost in your own house. In *Broken memories: case studis in memory impairmen* (R. Campbell and M. A. Conway eds), pp. 195–208. Oxford: Blackwell.

Hanley, J. R., Young, A. W. and Pearson, N. A. (1991). Impairment of the visuospatial sketch pad. *Quarterly Journal of Experimental Psychology, Section A*, **43(1)**, 101–25.

Hari, R., Hännien, R., Mäkinen, T., Jousmäki, V., Forss, N., Seppä, M. and Salonen, O. (1998). Three hands: fragmentation of human bodily awareness. *Neuroscience Letters*, **240**, 131–4.

Harlow, J. M. (1868). Recovery from the passage of an iron bar through the head. *Massachusetts Medical Society Publications*, **2**, 327–46.

Hartley, T. and Houghton, G. (1996). A linguistically constrained model of short-term memory for nonwords. *Journal of Memory and Language*, **35**, 1–31.

Hartman, A., Pickering, R. M. and Wilson, B. A. (1992). Is there a central executive deficit after severe head injury? *Clinical Rehabilition*, **6**, 133–40.

Hasher, L. and Zacks, R. T. (1979). Automatic and effortful processes in memory. *Journal of Experimental Psychology: General*, **108**, 356–88.

Hasher, L. and Zacks, R. T. (1988). Working memory, comprehension and aging: a review and a new view. In *The psychology of learning and motivation*, vol. 22 (G. Bower ed.), pp. 195–225. New York: Academic Press.

Hatano, G. and Osawa, K. (1983a). Digit memory of grand experts in abacus-derived mental calculation. *Cognition*, **15**, 95–110.

Hatano, G. and Osawa, K. (1983b). Japanese abacus experts memory for numbers is disrupted by mechanism of action. *Journal of Clinical Psychology*, **58(1)**, 61–75.

Hebb, D. O. (1949). *Organisation of behaviour*. New York: Wiley.

Hebb, D. O. (1961). Distinctive features of learning in the higher animal. In *Brain mechanisms and learning* (J. F. Delafresnaye ed.), pp. 37–46. Oxford: Oxford University Press.

Hebb, D. O. (1968). Concerning imagery. *Psychological Review*, **75**, 466–77.

Heims, H. C., Critchley, H. D., Mathias, C. J., Dolan, R. J. and Cipolotti, L. (2004). Social and motivational functioning is not critically dependent on autonomic responses: neuropsychological evidence from patients with pure autonomic failure. *Neuropsychologia*, **42**, 1979–88.

Hendry, L. and Tehan, G. (2005). An item/order trade-off explanation of word length and generation effects. *Memory*, **13**, 364–71.

Henry, L. A. (1991). The effect of word length and phonemic similarity in young children's short term memory. *Quarterly Journal of Experimental Psychology*, **43A**, 35–52.

Henson, R. (2001). Neural working memory. In *Working memory in perspective* (J. Andrade ed.), pp. 151–74. Hove, Sussex: Psychology Press.

Henson, R. N. A. (1998). Short-term memory for serial order. The Start-End Model. *Cognitive Psychology*, **36**, 73–137.

Henson, R. N. A., Norris, D. G., Page, M. P. A. and Baddeley, A. D. (1996). Unchained memory: error patterns rule out chaining models of immediate serial recall. *Quarterly Journal of Experimental Psychology*, **49A (1)**, 80–115.

Hertel, P. T. and Hardin, T. S. (1990). Remembering with and without awareness in a depressed mood: evidence of deficits in initiative. *Journal of Experimental Psychology: General*, **119**, 45–59.

Hertel, P. T. and Rude, S. S. (1991). Depressive deficits in memory: focusing attention improves subsequent recall. *Journal of Experimental Psychology: General*, **120**, 301–9.

Heuer, F., Fischman, D. and Reisberg, D. (1986). Why does vivid imagery hurt colour memory? *Canadian Journal of Psychology*, **40**, 161–75.

Hinson, J. M., Jameson, T. J. and Whitney, P. (2002). Somatic markers, working memory and decision making. *Cognitive, Affective and Behavioural Neuroscience*, **2**, 341–53.

Hinson, J. M., Jameson, T. J. and Whitney, P. (2003). Impulsive decision making and working memory. *Journal of Experimental Psychology: Learning, Memory and Cognition*, **29**, 298–306.

Hinton, G. E. and Parsons, L. M. (1988). Scene-based and viewer-centered representations for comparing shapes. *Cognition*, **30**, 1–35.

Hinton, G. E. and Plaut, D. C. (1987). *Using fast weights to deblur old memories*. Paper presented at the Proceedings of the Ninth Annual Conference of the Cognitive Science Society, Seattle, WA.

Hintzman, D. L. (1967). Articulatory coding in short-term memory. *Journal of Verbal Learning and Verbal Behavior*, 6, 312–16.

Hiroto, D. S. and Seligman, M. E. P. (1975). Generality of learned helplessness in man. *Journal of Personality and Social Psychology*, 37, 1–11.

Hitch, G. J. and Baddeley, A. D. (1976). Verbal reasoning and working memory. *Quarterly Journal of Experimental Psychology*, 28, 603–21.

Hitch, G. J., Halliday, M. S., Dodd, A. and Littler, J. E. (1989). Development of rehearsal in short-term memory: differences between pictorial and spoken stimuli. *British Journal of Developmental Psychology*, 7, 347–62.

Hitch, G. J., Towse, J. N. and Hutton, U. (2001). What limits children's working memory span? Theoretical accounts and applicaions for scholastic development. *Journal of Experimental Psychology: General*, 130, 184–98.

Hodgins, D. C., el-Guebaly, N. and Armstrong, N. (1995). Prospective and retrospective reports of mood states before relapse to substance abuse. *Journal of Consulting and Clinical Psychology*, 63, 400–7.

Holding, D. H. (1989). Counting backward during chess move choice. *Bulletin of Psychonomic Society*, 27, 421–4.

Hope, D. A., Rapee, R. M., Heimberg, R. G. and Dombeck, M. J. (1990). Representations of the self in social phobia - Vulnerability to social threat. *Cognitive Therapy and Research*, 14(2), 177–189.

Houghton, G. (1990). The problem of serial order: a neural network model of sequence learning and recall. In *Current research in natural language generation* (R. Dale and C. Mellish and M. Zock eds), pp. 287–319. London: Academic Press.

Hsi, S., Linn, M. C. and Bell, J. E. (1997). The role of spatial reasoning in engineering and the design of spatial instruction. *Journal of Engineering Education*, 86(2), 151–8.

Hull, C. L. (1943). *The principles of behaviour*. New York: Appleton-Century.

Hulme *et al.* (2004). *Journal of Experimental Psychology: Learning, Memory and Cognition*, 30, 98–106

Hulme, C., Neath, I., Stuart, G., Shostak, L., Suprenant, A. M. and Brown, G. D. A. (in press). The distinctiveness of the word-length. *Journal of Experimental Psychology: Learning, Memory and Cognition*.

Hulme, C., Roodenrys, S., Schweickert, R., Brown, G. D. A., Martin, S. and Stuart, G. (1997). Word-frequency effects on short-term memory tasks: evidence for a redintegration process in immediate serial recall. *Journal of Experimental Psychology: Learning, Memory and Cognition*, 23(5), 1217–32.

Hulme, C., Suprenant, A. M., Bireta, T. J., Stuart, G. and Neath, I. (2004). Abolishing the word-length effect. *Journal of Experimental Psychology: Learning, Memory and Cognition*, 30, 98–106.

Hulme, C., Thomson, N., Muir, C. and Lawrence, W. A. (1984). Speech rate and the development of short-term memory span. *Journal of Experimental Child Psychology*, 38, 241–53.

Hume, D. (1739/1978). *A treatise of human nature*. Oxford: Oxford University Press.

Hummel, J. (1999). The binding problem. In *The MIT encyclopedia of cognitive sciences* (R. A. W. F. C. Keil ed.), pp. 85–86. Cambridge, MA: MIT Press.

Huttenlocher, J., Hedges, L. V. and Duncan, S. (1991). Categories and particulars: prototype effects in estimating spatial location. *Psychological Review*, **98**, 352–76.

Igel, A. and Harvey, L. O., Jr (1991). Spatial distortions in visual perception. *Gesalt Theory*, **13(4)**, 210–31.

Imber, S. D., Pilkonis, P. A., Sotsky, S. M., Elkin, I., Watkins, J. T., Collins, J. F., Shea, T. M., Leber, W. R. and Glass, D. R. (1990). Mode-specific effects among three treatments for depression. *Journal of Consulting and Clinical Psychology*, **58**, 352–9.

Intons-Peterson, M. J. (1996). Linguistic effects in a visual manipulation task. *Psychologische Beitrage*, **38**, 251–78.

Irwin, D. E. and Andrews, R. V. (1996). Integration and accumulation of information across saccadic eye movements. In *Attention and performance XVI: information integration in perception and communication* (T. Inui and J. L. McClelland eds), pp. 125–55. Cambridge, MA: MIT Press.

Jahanshahi, M., Dirnberger, G., Fuller, R. and Frith, C. D. (2000). The role of the dorsolateral prefrontal cortex in random number generation: a study with positron emission tomography. *Neuroimage*, **12(6)**, 713–25.

James, W. (1890). *The principles of psychology*. New York: Henry Holt.

Jarrold, C., Baddeley, A. D. and Hewes, A. K. (1999). Dissociating working memory: evidence from Down's and Williams' syndrome. *Neuropsychologia*, **37**, 637–51.

Jarrold, C., Baddeley, A. D., Hewes, A. K., Leeke, T. and Phillips, C. (2004). What links verbal short-term memory performance and vocabulary level? Evidence of changing relationships among individuals with learning disabilities. *Journal of Memory and Language*, **50**, 134–48.

Jarrold, C., Hewes, A. and Baddeley, A. D. (2000). Do two separate speech measures constrain verbal short-term memory in children? *Journal of Experimental Psychology*, **26(6)**, 1626–37.

Jeannerod, M. (1994). The representing brain: neural correlates of motor intention and imagery. *Behavioral and Brain Sciences*, **17(2)**, 187–245.

Jeannerod, M., Decety, J. and Michel, F. (1994). Impairment of grasping movements following a bilateral posterior parietal lesion. *Neuropsychologia*, **32(4)**, 369–80.

Jefferies, E., Frankish, C. and Lambon Ralph, M. A. (2006). Lexical and semantic influences on item and order memory in immediate serial recognition: evidence from a novel task. *Quarterly Journal of Experimental Psychology*, **59**, 949–64.

Jefferies, E., Lambon Ralph, M. A. and Baddeley, A. D. (2004a). Automatic and controlled processing in sentence recall: the role of long-term and working memory. *Journal of Memory and Language*, **51**, 623–43.

Jefferies, E., Patterson, K., Jones, R. W., Bateman, D. and Lambon Ralph, M. A. (2004). A category-specific advantage for numbers in verbal short-term memory: evidence from semantic dementia. *Neuropsychologia*, **42(5)**, 639–60.

Jersild, A. T. (1927). Mental set and shift. *Archives of Psychology, Whole no.* **89**.

John, E. R., Prichep, L. S., Kox, W., Valdes-Sosa, P., Bosch-Bayard, J., Aubert, E., Tom, M., diMichele, F. and Gugino, L. D. (2001). Invariant reversible QEEG effects of anesthetics. *Consciousness and Cognition*, **10**, 165–83.

Johnson, E. J. and Tversky, A. (1983). Affect, generalisation and the perception of risk. *Journal of Personality and Social Psychology*, **45**, 20–31.

Johnston, R. S., Rugg, M. D. and Scott, T. (1987). Phonological similarity effects, memory span and developmental reading disorders: the nature of the relationship. *British Journal of Psychology*, **78**, 205–11.

Jones, D. M. (1993). Objects, streams and threads of auditory attention. In *Attention: selection, awareness and control* (A. D. Baddeley and L. Weiskrantz eds), pp. 87–104. Oxford: Clarendon Press.

Jones, D. M. and Macken, W. J. (1993). Irrelevant tones produce an irrelevant speech effect: implications for phonological coding in working memory. *Journal of Experimental Psychology: Learning, Memory and Cognition*, **19**, 369–81.

Jones, D. M. and Macken, W. J. (1995). Phonological similarity in the irrelevant speech effect. Within- or between-stream similarity? *Journal of Experimental Psychology: Learning, Memory and Cognition*, **21 or 27?** 103–15.

Jones, D. M. and Tremblay, S. (2000). Interference In memory by process or content? A reply to Neath. *Psychonomic Bulletin and Review*, **7**, 544–58.

Jones, D. M., Beaman, P. and Macken, W. J. (1996). The object-orientated episodic record model. In *Models of short-term memory* (S. Gathercole ed.), pp. 209–38. Hove, Sussex: Psychology Press.

Jones, D. M., Farrand, P., Stuart, P. and Morris, N. (1995). Functional equivalence of verbal and spatial information in serial short-term memory. *Journal of Experimental psychology: Learning, Memory and Cognition*, **21**, 1008–18.

Jones, D. M., Hughes, R. W. and Macken, W. J. (2006). Perceptual organization masquerading as phonological storage: further support for a perceptual-gestual view of short-term memory. *Journal of Memory and Language*, **54**, 265–81.

Jones, D. M., Macken, W. J. and Mosdell, N. A. (1997). The role of habituation in the disruption of recall performance by irrelevant sound. *British Journal of Psychology*, **88**, 549–64.

Jones, D. M., Macken, W. J. and Murray, A. C. (1993). Disruption of visual short-term memory by changing-state auditory simuli: The role of segmentation. *Memory and Cognition*, **21(3)**, 318–66.

Jones, D., Macken, W. J. and Nicholls, A. P. (2004). The phonological store of working memory: Is it phonological and is it a store? *Journal of Experimental Psychology: Learning, Memory and Cognition*, **30(3)**, 656–74.

Jones, E. E. and Harris, V. A. (1967). The attribution of attitudes. *Journal of Experimental Social Psychology*, **3**, 1–24.

Jonides, J., Schumacher, E. H., Smith, E. E., Koeppe, R. A., Awh, E., Reuter-Lorenz, P. A., Marshuetz, C. and Willis, C. R. (1998a). The role of a parietal cortex in verbal working memory. *The Journal of Neuroscience*, **18**, 5026–34.

Jonides, J., Schumacher, E. H., Smith, E. E., Lauber, E. J., Awh, E., Minoshima, S. and Koeppe, R. A. (1997). Verbal working memory load effects regional brain activation as measured by PET. *Journal of Cognitive Neuroscience*, **9**, 462–75.

Jonides, J., Smith, E. E., Koeppe, R. A., Awh, E., Minoshima, S. and Mintun, M. (1993). Spatial working memory in humans as revealed by PET. *Nature*, **363**, 623–5.

Jordan, M. I. (1986). *Attractor dynamics and parallelism in a connectionist sequential machine*. Paper presented at the Eight Annual Conference of the Cognitive Science Society.

Judd, C. H. (1908). The relation of special training to general intelligence. *Educational Review*, **36**, 28–42.

Just, M. A. and Carpenter, P. A. (1992). The capacity theory of comprehension: individual differences in working memory. *Psychological Review*, **99**, 122–49.

Kahn, R., Zarit, S. H., Hilbert, N. M. and Niederehe, G. (1975). Memory complaint and impairment in the aged. *Archives of General Psychiatry*, **32**, 1569–73.

Kahneman, D. (1973). *Attention and effort*. Englewood Cliffs, N.J: Prentice Hall.

Kail, R. (1988). Developmental functions for speeds of cognitive processes. *Journal of Experimental Child Psychology*, **45**, 339–64.

Kail, R. (1992). Processing speed, speech rate and memory. *Developmental Psychology*, **28**, 899–904.

Kail, R. and Park, Y. (1994). Processing time, articulation time and memory span. *Journal of Experimental Child Psychology*, **57**, 281–91.

Kane, M. J. and Engle, R. W. (2000). Working-memory capacity, proactive interference and divided attention: limits on long-term memory retrieval. *Journal of Experimental Psychology: Learning, Memory and Cognition*, **26**(2), 336–58.

Kane, M. J. and Engle, R. W. (2002). The role of prefrontal cortex in working-memory capacity, executive attention and general fluid intelligence: an individual differences perspective. *Psychonomic Bulletin and Review*, **4**, 637–71.

Kane, M. J., Bleckley, M. K., Conway, A. R. A. and Engle, R. W. (2001). A controlled-attention view of working-memory capacity. *Journal of Experimental Psychology: General*, **130**(2), 169–83.

Katkin, E. S., Wiens, S. and Ohman, A. (2001). Nonconscious fear conditioning, visceral perception and the development of gut feelings. *Psychological Science*, **12**, 366–70.

Kavanagh, D. J. and Bower, G. H. (1985). Mood and self-efficacy: Impact of joy and sadness on perceived capabilities. *Cognitive Therapy and Research*, **9**, 507–25.

Kavanagh, D. J., Andrade, J. and May, J. (2005). Imaginary relish and exquisite torture: the elaborated intrusion theory of desire. *Psychological Reveiw*, **112**(2), 446–67.

Kelley, A. E. (2004). Ventral striatal control of appetitive motivation: role in ingestive behavior and reward-relating learning. *Neuroscience and Biobehavioral Reviews*, **27**, 765–76.

Kello, C. T. (2003). The emergence of a double dissociation in the modulation of a single control parameter in nonlinear dynamical system. *Cortex*, **39**, 132–4.

Kelso, J. A. S. (1995). *Dynamic patterns: the self-organization of brain and behavior*. Cambridge, MA: MIT Press.

Kemps, E., Tiggemann, M., Woods, D. and Soekov, B. (2004). Reduction of food cravings through concurrent visuo-spatial processing. *International Journal of Eating Disorders*, **36**, 31–40.

Kennard, C. and Swash, M. (1989). *Hierarchies in neurology: a reappraisal of Jacksonian concept*. London: Springer-Verlag.

Keppel, G. and Underwood, B. J. (1962). Proactive inhibition in short-term retention of single items. *Journal of Verbal Learning and Verbal Behavior*, **1**, 153–61.

Kiewra, K. A. and Benton, S. L. (1988). The relationship between information-processing ability and note taking. *Comtemporary Educational Psychology*, **13**, 33–44.

Kilts, C. D., Schweitzer, J. B., Quinn, C. K., Gross, R. E., Faber, T. L., Muhammad, F., Ely, T. D., Hoffman, J. M. and Drexler, K. P. G. (2001). Neural activity related to drug craving in cocaine addiction. *Archives of General Psychiatry*, **58**, 334–41.

Kimberg, D. Y., D'Esposito, M. and Farah, M. J. (1997). Executive control, working memory and the frontal lobes. *Current Directions in Psychological Science*, **6**, 185–92.

King, J. and Just, M. A. (1991). Individual differences in syntactic processing: the role of working memory. *Journal of Memory and Language*, **30**, 580–602.

Kintsch, W. and Buschke, H. (1969). Homophones and synonyms in short-term memory. *Journal of Experimental Psychology*, **80**, 403–7.

Kintsch, W. and van Dyck, T. (1977). Toward a model of text comprehension and production. *Psychological Review*, **85**, 63–94.

Kjaer, T. W., Lou, H. C., Nowak, M., Wildschidz, G. and Friberg, L. (1997). Consciousness quality and quantity. *Society for Neuroscience Abstracts*, **23**, Abstr. 192.112.

Kjaer, T. W., Nowak, M. and Lou, H. C. (2002). Reflective self-awareness and conscious states: PET evidence for a common midline parietofrontal core. *NeuroImage*, **17**, 1080–6.

Klauer, K. C. and Zhao, Z. (2004). Double dissociaions in visual and spatial short-term memory. *Journal of Experimental Psychology: General*, **133**, 355–81.

Klingberg, T. (1998). Concurrent performance of two working memory tasks: potential mechanisms of interference. *Cerebral Cortex*, **8**, 593–601.

Klingberg, T., Fernell, E., Olesen, P. J., Johnson, M., Gustafsson, P., Dahlström, K., Gillberg, C. G., Forssberg, H. and Westerberg, H. (2005). Computerized training of working memory in children with ADHD – a randomized, controlled trial. *Journal of American Academy of Child Adolescent Psychiatry*, **44**, 177–86.

Knapska, E., Walasek, G., Nikolaev, E., Neuhäusser-Wespy, F., Lipp, H., Kaczmarek, L. and Werka, T. (2006). Differential involvement of the central amygdala in appetitive versus aversive learning. *Learning and Memory*, **30**, 192–200.

Köhler, S. and Moscovitch, M. (1997). Unconscious visual processing in neuropsychological syndromes: a survey of the literature and evaluation of models of consciousness. In *Cognitive neuroscience* (M. D. Rugg ed.), pp. 305–73. Hove, Sussex: Psychology Press.

Kosslyn, S. M. (1978). Measuring the visual angle of the mind's eye. *Cognitive Psychology*, **10**, 356–89.

Kosslyn, S. M. (1980). *Image and mind*. Cambridge, MA: Harvard University Press.

Kosslyn, S. M. (1994). *Image and brain: the resolution of the imagery debate*. Cambridge, MA: MIT Press.

Kosslyn, S. M. and Shwartz, S. P. (1977). A simulation of visual imagery. *Cognitive Science*, **1**, 265–95.

Kosslyn, S. M. N. M., Alpert, W. L., Thompson, V., Maljkovic, S. B., Weise, C. F., Chabris, S. E., Hamilton, S. E. and Buonanno, F. S. (1993). Visual mental imagery activates topographically organised cortex: PET investigations. *Journal of Cognitive Neuroscience*, **5**, 263–87.

Kosslyn, S. M., Cave, C. B., Provost, D. and Von Gierke, S. (1988). Sequential processes in image generation. *Cognitive Psychology*, **20**, 319–43.

Kosslyn, S., Pascual-Leone, A., Felician, O., Camposano, S., Keenan, J. P. and Thompson, W. L. (1999). The role of area 17 in visual imagery: convergent evidence from PET and TMS. *Science*, **284**, 167–70.

Krosnick, J. A., Betz, A. L., Jussin, L. J. and Lynn, A. R. (1992). Subliminal conditioning of attitudes. *Personality and Social Psychology Bulletin*, **18**, 152–62.

Kuhl, J. (2000). A functional-design approach to motivation and self-regulation: the dynamics of personality systems interactions. In *Handbook of self regulation* (S. Boekaert and P. R. Pintrich and M. Zeidner eds), pp. 111–69. San Diego, CA: Academic Press.

Kunda, Z. (1990). The case for motivated reasoning. *Psychological Bulletin*, **108**, 480–98.

Kutas, M. and Dale, A. (1997). Electrical and magnetic readings of mental functions. In *Cognitive neuroscience* (M. D. Rugg ed.). Cambridge, MA: MIT Press.

Kyllonen, P. C. and Christal, R. E. (1990). Reasoning ability is (little more than) working memory capacity. *Intelligence*, **14**, 389–433.

Kyllonen, P. C. and Stephens, D. L. (1990). Cognitive abilities as determinants of success in acquiring logic skill. *Learning and Individual Differences*, **2(2)**, 129–60.

L'Hermite, F. (1983). 'Utilisation behaviour' and its relation to lesions of the frontal lobe. *Brain*, **106**, 237–55.

LaPointe, L. B. and Engle, R. W. (1990). Simple and complex word spans as measures of working memory capacity. *Journal of Experimental Psychology: Learning, Memory* and *Cognition*, **16**, 1118–33.

Larsen, J. and Baddeley, A. D. (2003). Disruption of verbal STM by irrelevent speech, articulatory suppression and manual tapping: do they have a common source? *quarterly Journal of Experimental Psychology A*, **56(8)**, 1249–1268.

Larsen, J. D., Baddeley, A. D. and Andrade, J. (2000). Phonological similarity and the irrelevant speech effect: Implications for models of short-term verbal memory. *Memory*, **8**, 145–57.

Lashley, K. S. (1951). The problem of serial order in behaviour. In *Cerebral mechanisms in behaviour: the Hixon symposium* (L. A. Jeffress ed.). New York: John Wiley.

Latane, D. and Darley, J. (1968). *The unresponsive bystander: Why doesn't he help?* NY: Appelton-Century-Crofts.

Lavie, N. (1995). Perceptual load as a necessary condition for selective attention. *Journal of Experimental Psychology: Human Perception and Performance*, **21**, 451–68.

Lavie, N. (2000). Selective attention and cognitive control: dissociating attentional functions through different types of load. In S. Monsell and J. Driver (eds), *Attention and Performance XVIII* (pp. 175–194). Cambridge, Massachusetts: MIT Press.

Lawrence, B. M., Myerson, J. and Abrams, R. A. (2004). Interference with spatial working memory: an eye movement is more than a shift of attention. *Psychonomic Bulletin and Review*, **11**, 488–94.

Lawrence, B. M., Myerson, J., Oonk, H. M. and Abrams, R. A. (2001). The effects of eye and limb movements on working memory. *Memory*, **9**, 433–44.

Lazarus, R. S. (1982). Thoughts on the relationship between emotion and cognition. *American Psychologist*, **37**, 1019–24.

Le Compte, D. C. and Shaibe, D. M. (1997). On the irrelevance of phonological similarity to the irrelevant speech effect. *Quarterly Journal of Experimental Psychology*, **50A**, 100–18.

LeDoux, J. E. (1996). *The emotional brain*. New York: Simon and Schuster.

Lee, C. L. and Estes, W. K. (1981). Item and order information in short-term memory: evidence for multilevel perturbation processes. *Journal of Experimental Psychology: Human Learning and Memory*, **7**, 149–69.

Lee, C. L. and Estes, W. K. (1997). Order and position in primary memory for letter strings. *Journal of Verbal Learning and Verbal Behavior*, **16**, 395–418.

Leopold, D. A. and Logothetis, N. K. (1999). Multistable phenomena: changing views in perception. *Trends in Cognitive Science*, **3**, 254–64.

Lépine, R., Barrouillet, P. and Camos, V. (2005). What makes working memory spans so predictive of high-level cognition? *Psychonomic Bulletin and Review*, **12**, 165–70.

Leventhal, H. (1980). Toward a comphrensive theory of emotion. In *Advances in experimental social psychology*, vol. 13, (L. Berkowitz ed.), pp. 139–207. New York: Academic Press.

Leventhal, H. and Scherer, K. (1987). The relationship of emotion to cognition: a functional approach to a semantic controversy. *Cognition and Emotion*, **1**, 3–28.

Levey, A. B., Aldaz, J. A., Watts, F. N. and Coyle, K. (1991). Articulatory suppression and the treatment of insomnia. *Behaviour Research and Therapy*, **29**, 85–89.

Levy, B. A. (1971). The role of articulation in auditory and visual short-term memory. *Journal of Verbal Learning and Verbal Behavior*, **10**, 123–32.

Levy, E. A. and Mineka, S. (1998). Anxiety and mood-congruent autobiographical memory: A conceptual failure to replicate. *Cognition* and *Emotion*, **12**, 625–34.

Lewandowsky, S. and Murdock, B. B. (1989). Memory for serial order. *Psychological Review*, **96**, 25–57.

Lewandowsky, S., Brown, G. D. A., Wright, T. and Nimmo, L. M. (2006). Timeless memory: Evidence against temporal distinctiveness models of short-term memory for serial order. *Journal of Memory and Language*, **54**, 20–38.

Lewin, K. (1951). *Field theory in social science*. New York: Harper.

Lewinsohn, P. M. (1975). The behavioral study and treatment of depression. In *Progress in behavior modification* (M. Hersen, R. M. Eisler and P. M. Miller eds), pp. 19–64. : Academic Press.

Lewis, A. J. (1934). Melancholia: clinical survey of depressive states. *Journal of Mental Science*, **80**, 1–43.

Libet, B. (1985). Unconscious cerebral initiative and the role of conscious will in voluntary action. *Behavioral and Brain Sciences*, **8**, 529–66.

Libet, B., Gleason, C. A., Wright, E. W. and Pearl, D. K. (1983). Time of conscious intention to act in relation to onset of cerebral activity (readiness-potential): the unconscious initiation of a freely voluntary act. *Brain*, **106**, 623–42.

Lindenberger, U. and Pötter, U. (1998). The complex nature of unique and shared effects in hierarchical linear regression: implications for developmental psychology. *Psychological Methods*, **3**, 218–30.

Linn, M. C. and Petersen, A. C. (1985). Emergence and characterization of sex differences in spatial ability: a meta-analysis. *Child Development*, **56**, 1479–98.

Lobley, K. K., Baddeley, A. D. and Gathercole, S. E. (2005). Phonological similarity effect in verbal complex span. *Quarterly Journal of Experimental Psychology*, **58A**, 1462–78.

Loess, H. and Waugh, N. C. (1967). Short-term memory and inter-trial interval. *Journal of Verbal Learning and Verbal Behaviour*, **6**, 455–60.

Loftus, E. F. (1979). *Eyewitness Testimony*. Cambridge, Mass.: Harvard University Press.

Logie, R. H. (1986). Visuo-spatial processing in working memory. *Quarterly Journal of Experimental Psychology* **38A**, 229–47.

Logie, R. H. (1995). *Visuo-spatial working memory*. Hove, Sussex: Lawrence Erlbaum Associates, Ltd.

Logie, R. H. and Marchetti, C. (1991). Visual-spatial working memory: Visual, spatial or central executive? In *Mental images in human cognition* (R. H. Logie and M. Denis eds), pp. 105–115. Amsterdam: North Holland Press.

Logie, R. H., Cocchini, G., Della Sala, S. and Baddeley, A. (2004). Is there a specific capacity for dual task co-ordination? Evidence from Alzheimer's disease. *Neuropsychology*, **18**(3), 504–13.

Logie, R. H., Della Sala, S., Wynn, V. and Baddeley, A. D. (2000). Visual similarity effects in immediate serial recall. *Quarterly Journal of Experimental Psychology*, **53A**(3), 626–46.

Logie, R. H., Zucco, G. M. and Baddeley, A. D. (1990). Interference with visual short-term memory. *Acta Psychologica*, **75**, 55–74.

Longoni, A. M., Richardson, J. T. E. and Aiello, A. (1993). Articulatory rehearsal and phonological storage in working memory. *Memory and Cognition*, **21**, 11–22.

Lovatt, P., Avons, S. E. and Masterson, J. (2000). The word length effect and disyllabic words. *Quarterly Journal of Experimental Psychology*, **53A**(1), 1–22.

Luck, S. J. and Vogel, E. K. (1997). The capacity of visual working memory for features and conjunctions. *Nature*, **390**, 279–81.

Lumer, E. D., Friston, K. J. and Rees, G. (1998). Neural correlates of perceptual rivalry in the human brain. *Science*, **280**, 1930–4.

Luria, A. R. (1959). The directive function of speech in development and dissolution, Part I. *Word*, **15**, 341–52.

Lustig, C., May, C. P. and Hasher, L. (2001). Working memory span and the role of proactive interference. *Journal of Experimental Psychology: General*, **130**(2), 199–207.

Luzzatti, C., Vecchi, T., Agazzi, D., Cesa-Bianchi, M. and Vergani, C. (1998). A neurological dissociation between preserved visual and impaired spatial processing in mental imagery. *Cortex*, **34**, 461–9.

MacDonald, M. C., Just, M. A. and Carpenter, P. A. (1992). Working memory constraints on the processing of syntactic ambiguity. *Cognitive Psychology*, **24**, 56–98.

Macdonald, R. R. and Labuc, S. (1982). *Parachuting stress and performance*. Army Personnel Research Establishment Memorandum 82M511. London: HMSO.

Mack, A. and Rock, I. (1998). *Inattentional blindness*. Cambridge, MA: MIT Press.

Macken, W. J. and Jones, D. M. (1995). Functional characteristics of the inner voice and the inner ear: single or double agency? *Journal of Experimental Psychology: Learning, Memory and Cognition*, **21**, 436–48.

Macken, W. J. and Jones, D. M. (2003). Reification of phonological storage. *Quarterly Journal of Experimental Psychology*, **56A**, 1279–88.

Mackintosh, N. J. (1998). *IQ and human intelligence*. Oxford: Oxford University Press.

MacLeod, C. and Donnellan, A. M. (1993). Individual-differences in anxiety and the restriction of working-memory capacity. *Personality and Individual Differences*, **15**(2), 163–73.

MacLeod, C. and Mathews, A. (1988). Anxiety and the allocation of attention to threat. *Quarterly Journal of Experimental Psychology*, **40A**(4), 653–70.

MacLeod, C. and Mathews, A. (2004). Selective memory effects in anxiety disorders. In D. Reisberg and P. Hertel (eds), *Memory and Emotion* (pp. 155–85). Oxford: Oxford University Press.

MacLeod, C. and Rutherford, E. M. (1992). Anxiety and the selective processing of emotional information - mediating roles of awareness, trait and state variables, and personal relevance of stimulus materials. *Behaviour Research and Therapy*, **30**(5), 479–91.

MacLeod, C., Mathews, A. and Tata, P. (1986). Attentional bias in emotional disorders. *Journal of Abnormal Psychology*, **95**(1), 15–20.

Madigan, R. J. and Bollenbach, A. K. (1982). Effects of induced mood on retrieval of personal episodic and semantic memories. *Psychological Reports*, **50**, 147–57.

Magee, B. (1987). *The great philosophers*. Oxford: Oxford University Press.

Maguire, E. A., Vargha-Khadem, F. and Mishkin, M. (2001). The effects of bilateral hippocampal damage on fMRI regional activations and interactions during memory retrieval. *Brain*, **124**, 1156–70.

Maia, T. V. and McClelland, J. L. (2004). A re-examination of the evidence for the somatic market hypothesis: what participants know in the Iowa gambling task. *Proceedings of the National Academy of Sciences*, **101**, 16075–80.

Mandler, G. (1967). Organization and memory. In *The psychology of learning and motivation: advances in research and theory*, vol. 1 (K. W. Spence and J. T. Spence eds), pp. 328–72. New York: Academic Press.

Manes, F., Sahakian, B. J., Clark, L., Rogers, R., Antoun, N., Aitken, M. and Robbins, T. W. (2002). Decision-making processes following damage to the prefrontal cortex. *Brain*, **125**, 624–39.

Marcel, A. J. (1983). Conscious and unconscious perception: Experiments on visual masking and word recognition. *Cognitive Psychology*, **15**, 197–237.

Marcel, A. J. (1998). Blindsight and shape perception: deficit of visual consciousness or of visual function? *Brain*, **121**, 1565–88.

Marcel, A. J. (2003). The sense of agency: awareness and ownership of actions and intentions. In *Agency and self awarness* (J. Roessler and N. Eilan eds). Oxford: Oxford University Press.

Marcel, A. J. and Bisiach, E. (eds) (1988). *Consciousness in contemporary science*. Oxford: Clarendon Press.

Margo, A., Helmsley, D. R. and Slade, P. D. (1981). The effects of varying auditory input on schizophrenic hallucinations. *British Journal of Psychiatry*, **139**, 122–7.

Marlatt, G. A. and Gordon, J. R. (1980). Determinants of relapse: implications for the maintenance of behavior change. In *Behavioral medicine: changing health lifestyles* (P. O. Davidson and S. M. Davidson eds), pp. 410–52. New York: Brunner/Mazel.

Marlatt, G. A. and Gordon, J. R. (1985). *Relapse preventation*. New York: Guilford Press.

Marshall, G. D. and Zimbardo, P. G. (1979). Affective consequences of inadequately explained physiological arousal. *Journal of Personality and Social Psychology*, **37**, 970–88.

Martin, R. C. and Breedin, S. D. (1992). Dissociations between speech perception and phonological short-term memory deficits. *Cognitive Neuropsychology*, **9**, 509–34.

Martin, R. and Freedman, M. (2001). The neuropsychology of verbal working memory: The ins and outs of phonological and lexical-semantic retention. In H.L. Roediger, J.S. Nairne, I. Neath and A.M. Suprenant (eds). The Nature of Remembering: Essays in honor of Robert G. Crowder. Washington DC: American Psychological Association Press. pp. 331–49.

Maszk, P., Eisenberg, N. and Guthrie, I. K. (1999). Relations of children's social status to their emotionality and regulation: a short-term longitudinal study. *Merrill-Palmer Quarterly*, **45**, 468–92.

Mathews, A. and Mackintosh, B. (1998). A cognitive model of selective processing in anxiety. *Cognition Therapy and Research*, **22**, 539–60.

Mathews, A. and MacLeod, C. (1985). Selective processing of threat cues in anxiety-states. *Behaviour Research and Therapy*, **23(5)**, 563–69.

Mathews, A. and MacLeod, C. (1986). Discrimination of threat cues without awareness in anxiety-states. *Journal of Abnormal Psychology*, **95(2)**, 131–38.

Mathews, A. and Macleod, C. (1994). Cognitive approaches to emotion and emotional disorders. *Annual Review of Psychology*, **45**, 25–50.

Maude-Griffin, P. M. and Tiffany, S. T. (1996). Production of smoking urges through imagery: The impact of affect and smoking abstinence. *Experimental and Clinical psychopharmacology*, **4**, 198–208.

May, J., Andrade, J., Panabokke, N. and Kavanagh, D. (2004). Images of desire: Cognitive models of craving. *Memory*, **12**, 447–61.

McConnell, J. and Quinn, J. G. (2000). Interferene in visual working memory. *Quarterly Journal of Experimental Psychology*, **53A**, 53–67.

McGeoch, J. A. and Irion, A. L. (1952). *The psychology of human learning*. New York: Longmans.

McGeogh, J. A. (1932). Forgetting and the law of disuse. *Psychological Reveiw*, **39**, 352–70.

McGlinchey-Beroth, R., Milberg, W. P., Verfaellie, M., Alexander, M. and Kilduff, P. T. (1993). Semantic processing in the neglected visual field: evidence from a lexical decision task. *Cognitive Neuropsychology*, **10**, 79–108.

McGuire, P. K., Shah, G. M. S. and Murray, R. M. (1993). Increased blood flow in Broca's area during auditory hallucinations in schizophrenia. *Lancet*, **342**, 703–6.

McKenna, P., Ornstein, T. and Baddeley, A. (2002). Schizophrenia. In *The handbook of memory disorders*, 2nd edn (A. D. Baddeley, M. D. Kopelman and B. A. Wilson (eds), pp. 413–36). Chichester: Wiley.

McNally, R. J., Foa, E. B. and Donnell, C. D. (1989). Memory basis for anxiety information in patients with panic disorder. *Cognition and Emotion*, **3**, 27–44.

Mecklinger, A., von Cramon, D. Y., Springer, A. and Matthes-von Cramon, G. (1999). Executive control functions in task switching: evidence from brain-injured patients. *Journal of Experimental and Clinical Neuropsychology*, **21(5)**, 606–19.

Meiser, T. and Klauer, K. C. (1999). Working memory and changing-state hypothesis. *Journal of Experimental Psychology: Learning, Memory and Cognition*, **25(5)**, 1272–99.

Mellet, E., Tzourio, N., Denis, M. and Mazoyer, B. (1995). A positron emission topography study of visual and mental spatial exploration. *Journal of Cognitive Neurscience*, **7**, 433–45.

Melton, A. W. (1962). Editorial. *Journal of Experimental Psychology*, **64**, 553–7.

Melton, A. W. (1963). Implications of short-term memory for a general theory of memory. *Journal of Verbal Learning and Verbal Behavior*, **2**, 1.21.

Merikle, P. M. and Joordens, S. (1997). Parallels between perception without attention and perception without awareness. *Consciousness and Cognition*, **6**, 219–36.

Merikle, P. M., Joordens, S. and Stolz, J. A. (1995). Measuring the relative magnitude of unconscious influences. *Consciousness and Cognition*, **4(4)**, 422–39.

Messe, R. M. (2000). Is depression an adaptation? *Archives of General Psychiatry*, **57**, 14–19.

Meyer, D. and Kieras, D. (1999). Insights into working memory from the perspective of computational cognitive architectures for modelling human performance. In *Models of working memory: mechanisms of active maintenance and executive control* (A. Miyake and P. Shah eds). New York: Cambridge University Press.

Miles, T. R. (1993). *Dyslexia: the pattern of difficulties*, 2nd edn. London: Whurr.

Milgram, S. (1963). Behavioral study of obedience. *Journal of Abnormal and Social Psychology*, **67**, 371–8.

Miller, E. K., Erickson, C. A. and Desimone, R. (1996). Neural mechanisms of visual working memory in prefrontal cortex of the macaque. *Journal of Neuroscience*, **16**, 5154–67.

Miller, G. A. (1956). The magical number seven, plus or minus two: some limits on our capacity for processing information. *Psychological Review*, **63**, 81–97.

Miller, G. A., Galanter, E. and Pribram, K. H. (1960). *Plans and the structure of behavior*. New York: Holt, Rinehart and Winston.

Miller, J. G. (1984). Culture and the development of everyday social explanation. *Journal of Personality and Social Psychology*, **46**, 961–78.

Miller, J. G. (1987). Cultural influences on the development of conceptual differentiation in person description. *British Journal of Developmental Psychology*, **5**, 309–19.

Milner, A. D., Paulignan, Y., Dijkerman, H. C., Michel, F. and Jeannerod, M. (1999). A paradoxical improvement of misreaching in optic ataxia: new evidence for two separate neural systems for visual localization. *Proceedings of the Royal Society of London, Series B*, **266**, 2225–9.

Milner, B. (1966). Amnesia following operation on the temporal lobes. In *Amnesia* (C. W. M. Whitty and O. L. Zangwill eds), pp. 109–33. London: Butterworths.

Milner, B. (1971). Interhemispheric differences in the localization of psychological processes in man. *British Medical Bulletin*, **27**, 272–7.

Milner, B. (1982). *Some cognitive effects of frontal-lobe lesions in man*. Paper presented at the Philosophical Transactions of the Royal Society, London.

Milner, B. A. (1964). Some effects of frontal leucotomy in man. In *The frontal granular cortex and behavior* (J. M. Warren and K. Akert eds), pp. 313–34. New York: McGraw Hill.

Milner, B. A. (1982). Some cognitive effects of frontal-lobe lesions in man. *Philosophical Transactions of the Royal Society, London B*, **298**, 211–26.

Mischel, W., Ebbesen, E. B. and Zeiss, A. R. (1976). Determinants of selective memory about the self. *Journal of Consulting and Clinical Psychology*, **44**, 92–103.

Mishkin, M., Ungerleider, L. G. and Macko, K. A. (1983). Object vision and spatial vision: two cortical pathways. *Trends in Neurosciences*, **6**, 414–17.

Miyake, A. and Shah, P. (1999a). *Models of working memory: mechanisms of active maintenance and executive control*. New York: Cambridge University Press.

Miyake, A. and Shah, P. (1999b). Toward unified theories of working memory: emerging general consensus, unresolved theoretical issues and future directions. In *Models of working memory: mechanisms of active maintenance and executive control* (A. Miyake and P. Shah eds), pp. 28–61. Cambridge: Cambridge University Press.

Miyake, A., Friedman, N. P., Emerson, M. J., Witzki, A. H., Howerter, A. and Wager, T. D. (2000). The unity and diversity of executive functions and their contributions to complex 'frontal lobe' tasks: A latent variable analysis. *Cognitive Psychology*, **41**, 49–100.

Miyake, A., Friedman, N. P., Rettinger, D. A., Shah, P. and Hegarty, P. (2001). How are visuospatial working memory, executive functioning and spatial abilities related? A latent-variable analysis. *Journal of Experimental Psychology: General*, **130(4)**, 621–40.

Mogg, K. and Bradley, B. P. (1998). A cognitive-motivational analysis of anxiety. *Behaviour Research and Therapy*, **36**, 809–848.

Mogg, K. and Bradley, B. P. (2005). Attentional bias in generalised anxiety disorder versus depressive disorder. *Cognitive Therapy and Research*, **29**, 29–45.

Mogg, K., Bradley, B. P., Field, M. and De Houwer, J. (2003). Eye movements to smoking-related pictures in smokers: relationship between attentional biases and implicit and explicit measures of stimulus valence. *Addiction*, **98(6)**, 825–36.

Mogg, K., Bradley, B. P., Williams, R. and Mathews, A. (1993). Subliminal processing of emotional information in anxiety and depression. *Journal of Abnormal Psychology*, **102(2)**, 304–11.

Mogg, K., Mathews, A. and Weinman, J. (1987). Memory bias in clinical anxiety. *Journal of Abnormal Psychology*, **96**, 94–8.

Mogg, K., Mathews, A., Bird, C. and MacGregor-Morris, R. (1990). Effects of stress and anxiety on the processing of threat stimuli. *Journal of personality and Social Psychology*, **59(6)**, 1230–7.

Mogg, K., Millar, N. and Bradley, B. P. (2000). Biases in eye movements to threatening facial expressions in generalized anxiety disorder and depressive disorder. *Journal of Abnormal Psychology*, **109**, 695–704.

Mohr, H. M. and Linden, D. E. J. (2005). Separation of the systems for colour and spatial manipulation in working memory revealed by a dual task procedure. *Journal of Cognitive Neuroscience*, **17**, 355–66.

Monsell, S. (1996). Control of mental processes. In *Unsolved mysteries of the mind: tutorial essays in cognition* (V. Bruce ed.), pp. 93–148. Hove, Sussex: Erlbaum UK.

Monsell, S. (2005). The chronometrics of task-set control. In *Measuring the mind: speed, control and age* (J. Duncan and L. Phillips and P. McLeod eds), pp. 161–90. Oxford: Oxford University Press.

Monti, P. M., Rohsenow, D. J., Rubonis, A. V., Niaura, R. S., Sirota, A. D., Colby, S. M. and Abrams, D. B. (1993). Alcohol cue reactivity: Effects of detoxification and extended exposure. *Journal of Studies on Alcohol*, **54**, 235–45.

Moray, N. (1959). Attention in dichotic listening: affective cues and the influence of instructions. *Quarterly Journal of Experimental Psychology*, **11**, 56–60.

Morey, C. C. and Cowan, N. (2005). When do visual and verbal memory conflict? The importance of working memory load and retrieval. *Journal of Experimental Psychology: Learning, Memory and Cognition*, **31**, 703–13.

Morris, J. S., Öhman, A. and Dolan, R. J. (1999). A subcortical pathway to the right amygdala mediating 'unseen' fear. *Proceedings, National Academy of Sciences of the United States of America*, **96(4)**, 1680–5.

Morris, M. and Peng, K. (1994). Culture and cause: American and Chinese attributions for social and physical events. *Journal of Personality and Social Psychology*, **67**, 949–71.

Morris, R. G. (1984). Dementia and the functioning of the articulatory loop system. *Cognitive Neuropsychology*, **1**, 143–57.

Morris, R. G. (1986). Short-term forgetting in senile demential of the Alzheimer's type. *Cognitive Neuropsychology*, **3**, 77–97.

Mowbray, G. H. and Rhoades, M. V. (1959). On the reduction of choice reation times with practice. *Quarterly Journal of Experimental Psychology*, **11**, 16–23.

Mueller, S. T., Seymour, T. L., Kieras, D. E. and Meyer, D. E. (2003). Theoretical implications of articulatory duration, phonological similarity and phonological complexity in verbal working memory. *Journal of Experimental Psychology: Learning, Memory and Cognition.*

Muraven, M. and Baumeister, R. F. (2000). Self-regulation and depletion of limited resources: Does self-control resemble a muscle? *Psychological Bulletin*, **126**, 247–59.

Muraven, M., Baumeister, R. F. and Tice, D. (1999a). Longitudinal improvement of self-regulation through practice: building self-control through repeated exercise. *Journal of Social Psychology*, **139**, 446–57.

Muraven, M., Collins, R. L. and Neinhaus, K. (1999b). Self-control and alcohol restraint: a test of the self control strength model. Unpublished manuscript.

Muraven, M., Tice, D. M. and Baumeister, R. F. (1998). Self-control as limited resource: regulatory depletion patterns. *Journal of Personality and Social Psychology*, **74**, 774–89.

Murdock, B. B. (1993). TODAM2: a model for the storage and retrieval of item, associative and serial order information. *Psychological Review*, **100**, 183–203.

Murdock, B. B. J. (1965). Effects of a subsidary task on short-term memory. *British Journal of Psychology*, **56**, 413–19.

Murphy, F. C., Sahakian, B. J., Rubinsztein, J. S., Michael, A., Rogers, R. D., Robbins, T. W. and Paykel, E. S. (1999). Emotional bias and inhibtory control processes in mania and depression. *Psychological Medicine*, **29**, 1037–321.

Murray, D. J. (1967). The role of speech responses in short-term memory. *Canadian Journal of Psychology*, **21**, 263–76.

Murray, D. J. (1968). Articulation and acoustic confusability in short-term memory. *Journal of Experimental Psychology*, **78**, 679–84.

Mushiake, H., Inase, M. and Tanji, J. (1991). Neuronal activity in the primate premotor, supplementary and precentral motor cortex during visually guided and internally determined sequential movements. *Journal of Neurophysiology*, **66**, 705–18.

Nairne, J. S. (1990). A feature model of immediate memory. *Memory and Cognition*, **18**, 251–69.

Nairne, J. S. (2002). Remembering over the short-term: the case against the standard model. *Annual Review of Psychology*, **53**, 53–81.

Nairne (2003). Paper presented at Essex I have got his CV and only paper I can find for that year is Nairne, J.S. (2003, September). *The architecture of immediate retention: A multinomial model*. Keynote address at the British Psychological Society, Reading, England.

Naveh Benjamin, M., Craik, F. I. M. and Peratta, J. (2000). The effects of divided attention on encoding and retrieval processes: the resiliency of retrieval processes. *Quarterly Journal of Experimental Psychology*, **53**, 609–26.

Naveh-Benjamin, M. (1987). Coding of spatial location information: an automatic process? *Journal of Experimental psychology: Learning, Memory and Cognition*, **13**, 595–605.

Naveh-Benjamin, M. (1988). Recognition memory of spatial location information: another failure to support automaticity. *Memory and Cognition*, **16**, 437–45.

Naveh-Benjamin, M., Guez, J. and Marom, M. (2003). The effects of divided attention at encoding on item and associative memory. *Memory and Cognition*, **31**, 1021–35.

Naveh-Benjamin, M., Guez, J. and Shulman, S. (2004). Older adult's associative deficit in episodic memory: assessing the role of decline in attentional resources. *Psychonomic Bulletin and Review*, 11, 1067–73.

Neath, I. (2000). Modelling the effects of irrelevant speech on memory. *Psychonomic Bulletin and Review*, 7, 403–23.

Neath, I. and Nairne, J. S. (1995). Word-length effects in immediate memory: overwriting trace-decay theory. *Psychonomic Bulletin and Review*, 2, 429–41.

Neath, I., Suprenant, A. M. and Le Compte, D. C. (1998). Irrelevant speech eliminates the word length effect. *Memory and Cognition*, 26, 343–54.

Nebes, R. D. and Brady, C. B. (1992). Generalized cognitive slowing and severity of dementia in Alzheimers disease: implications for the interpretation of response-time data. *Journal of Clinical and Experimental Neuropsychology*, 2, 317–26.

Neisser, U. (1967a). *Cognitive psychology*. New York: Appleton-Century Crofts.

Neisser, U. (1967b). *Cognitive psychology*. Englewood Cliffs, NJ.: Prentice-Hall.

Neisser, U. and Fivush, R. (1994). *The remembering self: construction and accuracy in the self-narrative*. Cambridge: Cambridge University Press.

Neisser, U., Boodoo, G., Bouchard, T. J. J., Boykin, A. W., Brody, N., Ceci, S. J., Halpern, D. F., Loehlin, J. C., Perloff, R., Sternberg, R. J. and Urbina, S. (1996). Intelligence: knowns and unknowns. *American Psychologist*, 51, 77–101.

Nelson, K. A. (1989). Remembering: A functional developmental perspective. In P. R. Solomon and G. R. Goethals and C. N. Kelley and B. R. Stephens (eds), *Memory: Interdisciplinary approaches* (pp. 127–50). New York: Springer-Verlag.

Nelson, T. O. and Chaiklin, S. (1980). Immediate memory for spatial location. *Journal of Experimental Psychology: Human Learning and Memory*, 6, 529–45.

Newell, A. and Simon, H. A. (1972). *Human problem solving*. Englewood Cliffs, N J: Prentice-Hall.

Newton, T. L. and Contrada, R. J. (1992). Repressive coping and verbal/autonomic response dissociation: The influence of social context. *Journal of Personality and Social Psychology*, 62, 159–67.

Nicolson, R. (1981). The relationship between memory span and processing speed. In *Intelligence and learning* (M. Friedman, J. P. Das and N. O'Connor eds), pp. 179–84. New York: Plenum Press.

Nimmo, L. M. and Lewandowsky, S. (in press-a). Distinctiveness revisited: unpredictable temporal isolation does benefit short-term serial recall of heard and seen events. *Memory and Cognition*.

Nimmo, L. M. and Lewandowsky, S. (2006). From brief gaps to very long pauses: Temporal isolation does not benefit serial recall. *Psychonomic Bulletin and Review*, 12, 999–1004.

Nimmo, L. M. and Lewandowsky, S. (in press-b). From brief gaps to very long pauses: temporal isolation does not benefit serial recall. *Psychonomic Bulletin and Review*.

Nisbett, R. (1993). Violence and US regional culture. *American Psychologist*, 48, 441–89.

Nisbett, R. E., Peng, K. P., Choi, I. and Norenzayan, A. (2001). Culture and systems of thought: holistic vs. analytic cognition. *Psychological Review*, 108, 291–310.

Nohara, D. M. (1965). Variety of responses and reactive inhibition. *Psychonomic Science*, 2, 301–2.

Nolde, S. F., Johnson, M. K. and D'Esposito, M. (1998). Left prefrontal activation during episodic remembering: an event-related fMRI study. *NeuroReport*, 9, 3509–14.

Nolde, S. F., Johnson, M. K. and Raye, C. L. (1998). The role of prefrontal cortex during tests of episodic memory. *Trends in Cognitive Sciences*, **2**, 399–406.

Nolen-Hoeksema, S. (1991). Responses to depression and their effects on the duration of depressive episodes. *Journal of Abnormal Psychology*, **100**, 569–82.

Nolen-Hoeksema, S. and Morrow, J. (1991). A prospective study of depression and distress following a natural disaster: the 1989 Loma Prieta earthquake. *Journal of Personality and Social Psychology*, **61**, 115–21.

Nolen-Hoeksema, S., Morrow, J. and Fredrickson, B. L. (1993). Response styles and the duration of episodes of depressed mood. *Journal of Abnormal and Social Psychology*, **102**, 20–8.

Norman, D. A. and Shallice, T. (1983). Attention to action – willed and automatic control of behaviour. *Bulletin of the Psychonomic Society*, **21**(5), 354–54.

Norman, D. A. and Shallice, T. (1986). Attention to action: willed and automatic control of behaviour. In *Consciousness and self-regulation. Advances in research and theory*, vol. 4 (R. J. Davidson, G. E. Schwarts and D. Shapiro eds), pp. 1–18. New York: Plenum Press.

Norretranders, T. (1999). *The user illusion, cutting consciousness down to size*, translated by J. Sydenham. Harmondsworth: Penquin.

Norris, D., Baddeley, A. D. and Page, M. P. A. (2004). Retrospective effects of irrelevent speech on serial recall from short-term memory. *Journal of Experimental Psychology*, **30**, 1093–105.

North, N. T. and O'Carroll, R. E. (2001). Decision making in patients with spinal cord damage: afferent feedback and the somatic marker hypothesis. *Neuropsychologia*, **39**, 521–4.

Nyberg, L., Cabeza, R. and Tulving, E. (1996). PET studies of encoding and retrieval: the HERA model. *European Journal of Cognitive Psychology*, **8**, 163–83.

O'Regan, J. K., Rensink, R. A. and Clark, J. J. (1999). Change-blindness as a result of 'mudsplashes'. *Nature*, **398**(6722), 34.

Oatley, K. and Johnson-Laird, P. (1987). Towards a cognitive theory of emotions. *Cognition and Emotion*, **1**, 29–50.

Oh, S.-H. and Kim, M.-S. (2004). The role of spatial working memory in visual search efficiency. *Psychonomic Bulletin and Review*, **11**, 275–81.

Ohmän, A. (1993). Fear and anxiety as emotional phenomena: Clinical phenomenology, evolutionary perspectives, and information processing mechanisms. In M. Lewis and J. M. Haviland (eds), *Handbook of Emotions* (pp. 511–36). New York: Guildford.

Ohmän, A. (1996). Preferential preattentive processing of threat in anxiety: Preparedness and attentional biases. In R. M. Rapee (ed.), *Current controversies in the anxiety disorders* (pp. 253–90). New York: Guildford Press.

Öhman, A. and Soares, J. J. F. (1994). 'Unconscious anxiety': phobic responses to masked stimuli. *Journal of Abnormal Psychology*, **103**, 231–40.

Öhman, A. and Soares, J. J. F. (1998). Emotional conditioning to masked stimuli: expectancies for aversive outcomes following non-recognized fear-relevant stimuli. *Journal of Experimental Psychology: General*, **127**, 69–82.

Ojemann, G. A. (1978). Organization of short-term verbal memory in language areas of human cortex: evidence from electrical stimulation. *Brain and Language*, **5**, 331–40.

Ojemann, G. A. (1994). Cortical stimulation and recording in language. In *Localisation and neuroimaging in neuropsychology* (A. Kertesz ed.), pp. 35–55. New York: Academic Press.

Olton, D. S. (1979). Mazes, maps and memory. *American Psychologist,* **34,** 583–96.

Osgood, C. E. (1949). The similarity paradox in human learning: A resolution. *Psychological Review,* **56,** 132–43.

Owen, A. M. (1997). The functional organisation of working memory processes within the human lateral frontal cortex: the contribution of functional neuroimaging. *European Journal of Neuroscience,* **9,** 1329–39.

Owen, A.M., McMillan, K.M., Laird, A.R. and Bullmore, E. (2005). N-Back working memory paradigm: A meta-analysis of normative functional neuroimaging studies. *Human Brain Mapping,* **25,** 46–59.

Page, M. P. A. and Norris, D. (1998). The primacy model: A new model of immediate serial recall. *Psychological Review,* **105,** 761–81.

Page, M. P. A. and Norris, D. G. (2003). The irrelevant sound effect: what needs modeling and a tentative model. *Quarterly Journal of Experimental Psychology* **56A,** 1289–300.

Paivio, A. (1969). Mental imagery in associative learning and memory. *Psychological Review,* **76,** 241–63.

Paivio, A. (1971). Imagery and Verbal Processes.

Paivio, A., Yuille, J. C. and Madigan, S. (1968). Concreteness imagery and meaningfulness values for 925 nouns. *Journal of Experimental Psychology Monograph Supplements,* **76**(1, Pt. 2).

Pall, J. (1999).

Panabokke, N., May, J., Eade, D., Andrade, J. and Kavanagh, D. (2004). Visual imagery tasks suppress craving for cigarettes. *Unpublished manuscript:* University of Sheffield, Sheffield, England.

Panksepp, J. (1998). *Affective neuroscience: the foundations of human and animal emotions.* Oxford: Oxford University Press.

Papagno, C. and Vallar, G. (1992). Phonological short-term memory and the learning of novel words: The effects of phonological similarity and item length. *Quarterly Journal of Experimental Psychology,* **44A,** 47–67.

Papagno, C. and Vallar, G. (1995). Verbal short-term memory and vocabulary learning in polyglots. *Quarterly Journal of Experimental Psychology,* **48A,** 98–107.

Papagno, C., Valentine, T. and Baddeley, A. D. (1991). Phonological short-term memory and foreign-language vocabulary learning. *Journal of Memory and Language,* **30,** 331–47.

Parasuraman, R. (1984). Sustained attention in detection and discrimination. In *Varieties of attention* (R. Parasuraman and D. R. Davies eds), pp. 243–71. Orlando, FL: Academic Press.

Parkin, A. J. (1996). *Explorations in Cognitive neuropsychology.* Oxford: Blackwell.

Parkin, A. J. (1998). The central executive does not exist. *Journal of the International Neuropsychology Society,* 4.

Parkinson, L. and Rachman, S. (1981). The nature of intrusive thoughts. *Advances in Behavior Research and Therapy,* **3,** 101–10.

Parra, C., Esteves, F., Flykt, A. and Öhman, A. (1997). Pavolovian conditioning to social stimuli: backward masking and the dissociation of implicit and explicit cognitive processes. *European Psychologist,* **2,** 106–17.

Pashler, H. (1998). *The psychology of attention.* Cambridge, MA: MIT Press.

Passingham, R. E. (1998). The specializations of the human neocortex. In *Comparative neuropsychology* (A. D. Milner ed.), pp. 271–98. Oxford: Oxford University Press.

Paulesu, E., Frith, C. D. and Frackowiak, R. S. J. (1993). The neural correlates of the verbal component of working memory. *Nature*, **362**, 342–5.

Pearson, D. G. (2001). Imagery and visuo-spatial sketchpad. In *Working memory in perspective* (J. Andrade ed.), pp. 33–59. Hove, Sussex: Psychology Press.

Pearson, D. G. and Sahraie, A. (2003). Oculomotor control and the maintenance of spatially and temporally distributed events in visuo-spatial working memory. *Quarterly Journal of Experimental Psychology*, **56A**, 1089–111.

Pearson, D. G., Logie, R. H. and Gilhooly, K. J. (1999). Verbal representations and spatial manipulation during mental synthesis. *European Journal of Cognitive Psychology*, **11(3)**, 295–314.

Penfield, W. (1958). *The excitable cortex in conscious man*. Liverpool, England: Liverpool University Press.

Penrose, R. (1994). *Shadows of the mind*. Oxford: Oxford University Press.

Perry, R. J. and Hodges, J. R. (1999). Attention and executive deficits in Alzheimer's disease: a critical review. *Brain*, **122**, 383–404.

Perry, R. J., Watson, P. and Hodges, J. R. (2000). The nature and staging of attention dysfunction in early (minimal and mild) Alzheimer's disease: relationship to episodic and semantic memory impairment. *Neuropsychologia*, **38**, 252–71.

Perry, W., Potterat, E. G. and Braff, D. L. (2001). Self-monitoring enhances Wisconsin Card Sorting Test performance in patients with schizophrenia: performance is improved by simply asking patients to verbalize their sorting strategy. *International Neuropsychological Society*, **7(3)**, 344–52.

Peterson, L. R. and Johnson, S. T. (1971). Some effects of minimizing articulation on short-term retention. *Journal of Verbal Learning and Verbal Behavior*, **10**, 346–54.

Peterson, L. R. and Peterson, M. J. (1959). Short-term retention of individual verbal items. *Journal of Experimental Psychology*, **58**, 193–8.

Petrides, M. and Milner, B. (1982). Deficits on subject-ordered tasks after frontal and temporal lobe lesions in man. *Neuropsychologia*, **20**, 601–14.

Petrides, M., Alivasatos, B., Evans, A. C. and Meyer, E. (1993a). Dissociation of human mid-dorsolateral from posterior dorsolateral frontal cortex in memory processing. *Proceedings of the National Academy of Sciences, USA*, **90**, 873–7.

Phillips, W. A. (1974). On the distinction between sensory storage and short-term visual memory. *Perception and Psychophysics*, **16**, 283–90.

Phillips, W. A. and Baddeley, A. D. (1971). Reaction time and short-term visual memory. *Psychonomic Science*, **22**, 73–4.

Phillips, W. A. and Christie, D. F. M. (1977a). Components of visual memory. *Quarterly Journal of Experimental Psychology*, **29**, 117–33.

Phillips, W. A. and Christie, D. F. M. (1977b). Interference with visualisation. *Quarterly Journal of Experimental Psychology*, **29**, 637–50.

Pinto da Costa, A. and Baddeley, A. D. (1991). Where did you park your car? Analysis of a naturalistic long-term recency effect. *European Journal of Cognitive Psychology*, **3**, 297–313.

Plunkett, K. and Marchman, V. (1993). From rote learning to system building: acquiring verb morphology in children and connectionist nets. *Cognition*, **48**, 21–69.

Posner, M. I. (1967). Short-term memory systems in human information processing. *Acta Psychologica*, **27**, 267–84.

Posner, M. I. and Fan, J. (2004). Attention as an organ system. In *Topics in integrative neuroscience: from cells to cognition* (J. R. Pomeratz and M. C. Crair eds), Cambridge: Cambridge University Press.

Posner, M. I. and Keele, S. W. (1967). Decay of visual information from a single letter. *Science*, **158**, 137–9.

Posner, M. I. and Konick, A. F. (1966). Short term retention of visual and kinesthetic information. *Journal of Organization Behavior and Human Performance*, **1**, 71–86.

Posner, M. I. and Mitchell, R. F. (1967). Chronometric analysis of classification. *Psychological Review*, **74**, 392–409.

Posner, M. I. and Petersen, S. E. (1990). The attention system of the human brain. *Annual Review of Neuroscience*, **13**, 25–42.

Posner, M. I. and Raichle, M. E. (1994). *Images of mind*. New York: Scientific American Library.

Postle, B. R., Idzikowski, C., Della Sala, S., Logie, R. H. and Baddeley, A. D. (2006). The selective disruption of spatial working memory with eye movements. *Quarterly Journal of Experimental Psychology*, **59**, 100–20.

Postman, L. (1975). Verbal learning and memory. *Annual Review of Psychology*, **26**, 291–335.

Postman, L. and Underwood, B. J. (1973). Critical issues in interference theory. *Memory and Cognition*, **1**, 19–40.

Potts, R., Camp, C. and Coyne, C. (1989). The relationship between naturally occuring dysphoric moods, elaborative encoding and recall performance. *Cognition and Emotion*, **3**, 197–205.

Poulton, E. C. (1958). Time for reading and memory. *British Journal of Psychology*, **49**, 230–45.

Powell, J., Bradley, B. and Gray, J. (1992). Classical conditioning and cognitive determinants of subjective craving for opiates: An investigation of their relative contributions. *Journal of Addiction*, **87**, 1133–44.

Prabhakaran, V., Narayanan, K., Zhao, Z. and Gabrielli, J. D. E. (2000). Integration of diverse information in working memory in the frontal lobe. *Nature of Neuroscience*, **3**, 85–90.

Price, J., Sloman, L., Gardiner, R., Gilbert, P. and Rohde, P. (1994). The social competition hypothesis of depression. *British Journal of Psychiatry*, **164**, 309–15.

Pucak, M. L., Levitt, J. B., Lund, J. S. and Lewis, D. A. (1996). Patterns of intrinsic and associational circuitry in monkey prefrontal cortex. *Journal of Comparative Neurology*, **376**, 614–30.

Pulkkinen, L. and Hamalainen, M. (1995). Low self-control as a precursor to crime and accidents in a Finnish longitudinal study. *Criminal Behaviour and Mental Health*, **5**, 424–38.

Pyszczynski, T. and Greenberg, J. (1987). Self- regulatory preservation and the depressive self-focusing style: a self-awareness theory of reactive depression. *Psychological Bulletin*, **102**, 122–38.

Quinn, G. and McConnell, J. (1996a). Exploring the passive visual store. *Psychologische Beitrage*, **38(314)**, 355–67.

Quinn, G. and McConnell, J. (1996b). Irrelevant pictures in visual working memory. *Quarterly Journal of Experimental Psychology*, **49A(1)**, 200–15.

Quinn, J. G. and McConnell, J. (1999). Manipulation of interference in the passive visual store. *European Journal of Cognitive Psychology*, **11**, 373–89.

Quinn, J. G. and **Ralston, G. E.** (1986). Movement and attention in visual working memory. *Quarterly Journal of Experimental Psychology* **38A**, 689–703.

Rabbitt, P. M. A. (1997). Introduction: methodologies and models in the study of executive function. In *Methodology of frontal and executive function* (P. Rabbitt ed.), pp. 1–59. Hove, Sussex: Psychology Press.

Raffone, A. and **Wolters, G.** (2001). A cortical mechanism for binding in visual working memory. *Journal of Cognitive Neuroscience*, **13(6)**, 766–85.

Ramachandran, V. S. (1996). Synaesthesia in phantom limbs induced with mirrors. *Proceedings of the Royal Society of London*, **263**(377–86).

Ramachandran, V. S. and **Hirstein, W.** (1998). The perception of phantom limbs – The D. O. Hebb lecture. *Brain*, **121**, 1603–30.

Ranganath, C. and **Paller, K. A.** (2000). Neural correlates of memory retrieval and evaluation. *Cognitive Brain Research*, **9(2)**, 209–22.

Rao, N. (1997). *Facilitating development in preschoolers with Down's syndrome in Hong Kong: a controlled evaluation study of the effects on centre-based intervention*, vol. 24). Oxford, UK: Blackwell.

Raymond, J. E., **Shapiro, K. L.** and **Arnell, K. M.** (1992). Temporary suppression of visual processing in an RSVP task: An attentional blink? *Journal of Experimental Psychology: Human Perception and Performance*, **18**, 849–60.

Reason, J. T. and **Mycielska, K.** (1982). *Absent-minded? The psychology of memory lapses and everyday errors.* Englewood Cliffs, NJ: Prentice Hall.

Reber, A. S. (1993). *Implicit learning and tacit knowledge.* Oxford: Oxford University Press.

Rehm, L. P., **Kaslow, N. J.** and **Rabin, A. S.** (1987). Cognitive and behavioural targets in a self-controlled therapy program for depression. *Journal of Consulting and Clinical Psychology*, **55**, 60–7.

Reisberg, D., **Clayton, C. L.**, **Heuer, F.** and **Fischman, D.** (1986). Visual memory: when imagery vividness makes a difference. *Journal of Mental Imagery*, **10**, 51–74.

Rensink, R. A. (2000). The dynamic representation of scenes. *Visual Cognition*, **7**, 17–42.

Rensink, R. A., **O'Regan, J. K.** and **Clark, J. J.** (1997). To see or not to see: the need for attention to perceive changes in scenes. *Psycological Science*, **8**, 368–73.

Riby, L. M., **Perfect, T. J.** and **Stollery, B. T.** (2004). Dual task performance in older adults: a meta-analysis. *European Journal of Cognitive Psychology*, **16**, 683–91.

Richardson, J. T. E. (1999). *Mental imagery.* Hove, Sussex: Psychology Press.

Rizzolatti, G. and **Arbib, M. A.** (1998). Language within our grasp. *Trends in Neurosciences*, **21(5)**, 188–94.

Robbins, T. Anderson, E., **Barker, D.**, **Bradley, A.**, **Fearneyhough, C.**, **Henson, R.**, **Hudson, S.** and **Baddeley, A.** (1996). Working memory in chess. *Memory and Cognition*, **24(1)**, 83–93.

Roberts, A. C., **Robbins, T. W.** and **Weiskrantz, L.** (1998). *The pre-frontal cortex: executive and cognitive functions.* Oxford: Oxford University Press.

Roberts, R. J., **Hager, L.** and **Heron, C.** (1994). Prefrontal cognitive processes: working memory and inhibition in the antisaccade task. *Journal of Experimental Psychology: General*, **123**, 374–93.

Rochon, E., **Waters, G. S.** and **Caplan, D.** (2000). The relationship between measures of working memory and sentence comprehension in patients with Alzheimer's disease. *Journal of Speech, Language and Hearing Research*, **43**, 395–413.

Rogers, P. J. and **Green, M. W.** (1993). Dieting, dietary restraint and cognitive performance. *British Journal of Clinical Psychology*, **32**, 113–6.

Rodgers, R. D. and **Monsell, S.** (1995). Costs of a predictable shift between simple cognitive tasks. *Journal of Experimental Psychology: General*, **124**, 207–31.

Roediger, H. L. (1990). Implicit memory: Retention without remembering. *American Psychologist*, **45**, 1043–56.

Rosen, V. M. and **Engle, R. W.** (1997). The role of working memory capacity in retrieval. *Journal of Experimental Psychology: General*, **126**, 211–27.

Rossi-Arnaud, C., Pieroni, L. and **Baddeley, A. D.** (2006). Symmetry and binding in visuo-spatial working memory. *Journal of Cognitive Neuroscience*, **139**, 393–400.

Roth, P. (1991). *Patrimony*. New York: Simon, Schuster and Roy.

Rotton, J. (1983). Affective and cognitive consequences of malodorous pollution. *Basic and Applied Social Psychology*, **4(2)**, 171–91.

Rubenstein, J., Meyer, D. E. and **Evans, J. E.** (2001). Executive control of cognitive processes in task switching. *Journal of Experimental Psychology: Human Perception and Performance*, **27**, 763–97.

Rubin, D. C. and **Wenzel, A. E.** (1996). One hundred years of forgetting: on a quantative description of retention. *Psychological Reveiw*, **103**, 734–60.

Ruchkin, D. S., Grafman, J., Cameron, K. and **Berndt, R. S.** (2003). Working memory retention systems: a state of activated long-term memory. *Behavioral and Brain Sciences*, **26**, 709–77.

Rude, S. S., Hertel, P. T. and **Jarrold, W.** (1999). Depression-related impairments in prospective memory. *Cognition and Emotion*, **13(3)**, 267–76.

Rugg, M. D. (1995). ERP studies of memory in electrophysiology of mind: event-related brain potentials and cognition. In (M. D. Rugg and M. G. H. Coles eds) pp. 132–70. Oxford: Oxford University Press.

Rundus, D. (1971). Analysis of rehearsal process in free recall. *Journal of Experimental Psychology*, **89**, 63–77.

Ryan, J. (1969). Temporal grouping, rehearsal and short-term memory. *Quarterly Journal of Experimental Psychology*, **21**, 148–55.

Saariluoma, P. (1995). *Chess players' thinking: a cognitive psychological approach*. London: Routledge.

Saito, S. (1994). What effect can rhythmic finger tapping have on the phonological similarity effect? *Memory and Cognition*, **22**, 181–7.

Saito, S. (1997). When articulatory suppression does not supress the activity of the phonological loop. *British Journal of Psychology*, **88**, 565–78.

Saito, S. (1998). Phonological loop and intermittent activity: a whistle task as articulatory suppression. *Canadian Journal of Experimental Psychology*, **52**, 18–24.

Saito, S. and **Baddeley, A. D.** (2004). Irrelevant sound disrupts speech production: exploring the relationship between short-term memory and experimentally induced slips of the tongue. *Quarterly Journal of Experimental Psychology*, **57A(7)**, 1309–40.

Saito, S. and **Miyake, A.** (2004). On the nature of forgetting and the processing-storage relationship in reading span performance. *Journal of Memory and Language*, **50**, 425–43.

Salamé, P. (1990). Effects of music, speech-like noise and irrelevant speech on immediate memory. In *Noise as a public health problem, vol. 4 New advances in noise research part 1*

(B. Bergland and T. Lindvall eds), pp. 411–23. Stockholm, Sweden: Swedish Council for Building Research.

Salamé, P. and Baddeley, A. D. (1982). Disruption of short-term memory by unattended speech: implications for the structure of working memory. *Journal of Verbal Learning and Verbal Behaviour*, 21, 150–64.

Salamé, P. and Baddeley, A. D. (1986). Phonological factors in STM: similarity and the unattended speech effect. *Bulletin of the Psychonomic Society*, 24, 263–5.

Salamé, P. and Baddeley, A. D. (1989). Effects of background music on phonological short-term memory. *Quarterly Journal of Experimental Psychology*, 41A, 107–22.

Salamé, P. and Baddeley, A. D. (1990). The effects of irrelevant speech on immediate free recall. *Bulletin of the Psychonomic Society*, 28, 540–2.

Salkovskis, P. M. and Reynolds, M. (1994). Thought suppression and smoking cessation. *Behaviour Research and Therapy*, 32, 192–201.

Salthouse, T. A. (1992). *Mechanisms of age-cognition relations in adulthood*. Hillsdale, NJ: Lawrence Erlbaum Associates.

Salthouse, T. A. (1996). The processing-speed theory of adult age differences in cognition. *Psychological Review*, 103, 403–28.

Salthouse, T. A., Fristoe, N., McGuthry, K. E. and Hambrick, D. Z. (1998). Relation of task switching to speed, age and fluid intelligence. *Psychology and Aging*, 13, 445–61.

Salway, A. F. S. and Logie, R. H. (1995). Visuospatial working memory, movement control and executive demands. *British Journal of Psychology*, 86, 253–69.

Sanz, J. (1996). Memory biases in social anxiety and depression. *Cognition* and *Emotion*, 10, 87–105.

Schachter, S. and Singer, J. E. (1962). Cognitive, social and physiological determinants of emotional state. *Psychological Review*, 69, 379–99.

Schacter, D. L. (1994). Priming and multiple memory systems: Perceptual mechanisms of implicit memory. In *Memory systems* (D. L. Schacter and E. Tulving eds), pp. 233–68. Cambridge MA: MIT Press.

Schank, R. C. and Abelson, R. (1977). *Scripts, plans, goals and understanding*. Hillsdale, NJ: Lawrence Erlbaum Associates Inc.

Schare, M. L., Lisman, S. A. and Spear, N. E. (1984). The effects of mood variation on state-dependent retention. *Cognitive Therapy and Research*, 8, 387–408.

Scherer, K. R. (1984). Emotion as a multicomponent process: a model and some cross-cultural data. In *Review of personality and social psychology*, vol. 5 (P. Shaver ed.), pp. 37–63. Beverly Hills, CA: Sage.

Schmeichel, B. J., Vohs, K. D. and Baumeister, R. F. (2003). Intellectual performance and ego depletion: role of the self in logical reasoning and other information processing. *Journal of Personality and Social Psychology*, 85(1), 33–46.

Schmidt, B. K., Vogel, E. K., Woodman, G. F. and Luck, S. J. (2002). Voluntary and automatic attentional control of visual working memory. *Perception and Psychophysics*, 64(5), 754–63.

Schneider, W. and Shiffrin, R. M. (1977). Controlled and automatic human information processing: I. Detection, search and attention. *Psychological Review*, 84, 1–66.

Schotte, D. E., McNally, R. J. and Turner, M. L. (1990). A dichotic-listening analysis of body-weight concern in bulimia nervosa. *International Journal of Eating Disorders*, 9(1), 109–13.

Schumacher, E. H., Lauber, E., Awh, E., Jonides, J., Smith, E. E. and Koeppe, R. A. (1996). PET evidence for an amodal verbal working memory system. *Neuroimage*, 3(2), 79–88.

Schumann-Hengsteler, R. (1992). The development of visuo-spatial memory: how to remember location. *International Journal of Behavioral Development*, 15, 455–71.

Schwarz, N. and Clore, G. L. (1983). Mood, misattribution and judgements of well-being: informative and directive functions of affective states. *Journal of Personality and Social Psychology*, 45, 513–23.

Schwarz, N., Strack, F., Kommer, D. and Wagner, D. (1987). Soccer, rooms and the quality of your life: mood effects on judgements of satisfaction with life in general and with specific life-domains. *European Journal of Social Psychology*, 17, 69–79.

Schweikert, R. (1993). A multinomial processing tree model for degradation and redintegration in immediate recall. *Memory and Cognition*, 21, 168–75.

Scogin, F., Storandt, M. and Lott, L. (1985). Memory-skills training, memory complaints and depression in older adults. *Journal of Gerontology*, 40, 562–8.

Selfridge, O.G. (1955). Pattern recognition and modern computers. *Proceedings of the Western Joint Computer Conference, New York: Institute of Electrical and Electronics Engineers.*

Seligman, M. E. P. (1975). *Helplessness: on depression, development and death.* San Francisco, CA: Freeman.

Service, E. (2000). Phonological complexity and word duration in immediate recall: different paradigms answer different questions. A comment on Cowan, Nugent, Elliott and Geer. *Quarterly Journal of Experimental Psychology*, 53A(3), 661–5.

Shah, P. and Miyake, A. (1996). The separability of working memory resources for spatial thinking and language processing: an individual differences approach. *Journal of Experimental Psychology: General*, 125, 4–27.

Shallice, T. (1988). *From neuropsychology to mental structure.* Cambridge: Cambridge University Press.

Shallice, T. (2002). Fractionation of the supervisory system. In *Principles of frontal lobe function* (D. T. Stuss and R. T. Knight eds), pp. 261–77. New York: Oxford University Press.

Shallice, T. and Burgess, P. W. (1991). Deficits in strategy application following frontal lobe damage in men. *Brain*, 114, 727–41.

Shallice, T. and Burgess, P. W. (1996). The domain of supervisory processes and temporal organization of behaviour. *Philosophical Transactions of the Royal Society of London Series B*, 351(1346), 1405–11.

Shallice, T. and Warrington, E. K. (1970). Independent functioning of verbal memory stores: a neuropsychological study. *Quarterly Journal of Experimental Psychology*, 22, 261–73.

Shallice, T., Burgess, P. W., Schon, F. and Baxter, D. M. (1989). The origins of utilisation behaviour. *Brain*, 112, 1587–98.

Shallice, T., Fletcher, P., Frith, C. D., Grasby, P. M., Frackowiak, R. S. J. and Dolan, R. J. (1994). Brain regions associated with acquisition and retrieval of verbal episodic memory. *Nature*, 368, 633–5.

Shanks, D. R. and St. John, M. F. (1994). Characteristics of dissociable human learning systems. *Behavioral and Brain Sciences*, 17, 367–94.

Shankweiler, D., Liberman, I. Y., Mark, L. S., Fowler, C. A. and Fischer, F. W. (1979). The speech code and learning to read. *Journal of Experimental Psychology: Human Learning and Memory*, 5, 531–45.

Shaw, R. (2003). The agent-environment interface: Simon's indirect or Gibson's direct coupling? *Ecological Psychology*, **15**, 37–106.

Sheline, Y. I., Barch, D. M., Donnelly, J. M., Ollinger, J. M., Snyder, A. Z. and Mintun, M. A. (2001). Increased amygdala response to masked emotional faces in depressed subjects resolves with antidepressant treatment: an fMRI study. *Biological Psychiatry*, **50**, 651–8.

Shepard, N. and Metzler, J. (1971). Mental rotation of three-dimensional objects. *Science*, **171**, 701–3.

Shepard, R. N. and Cooper, L. A. (1982). *Mental images and their transformations*. Cambridge, MA, London: MIT Press.

Shepard, R. N. and Feng, C. (1972). A chronometric study of mental paper-folding. *Cognitive Psychology*, **3**, 228–43.

Sherrod, D. R. (1974). Crowding, perceived control and behavioral aftereffects. *Journal of Applied Social Psychology*, **4**, 171–86.

Shiel, A., Wilson, B. A., McLellan, L., S., H. and Watson. (2000). *The Wessex Head Injury Matrix (WHIM)*. Bury St Edmunds: Thames Valley Test Company.

Shiffrin, R. M. and Cook, J. R. (1978). Short-term forgetting of item and order information. *Journal of Verbal Learning and Verbal Behavior*, **17**, 189–218.

Shrauger, J. S. and Rosenberg, S. E. (1970). Self-esteem and the effects of success and failure feedback on performance. *Journal of Personality*, **38**, 404–17.

Shrauger, J. S. and Schoeneman, T. J. (1979). Symbolic interactionist view of self-concept: through the looking glass darkly. *Psychological Bulletin*, **86**, 549–73.

Shrauger, J. S. and Sorman, P. B. (1977). Self-evaluation, initial success and failure and improvement as determinants of persistence. *Journal of Consulting Psychology and Clinical Psychology*, **45**, 784–95.

Shute, R. (1991). *Psychology in vision care*. Oxford: Butterworth Heinemann.

Shweder, R. A. and Bourne, E. (1982). Does the concept of the person vary cross-culturally? In A. J. Marsella and G. White (eds), Cultural conceptions of mental health and therapy (pp. 97–137). Boston: Reidel.

Silbersweig, D. A., Stern, E., Frith, C., Cahill, C., Holmes, A., Grootoonk, S., Seaward, J., McKenna, P., Chua, S. E., Schnorr, L., Jones, T. and Frackowiak, R. S. J. (1995). A functional neuroanatomy of hallincinations in schizophrenia. *Nature*, **378**, 176–9.

Simons, A. D., Garfield, S. L. and Murphy, G. E. (1984). The process of change in cognitive therapy and pharmacotherapy for depression: Changes in mood and cognition. *Archives of General Psychiatry*, **43**, 43–8.

Singer, W. (1999). Binding by neural synchrony. In *The MIT encyclopedia of the cognitive sciences* (R. A. W. F. C. Keil ed.), pp. 81–4. Cambridge, MA: MIT Press.

Singer, W. and Gray, C. M. (1995). Visual feature integration and the temporal correlation hypthesis. *Annual Review of Neuroscience*, **18**, 555–86.

Smith, E. E. and Jonides, J. (1996). Working memory in humans: neuropsychological evidence. In *The cognitive neurosciences* (M. Gazzaniga ed.), pp. 1009–20. Cambridge, MA: MIT Press.

Smith, E. E. and Jonides, J. (1997). Working memory: a view from neuroimaging. *Cognitive Psychology*, **33**, 5–42.

Smith, E. E. and Jonides, J. (1999). Storage and executive processes in the frontal lobes. *Science*, **283**, 1657–61.

Smith, E. E., Jonides, J. and Koeppe, R. A. (1996). Dissociating verbal and spatial working memory using PET. *Cerebral Cortex*, **6**, 11–20.

Smith, E. E., Jonides, J., Koeppe, R. A., Awh, E., Schumacher, E. H. and Minoshima, S. (1995). Spatial vs. object working memory: PET investigations. *Journal of Cognitive Neuroscience*, **7**, 337–56.

Smith, E., Jonides, J. and Koeppe, R. A. (1996). Dissociating verbal and spatial working memory using PET. *Cerebral Cortex*, **6**, 11–20.

Smyth, M. M. and Pendleton, L. R. (1989). Working memory for movement. *The Quarterly Journal of Expermental Psychology*, **41A**, 235–50.

Smyth, M. M. and Pendleton, L. R. (1990). Space and movement in working memory. *Quarterly Journal of Experimental Psychology*, **42A**, 291–304.

Smyth, M. M. and Scholey, K. A. (1992). Determining spatial span: the role of movement time and articulation rate. *Quarterly Journal of Experimental Psychology*, **45A**, 479–501.

Smyth, M. M. and Waller, A. (1998). Movement imagery in rock climbing: Patterns of interference from visual, spatial and kinaesthetic secondary tasks. *Applied Cognitive Psychology*, **12**, 145–115.

Smyth, M. M., Hay, D. C., Hitch, G. J. and Horton, N. J. (2005). Serial position memory in the visuo-spatial domain: reconstructing sequences of unfamiliar faces. *Quarterly Journal of Experimental Psychology*, **58A**, 909–30.

Smyth, M. M., Pearson, N. A. and Pendleton, L. R. (1988). Movement and working memory: patterns and positions in space. *Quarterly Journal of Experimental Psychology*, **40A**, 499–514.

Snowling, M., Chiat, S. and Hulme, C. (1991). Words, nonwords and phonological processes: Some comments on Gathercole, Willis, Emslie and Baddeley. *Applied Psycholinguistics*, **12(3)**, 369–73.

Snyder, M. and White, P. (1982). Moods and memories: elation, depression and the remembering of the event of one's life. *Journal of Personality*, **50**, 142–67.

Solarz, A. K. (1960). Latency of instrumental responses as a function of compatibility with the meaning of eliciting verbal signs. *Journal of Experimental Psychology*, **59**, 239–45.

Spacapan, S. and Cohen, S. (1983). Effects and aftereffects of stressor expectations. *Journal of Personality and Social Psychology*, **45**, 1243–54.

Spearman, C. (1927). *The abilities of man*. London: Macmillan.

Spector, A. and Beiderman, I. (1976). Mental set and mental shift revisited. *American Journal of Psychology*, **89**, 669–79.

Speidel, G. E. (1993). Phonological short-term memory in individual differences in learning to speak: bilingual case study. *First Language*, **13**, 69–91.

Spence, K. W. (1937). The differential response in animals to stimuli varying within a single dimension. *Psychological Review*, **44**, 430–44.

Sperling, G. (1960). The information available in brief visual presentations. *Psychological Monographs: General and Applied*, **74**, 1–29.

Sperling, G. and Speelman, R. G. (1970). Acoustic similarity and auditory short-term memory: experiments and a model. In *Models of human memory* (D. A. Norman ed.), pp. 149–202. New York: Academic Press.

Spinnler, H., Della Sala, S., Bandera, R. and Baddeley, A. D. (1988). Dementia, ageing and the structure of human memory. *Cognitive Neuropsychology*, **5**, 193–211.

Squire, L. R. (1992). Declarative and non-declarative memory: multiple brain systems supporting learning and memory. *Journal of Cognitive Neuroscience*, **4**, 232–43.

Steenhuis, E. and Goodale, M. A. (1988). The effects of time and distance on accuracy of target-directed locomotion: does an accurate short-term memory for spatial location exist? *Journal of Motor Behaviour*, **20**, 399–415.

Stephan, K. M., Fink, G. R., Passingham, R. E., Silbersweig, D., Ceballos-Baumann, A. O., Frith, C. D. and Frackowiak, R. S. J. (1995). Functional anatomy of the mental representation of upper extremity movements in healthy subjects. *Journal of Neurophysiology*, **73**, 373–86.

Sternberg, S. (1966). High-speed scanning in human memory. *Science*, **153**, 652–4.

Stuss, D. T. and Knight, R. T. (2002). *Principles of frontal lobe function*. New York: Oxford University Press.

Sully, J. (1892). *The human mind: a textbook of psychology*. London: Longmans, Green.

Sweeney, J. A., Mintun, M. A., Kwee, S., Wiseman, M. B., Brown, D. L., Rosenberg, D. R. and Carl, J. R. (1996). Position emission tomography study of voluntary saccadic eyemovements and spatial working memory. *Journal of Neuophysiology*, **75**, 454–68.

Tam, L. and Ward, G. (2000). A recency-based account of the primacy effect in free recall. *Journal of Experimental Psychology: Learning, Memory and Cognition*, **26**, 1589–625.

Tangney, J. P., Baumeister, R. F. and Boone, A. (2004). High self-control predicts good adjustment, less pathology, better grades and interpersonal success. *Journal of Personality*, **72**, 271–324.

Taylor, S. E. and Brown, J. D. (1988). Illusion and well-being: a social psychological perspective on mental health. *Psychological Bulletin*, **103(2)**, 193–210.

Taylor, S. E. and Brown, J. D. (1999). Illusion and well-being: a social psychological perspective on mental health. In *The self in social psychology* (R. F. Baumeister ed.). Philadelphia, PA: Psychology Press.

Teasdale, G. and Jennett, B. (1974). Assessment of coma and impaired consciousness: a practical scale. *Lancet*, **2(7872)**, 81–4.

Teasdale, J. D. (1988). Cognitive vulnerbility to persistent depression. *Cognition and Emotion*, **2**, 247–74.

Teasdale, J. D. and Barnard, P. J. (1993). *Affect, cognition and change: remodelling depressive thought*. Hove, Sussex: Lawrence Erlbaum Associates.

Teasdale, J. D., Dritschel, B. H., Taylor, M. J., Proctor, L., Lloyd, C. A., Nimmo-Smith, I. and Baddeley, A. D. (1995). Stimulus-independent thought depends on central executive resources. *Memory and Cognition*, **23**, 551–9.

Teasdale, J. D., Proctor, L., Lloyd, C. A. and Baddeley, A. D. (1993). Working memory and stimulus-independent thought: effects of memory load and presentation rate. *European Journal of Cognitive Psychology*, **5**, 417–33.

Teasdale, J. D., Segal, Z. V., Williams, J. M. G., Ridgeway, V. A., Soulsby, J. M. and Lau, M. A. (2000). Prevention of relapse/recurrence in major depression by mindfulness-based cognitive therapy. *Journal of Consulting and Clinical Psychology*, **68**, 615–23.

Teasdale, J. D., Taylor, R. and Fogarty, S. J. (1980). Effects of induced elation depression on the accessibility of memories of happy and unhappy experiences. *Behaviour Research and Therapy*, **18**, 339–46.

Tehan, G., Hendry, L. and Kocinski, D. (2001). Word length and phonological similarity effects in simple, complex and dealyed serial recall tasks: implications for working memory. *Psychology Press*, **9**, 333–48.

Thierry, B., Steru, L., Chermat, R. and Simon, P. (1984). Searching-waiting strategy: a candidate for an evolutionary model of depression? *Behavioural and Neural Biology*, **41**, 180–9.

Thomson, J. A. (1983). Is continuous visual monitoring necessary in visually-guided locomotion. *Journal of Experimental Psychology*, **9**, 427–33.

Thorn, A. S. C. and Gathercole, S. (1999). Language-specific knowledge and short-term memory in bilingual and non-bilingual children. *Quarterly Journal of Experimental Psychology*, **52A**, 303–24.

Tiffany, S. T. and Hakenewerth, D. M. (1991). The production of smoking urges through an imagery manipulation: Psychophysiological and verbal manifestations. *Addictive Behaviors*, **16**, 389–400.

Thurstone, L. L. (1940). *The vectors of mind*. Chicago, IL: University of Chicago Press.

Tong, F., Nakayama, K., Vaughan, J. T. and Kanwisher, N. (1998). Binocular rivalry and visual awareness in human extrastriate cortex. *Neuron*, **21**, 753–9.

Towse, J. N. (1998). On random generation and the central executive of working memory. *British Journal of Psychology*, **89**, 77–81.

Towse, J. N. and Hitch, G. J. (1995). Is there a relationship between task demand and storage space in tests of working memory capacity? *Quarterly Journal of Experimental Psychology*, **48A(1)**, 108–24.

Towse, J. N., Hitch, G. J. and Hutton, U. (1998). A reevaluation of working memory capacity in children. *Journal of Memory and Language*, **39**, 195–217.

Treisman, A. (1993). The perception of features and objects. In *Attention: selection, awareness and control* (A. Baddeley and L. Weiskrantz eds), pp. 5–35. Oxford: Clarendon Press.

Treisman, A. and Gelade, G. (1980). A feature-integration theory of attention. *Cognitive Psychology*, **12**, 97–136.

Tremblay, S. and Jones, D. M. (1998). Habituation versus changing state explanations of the irrelevant sound effect: Evidence from the effects of token set size. *Journal of Experimental Psychology: Learning, Memory and Cognition*, **24**, 659–71.

Tremblay, S., Macken, W. J. and Jones, D. M. (2000). Elimination of the word length effect by irrelevant sound revisited. *Memory and Cognition*, **29(5)**, 841–6.

Tresch, M. C., Sinnamon, H. M. and Seamon, J. G. (1993). Double dissociation of spatial and object visual memory: evidence from selective interference in intact human subject. *Neuropsychologia*, **31(3)**, 211–19.

Trieman, R. and Danis, C. (1988). Short-term memory errors for spoken syllables are affected by the linguistic structure of the syllables. *Journal of Experimental Psychology – Learning Memory and Cognition*, **14**, 145–52.

Tulving, E. (1962). Subjective organisation in free recall of 'unrelated' words. *Psychological Review*, **69**, 344–54.

Tulving, E. (1989). Memory: performance, knowledge and experience. *European Journal of Cognitive Psychology*, **1**, 3–26.

Tulving, E. (2002). Episodic memory: from mind to brain. *Annual Review of Psychology*, **53**, 1–25.

Tulving, E., Kapur, S., Craik, F. I. M., Moscovitch, M. and Houle, S. (1994). Hemispheric encoding/retrieval asymmetry in episodic memory – positron emission tomography findings. *Proceedings of the National Academy of Sciences, USA*, **91**(6), 2016–20.

Tune, G. S. (1964). A brief survey of variables that influence random generation. *Perceptual and Motor Skills*, **18**, 705–10.

Turner, M. L. and Engle, R. W. (1989). Is working memory capacity task dependent? *Journal of Memory and Language*, **28**, 127–54.

Turvey, M. T. (2004). Space (and its perception): the first and final frontier. *Ecological Psychology*, **16**, 25–9.

Turvey, M. T., Brick, P. and Osborn, J. (1970). Proactive interference in short-term memory as a function of prior-item retention interval. *Quarterly Journal of Experimental Psychology*, **22**, 142–7.

Tzeng, O. J. L. (1973). Positive recency effects in delayed free recall. *Journal of Verbal Learning and Verbal Behavior*, **12**, 436–9.

Underwood, B. J. (1957). Interference and forgetting. *Psychological Review*, **64**, 49–60.

Underwood, B. J. and Postman, L. (1960). Extra experimental sources of interference in forgetting. **67**, 73–95.

Vallar, G. and Baddeley, A. D. (1982). Short-term forgetting and the articulatory loop. *Quarterly Journal of Experimental Psychology*, **34A**, 53–60.

Vallar, G. and Baddeley, A. D. (1984). Fractionation of working memory. Neuropsychological evidence for a phonological short-term store. *Journal of Verbal Learning and Verbal Behaviour*, **23**, 151–61.

Vallar, G. and Baddeley, A. D. (1987). Phonological short-term store and sentence processing. *Cognitive Neuropsychology*, **4**, 417–38.

Vallar, G. and Papagno, C. (1993). Preserved vocabulary acquisition in Down's syndrome: the role of phonological short-term memory. *Cortex*, **29**, 467–83.

Vallar, G. and Papagno, C. (2002). Neuropsychological impairments of verbal short-term memory. In *Handbook of memory disorders*, 2nd edn (A. D. Baddeley, M. D. Kopelman and B. A. Wilson eds), pp. 249–70. Chichester: Wiley.

Vallar, G. and Shallice, T. (eds). (1990). *Neuropsychological impairments of short-term memory*. Cambridge: Cambridge University Press.

Vallar, G., Corno, M. and Basso, A. (1992). Auditory and visual verbal short-term memory in aphasia. *Cortex*, **28**, 383–9.

Vallar, G., Papagno, C. and Baddeley, A. D. (1991). Long-term recency effects and phonological short-term memory: a neuropsychological case study. *Cortex*, **27**, 323–6.

van den Hout, M., Muris, P., Salemink, E. and Kindt, M. (2001). Autobiographical memories become less vivid and emotional after eye movements. *British Journal of Clinical Psychology*, **40**, 121–30.

Velten, E. (1968). A laboratory task for induction of mood states. *Behavioral Research and Therapy*, **6**, 473–82.

Vogel, E. K., Woodman, G. F. and Luck, S. J. (2001). Storage of features, conjunctions and objects in visual working memory. *Journal of Experimental Psychology: Human Perception and Performance*, **27**(1), 92–114.

Vogel, E. K., Woodman, G. F. and Luck, S. J. (in press). The time course of consolidation in visual working memory. *Journal of Experimental Psychology: Human Perception and Performance*.

von der Malsberg, C. (1995). Binding in models of perception and brain function. *Current Opinion in Neurobiology*, **5**, 520–6.

Von Restorff, H. (1933). Über die Wirkung von Bereichsbildungen im Spurenfeld. *Psychologisch Forschung*, **18**, 299–342.

Vreugdenburg, L., Bryan, J. and Kemps, E. (2003). The effect of self-initiated weight-loss dieting on working memory: the role of preoccupying cognitions. *Appetite*, **41(3)**, 291–300.

Vygotsky, L. S. (1962). *Thought and language*, translated by E. Hanfmann and G. Vakar. Cambridge, MA: MIT Press.

Wagar, B. M. and Dixon, M. J. (2005). Past experience influences object representation in working memory. *Brain and Cognition*, **57**, 248–56.

Walker, I. and Hulme, C. (1999). Concrete words are easier to recall than abstract words: evidence for a semantic contribution to long-term serial recall. *Journal of Experimental Psychology: Learning, Memory and Cognition*, **25**, 1256–71.

Walker, N. K. and Burkhardt, J. F. (1965). The combat effectiveness of various human operator controlled systems. *Proceedings of the17th U.S. Military Operation Research Symposium*.

Walker, P. and Cuthbert, L. (1998). Remembering visual feature conjunctions: visual memory for shape-colour associations is object-based. *Visual Cognition*, **5(4)**, 409–55.

Walker, P., Hitch, G. J., Doyle, A. and Porter, T. (1994). The development of short-term visual memory in young children. *International Journal of Behavioral Development*, **17**, 73–89.

Walters, A. J., Shiffman, S., Bradley, B. P. and Mogg, K. (2003). Attentional shifts to smoking cues in smokers. *Addiction*, **98(10)**, 1409–17.

Ward, G. (2001). A·critique of the working memory model. In *Working memory in perspective* (J. Andrade ed.), pp. 219–39. Hove, Sussex: Psychology Press.

Warren, C. and Cooper, P. J. (1988). Psychological efects of dieting. *British Journal of Clinical Psychology*, **27**, 269–70.

Warrington, E. K. and Baddeley, A. D. (1974). Amnesia and memory for visual location. *Neuropsychologia*, **12**, 257–63.

Warrington, E. K. and Weiskrantz, L. (1968). New methods of testing long-term retention with special reference to amnesic patients. *Nature*, **217**, 972–4.

Wason, P. and Johnson-Laird, P. (1972). *Psychology of reasoning: structure and content*. Cambridge, MA.: Harvard University Press.

Waters, G. S. and Caplan, D. (1996). The capacity theory of sentence comprehension: Critique of Just and Carpenter (1992). *Psychological Review*, **103**, 761–72.

Waters, G. S. and Caplan, D. (2004). Verbal working memory and online-syntactic processing; evidence from self-based listening. *Quarterly Journal of Experimental Psychology*, **57A**, 129–63.

Watkins, M. J. and Peynircioglu, Z. F. (1983). Three recency effects at the same time. *Journal of Verbal Learning and Verbal Behavior*, **22**, 375–84.

Watts, F. N. (1993). Problems of memory and concentration. In *Symptoms of depression* (C. G. Costello ed.). New York: John Wiley.

Watts, F. N., Trezise, L. and Sharrock, R. (1986). Processing of phobic stimuli. *British Journal of Clinical Psychology*, **25**, 253–9.

Waugh, N. C. and Norman, D. A. (1965). Primary memory. *Psychological Review*, **72**, 89–104.

Wegner, D. M. (1994). Ironic processes of mental control. *Psychological Review*, **101**, 34–52.

Weinberger, D. A. (1990). The construct validity of the repressive coping style. In J. L. Singer (ed.), *Repression and dissociation: Implications for personality theory, psychopathology, and health.* (pp. 337–386). Chicago: University of Chicago Press.

Weingartner, H., Cohen, R. M., Murphy, D. L., Martello, J. and Gerdt, C. (1981). Cognitive processes in depression. *Archives of General Psychiatry*, **38**, 42–47.

Weiskrantz, L. (1986). *Blindsight: a case study and implications.* Oxford: Oxford University Press.

Weiskrantz, L. (1997). *Consciousness loss and found: a neuropsychological exploration.* Oxford: Oxford University Press.

Weiskrantz, L., Elliot, J. and Darlington, C. (1971). Preliminary observations of tickling oneself. *Nature*, **230**, 598–99.

Welford, A. T. (1956). *Ageing and human skill.* London: Oxford University Press.

Weltman, G., Christianson, R. A. and Egstrom, G. H. (1970). Effects of environment and experience on underwater work performance. *Human Factors*, **12**, 587–98.

Weltman, G., Smith, J. E. and Egstrom, G. H. (1971). Perceptual narrowing during simulated pressure chamber-exposure. *Human Factors*, **13**, 99–107.

Wheeler, M. E. and Treisman, A. M. (2002). Binding in short-term visual memory. *Journal of Experimental Psychology: General*, **131**, 48–64.

Wickelgren, W. A. (1964). Size of rehearsal group and short-term memory. *Journal of Experimental Psychology*, **68(4)**, 413–19.

Wickelgren, W. A. (1965). Short-term memory for phonemically similar lists. *American Journal of Psychology*, **78**, 567–74.

Wickelgren, W. A. (1969). Auditory or articulatory coding in verbal short-term memory. *Psychological Review*, **76**, 232–5.

Wickens, D. D., Born, D. G. and Allen, C. K. (1963). Proactive inhibition and item similarity in short-term memory. *Journal of Verbal Learning and Verbal Behavior*, **2**, 440–5.

Williams, J. M. G. (1984). *The psychological treatment of depression: a guide to the theory and practice of cognitive-behaviour therapy.* London: Croom Helm.

Williams, J. M. G. and Broadbent, K. (1986). Distraction by emotional stimuli - Use of a Stroop task with suicide attempters. *British Journal of Clinical Psychology*, **25**, 101–110.

Williams, J. M. G. and Scott, J. (1988). Autobiographical memory in depression. *Psychological Medicine*, **18**, 689–95.

Williams, J. M. G., Mathews, A. and MacLeod, C. (1996). The emotional Stroop task and psychopathology. *Psychological Bulletin*, **120**, 3–24.

Williams, J. M. G., Watts, F. N., MacLeod, C. and Mathews, A. (1988). *Cognitive psychology and emotional disorders.* New York: John Wiley and Sons.

Williams, J. M. G., Watts, F. N., MacLeod, C. and Mathews, A. (1997). *Cognitive Psychology and emotional disorders* (1st ed.). Chichester: Wiley.

Williams, J. M. G., Watts, F. N., MacLeod, C. and Mathews, A. (1997). *Cognitive psychology and emotional disorders*, 2nd edn. Chichester: Wiley.

Wilson, B. A. and Baddeley, A. D. (1988). Semantic, episodic and autobiographical memory in a post-meningitic amnesic patient. *Brain and Cognition*, **8**, 31–46.

Wilson, B. A., Baddeley, A. D. and Young, A. W. (1999). LE, a person who lost her 'mind's eye'. *Neurocase*, **5**, 119–27.

Wilson, B. A., Shiel, A., McLellan, L., Horn, S. and Watson, M. A. (2001). Monitoring recovery of cognitive function following severe traumatic brain injury. *Brain Impairment*, **2**, 22–8.

Wilson, F. A., Scalaidhe, S. P. and Goldman-Rakic, P. S. (1993). Dissociation of object and spatial processiing domains in primate pre-frontal cortex. *Science*, **260**, 1955–8.

Wing, A. M., Lewis, V. J. and Baddeley, A. D. (1979). The slowing of handwriting by letter repetition. *Journal of Human Movement Studies*, **5**, 182–8.

Wise, R. J., Katkin, E. S., Wiens, S. and Öhman, A. (2001). Nonconcious fear conditioning, visceral perception and the development of gut feelings. *Psychological Science*, **12**, 366–70.

Wolford, G. and Hollingsworth, S. (1974). Evidence that short-term memory is not the limiting factor in tachistoscopic full-report procedure. *Memory and Cognition*, **2**, 796–800.

Wolpert, D. M. and Kawato, M. (1998). Multiple paired forward and inverse models for motor control. *Neural Networks*, **11(7–8)**, 1317–29.

Wolpert, D. M., Ghahramani, Z. and Jordan, M. I. (1995). An internal model for sensorimotor integration. *Science*, **269**, 1880–2.

Woodin, M. E. and Heil, J. (1996). Skilled motor performance and working memory in rowers: Body patterns and spatial positions. *Quarterly Journal of Experimental Psychology*, **49A**, 357–78.

Woodman, G. F. and Luck, S. J. (2004). Visual search is slowed when visuospatial working memory is occupied. *Psychonomic Bulletin and Review*, **11**, 269–74.

Woodman, G. F., Vecera, S. P. and Luck, S. J. (2003). Perceptual organization influences visual working memory. *Psychonomic Bulletin and Review*, **10(1)**, 80–87(88).

Woodman, G. F., Vogel, E. K. and Luck, S. J. (2001). Visual search remains efficient when visual working memory is full. *Psychological Science*, **12**, 219–24.

Wutz, R. H. and Olds, J. (1963). Amygdaloid stimulation and operant reinforcement in the rat. *Journal of Comparative and Physiological Psychology*, **56**, 941–9.

Wyer, R. S. and Frey, D. (1983). The effects of feedback about self and others on the recall and judgments of feedback-relevant information. *Journal of Experimental Social Psychology*, **19(6)**, 540–59.

Yerkes, R. M. and Dodson, J. D. (1908). The relation of strength of stimulus to rapidity of habit formation. *Journal of Comparative* and *Physiological Psychology*, **18**, 459–82.

Yntema, D. B. and Trask, F. P. (1963). Recall as a search process. *Journal of Verbal Learning and Verbal Behavior*, **2**, 65–74.

Zajonc, R. B. (1984). On the primacy of affect. *American Psychologist*, **39**, 117–23.

Zinser, M. C., Baker, T. B., Sherman, J. E. and Cannon, D. S. (1992). Relation between self-reported affect and drug urges and cravings in continuing and withdrawing smokers. *Journal of Abnormal Psychology*, **101**, 617–29.

Zuckerman, M. (1979). *Sensation seeking: beyond the optimal levl of arousal.* Hillsdale, NJ: Erlbaum.

Zwaan, R. A. and Truitt, T. P. (1998). Smoking urges affect language processing. *Experimental and Clinical Psychopharmacology*, **6**, 325–30.

Index